Love Me Now

Love Me Now

Memoir

Joanne T. Pisoni Amoroso

Amoroso Publications
Green Valley, Arizona

Contact the author at:
Lovemenowbook@Gmail.com

This edition was prepared for publication by
Ghost River Images
5350 East Fourth Street
Tucson, Arizona 85711
www.ghostriverimages.com

Cover design by
Joanne T. Pisoni Amoroso

Oil crayon pastel original by Angela Yarra Amoroso

ISBN 978-1-7324125-0-7

Library of Congress Control Number: 2018906602

Printed in the United States of America
September 2018

Table of Contents

Dedication

For my daughter and inspiration, Angela/Yarra, and to Kris Kolff, my stalwart son-in-law, both of whom dedicated themselves to a loving, intentional, courageous, and frequently chaotic, journey. Kris encouraged me to use "absolute honesty" in relating this story of evolving, enduring relationships.

To caregivers worldwide, with appreciation and awareness of your generosity. Reflections of your story may be found in the pages of this book.

Joanne T. Pisoni Amoroso

Dear Reader,

My daughter was known by many names, depending on where and with whom she was living. Baptized, Angela Marie Amoroso, she was called Angie and Ange in her childhood in the US and Anque as a teen in Peru, then Suki in India and Australia, and, lastly, Yarra in Australia and New Zealand.

Prologue

Their Own Way to God, Motueka, New Zealand, 2007

Our B&B is only two blocks from St. Peter's church and school. I join red-cheeked, winter-hardy parishioners sitting facing each other. Mass is held daily at 8:30 in a small side chapel. When I walk in, some look up from their prayers. I suspect they already know who I am and why I am here. "Americans," I imagine them advising their friends. "Their daughter's in hospital."

According to the bulletin I pick up, Father Patrick is the celebrant. He reads today's gospel from the Bible, John 8:1-11, which is about the woman caught in adultery who is condemned to be stoned by the Pharisees. To my surprise, he begins his sermon with "We New Zealanders are good at the whitewash." He presents a case of three policemen who went unpunished in the rape of a young woman and the injustice and danger of that omission. He concludes that a Christian's role is defending justice for all. I mull this over. *This priest is not afraid to tell it like it is. Maybe this is the priest I want to talk to, to pour out my feelings...please God, maybe.*

I listen intently. I hope. I pray. Midway through the Mass, Father asks us to offer each other the sign of peace. I turn to extend my hand to those parishioners seated around me. We greet each other with, "The peace of Christ be with you." I look into the inquisitive eyes of shy parishioners who remind me I'm *"those people" again.*

I return the smiles of the more cordial, feeling grounded by sharing our familiar ritual. I'm hopeful as I see Father Patrick standing at the door, shaking hands, smiling and chatting. I catch his bright blue eyes glancing in my direction and step up.

"I'm Joanne Amoroso, Father. My daughter is in the hospital here. I'd like to talk with you, if you have time."

He nods, "Surely, just stop by the office and ask Marie to make an appointment." He pauses. "Is it urgent?"

"I'd like to get some copies of prayers for the dying. I want to read them myself while I'm sitting with my daughter."

His smile disappears. "Will you be at Mass tomorrow?"

I nod. "I'd also just like to talk with you." I hear my voice diminishing. I take a breath and say out loud, "I need some guidance."

"Never mind the appointment," Father responds. "Just meet me after Mass."

It is "breath clouds cold" next morning. I crunch my hands into my jacket pockets. Inside Father's office, a few logs glow red behind an ornate grill. The high, wide walls are totally lined with shelves of books. Surprisingly, the room feels comfortable, no drafts. I wonder if the books provide insulation.

Father's desk is piled with stacks of papers, notebooks, folders, and books. "Thank you for making time to see me, I say."

"I'm happy to do whatever I can. Would you like to hang your coat?" He points to a standing wooden rack with many curved hooks. A dark black, heavy coat already hangs there. "Pardon the mess." He spreads his hands over his desk. "I make choices. Sometimes… my desk…doesn't get chosen." He smiles and shrugs a shoulder. He looks at me with soft blue eyes. The smile disappears. "How can I help you…Joanne, isn't it? I get to know the children as I watch them come to school. Do you mind if we sit here by the window?" He motions to two grey-blue, padded armchairs.

"No, I enjoy watching the children. I spent some time volunteering at St. Joseph's a few years ago, listening to the student readers."

"Oh, you know Father Ed then?"

"Oh, yes, quite well. We appreciated his sermons."

"Yes, no one sleeps during his sermons, I hear." He presses his fingertips together under his chin. "Well, Joanne, you'd like to tell me about your daughter, is that right?"

"That's right, Father. Her name is Yarra, baptized Angela Marie. Later, she chose Yarra for herself." I smile. "That tells you a bit about her."

"Independent, was she?"

"Not that so much, but she knew how to make her way in the world."

"And what's her present situation?"

"She's moribund, Father. She's lived an incredible, full life with MS for fourteen years. We've been with her here in New Zealand part of each year since 1998. Now she's dying. She's at the community hospital."

"I'm sorry to hear that, Joanne. Is she here alone?"

"No, her husband, Kris, and his Dutch immigrant family came here after World War II."

"Good, good, and how about you? Are you here by yourself?"

"No, my husband, Chris, who is a doctor–I'm a nurse by the way–and my eldest daughter, Chiara, are here. We're staying at the bed and breakfast just two blocks away."

"Yes, I heard some Americans were staying there." He grins and tips his head. "News gets around in a small town."

"The nurses have arranged it so we can be at her bedside around the clock. I'm morning shift. I walk over to Mass before I go to the hospital. The parishioners are so kind; some have even offered us transportation."

"And how are you doing?"

"I…she…well…it's hard; Yarra can't speak. Thanks to Chiara, who thought about recording Yarra's last wishes when she could still speak, Yarra has had signed advanced directives since 2004."

"That's unusual, for here," says Father.

"We did some checking into the local system. After Chris met with a hospice doctor, we hired a lawyer to come to the house to fill out forms for advance directives. We hoped Yarra's last wishes would be carried out. The thing is, she's outlived all her parameters, Father." I hear my own clinical voice. *How can I tell it all? There is so much more to Yarra than any conversation.* "She has loved life."

I look out the window. The kids in their knit hats make a colorful parade as they tromp by in their boots, book bags on their backs and chins buried into their collars. *Like Yarra, yes, just like Yarra "soldiering on," as the New Zealanders say.*

"Now her husband and those who know her best, her daily caregivers and long-time friends, feel she is leaving her body. They feel she is ready to go."

He looks at me with gentle eyes. In a soft, metered tone he says, "And are you ready?"

"I think so. We came from the US because we want to be with her in her dying. We've talked about her dying for years with priests, theologians, hospice doctors and psychologists. When we realized we were coming to this point, I contacted an ethicist from Nelson. She talked with me alone, as Chris was away in the US for surgery at that time. She was very helpful. She explained New Zealand policies at end-of-life and told us advance directives are not binding in New Zealand. She said a committee of physicians, caregivers, and the family is formed."

The school bell rings. We both look out the window. A few late arrivers bustle in the door. Father brings us back to our conversation.

"And what did you think of that?"

What do I think? I take a long breath. "Yarra couldn't eat in 2001. She coughed and choked terribly and lost weight. A feeding tube was proposed, a 'Mic-key tube.'" I grin, "Yarra liked the name." Before it was inserted, the doctor told her, 'If you don't like it, you can have it taken out at any time…fifteen-minute procedure.'"

I'm remembering Yarra. Her face flushed, high on steroids, looking up at the doctor as he waves his arm as if he's removing the tube. He sounded so glib.

"I remember saying to myself, '*Doctor, there will be many difficult decisions to be made when that day comes.'"*

Father is very attentive, still. *Go on Joanne, he's waiting.* I sit up in my seat and add, "Chris and I considered the insertion of the feeding tube an intervention of extraordinary means, if you will. We believe she would have died without it. It has kept her alive all these years."

"Now the doctor will close the tube, with Yarra's approval, as best we can tell." I shake my head side to side. "The head nods and eye blinks she once used for communication are no longer reliable. Her husband and her closest friends spent days trying to determine if they understood correctly that she was 'ready to leave her body,' as they say, and that she understood what they would tell her doctor and the family. Now with her husband's approval and ours, the doctor will suspend feedings and liquids. She'll only be given palliative medication."

Father Patrick sits with this. He takes off his glasses and drops his chin. The ceiling light reflects on thin reddish strands falling over his forehead. He rubs his brow. We're both silent.

"Chris talks frequently with a doctor friend, Dr. Joseph Fennelly, who has made his life a spiritual practice of assisting dying patients and the families. He assured us there are no right or wrong decisions in palliative care. He said, 'All the decisions are difficult. You do the best you can and you pray.'"

Father responds, "Good advice, and it looks like you are doing just that, though it isn't easy to let go. The days ahead will be trying."

"Yes, this time it's our daughter." I pause. "In the past, whenever we could, we went to be with our sick and dying relatives. It's gotten to be something we can do. We finally came to see it as being like being midwives for birthing. We want to be with and assist our daughter in her transition through dying. I thought we could be strong, but by now I know I can't possibly gauge what that will mean to us emotionally."

The priest sits with his hands folded as if in prayer. *Maybe he is praying.*

"The hospital staff has been wonderful. They're taking care of us all."

Father nods. "Yes, I know they do very good work over at the hospital. Several of the nurses are from our parish. Have you met Andrea?" I feel from his relaxed response that I'm on safe ground with him.

"Yes, I know Andrea. She even offered us lodging. Everyone has been generous to us."

He looks at his appointment book, open on the desk. "Would you like me to bring the Last Sacraments to your daughter?"

I take a deep breath. "Thank you, Father. Yarra, in her travels, learned much about spiritual practices other than our Catholic religion; she chose another path. It took a while for us to become settled with her decision."

Father's blue eyes look straight at me. He is pondering, silent. In another part of the building a phone rings. I hear a female voice responding, but I don't hear words.

I feel as if I'm waiting to hear what Father is thinking.

"Oh, Joanne," he sighs. "It's so difficult, I know. I hear this story from many parents. Children leave the faith and take up their own ways of thinking about life. Often it breaks families apart."

I feel tears forming in my eyes. *He knows. I nod to Father Patrick.*

"It's good you have been able to come to peace with her decision." He extends his upturned hand. "How important it is that you and your husband and your other daughter, too, can be here to support her and her husband."

"Thank you, Father."

Father Patrick is sitting, relaxed, no signs he is ready to end the conversation.

"There is something else. We would like a service of some kind. I don't know if I will be responsible for planning it…setting it up. I don't think it will be in a church. I guess I just wanted to tell you that. We'll be at the service, whatever and wherever it is."

"Joanne, don't worry about your daughter. Let's see what God has in store." He looks kindly at me, "Over the years, I've learned everyone finds their own way to God."

I walk out onto a small porch. Cold, moisture-laden air smacks my teary cheeks. The pavement is wet, glaring in slashes of sunlight which slant through bare, black branches overhead. I feel as if I'm floating back in time. Ange/Yarra was always showing us her way.

> *I remember phone calls from watchful acquaintances, like Jim's phone call from the Dainty Pastry. "Mrs. Amoroso, two little girls are here. I thought you'd like to know. One is named Angela; the other is Mary. They say they are going to Denver on the bus today," he chuckled. "But they came in to get a doughnut*

first. I'll keep them here with doughnuts, if it's all right with you...until you come?"

When she was eleven, the police were alerted by our frantic babysitter that Angela was missing. They saw her walking on Main Street around five in the evening and brought her home. Of course, Angela had a good explanation, "There was a new girl at school. She didn't know her way to her new house across from the swimming pool. That's a long way, Mom. So, I took her to the swimming pool, then she was OK."

The day after the class skating party, I saw her legs were covered with black and blue marks, "What on earth happened to your legs?" Angela laughed, "Nancy wanted to skate and no one else would skate with her. We kept falling down."

Before her 17th birthday, she was an American Field Service Exchange Student living in Cusco, Peru. Years later, her younger brother Chris Jr. said, "Angela led the way out." I didn't know what he meant until I, too, went to Ecuador in 1984 with a volunteer health program, Amigos de las Americas. He was right.

While at Colorado State University, she spent one summer working in a fish processing plant on the Kenai Peninsula, Alaska. Her next summer, she worked at the Lions Club school for the handicapped in Woodland, Colorado, as art director. Her satisfaction with this experience convinced her to major in art therapy.

She transferred to the School for International Living (SIT) in Brattleboro, Vermont, where she earned a degree, and she practiced it. All the while, she continued living in what our New Zealand friends call the Antipodes, places on the opposite side of the earth. She had an excellent art therapy internship in Sydney, Australia under two fine art therapists, Vivian Miller and Denise Barry.

After graduation from SIT, she tried the US for a while then lived in Australia and visited New Guinea. Then there was a long period where she lived in Australia. She sent bushels of quirky, hand-made postcards professing love to all the family and wrote to both grandmothers.

She had several health episodes, both mental and physical. We kept in close touch through phone calls and mail. We visited her and so did her brothers and sister.

Fortunately, she met Kris, a man who became her joyful soulmate and eventually her caring husband. She made many supportive, long-time friends. She found her own way, and here we are, with her. Maybe Father Patrick is right.

Chapter 1—Joanne and Angela 1971

"Those People," Big Elk Meadows, Colorado

It is my son Joe's ninth birthday party at Big Elk Meadows. We have invited his boyfriends for a fishing party, well aware that five, nine-year-olds are a rambunctious lot. Ange, seven, is along for the fun of it. I'm taking the boys in a rowboat, one at a time, to fish along the shore. I ask the others to stay on the dock, but they're not staying. They are frog hunting in the tall grass and splashing each other and yelling. Chini, our standard poodle, is having a great time barking and romping around them.

I pull in to pick up a new fisherman and help put worms on fishing hooks. Jimmie gets in the boat. The boys on shore start snickering. Jimmie grins at me, and before I complete a stroke, he pulls a garter snake out of his pocket. The boys on the dock howl with laughter.

"Oh no you don't," I yell. "Out of the boat. No boys with snakes in here." I row back to the pier. The aluminum boat bangs into the dock. "Who's next?"

Ange gets bored. She asks, "Mom, see that car down there?" She points to the end of the lake. "A man and lady are fishing down there. I'm going to go down there."

"OK, honey, just don't get in their way."

That evening, back in town, after the boys were delivered to their homes, she and I were doing some drawing. "Mom," she says softly, without looking up from her drawing, "you know those people fishing at the lake?"

"Yes?"

"They were complaining about the noise. They said, 'Did you hear all that ruckus those people were making? Did you hear that black dog with those people barking?'"

"Oh, hmm, what did you say?"

She kept her head down, absorbed in her drawing, "I didn't say anything." She lifted her crayon and looked at me. "Then they said, 'Well, they were scaring all the fish away.' They were real mad. Chini came down the path and sat down beside me. The lady said, 'Do you know those people with that dog?'"

"Hmm? What did you say then?"

"I said, 'I am those people.'" Ange paused. "I turned around and walked away."

I played the scene over in my mind as I lay awake in bed. *"Those people...." She knows who she is, and she knows who we are. And she's not afraid to say so.*

Home by the Light of a Star, Big Elk Meadows, Colorado

"Come on, kids, get your backpacks. Let's head up to Kenny Mountain," calls Chris. Our friends, Lou and Joe Fennelly and kids from New Jersey, are visiting at our cabin. Chris and Joe and fourteen-year-old Angela, thirteen-year-old Brian, and eleven-year-olds, Chris, Jr. and Glen, are headed to a mountain park about a mile and a half away. The dads will get them settled into camp for the night, and Angela will stay with them.

Chris and Joe come back to the cabin to join Lou and me for a good evening of storytelling and card games. We haven't seen each other in years. It's almost midnight, and we are still chatting and laughing. We hear boots resounding on the porch. The door swings open, and there is Ange, looking disgusted, followed by three grumpy boys.

"What are you doing here? What's happened?"

"Chris Jr. had a belly ache," Ange explains. He thinks he's getting appendicitis. He had to come home."

"My gosh, Ange, how did you find your way down in the dark?"

"I couldn't see anything with my puny flashlight. We just kept walking downhill. When that bright star came out, the one that always comes out over the mountain across from our cabin, I knew the way home."

When Ange began her world wanderings, I watched the evening sky for Venus, her "bright star," assured by an inner knowing she would be able to find her way home.

Unmasking

On Halloween eve, I ask Ange to drive me to meet a teacher friend at the mall so we can wear our witch costumes together. My long, glued-on, black fingernails and strands of a stringy grey wig falling from under a broad-brimmed hat preclude my safe driving. Ange has just gotten her driver's license and is only too happy to do the driving. I keep quiet so she can concentrate.

"Mom," she says with a gentle, pondering tone, "I bet I'm the only sixteen-year old driving her mom around town on Halloween."

A silent, eerie moment passes. "Yes, probably so." It is uncanny. An uncertain feeling I've held about our relationship—that I know more about her than I know is real in this lifetime. I risk asking the question, "Ange, do you ever feel we lived together?" I hesitate. "Before?"

She answers as casually as if I'd asked her, "Do you have any homework?"

"Yes, Mom, I do, all the time. I feel like you were my sister, or I was your auntie."

I had much to ponder as I waited for Kathy, my costumed companion. *Did I do things with Ange that I wished I had done as a child? Did I wish I had done the zany things she chooses to do, with her "caution-to-the-wind" way? But tonight, Joanne, you're the one here in a witch's costume, and she's driving.*

Her simple declaration was a gift. Later, when she distanced herself from us, that nonchalant statement helped me. I knew that we both felt we were joined by another bond, however illusionary, from some previous, unknown time together, and we would be all right.

When's This Kid Going to Get a Job?

Chiara and Joe both had responsible jobs by ninth grade, Chiara as a pool lifeguard and Joe at the bicycle shop, as shopkeeper, alone on Saturdays. I'm still waiting for Ange to make a move. Yet, she had been Chris and John's "little mama" practically since they were born. I can't fault her for not moving to more babysitting, and I hoped she wouldn't be tempted to go to the ice cream shop.

The spring of her junior year she came home smiling and waving an envelope. "Hey, I got a job with the City of Longmont."

"Great, what's that?"

"Art director for the summer playground program!"

"Super, Ange. That sounds like an interesting job. Did you say art director?"

"Yeah, eight weeks. I get to choose all the projects and make the supply list for all materials. Five different parks and different groups of kids."

"And how are you going to get all your supplies around town? Do they have storage sheds?"

"No," she giggled. "Now that I have my license, I was hoping I could use the truck."

I gulped. *Well, there it is, Joanne. You wanted her to get a responsible job.*

She had a great summer. She learned advance preparation and time management. She observed different behaviors in the kids from the various socio-economic parts of town. Her projects were well received. Except perhaps for the last-minute Father's Day gifts; plaster of Paris ashtrays fashioned in empty tuna cans, then painted with the only paint color left, brown.

Ange brought one home for me to see. "Oh Mom I had them all laid out on the table. When the kids saw those brown lumps, they just started laughing and laughing, but they took them home to their dads, I guess."

The City of Longmont personnel may have seen what I saw—

Ange loved working with kids. She respected them. She was rehired to teach a Christmas gift-making, after-school class for disabled junior high students. She chose a tooled leather phone book cover for the project. She gave the sample she made to us for Christmas, and we used it for years.

There were six students of varying ages and abilities in the class. Ange gave a hand-written list to each student:

Come in, sit down, and start your project as soon as possible.

Not too much talking.

No leaving the table, unless you have to go to the bathroom.

No getting things out of the vending machine unless you didn't get lunch.

She asked me to visit her class. One afternoon, I walked in quietly and sat at the far end of the table. The students were intently engaged tapping metal design stamps on wet leather.

Ange quietly moved from student to student, assisting them if needed. She handed me a leather stamping magazine, "This is what they will look like, Mom."

Hearing that, one boy across the table stopped his work, raised his head and looked curiously at me. He called to Ange, "Is dat you mudda?"

She replied, "Yes, that's my mom."

The boy's eyes filled with mischief, his gleeful words floated in my direction, "You dah-tas..." he paused for emphasis, "craeezee." The students erupted in laughter. Ange flashed her dancing eyes around the table.

Ange Flies Away, 1979

Within a month, Ange would burst into the house, waving a set of papers saying, "You have to read this. I really want to go. Please come to the meeting."

It was a flyer for volunteers to American Field Service. We believed it was good for our kids to see how other people lived. AFS asked if there was a place she preferred not to be sent. She requested she not be assigned to high altitude or places where "people ate a lot of fish." In a month's time, she would be on her way to Cusco, Peru, elevation 11,000 feet. On Christmas Eve, she was served "fish eyeball" soup. It was the beginning of her exploring the world and new ways of living.

Only Ange's letters, full of information but long in arriving, kept us scantily apprised of her present situation. Telephone communication was difficult. The operators spoke little English. We spoke little Spanish. One of Ange's host family's names sounded like "librera." We were connected with the Cusco Library three times. Once, the telephone lines were not in service because the whole country was watching Peru in the televised world soccer games, including telephone operators.

She left one family because they insisted on giving her penicillin every time she got a cold. The second family dressed her up in fancy clothes to "parade her around" and locked her in her room when they left the house. A call to them resulted in a curt "estas en la calle" (She's on the street). Our frantic telegram inquiry to AFS resulted in an unsettling reply. "Don't worry, your daughter is with Jorge Romero."

Great. Whoever the heck Jorge Romero is!

Finally, Ange called. She has been taken in by the current mayor of Cusco, his wife, and three daughters. She bonded immediately with Carmella, the mother, and the girls, all students and all close to her age. Our local representative visited her in Cusco and returned to tell us, "Ange is devastated but does not want to leave." We had no idea what that meant, and he was not forthcoming.

I cut a branch off the Christmas tree and hung it with a few colored baubles from the ceiling in a corner of our living room to await her return in January. She arrived at the Denver airport dressed in a brown llama-yarn poncho and a red Peruvian hat, as slender as we had ever seen her, and carrying a stuffed baby llama.

After hugs, tears and flowers, we asked of the llama, "How did you ever get that on the plane?"

"Oh, I just did what they taught me in Peru. I batted my eyes at the pilot, and he took the llama himself into the cockpit."

Oh, great, that's all foxy Ange needed for her bag of tricks. Ange was no saint. She was sweet and funny, secretive and thoughtful, as well as conniving. She rarely asked us for permission to do things unless it involved our providing the money. Even so, we were rarely angry with her. She relied on her friends and her siblings for advice and help. She said her friend, Alice, "saved my life in Peru." We heard rumbles about her owing money to one of her siblings.

Two weeks after she was home, Ange and a friend, Moe, came to the front door after school. "Mom, I want to talk to you." We sat down in the living room. Ange told me she was addicted to drugs and alcohol and needed to go to a rehab center. Her explanation: "When the kids had a party, the parents locked the kids in the house and left them alone so they would 'be safe.'"

Denver General Rehabilitation staff decided that 18 years of age was too old for the juvenile program. Ange, instead, heard six weeks of stories of long-time users and their difficult life-long struggles. She recovered and, to my knowledge, never had a problem with addiction—excluding chocolate and coffee, of course.

I did a lot of praying when she went out with her gang. We went to follow-up meetings, which were usually attended by older people. We trusted her. We sporadically attended 12 Step programs. Eventually, Ange was told she was not addicted, but "situationally habituated."

Woodland Camp for the Handicapped, 1984

In Woodland Camp For the Handicapped for While in drug and alcohol rehabilitation, Ange missed the first five weeks of her senior high school year. Her English teacher declared with certainty, "She'll never get all her homework done. She can't graduate this year."

When she returned home from the rehabilitation center, her classmates and friends gathered round after school at our house to help her study and get reams of homework done. She graduated from Longmont High with her class.

During high school, Ange met Mimi Farrelly-Hansen, a local art therapist, who befriended her and introduced her to art therapy. As a child, anytime Chris and I went out in the evening, she left scribbled drawings and notes on white tissues on her nightstand beside the bed. Intuitively, Ange had been using art for her own healing since she was seven. Mimi saw that in Ange and encouraged her to consider art therapy as a possible career choice.

The summer after high school graduation, Ange applied for a job at Colorado Lions Club Camp in Woodlands, Colorado, a camp for people with disabilities. She was hired for a summer job teaching art. For the first three weeks, there was a set of students divided by age and inclusive of all disabilities. Later in the summer, the sight-impaired and the hearing-impaired would attend.

It sounded like a complicated assignment, but she was accepted. Again, she was responsible for designing the projects, ordering the supplies and instructing the classes. I gratefully assisted her in thinking up projects that could be completed or experienced by special needs students. The school nurse was Ange's assistant.

Two projects for the blind, for example, were making "soap on a rope" for showering and creating a giant papier-mâché egg and painting it. Then, the students created a long rope from torn fabrics and wove a nest by winding the rope around three trees. They placed the giant egg in the nest. The projects were visual, tactile, sensual—and a success. Ange created weeks of projects. When she called home, her voice was high with excitement. She was in her glory, up to her ears in art projects and special students.

She made a visit home while she was at Woodland. She got out of the old Volvo, stood in our driveway, threw up her arms and yelled, "I taught them how to wash their pits!"

After hugs, she told us the story, "The female students always wanted to sit close to me. They keep saying, 'You smell so good.'

I noticed they didn't smell good. I asked the school nurse to let me check out shower time. We went together into the shower room. We saw the students were afraid of getting under the noisy showers and walking on the slippery floor. They couldn't move around to wash all their bodies, under their arms and down below. The nurse made arrangements to get the shower streams adjusted and put mats on the floors."

I'd never seen Ange so pleased and proud. She so thoroughly enjoyed the whole experience. Her vacation opened her to a life vocation, working with people with disabilities, preferably in art therapy.

College and Beyond

Angela was admitted to Colorado State University in 1983 with the lowest SAT score of any student previously accepted. Her admission was based on her Peruvian foreign student experience, the confidence of the counselor who interviewed her and, who knows, perhaps a little "eye batting."

College at CSU was a struggle. She moved out of the dorms, as there was too much temptation to waste time partying. She moved to a small apartment and discovered one day when she walked in her apartment that, "Nothing happens in that apartment unless I do it." She helped a dear friend with newborn twins. She bought an electric scooter, which scared us all.

Her experiences at CSU were varied. She enjoyed social studies very much, answered the crisis line for credit and reported, "My social studies teacher said, 'If you students, years from now when your children are grown, would not replace the family room furniture, but send your children off to foreign lands, the world would be a better place.'" Angela took the message to heart.

Math was her biggest challenge. She could take the pass-fail required math test as many times as necessary until she passed or gave up. She didn't give up. She repeated the test eight times before passing.

She excelled in art and brought home her artwork and the stories. One stark piece was a charcoal drawing of an anatomically perfect, twisted human tongue, centered on a sheet of white 14" by 20" paper.

"Ange, what's this?"

"My class assignment," she giggled. "The teacher said, 'Draw anything you've seen here on campus in the last twenty minutes, then bring them up to the desk as you finish. We'll spend the rest of the class reviewing.' When the teacher came to mine, he held it up and asked, 'Whose is this? Where did this come from?' I said, 'It's mine. I saw it in the hall, outside the men's bathroom.'"

I gasped.

Ange laughed. "The kids went crazy. The teacher said, 'Class is over.'"

The following summer Angela applied for a job in a fish factory on the Kenai Peninsula in Alaska. She walked out of our driveway with 100 pounds in her giant red backpack. She lived in a modified boxcar. She almost fainted the first day on the gutting line. She learned the company was looking for a Spanish-speaking person to work in sales with Japanese merchants, in "the roe room." The Spanish she had learned in Peru got her off the "blood and guts" production line.

In the fall, Angela called to say she would be late returning to CSU. The salmon run had not been good, and she wanted to stay for another processing season. Three of our children were enrolled in college. We didn't mind a break.

Angela realized traditional school wasn't for her. When she returned, she sought advice from the same counselor at CSU who had interviewed her for admission. He understood her needs and suggested the School for International Training in Brattleboro, Vermont. It was the right school for Angela.

In a letter to all relatives in 1984, Angela wrote, "I'm at the Experiment in International Living in Brattleboro, Vermont, preparing for an internship, hopefully, in art therapy somewhere in the world. Any of you have contacts? Let me know."

The Guided Tour

In the summer of 1984, our son John and I enrolled as health volunteers in Amigos de Las Americas; John supervising latrine building in the Dominican Republic, and me, in Ecuador in an eyeglass distribution program and briefly as a nurse assistant in a cataract program. I returned home just days after Angela left for School for International Training in Vermont. I'd hoped to chat with her and compare notes about her senior high trip to Peru in 1979 with American Field Service, but I missed her.

Angela's Bachelor of Arts degree in International Living included an internship in art therapy in Sydney, Australia under two excellent art therapists, Denise Barry and Vivien Miller.

Her Christmas card said, "Australia is wonderful. The people fill me with fascination, and the environment is like a fairy tale."

Later, when I saw a magazine article about the Milford Trek in New Zealand, I showed it to Chris. "Look at this, Honey. Sounds like a great hike, only five days, supported, overnight lodgings, and we could stop to see Angela in Sydney."

I remember Angela's excited voice when we phoned her during her art therapy internship in Sydney. I told her we were traveling to New Zealand to do the Milford, and we would come to Australia to visit her. She bawled into the phone, "Mom, you can't come to Australia and not go to the Great Barrier Reef; it's the chance of a lifetime."

I knew of the Great Barrier Reef, but vaguely. Angela raved on about how we could go on a resort boat and see all kinds of ocean creatures. "I can arrange it for you, Dad; I've done it, and it's wonderful." But "Dad," Chris, doesn't enjoy boats. He prefers race walking around the beach.

I enjoyed the "Silver Queen," a large tour boat that provided a glass-bottom rowboat for viewing the magnificent sea creatures that the guide brought to the surface, such as a "six-pound pink baloney" with tiny green flowers growing on it and a bright blue starfish. I wanted more and inquired.

"Yes, there is a resort dive available with a personal guide for uncertified divers." I certainly fit the "uncertified" part. I'd never gone scuba diving, but, assured that the guide would stay close at hand, I was willing. My day with five experienced divers from around the world included two dives and diving to the ocean floor to cautiously poke a finger toward an enormous ocean clam. Chris described it later to friends, "Joanne rates her life experiences, and, right now, this scuba dive far surpasses her marriage to me."

It was a terrific time together. Angela came with us to New Zealand. We spent evenings in excellent backpackers' hostels and we drove through beautiful New Zealand to Milford. When we arrive at our hotel, there was a message for me from my brother, Joe. Our father, who had been languishing for months in a nursing home, is "not doing well. Will telegraph tomorrow before you start your walk." In the morning, he wrote, "Dad doing some better. Go, enjoy your walk."

During our five-day trek, the South Island of New Zealand experiences torrential rains. The waterfalls are stupendous. At tea break, the river rises ten inches. The water flows over our path above our knees. From behind me, I hear a guide scream, "Chris! Stop! You're walking into the river."

I turn and see Chris jump back into our line of sodden stragglers, and he is saved.

We gratefully exit the trek, and spy Angela waiting with a big smile. She calls out, "Congratulations, you two. You made it!" She stretches her arms out to hug us both.

I sense guardedness about her. "Daddy?" I ask. She nods and says in a hushed tone, "So sorry, Mom, Grandpa died two days ago."

It hits me…*Daddy is gone*. Tears well up. Chris puts his arm behind me, draws me to him. Angela pulls us out of the path of other hikers jostling past with their gear bags.

"Chiara and Joe are with Grandma. She told me to tell you they are taking care of everything for her. You should have heard her voice, Mom. She is doing OK." Angela embraces the two of us again. I feel her calmness, and I'm glad she's with us.

On our last evening of traveling toward Christchurch Airport, Angela and I share a room in a backpackers' hostel. I have seen how self-assured she is as we travel. As we are changing into our pajamas, I ask her, "Angela, how do you know who to travel with and how to travel safely?"

She flashes a confident smile, "I talk with everyone, Mom, you know me. I find out who the safe travelers are and," she laughs, "I have eyes in the back of my head."

Chris and I have a very brief flight to Sydney. I feel spent and sad. The bustle in the airport exhausts me.

"Chris, there's a patio outside the entry. Do I have time to go outside for a breath of air and some quiet time?"

"Plenty of time. Are you OK going alone?"

"Yes, I prefer to go alone, OK? I'll stay close."

"OK, check your watch. Be back at this terminal in forty-five minutes."

A vast expanse of sun-filled, blue sky arches overhead. I take a deep breath. Warm tears course down my cheeks. I'm miles away. I see Dad in my mind's eye, in his casket at the funeral home. I wonder about Mom and when I will be going home.

"Madame," I hear a man's voice, a formal, accented, "Madame? " at my side. A soldier in blue uniform greets me with a salute and a soft, steady, look. "Raymond, of the RAF, at your service."

Surprised and bewildered as to how to respond, I reply, "Oh…so kind, thank you…there's nothing…." My voice trails off. "I'm OK, really, I just need a breath of air." I wipe my eyes and my sniffles.

Raymond waits, his eyes still questioning, "Do you feel safe here, Madame?"

"Yes, thank you, I just learned…I've gone to see my father as often as I could for years, and now this morning…while I'm away from home…I've just completed a five-day trek in the Milford Sound." I take a breath. "When I ended the trek, I learned my father had died."

The young man's face changes from concern to surprise and then softens.

"Madame, I am truly sorry for your grief. I surely do know how you feel." He pauses and clears his throat. "This is, if I must say, extraordinary. Last year, I experienced the same. I visited my father every month, and he, too, died while I was out of country. My heartfelt condolences."

I can only look at him in wonder. *Extraordinary indeed.* I raise my fingers to my lips, pondering.

He glances at his watch, "Is there anything I can do for you? If not, I'll leave now, I must catch my flight."

I nod my head. "Raymond, thank you so much. My husband is here with me. I'll find a bench. I'll be OK." I regain my senses, extend my hand and grasp his and add, "I'm so sorry for your loss, as well, and your courtesy has also been something I will never forget."

He gives a small salute and disappears in the crowd.

I sit gently, trying to take in our similar circumstances. *How could that happen?* I hear footsteps approaching. Here comes Raymond, with arm outstretched. "This is for your flight home." He offers me a red rose wrapped in green tissue. My throat tightens.

His soft blue eyes hold my attention. "If I may take the liberty, Madame, to share again, some of my experience." I nod.

"Since my father's passing, as he did, I've come to see my life as…" he hesitates, looks down, "as a guided tour." He smiles a wistful smile and, with another gentle salute, disappears into the crowd.

NO,L NO,L NO,

Spare a minute and
you'll find peace.

1986, the year of peace – I hope you
will join me this holiday season
and reflect on our world, one world,
at peace. I'm working hard down-
under to keep my balance so I can
finish my senior year. Australia is
wonderful. The people fill me with
fascination and the environment is like
a grand fairytale. You all are dear
in my memory and to you I send
my love.

Merry Merry &
New Year Cheers
~ Angela ~

Graduation SIT, Brattleboro, VT, 1987

Everything is exciting for the grandmas who are infrequent travelers. Never before have they traveled together on a family trip. For my mom, Lucy Pisoni, it is the first time to attend a grandchild's college graduation. Chris and I flew to Brockway, Pennsylvania to pick up Lucy and then drove to Erie for Chris' mom, Alberta. We spent another three hours visiting as we all drove to Rochester, New York. When the motel elevator doors opened, both the moms gasped, "Oh, what a pretty elevator…mirrors…etched walls."

On the following morning's drive when Chris comments that we had already crossed two state lines and would cross three more before our destination in Brattleboro, they could hardly contain themselves. Driving through five states in two days, they counted on their fingers: Pennsylvania, New York, Massachusetts, New Hampshire, and Vermont.

In the evening, son Joe arrives. He asks the grandmothers, "Would you two like to go to late breakfast with me? That way we'll be rested for graduation and the dinner later on. What d'ya you think?"

All three of them beam.

"Sure, Joe," Guggie says, "Breakfast with my grandson—why not?"

"OK, see you in the morning, 10:30."

Saturday morning, the audience of board members, teachers, parents, and fellow students are seated on folding chairs in a crowded semi-circle, inside a white canvas tent. The men wear suits and the women pastel wool, spring suits. I'm comfortable in a tobacco green, lightweight suit. It's only ten o'clock, and it's already getting warm.

The graduates are presenting their senior projects: reports of their work in various international settings where they have spent the last six months. One by one, they appear from behind a white backdrop. Chris tilts the program toward me. Angela is up next with, "The Aboriginal Dreamtime in Relation to Aboriginal Art."

The white curtain sways. She slides out. Her dark, lustrous, wavy hair drops around her bare shoulders. She's wearing her favorite multicolored sheer skirt. She is tan, barefoot, and bare breasted. Her chest is painted in bright swirls of green, yellow and white paint. She stands in front of a staid crowd of conservatively and totally dressed students and students' relatives.

Oh, my God! How did I get a kid like this? "Cover up" was Mom's watchword. I catch my breath. I clamp my teeth. My arms drop to the side of my folding chair. I grip my fingers around the metal seat to hold myself upright. *Where did she get the idea to do this? And the nerve.* I strain to hear what she says about representing some percentage of the world's female population.

Oh, yes, I get that loud and clear, and you also represent Angela.

My throat is tight. I force myself to breathe.

A memory flashes. When my girl cousins and I went upstairs to the bedroom to change into shorts for wading, each of us faced into a corner or hid in the closet or wiggled out of panties under our cotton slips, so as not to reveal one square inch of bare skin.

There stands my daughter. Welcoming us as benignly as a princess, she holds a woven circular tray with brown lumps of something on it. *I'm feeling very warm. I think I may faint.* I hold on tight. *Breathe, breathe.* Chris has not moved nor whispered a word or sound.

She speaks in a mellifluous voice everyone in our family recognizes as the one she uses when she has been deeply moved by something or wants to impart some wisdom she perceives. Or when she wants to con us.

Yes, I get that. The dreamtime...*She's talking about the dreamtime*. I feel a drop of perspiration trickle down my hairline. I tip my head slightly to keep it from the corner of my eye. I see a male student lean forward with a wicked grin. He's trying to catch our reaction. Chris' chin is set straight forward. He hasn't moved. His hands are in his lap.

In the background, a video camera grinds away, saving it all for posterity and surely for any absent board members. Angela speaks about Aboriginal life in Australia and their perception of life. She talks in a modulated, studious voice about her experience with Aborigines and describes their worldview, a very different and spiritually rich view from which we on the outside could learn and benefit.

Is she really going to pull this off? Is she really going to get away with this? I can't concentrate on anything she's saying. Is she really making a point, or is she just trying to pull the wool over our eyes? In this moment, I wish I could pull something over my eyes, but so far, she's getting away with her gig.

She picks up the tray. Angela instructs all to pause, imagine, and create our vision of the world. From a walnut-sized lump of brown clay? Angela continues her mellifluous patter, not a word of which I can remember. Somewhere it will be recorded, probably. It will be typed up quite eruditely, if…she graduates.

Oh, no. She's coming into the audience. She begins to speak very seriously, reverently, offering a lump of clay to each person, as if she were distributing Holy Communion. Beyond the tray I see her tan, tea-cup sized breasts. I keep my eyes lowered as she passes the tray into our row. *I don't dare look her in the eyes. We both may lose it.*

As much as I can see crosswise from my lowered eyelids, everyone else, including the students who are struggling to maintain composure, is also looking studiously down at the lumps in their hands and not at the girl who leans forward and twists among them with her dubious offerings. Her long black hair brushes across the cupped curves of her breasts inches from their eyes.

After a few silent minutes, the people around us either mash the clay or stare at it intently. Or stare at the young woman in the front of the room. *I'm glad we don't know anyone.*

Angela works her way through narrow aisles of folding chairs, offering everyone a portion of clay. She fingers each piece, graciously focusing on each as if it imparted some wisdom special to her. I can't look at her. Cautiously…I drop my clay ball into her hand. She straightens and holds the tray with the clay pieces high, moves to the front of the room where, mercifully, the next student is waiting to present his paper.

Chapter 2—Love Me Now

Georgia-New Mexico-Sydney, 1988

Unintentionally, she's been preparing me with her zany experiences for years. I've learned to expect the unexpected, stay open, really open, to surprises and to breathe and pray.

After SIT graduation, she tried several stateside ventures. The first was an attempt to establish a strawberry farm in rural Georgia with Anita and Debbie, classmates from SIT, and Ange's brown-skinned, well-educated, well-mannered boyfriend. They learned first-hand how the world works in rural Georgia.

When I call and reach her "under the trailer, trying to fix the plumbing," I ask, "How's the relationship going?"

Ange murmurs, "It's not going so good, Mom. He's only been out of New York City once, and that was the time he came to visit us in Colorado. It's way too hard for him here." She assures me, "Don't worry, we're on first-name basis with the sheriff."

Ange comes back to Longmont and tries working part-time in a department store during Christmas. She says "the materialism and madness stresses me to the max." I see her exhaustion and that she had learned more global values at SIT.

Big sister Chiara invites her to share her apartment in Santa Fe, New Mexico. Ange would help her with the work of establishing an art gallery for a Minnesota owner. Chiara phones, "We are having a good time together, Mom, but," she giggles, "I hold my breath when Ange walks across the floor with an expensive bowl in her hands. You know how she is."

Yes, I know how she is...constant chocolate stains on her clothes, dropped jelly jars, and glasses, bumping into tables.

Chiara goes on, "We're having so much fun together, making friends with the artists, and every evening we walk out to see the sunsets. I'm so glad she came."

For years after, "I'll see you in the sunsets" was their endearing phrase, but neither beloved sister nor sunsets could hold Ange in Santa Fe when a teacher-friend from SIT sent a notice about an Aboriginal Rock Art International Conference scheduled in Darwin, Australia in 1988. Ange told us she would send a letter to relatives and some of our friends asking for financial assistance for her plane ticket to Australia. We were grateful for those who responded. She purchased her tickets to an amazing adventure.

After the conference, she sends us a photo of herself while in camp with two dark-skinned women, standing in a jungle pond and probing knee-high water with long poles. She scribbles on the back, "Thumping for turtles on the bottom of the pond for soup, for tea. Don't worry, my new friends know where the crocodiles are."

She remains in Sydney. She teaches art therapy for teens in prison. She is excited and encouraged by the results of her work. *Color Your Day,* which we saw in notebook form, was one of her most successful exercises and won praise from her students, mentors, and supervisors.

She accompanies the teens and crew on a long sailboat trip to New Guinea.

Angela sends us a handwritten letter:

"Barque, St Paul...' Up You Go'"
This is the boat I was on when I was hired as an art therapist for disadvantaged teenagers in a developmental program in Byron Bay, Australia. There were twenty-five children, five staff, and a sailing crew. The boat was wood, with beautiful

sails, ropes, and nets. At certain times, we were free to climb up the masts, usually in the afternoon rest period. The masts were breathtakingly high. We clipped ourselves into the cross beams to sit and only unclipped when we were moving. We had safety ropes, but if you fall, you would be swinging about the mast.

We slept in the hull, sometimes on the deck, and we ate on the deck. We did art therapy down in the hold. There were some very emotional sessions. Sometimes, they would tell me some unbelievable life experiences like the death of a father or watching a mother deliver a stillborn baby. The tears would be flowing down their faces.

I'd say, "OK, this happened. You need to say all you need to say about it. You can say it to me. That's all that's necessary. Nothing else will happen."

I always had cookies at the end of the session. When they were done talking, I'd say, "OK, now you're free, up you go." I'd lead them up on deck and tell them, "Climb up there and see how far you can see." Sometimes, tears would still be streaming down their faces. They would know other people could see them crying, and they'd try to "get tough" to get ready to climb. I'd climb up with them, or, if they wanted, they went alone; that was fine, too. They took it as their challenge. The younger girls especially would say, "Come with me." Sometimes they stayed up, then I'd go up to get them, or the ship's captain would whistle them down, if the weather were changing.

I hope that growth happened through that experience, and they could continue growing as beautiful as they were.

We went out on the bow of the boat and hung in the nets under the bow. Dolphins would come play around the bow and leap around us. Two nights I slept outside with the girls; we laughed and laughed, told dirty stories and cramped all together in one spot. When we slept in the hold, we could hear the whales singing to each other.

We had a one-week session on "How to get in touch with yourself." Another week's session was "Your worst memory from childhood"— write it down, and share with one person, then have a sacred time of burning the slip of paper in the fire. It left all of us in tears.

Angela had found her element. We were happy and relieved.

During 1986 and 1989, Angela and Joe travel Australia. We hear only good things from the time the siblings spent together. We think she is doing fine in Sydney with Denise, but Angela writes of strange symptoms—tingling in her hands and distorted vision. I hear of several broken romances.

In 1989, we receive a letter from Denise who writes positively of Angela and the work she's doing with teens in prison, then adds, "I hope this does not cause you too much concern, but I think you should know that Angela is depressed and went off on her own."

Soon after, Angela sent a letter from Byron Bay telling us she'd come to "get a tan and meet some good people here who helped me." Many years later, I learn that "get a tan" was code for not wanting anyone to find her body "bleach-white."

"Maybe I will stay and start a children's art program. There's a doctor here who is interested. Would you be able to loan me some money to get it going?" We agree, hoping a valuable art-related project will settle her. The art program doesn't materialize. "We couldn't get supplies. It got too late. The summer children went back home. Maybe we'll get it started next summer," Angela explains.

We don't know what to make of it. We don't question her. We wait and wonder.

Shortly after, Angela writes saying she might be out of touch for a while. "I'm 'going walk-about' with Kris." Other times, she'd been out of touch in Alaska, in Peru. Where now?

She's never out of touch for long; there's always the funky handmade postcard from Australia saying, "Tell everyone I'm happy," or the pound package of black licorice logs or a message and a gift. The card says, "Since the kids left home, you deserve a more relaxing wind chime." A raffia rope strung with dried nut-pods clatters out of the package. The wind chime is unusual, soothing, like branches in the breeze, yet it reminds me of my wandering child… ah, yes, "unusual," too. Dear God…my prayer is interrupted by a flash, *Joanne, remember, she's the girl who came down Kenny Mountain…by the light of a star.*

Communication Gap

Joanne T. Pisoni Amoroso

Standing at the sink, I think of you
see your smiling face, your eyes,
your sunlit, tousled hair.

In the way that I know best
I want to tell you that I long
to be with you laugh, talk
and feel your love.

I find recipes, spices,
bags of chocolate chips.
I plan something to send,
set aside mailing boxes
but, of course, that's futile thinking….
given the distances
you'd forever be receiving stale crumbs.

I walk around the yard,
snip pine, crab apple, sumac,
ivy, basil, parsley, marigold, cosmos.
Risk postal fines so you could
pour home out of a plastic bag.

I scan catalogs, turn down page corners
thinking you'd like the colors of this beach towel
these funky socks, that book…
fur boots, that warm shirt,
but when you received it,
what would it say?

So, I send news clippings on God knows what …
topics that I think would interest you;
poems written on napkins;
letters that are too long; tapes;
impulsive post cards, or often when I think of you

I send nothing at all.
Feel how lonely it is to try to stay connected
to express that which, through years of living together,
came in the door unspoken.

I'm in bed reading when Angela calls from Australia. "Mom, I didn't want to leave without talking to you."

Oh, she's doing it; she's leaving. Where? With anyone?

"Oh, Angela, I'm so glad you called. How are you?"

"I'm good, Mom. The guy I'm with, Kris. He's very nice. His mom wrote a book about his family, they're Dutch. I'm sending you the book."

"Yeah? O-o-k, thanks. When are you leaving?"

"This afternoon."

"This afternoon?" My voice goes up. I catch my breath.

"Mom," she talks rapidly. "I don't have more coins to put in the phone. Say 'bye to Dad. I'm very excited. We're going to India, to Pune. Love you, Mom. Bye."

The line goes dead. She's gone.

Dazed, I drop the receiver in my lap. *She said she was going to Pune.*

I roll over and reach into my stash of old magazines. *Where was that article?* It's about a man named, Osho Rajneesh, in Oregon. The whole commune closed down after it was discovered the commune leaders had committed a number of serious crimes. Osho was deported. Many countries refused him entry. Eventually, he went to live at an ashram in Pune, India.

I paid attention to the magazine story. Close friends of ours had experience with cults. Some had lost young adult children to cults. One young woman was seriously ill after childbirth because the cult refused her blood transfusions for anemia. Another couple, a local hardware store owner, church people, turned their whole life, family, careers and belongings over to a cult. Their daughter went off to join a group embarking on a supposed space ship launching. She died overdosing on drugs.

We spend a week stunned and investigating locally for any professional with experience dealing with cults. We heard of a doctor in Santa Fe, who for many years had been Osho's personal physician. He tells us by phone of his own story of joining his mother in the cult. He said that unless the cult is very controlling, some people leave on their own, as he did. His mother chose to stay.

We locate Father Kent Burtner, a Dominican priest, whose chosen work is to counsel with former cult members and their parents. Over the phone, he gives us a tutorial on the wide range of cults and cult-like behaviors. For a week, Chris and I spend agonizing hours discussing what to do or should do, if anything.

Finally, we decide that Chris should go to Pune, India. Our son Chris Jr. chooses to interrupt a winning triathlon season, to go with Chris. Getting to the ashram was a long difficult trip requiring a twenty-hour air flight to India, a cross-country train trip, and finally a harrowing, long taxi ride in which the driver seemed intent on challenging death.

Once at Pune, Chris and Chris Jr. were required to have blood studies for AIDS and a medical exam. All of this is to check out Angela's safety.

Is such verification possible when your adult child steps away beyond safety boundaries as you know them? I'd rather have contact, rather have peace, do what I can when I can, than hash over hurts and lament the possibility of irreparable harm. My desires, but it was Chris and Chris Jr. who made the trip.

Once inside, they found starry-eyed Angela and became acquainted with Kris. Angela, now renamed "Suki" by Osho, had been trained in tending roses and was enchanted with her new work and the ashram lifestyle. "When I was with Osho, I learned to meditate," she later told me. Meditation served her well for life.

Angela/Suki and Kris return to Australia to the commune where she originally met Kris. At that time, she described the people in the commune as "kind people who took good care of me." We wonder in uncertainty for a year, if she is in a controlling cult. Fr. Burtner advises us to keep in touch. That has certainly not been a problem. Angela sends bushels of cards of her own creation and letters signed "Suki" to us and her siblings and signed "Angela" to the grandmothers.

We call often. The commune has one phone. When we reach someone, we hear a voice calling, "Does anyone know where…? "

What did he say? He didn't say "Angela?" I'm addressing her mail to Suki. Hope she gets it. More voices call in the distance. I can't make out the name. I imagine people running around in a forest. If they get her to the phone, I'll be happy.

Angela answers, giggling, "Mom, no one here gets phone calls from their parents."

Good, it's a reminder of who you are and who we are. Fr. Burtner's advice is working.

In 1990, Angela came to Colorado for Chiara's December wedding. She reveled in her Aussie accent and asserted her newly chosen lifestyle. All the young women in the wedding party wore long, white taffeta gowns with black velvet, off-the-shoulder bodices. Angela was the only member of the group wearing curly puffs of dark curls in the hollows under her tanned bare shoulders.

I choose to see her healthy and happy and be grateful.

In 1992, we plan to go to Australia to visit Angela. We ask Fr. Burtner to meet with us in the airport in San Francisco. We pour out our fears and ignorance of cults. He responds with a tutorial and reassurance.

His advice. "You really have to judge on a case-by-case basis. There may be a case and time where an individual's freedom is totally betrayed. When methods are used that deprive individuals of their ability to make a free choice. In another case, an individual's freedom, given slightly different circumstances, is not."

He also said, "If she's led a normal childhood until sixteen, chances are she will eventually tire of it and say, 'This isn't for me' and leave on her own."

Normal? I stopped looking for "normal" a long time ago. Chris has a joke when old friends ask, "How are the kids?" He replies, "On the average, they're doing well, but it's a hell of a range."

Did Angela have a "normal" upbringing? No matter what the circumstances, I'm sure I want to visit my daughter. That's normal.

Our first morning in Byron, Angela came to the motel with flowers and Australian fruit varieties such as rambutans, red ovals covered with spines; course-skinned lychees; and purple and yellow passion fruit—all new to us. She showed us how to open them and watched while we tasted them. She took us for a walk along the proverbial endless white sand beach, and it was stunning.

We went for lunch at a veggie café. We ate outdoors on a raised porch overlooking a white beach and deep blue ocean, a peaceful, magnificent experience.

"Mom and Dad," Angela looks at us seriously. "I've chosen a new name," she declares. "You can call me 'Yarra.' It suits me better."

"Yarra," we repeat. "Yarra."

Chris breathes out. "I like that."

I smile, "That's what your friends were saying when they called you to the phone. I couldn't make it out. That's a lovely name." *What to say? We're here, enjoying the day together—almost "normal."*

I met Kris Kolff the second day of our visit when he came with Yarra to the motel to drive us to the commune. He peeked out from under the broadest brimmed straw hat I'd ever seen. I'd not really seen his face.

Yarra confides, "He's got problems with the sun."

My impression is that he is having problems facing the American parents, with all the negatives that might hold for him, particularly the parents of a girl with whom he went off to India, to an ashram. Never mind the fact that he's twenty years older than Yarra. And where did the money to visit India come from? Was it the money she asked us for to establish and teach a children's art program? Sounds like you have the problem, Joanne.

"Chris has been for a walk around town. He's a walker. He's upstairs changing. He'll be ready in a few minutes." Kris nods.

I point to some carry bags and a box, near the door. "Here's lunch and some food for the day. Is there room for it in the car?" He looks at the boxes and bags I have next to the door.

"Not much leg room. Will they be OK in the boot?"

"Sure, you arrange the boxes, and I'll carry out the day bags."

He sets the boxes down behind the car and opens the trunk door. He turns to me, tilts his face up under the sun hat and looks into my eyes. His voice is strong and reassuring, "I want you to know that money you gave Yarra—that was…" He pauses momentarily, "her money. She wanted to go to India. She used it." He pauses again to emphasize, "her money."

There it is, out in the open. Kris' words come out so fast I catch my breath. They tumble in my head. I hold his gaze. He wants me to know he didn't use the money and wants to set things straight with us. He wants us to know he's an honest person. "Her money," not used for him.

I'm not surprised with Yarra's contrivance to do whatever was best for herself according to her own deliberations. She would do that. I'm surprised by this man, Kris, his openness and clarity. He, of the concealed eyes, cares about his integrity. He's risked a confrontation. He cares about this relationship, I think. Theirs…ours.

Kris heaves the boxes. With his broad shoulders and enormous hat, his face disappears under the lid. I stand mystified.

Chris comes bounding out the door mimicking the Australian, "Gud'aye, Gud'aye."

I jump, and my thoughts scatter.

Kris withdraws from under the lid, laughing and looking up at Chris.

We all pile in the car and drive to the commune.

Yarra points out her favorite beaches, walking paths, and trees. The rest of us are mostly silent. We really don't know each other except for when Chris and Chris Jr. visited with them in Osho's commune in Pune. Not a comfortable conversation point.

Best tell him we enjoyed reading his mother's book...except she wrote, "Kris was near graduation with a master's degree in business when his life took another direction." Best stop trying, Joanne; let things take their course.

Armed with wariness, we arrive at the commune, a place in the bush just up from the ocean. A few men and women are engrossed in slapping and smoothing stucco on a wooden-framed hut and splashing their tanned bodies and splashing their clothing as well. Kris comments, "We all build our own homes here."

The home being built looks substantial. It will have windows and a framed door. Other habitats are "jungle homes" of reeds, brush, and fronds. A woman peeks out through a doorway, as if she knows of our arrival but quickly withdraws. I imagine Yarra has told friends of our coming.

It is very quiet, very peaceful. A few other people look up from their open-air tasks as we walk in with Kris. A few smile. Some others keep to themselves as we walk towards what Yarra and Kris call, "Our home under a tree."

A fence woven of five-foot-long twigs and cord encloses a twenty-foot circle under a large overhanging shade tree. Inside the circle are tree stumps and a small wooden chair, baskets and boxes, a table, and a small open cabinet of shelves.

In my childhood, we girls created "play houses" under the trees in Pennsylvania. I hear our voices announcing, "Here's the kitchen and this is the living room." I can easily surmise the stumps are for sitting and serving surfaces for meals and tasks. Baskets encircling the fence hold books, clothing, utensils and blankets, replacing shelves and cabinets. I can't help but smile. It's so familiar to me, "playing house." And Yarra is here. Her reality is living out my fantasy.

Yarra pulls back a portion of the twig fence and looks up, smiling. "Welcome to our living space." I hear a bit of a dare in her voice. "Come sit down." She points to the only chair, for me. *This must be the "company chair." I feel I am "company."* Chris settles easily on a stump.

In the shade, Kris doffs his hat. He's handsome, puckish, with mischievous boyish features and yet sturdy. His shoulders are wide and square, lips smooth and broad and his nose sculpted. A mass of tousled, grey curls above unruly eyebrows frame expressive blue eyes. He moves with energized ease. Yet there are so many unknowns. We are wary around each other.

This guy had nothing to do with Yarra's past out-of-bounds choices—Peru, New Guinea, Alaska, Australia. Now, here with him, she seems safe. When she went to Pune, she called you to tell you she would be "out of touch for a while." Let it go. She looks happy. She is living a dream, loving her own life. In all of her photos she is looking straight on, smiling a broad "look at me" smile. She loves the guy, and he is very gentle with her.

It's delightful sitting here under overhanging branches. The living space is delineated from the surrounding bush by upright posts strung with woven brush carpets. They must have had fun working on it. Imagine, her furnishings are a kitchen table, tree stumps, hanging baskets, rows of storage baskets and tins. A small caravan on wheels is the only enclosed space. I start from my meandering when Yarra squeals, "Look Kris, there's a carpet python in my basket."

Python? I try to shrink myself back into a tiny wooden folding chair. "Come see, Mom: it looks just like a braided rug when it's all rolled up."

Yarra is grinning like an imp. She knows she has been pushing all my buttons. A snake in her "living room" might just push me over the edge.

Kris steps into the surrounding bush. He pulls a long branch from the grass and walks to the basket near where Yarra is sitting. He peers in, "You're right, it is a carpet snake. Sit still." He hooks the stick under the basket handle.

"Is it dangerous?" Chris asks, shifting to the side. Casually, Kris replies, "Oh, they can bite but aren't venomous. They are so beautiful; some people keep them as pets. We'll just put him out in the bush. He'll crawl away."

Yarra's eyes are dancing. She couldn't have planned a better entertainment for her parents.

"Come on, Mom." Yarra gets up. "Is your swimming suit in the car? Change in our bedroom in the camper. I want to take you to one of my favorite places. It's called Tea Tree Pond. You know the Tea Tree salve I use for everything? It's wonderful. Well, there's a big Tea Tree next to the water, you'll see. I usually come down here on my bike, it's not far. We'll be ready to jump in when we get there. I love it. It's magic."

We turn off the road onto the narrow path.

"Here we are!" Yarra announces as she strips off her top and shorts and walks to the edge of a totally black, 30-foot-wide pond.

Golden-tipped, parched grasses pierce the red-orange sand under our feet and encircle the pond. Tall trees with brilliant leaves glimmer in the intense sunshine. The air shimmers. It's eerily quiet. My antennae go up.

Earlier, when we came from the airport to the hotel, the bus driver drove across a shallow stream. He warned, "You folks stay out of these inviting ponds," he chortled. "The locals call them 'crocodile kitchens.' There was a big old bull laying out right here last week." He might have been making it all up, but one look at the black water of Tea Tree Pond, and I'm not taking any chances.

"But Yarra, the water's black!"

"It's the Tea Tree juice, Mom. So, good for you. Dive in, Mom."

She bends, hooks her thumbs, and forms a graceful arrow with her arms; the soles of her feet flip up, pink petals. She disappears under the dark liquid.

Oh, God, that may be the last I see of my daughter.

She surfaces, flings her wet hair around, cajoles, "It's wonderful, come on, Mom."

I want to join her, be part of her life here. I can't. "No way! It's too spooky for me."

I look around. *I'm disappointed. I wanted a dip in the water. I'm tired, but I'm not sitting down either. I want a head start if I need it.*

"I'll wait here, I'm OK." Yarra stretches her tan arms overhead in long, luxurious strokes.

I watched her swim away from me in Sydney harbor once during her art therapy internship. She called back over her shoulder, "Don't worry, Mom, I stay inside the shark nets."

That's Ange. No, Yarra. She sets her sights. She dives in.

Yarra's life in Australia was like children's play clay, semiliquid and multicolored. It changed shape and color to fit in any space in which it flowed, sometimes becoming an unpredictable thin stream. Until now, we only learned about it from her handmade notes, whimsical and beautiful, and signed consecutively Angela, Angie, Suki, and now, Yarra.

Laundry: A Song for Overseas Siblings

Christian R. Amoroso, Jr.

The weather has driven me inside today
where I was surprised to find my favorite clothes
in hapless piles, though my hand had placed them there.

I am a fool to wear them so often.

While others box theirs on basement shelves
for keepsake, I cannot let them go.
The bare denim of my jeans is almost through,
and, in the corner of my room, are the worn-heel boots
of our nights in town.

Under the bed lie my cotton T's.
Broke smooth, tattered soft, they bear the confidence of years and
late nights speaking closely.

I am glad to clean and sort them one more time,
even as they fade;
yet still I seem the victim of my own recklessness.

Today, I hung them out to dry as a warm Chinook stole
down the canyons.
It shook my memories from the line,
and I could not grasp them all at once. I lost my most
comforting chamois to the wind.

It took the wings of an albatross, spiraling high beyond the sky,
And I am sure it joined the jet stream;
yet, as I watched it go, I couldn't help but wonder if, maybe,
you would find it.

Seeing Spots, Longmont, Colorado, 1993

Ange has been home from Australia for two weeks, going to dentist appointments and resting. She is 30 years old. She walks up the sidewalk today just as I come out the door carrying arms full of six-foot-long Red Bark branches.

"Where are you going with those?"

"Going to the post office," I say. "I'm mailing them to Dorothy Johnson. She saw them when she visited us and thought they'd look good in her living room." Ange drops her jaw, flops her hands palms up, emphasizes every word, "You-Are-An-American-Woman."

"Did you forget. You sent me half a kilo of black licorice logs from Australia for my birthday last year."

We laugh in the first unguarded moment since she arrived.

"I'm awfully tired," she complains. "It's so hot. Took me forever to walk home. I'm going for a nap."

"OK, see you later, we're having fish and baked potatoes for supper."

I drive away wondering what has happened to the easy chatter that so often fell from our lips. Once Ange almost missed her plane to Alaska because we were gabbing away over one last "cuppa." Now, we have nothing to say. I try to engage her in our lives as we drive around town. Last week, when we drove by Powell's old house, I said to her, "The nicest young woman, Jeanine, lives there now, she has darling twin girls who play on the porch. Maybe you'll see them."

Ange looked straight ahead and replied, "I'm just not interested, Mom."

That just isn't Ange. Was she deliberately trying to stay out of our way of life? Still creating a secret scenario like when she visited us in Italy, after she'd been to Pune, visiting the Rajneesh?

In a diary we found, she had written, "My mother and sister would like to scratch my eyes out." Written for whose eyes? In my version, her mother and sister were trying very hard to get a passport extension form, either through the Italian or Swiss consulate, so she could re-enter Australia and not be stranded in India. Well, that was water under the bridge, but why was she home anyhow? To test the waters? To see if we could "live" with each other again? Not actually, of course, but at least treat each other with understanding? That wasn't going well, so far.

Her brother, Chris, is in a Denver hospital recovering from back surgery. He'll be home in a few days. She'll have a sibling to talk with if she wants that.

Or was she just home to get the fillings in her teeth replaced by an American dentist at a good price? That's what I think. She is convinced the mercury in the fillings might be causing the strange bladder symptoms and numbness in her fingers. The people living in the commune agreed with her. I don't know what to think. All Dr. Kellogg said was, "Some people try that." Not very enlightening, but that's what she wants, and she's paying what she can, so we stay out of it.

Sitting on our old telephone operator's chair after supper, talking to my friend Jeannie on the phone, I gaze across the kitchen carpet toward the sunroom windows. Ange is clearing the table. She crosses the floor carrying dishes to the sink. I see her foot drop. Her toes touch the floor before her heel, opposite what it should be. *Oh, my God, her foot dropped! I have to tell Chris.* I stop talking with Jeannie.

"Oh yes, Jeannie, I'm sorry. I dropped the phone. Well, yes, we are done talking anyway. I'll see you tomorrow." Stunned, I return the phone to the cradle. I hear the click, just like I saw the drop, quick and final.

All those quirky symptoms—urinary urgency, dribbling, the numb and weak fingers, twitching eyes and now a bona fide neurological sign, a foot drop. *Where was Chris? He has to know. I have to tell him.*

Before I can move, the phone rings. Son Chris says, "Mom, I talked to the doctor. He thinks my incision is healed well enough that I can come home tomorrow instead of Friday. Can you come get me?"

I close my eyes and try to speak normally. "Yeah, Son…great. We'll call you back after I talk with Dad. We'll be there."

I find Chris downstairs in the bedroom. "Honey, sit down, I have to tell you something important." We settle in the two green velvet, swivel rockers we purposely choose just for talks. With five kids, aging parents, and just everyday plans, we have so many serious discussions in those chairs. But this talk is heavy, really heavy, and there won't be much discussion or decision-making.

"Today, when Ange walked across the kitchen floor, I saw her foot drop."

Immediately, Chris switched to his doctor role with concern, "Oh, are you all right? Is Ange all right? Does she know?"

"No, I didn't say anything. I waited to talk with you first."

"Well, this is significant, good you caught it. I'll call Dr. Scaer right now and try to get an appointment as soon as possible. She leaves in two weeks, right?"

"Yes, and there's something else I need to tell you. Chris Jr. called. His surgeon will release him tomorrow, so he needs us to pick him up."

Chris leans back in the chair, closes his eyes, and sighs. "Wow. Well, let's talk with Ange first, then I'll call Scaer, see what he can do. We'll manage it."

Dr. Scaer is a compassionate, excellent neurologist and a good friend. Chris circles back to me with the news. "Dr. Scaer is going to work her in at nine tomorrow morning. I'll make rounds tonight. Call Chris Jr. and tell him we'll pick him up in the afternoon sometime. Maybe his cheery presence will clear the tension. We'll tell him what's going on on the way home."

At 11:30 next morning, the phone rings. Chris' voice is serious.

"Joanne, maybe you want to sit down, OK?"

My throat tightens. "OK, Chris, I'm sitting. Thanks."

"You probably guessed. We saw white spots all through Ange's brain and the myelin sheath of her spinal cord." He pauses. "It was awful. I'm so sorry, Hon. It's Multiple Sclerosis. Scaer was great, talked to us both about what that means. I thought I better tell you before we come home. Ange will probably sleep all the way home. We're both exhausted."

When Ange and Chris walk in the door, I know they'd seen the worst. Ange looks drained as she pulls herself up the steps to the landing. She lifts her chin and holds my eyes for a long moment. "At least…now, I know I'm not crazy."

She pauses long enough for me to give her a soft hug, pushes by and goes up to her room. I turn and hug Chris. "Thank you, Honey. That must have been very hard."

He nods "Very, very hard. She was great. Very polite to Dr. Scaer; he was so kind to her."

I remember it's past lunchtime. "Do you want some lunch, Hon?"

No. Think I'll go lie down for a bit if you're OK? We still have to drive to Denver for Chris Jr."

"Yeah, right. If you don't mind, I think I'll take a little rest, too. Wow. We'll talk with Ange before we leave, OK?"

After the first few discussions immediately after her diagnosis, Ange doesn't ask nor want to talk about it. She supplied herself with American goodies—T-shirts, shoes, good underwear, a nice cotton shirt for Kris. She is eager to get back with her husband. She schedules her plane trip; we take her to the airport, and I am left with an empty unease.

Communication is the same as usual, colorful, cleverly-reconstructed greeting cards and interesting letters, with no mention of her condition until 1994, when Kris calls to say Ange was "in hospital" in Sydney. He shares few details other than to say it was an awful, upsetting experience. She had a very painful spinal tap with accompanying terrible headaches and nausea. Worse, when she was discharged, the doctor's dismissive advice was, "Go home. Call us again if or when you have another attack."

Kris says, "Yarra wants to talk."

"Mom, Dad, I'm going to send you a poem about it. You'll see."

I stand silently, looking at Chris. "It's so hard when our adult kids become ill, and we can't do anything," I say finally. "At least I'm going to find out what's the latest, best treatment." Chris replies, "Maybe we can do something."

St. Vincents
hospital Sydney Australia
Nov. 94

not dark
not light
motionless I lay
tubes & needles dripping from
my arms
breath was it in or out?
not any more than a mouthful
and that pain, that band of
piercing across my forehead
threatens to strike - again
like a siren screaming.
Dont move,
not even an eyeball
scream help; impossible
flowed
tears (drop by drop)
by the corners of my eyes
Then, in a flash, the horizon
split open
pale yellow pale pink
reached out as to stroke me

a voice in my
head said I am morning, I am here,
you are here, this only this,
tips of the glorious lavender jackaranda trees
formed the blanket
upon which I floated above
again words "so much I give to you
now" yes - the only possible answer

St. Vincent's Hospital, Sydney, Australia Nov. 1994
Yarra Amoroso

Not dark
not light
motionless I lay
tubes, needles dripping from my arms
breathe was it in or out?
not any more than a mouthful
and that pain, that band
piercing across my forehead
threatening to strike again
like a siren screaming
Don't move!
not even an eyeball
scream help, impossible
tears by the corners of my eyes
flow drop by drop

Then, in a flash, the horizon split open
pale yellow, pale pink
reached out as to stroke me
a voice in my head
I am morning, I am here!
You are here, this only this

Tips of glorious lavender jacaranda trees
form the blanket upon which I float above
again words, "So much I give to you."
Now "Yes."
The only possible answer.

But to see her was to love her,
Love but her, and love her for ever.

—ROBERT BURNS (1759-1796)
Scottish poet

Yarra ♡

I love the way you can be a strong, wise woman one moment, and a playful child the next. Often it seems people are either one or the other, but you are both. Strength and softness I love these in you, Yarra

♡ Krishnaraj

(19/10/94)

Note from Kris to Yarra: Sydney, Australia (October 19,1994) "Yarra, I love the way you can be a strong wise woman one moment and a playful child the next. Often it seems people are one or the other, but you are both. Strength and softness. I love these in you, Yarra. Krisnaraj.

Love Me Now

Our sons, Joe, Chris Jr., and John, are living near Vail, Colorado, and they tell us they have been skiing for the Jimmie Heuga Multiple Sclerosis Center fundraiser the past few years. Through them, we learn of a weeklong introductory information program for MS patients and their families. We tell Kris and Yarra on our next phone call to Australia. They'll "think about it," but it isn't long before they plan a trip to America.

The Heuga Center waives the requirement that clients should have had a diagnosis of MS for at least a year before attempting the program, because Yarra lives in Australia and might be returning home for good.

All four of us attend a weeklong program where we hear many specialists speak and Yarra makes appointments with some of them. It is inspirational, informative, and reduces the many phone calls necessary to find specialists and travel to visit their offices, none of which are available or affordable in Australia. Kris and Yarra are introduced to the Multiple Sclerosis office in Denver, where they receive advice. They also make connections to psychological counseling and programs like therapeutic horse riding, adaptive skiing, rock climbing, swimming, and a local support group. Yarra is able to exercise regularly, and she swims at the local pool and rides therapy horses in Boulder, which she loves. In the summer and winter adaptive sports programs, she hikes and climbs, and learns to "sit-ski," which she raves about.

A counselor at the MS society in Denver remains with them for the two years it takes to make the decision on whether to stay in America or move to New Zealand, where Kris has family. We investigate options for the future, but in 1995, we cannot find longterm care facilities for young people in the US. That is one of the talking points in the two-year decision-making process. Their final decision is made one day when the counselor says to Kris and Yarra, "I'm not letting you out of this office until you make up your mind about where you are going to live."

Chris retires from his position as Medical Director at Kodak in Windsor, Colorado. It is his dream to live for a time permanently at the cabin where he can hike the mountains freely and frequently. I retire from teaching. We move an hour from Longmont to our foothills cabin in Big Elk Meadows, above Lyons, Colorado. Yarra and Kris stay with us for a time. They both enjoy living in the forest, but living in Longmont is much easier for them. Kris has a job at a natural food grocery store in Boulder, and Yarra has meetings in Boulder and Denver. We give them our old, trusty Toyota Camry, with the newly installed hand brakes just for Yarra, and it serves them very well. Kris takes a Master Gardening course and finds his most preferred work, gardening, in Longmont.

From Yarra's Diary, 1995, Big Elk Meadows

"Well this year holidays seem to have disappeared into one thing and the other.
Well, that's that and I move on.
But here-again sitting in my parents' gracious, "over the top" in ways,
Rocky Mountain cabin home-here with Kris
Feeling more our relationship I needing lots to help us.
My older bro, Joe and youngest brother, John
What stands out in all these thoughts is "Why?"
I don't know why I have this disease
I just want to live a normal settled life.
But I can see I'm going to have to work for that.
I look in the mirror-so pretty, my curls
roll around my face, my eyes straight
even though I just awoke.
Ahh, some wisdom
Coming through-Yarra-don't miss the magic-
Look, look out, look around you. Hey!
It's time to stay out of your little dream world
and be a part of this beautiful life.
How can this work?
Lower expectations

stick to simplicity, allow much space
use magic,
silence and stillness.
Love always more.
This life is short."

Yarra and Kris moved three times in two years. As Yarra's needs kept changing, they had to keep changing apartments. The entry at the latest place was down a flight of cement steps, which worried me very much, but Yarra, using a cane, managed.

As always, she did artwork at home but looked for other opportunities.

Our friend Jeannie came home from her volunteer work at Life Care Center of Longmont, an elder care facility, where she led an exercise program. Yarra sat on her front sidewalk steps. She told Jeannie that she was afraid she would not be able to make it down the hill to her apartment. Jeannie walked home with her. They talked.

Jeannie said there was a notice that Life Care was looking for a person to head "Memories in the Making," a national program for Alzheimer's patients. She would offer Yarra's name. Through Jeannie's intervention, Yarra's career choice came to being. That opportunity, combined with Yarra's intuitive, practical process of the application of art as therapy, changed and enhanced the rest of her life.

A group of six to ten clients, all in different stages of Alzheimer's, came to present awareness, in varying degrees, through the lessons Yarra planned for them. She used not only textured colors and paints and tactile materials but also flat pieces of red stone, twigs, boards, fabrics, anything she thought would stimulate their interest. Kris encouraged her by collecting these materials for her. They joked about his "scavenging" trips.

"Memories in the Making" program requires written comments on individual client's work for the program directors and family members. Yarra could not hand write. I went to transcribe her notes. In that way, we were a team. We stayed connected. I was amazed at her exceptional, creative, innate talent and her compassion for her clients.

"I think they know, Mom, that I'm like them in some ways. They see me come in with my walker. They see me drop things." She giggles. "We sit there and pee our diapers together."

As she shares paintings with me, I see how she creates innovative art projects. "My students can tell me what they are painting while they are absorbed in their work. Like one woman, when I asked her what she was painting said, 'That's my perfume bottle on my dresser.' As soon as she put her brush down and looked at the painting, she did not know who painted it or what it was."

Only one student was able to break through the time barrier: Hank.

"Look at this, Mom." She showed me a watercolor painting of green hills, trees, sky, a road and a dam with water behind it and the imposition of an open hand over the painting. "Hank's an engineer. When I saw what he'd drawn, I asked him to put his hand in the painting. He did and later he was able to look at it and say, 'It's a dam. I built that. That's my hand.'" Yarra shared the story with Hazel, Hank's wife, who later made a scrapbook for Yarra of her students' work.

December 6, 1997

Dear Yarra,

A gift for you -- a collection of photographs of some of the paintings your Alzheimer's Art Group have done during the year of 1997 -- and these are not all of them!

As the Art Therapist for these Alzheimer's residents, you have helped them so very much to bring out memories of their past. Everyone puts their own thoughts, memories and ideas into their paintings.

If you ever need a reference for future work with dementia patients, using the art therapy for which you are so good, I will be more than happy to give you a reference.

My husband, Hank, has very much benefited from your efforts and kind and gentle way of handling the moods that we all have at one time or another, but more prevelant with Alzheimer's residents.

I want to thank you sincerely for all you have done for him, as well as myself. Through you, I have learned to love every one of the "artists". Although Hank cannot express his thoughts as well as he did two years ago, when he started attending the Art Club, he still does something and I believe it is because of your gentle encouragement.

I wish you well in the future, and I do hope we can keep in touch.

With Love,

Hazel

Often, I don't know what is "going on" with Yarra. Is she just being her secretive self? Is it the hot summer weather or the recurring depression of MS? Something between her and Kris? Something I said or did? There are so many times I feel unknowing and helpless.

Yarra seems depressed and sad. It is at these times that I am so grateful for two of her childhood girlfriends, Sophie and Julie, who now live nearby. They share their precious time and energy with

Yarra. They visit regularly, run errands, shop, and help her with housekeeping, which is becoming seriously less manageable.

One afternoon, I arrive at her apartment ready to help her record her Alzheimer's client's painting, but instead she meets me at the door with, "Come see, Mom." She shows me a multicolored oil pastel crayon of a 10 by 12 inch bulbous, dark-colored heart, black-blue outlines, green, purple, blue and white in the swollen curves, surrounded by rich reds and orange and rose. "I did it after my rock climbing last week," she explains. She looks happy. The heart piece is glorious, so joyful. I love it, and, eventually, Kris and Yarra gave it to me.

Years later, after Yarra died, the sun shining down through our skylight, illuminated the painting on my wall in Arizona "just right." One side of the heart, along the left lower edge, was darker than the rest of the painting. As I looked closely, squinting my eyes into the dark shading my eyes filled with tears as I perceived the letters, "LOVE ME NOW."

I phoned Kris. What I didn't know, according to Kris, was that Yarra had been devastated after a Jimmie Huega Adaptive Sports Rock Climbing Class, when, after repeated attempts, she was not able to climb over a large, reclining rock surface. She was depressed for a time, until with her own deep, intense strokes of color and her own her powerful words of self-healing and self-acceptance "Love Me Now," enabled her to climb out of the experience of defeat.

In the fall of 1996, Yarra entered her clients' art pieces in a very successful nationally sponsored "Memories in the Making" art sale in a hotel in Denver. Professionals contributed striking matting and framing at an elegant dinner.

Yarra, Chris, and I attend the banquet. Sophie loaned Yarra a well-fitting, elegant black lace dress for the evening. Yarra's dark curls fall around her face. She looks both like a princess and a smart professional. It is the first highlight of her art therapy career. The sales of her clients' paintings bring in significant contributions.

We the family, Kris, Yarra's friends, and Jeannie, who initiated the job for Yarra, are overflowing with gratitude, pride, and happiness.

Yarra and Kris depart from the cabin in Big Elk Meadows for New Zealand in December, 1997. Brother John is driving them to

Denver International Airport two hours away. During the night, fresh snow has fallen. Kris and John spend an unexpected half-hour shoveling out our 1959 Ford pickup.

Kris and Yarra, using her trick to save on baggage, are wearing a couple layers of their heaviest sweaters and coats. The three of them pack themselves into the front seat and head down the wash-boarded, dirt, forest road. Approaching Highway 36, John notices a worrisome tug to the right. Flat tire!

John and Kris jump out and hastily replace the flat with a neglected, under-inflated spare tire. John fearfully guides the wounded truck, as fast as he dares, down the next 20 miles of windy mountain highway, with no guard rail and hundred foot drops, to the nearest gas station in Lyons. As John tells it, Yarra giggled the whole way, Kris sat in stunned silence, and, incredibly, they made it to the airport ontime.

preview by Marcus

CAN DO

EXHIBITION OF LIFE DRAWINGS BY YARRA AMOROSO AT CAFE METRO

Yarra Amoroso is already well known in the Green Dollar community. Although she and Kris only came back to Nelson about a year ago. There is something about Yarra that not many have known. Yarra is an artist. She's been doing that ever since but this will be her first exhibition.

It is always a daring task to exhibit one's art, more though when we learn that Yarra has only 10% feeling in her hands as a result of blocked nerve message due to multiple sclerosis.

To exhibit art means to exhibit one's innermost feelings and desires :

"I have deep respet for life and trust that my art will always express those feelings. It is always mysterously new and different."

Yarra's aim is to encourage others so that they too *"can do"*. The creative spark can easily be doused out; but luckily it is inherent in us. Yarra believes that giving this creativity an expression, gives life to the artist and those who share in it.

My artwork is finished whem it is exhibited.
To communicate with those who view it my art speaks it's own language unique to the viewer.
Every person takes away their own message.

Yarra's work can be viewed at the Metro Cafe, from 14 October untill 1st November.

All G$ members are welcome to the opening night on Wednesday 14th October 6:30pm

Yarra Can Do, Nelson New Zealand, 1998

Chapter 3—Vortex

The Brook, Nelson, NZ, 1998

Yarra and Kris have moved to New Zealand because Kris wanted to be with his mother, Tora, during the last months or years of her life. They have found a home redesigned for a special needs person, provided generously by the New Zealand government, in a tree-lined, quiet neighborhood. It's a nice-enough home with an access ramp, wide, sunny windows, a spacious porch off the dining area and a kitchen with open cupboards and raised counters. The bathroom is especially functional, a large room with a sealed, waterproof floor, an open overhead shower with curtain rail and a raised sink and stool. The home has been remodeled to ergonomic and safety specifications with New Zealand ingenuity by practical local tradesmen.

A small stream called "The Brook" flows through the neighborhood. At one time The Brook was the passage for transporting timber from the surrounding hills to Nelson Bay for export. The remnant stream is as beloved by the citizenry as an old grandfather and gives its name to the whole residential area. In the evenings, people stroll alone to the bridge and gaze at the stream for a "smoko" or a moment's peace, or go with their children to watch the water or feed the ducks.

We stay in a luxurious bed and breakfast, The Sussex House, very close to where Yarra and Kris are living. Between The Sussex House and their rental on a street called Silverbirch Grove, The Queen's Garden fills a block of earth and sky with the huge trunks and floating green canopies of heritage trees, nurtured and hung with medallions of identification. Flowering bushes brighten the lawn. The Maitai River, draped by swaying willow trees, glides along one side of our B&B.

When we get to Kris and Yarra's house, I notice boxes of belongings line the walls.

"We haven't had time to unpack them, and we don't have enough dressers. Besides we're looking for a different house."

"Really? This one seems much easier than the Second Avenue place in Longmont with those cement steps to go down. I always worried you'd fall."

"Yeah, it is. I'm still getting used to it, but I have a hard time coming up the ramp even with my cane."

I'd seen her struggles to hold the handrail with her weak right hand and grip the cane in her left. She bobbles as she lifts her feet up the incline over the rough wood. We discussed the advantages of using the walker. Why wasn't she using it? There's so much at risk with a fall, and she knows that.

"How's the neighborhood? Have you met anyone yet?" I ask, as we sit to share a cuppa. "Do you go for walks?"

"Well, the street dead-ends up there in the bush. Kris goes up the hill to tramp, but it's pretty rough. There's a young woman living up at the end of the street. I see her drive by. I walked up there once, to meet her. Did you see the mailbox with big, painted wooden flowers? Her husband built it, and she painted it. I love it. Did you see it?"

"I noticed bright colors when we drove in. I didn't know what it was. I'll check it out."

"It's a New Zealand thing. You'll see them, and some streets have all homemade post boxes. She was nice, but she works all the time. I haven't seen her again."

I don't know what to say. Angela doesn't feel welcome.

"Is this New Zealand tea? It's good."

Yarra giggles. "They call it gumboot tea because it's what all the workers drink. They have funny names for everything."

I carry my cup to the sink. Yarra presses her hands down hard on the table to push herself up. She turns and picks up her cup, it trembles in her hand. She stops to balance it on her cane handle, reaches for the sink and steadies herself before she turns on the water. As she washes the cup she looks out the window. I'm struggling to stay upbeat, but life looks precarious for her now.

"Mom, for eight months I've been looking out my kitchen window when I fix meals. I can see into the neighbor's window. I see her walking around in there. She never looks up. She never looks out her window to see me or wave."

What to say? What to do? Where to start?

I take my cup from the sink, grab a dishtowel, and finish drying the cups and spoons and pop them on the open shelf.

"How would you like to come to the B&B tomorrow for a "cuppa?" I think you'd like to see their dining room. The owners belong to a music group that plays here in town. All the instruments are hung on the walls. It's fun to see, and Carol is very welcoming. Sound good?"

"Yeah, I'll ask Kris, maybe I can have the car."

I didn't know she was still driving.

The car has a hand brake adaption. I've heard her say, "Kris needs to use the car."

I wonder if he's trying to reduce her driving.

"I'll call you after Kris comes home."

Chrissy and Lou's Party, 1999

Chris and I drive between pine-covered hills on either side of The Brook. "Pinus radiate" the locals scoff, a California pine, a timber crop. At maturity, they are harvested, and the locals are left with a view of denuded forests and stumps. Most of the one-level stucco cottages lining the streets are well shaded by mature trees unfamiliar to me.

On a drive through the valleys, I see an occasional tall, wooden Victorian house with porch swings and balconies with flower boxes. We pass open grassy spaces, lively with pick-up teams of rugby players and kite fliers. Picnickers crouch on blankets. They chat and nonchalantly swat at circling, shrieking seagulls, loudly demanding their share of lunch.

When we see the edge of a dark blue ocean on the horizon, we turn left on the Quay Road. Twenty-foot stacks of enormous, fresh cut, red and brown tree trunks lie like gigantic pick-up-sticks strewn over massive parking lots. A commercial ship attached to two thrumming tugboats glides slowly into a long, dark, weather-stained dock. We're fascinated to hear and see them each time we drive this way. A sky-scraping, magnetized crane swings its narrow filigree arm back and forth, lifting, positioning, and lowering boxed cargo of fish and fruit, railroad cars, lumber, and automobiles.

Hugging Quay Road on either side are small historical residences, interspersed with large buildings, originally fish processing factories or warehouses. A few buildings remain residences; some show B&B "Welcome" signs or have been converted into open-air, seafood restaurants.

Nelson Rescue Tower lifts its circular windows seaward. A shaded wall of dense, shiny-leafed magnolias and brilliant crimson, red-flowered pohutukawa trees line the highway. Kris is so good to teach me names, like "po-who-taa ka-wa," and I'm so proud to be able to pronounce them, but it's more than pride. I'm learning New Zealand by plant, by flower, by street, by town. The trees create a roadside awning before the road swings to Tahunanui (Ta-who-na-new-e), Maori for "sand beach," which, in Nelson, is a golden, curving swath of sand bordering the deep blue waves of Nelson Harbor under an arching, sun-filled, clear blue sky.

We both sigh.

"Lucky, aren't we?" Chris says.

"Lucky, maybe. I say, blessed. Did you know that Yarra laughed again, when I told her how happy I am she didn't marry someone from Cleveland?"

We find Kris' brother Lou and wife Chrissy's place by many parked, surrounding cars. No one is on the front porch. On the left, a steep, twisting, timber and rock stairs leads down to a back yard. One look at the irregular footing, and I demure, "Don't think I'll try that with my weak ankle."

We knock on the front door. "Maybe they're all outside, Chris. Should we just open the door?" We enter to a steep central stairway. Sunlight spills in the open door at the bottom of the stairs. A young woman, just entering, calls up, "Come on down. Everyone's out back."

On our way down, we hear chatter and laughter. We enter into the sunshine of a large green yard filled with bright colors and movement. Kids and adults are running around throwing Frisbees and chasing each other. Adults mill around chatting, drinks in hand. Everyone's engaged. A few people are seated under shade trees. We spy Kris smiling and talking with Yarra, who is seated in a sturdy wooden sun chair, watching the crowd.

Lou sees us hesitating by the door and comes to greet us, "Come down, come down. Join the crowd."

I follow him, "What a lovely, big back yard."

Lou says, "Actually, it was the front yard, but a trail came first, then a dirt road, then the house was built. Like many places in Nelson, when the official plot plan came from Britain, the road was put in elsewhere, and now the front of the house is the back. It works."

Yes, it works for some. Should I say something? Lou is a real estate evaluator. He should know the real story. Yes, I'll ask.

"I probably wouldn't notice, Lou, but I've been going around with Yarra. There are so many places which are inaccessible for her, despite the Handicap Access sign."

He gets the picture and smiles, "Yes, I know." He pauses, "Well, I was told, and I think you can find it in the library, about a history book, *On Zealand's Hills, Where Tigers Steal Along*." He raises his eyebrows. "You can tell by the title what the early settlers thought of New Zealand. There were very few certified surveyors in those days and lots of greedy people squabbling for power, but very little money. So, the original town leaders, trying to keep control, allowed a checkerboard plot plan to be laid over the hills, with no indication of elevations." Lou laughs, "That's what was sent to England for approval without any marking of elevations."

"Oh, now it's starting to make sense to me. I thought you'd know. Everyone else I asked just shrugged their shoulders and said, 'That's Nelson.'"

"Well, that's true, too, but the handicap access stuff is new, and people are slow to respond unless they know someone who needs help, I guess. It costs money. I've seen some of those places you're talking about."

Lou extends a hand, "Come say hello to Chrissy. Grab a plate. What can I get you to drink?"

The chatter is high; kids are laughing and chasing each other.

This is our new family, and a lively bunch from the looks of it. They all know each other intimately. It's going to take us a while.

A Step Too High, 1999

When Yarra drives up, I step off the porch to meet her. She looks stunning. She's shampooed her hair, and her luxuriant dark strands flip across a sundress of peach, yellow, and black floral print as she struggles to lift herself from the seat. She has one hand on her cane and one hand on the door handle. I can't really help her except to lug her up by the shoulders, and I don't want to ask, "Can I help you?" That could unleash a torrent or make her feel …who knows how. I wait.

Yarra finally overcomes gravity and pulls herself up on the door. She reaches for a large bag, too heavy for her to be carrying, and moves toward the porch. It is a beautiful day. The tops of tall pines along the street are glistening in backlit sunlight. She sees it, too.

"Pretty here, isn't it?" I remark. She nods. Rose's little trailer is parked beside the walk. "Oh, Kris and I always wanted to try one of those." She turns into the flower-lined entry, toward a cement step and the wooden porch. When she gets to the bottom of the step, she stops and looks at it in bewilderment. There's no railing. She's leaning on her cane.

Where to grab for support…to shift her weight while she lifts the other leg?

I see the problem. "Here Yarra, can you lean on my arm?"

She stares at the step, trying to figure it out. "I don't think I can do it, Mom. I'm worn out."

I grab a wicker chair from the porch and swing it down behind her. "Just sit here awhile Ange… Yarra."

I know that she wants to be called Yarra, but I can't help slipping into Ange.

I sit on the porch step. I could be on the far side of the moon. I can't imagine what she is thinking, how she feels. I'm shaken myself. One step, and she couldn't manage it. Yarra lifts her eyes and gives a wry smile.

"Does that happen very often?"

"Yes, Kris has been helping me up the steps to the house."

She should be using the walker all the time, but a walker isn't going to help her on steps.

"Do you feel OK enough to go around to the back yard? They have a little pool, and there are shade trees. Carol will be glad to bring our tea out there."

"That sounds good, let's try it." She pulls herself up and begins to shuffle along a narrow cement path. I walk behind her.

I feel so far away. A curtain has dropped between us. She's on the other side. I can do something that she can't.

I go in the house and find our hostess. "Carol, could you bring our tea out back? Ange…Yarra couldn't make it up the steps, so we're sitting out there."

Carol looks uncertain "Oh, it's not swept up out there. We just use it for family mostly. Sorry, but no problem. I'll be right out."

Golden-crusted, apricot scones with whipped cream and tea occupy Yarra and me as we spoon cream over broken, warm pieces and settle down to sip our tea. She looks at the hill peeking over the roof. "See that white house with green trim in the sunlight? Kris and I went there. It's for sale."

"How was it?" I ask.

"It took too long to drive up there, a half hour, and everything is on a slant. I wouldn't be able to walk anyplace. Tomorrow, we're going to look at another place, if you want to come. You know that place on Sheldon Street that looks like a castle. I heard it's pretty run down, but ever since we came to Nelson, I've wanted to live there."

A Tui's melodious trill contrasts the constant quack and squawk of ducks and gulls feeding at the Maitai River. Long willow branches hang limp in the stillness. "Sure, we saw it when we drove by yesterday. I never thought of a New Zealand castle. You'd love that, wouldn't you?"

Yarra's scone is half-eaten on the plate. The sun has moved above us from behind the roof peak. It's getting too warm for me, not good for Yarra. She's collapsed deep into the lounge chair."How are you doing now?" I ask.

"Tired, Mom, tired. I need to get home."

"OK, hon, let me help you out of that deep chair." I lean down, encircle her with my arm and pull. "It was pretty rough today, wasn't it? Sorry."

Castles in the Sky

In the morning, Kris picks us up to go see a house Yarra has her eyes on. "I think this may be one of Yarra's pipe dreams." Kris says as he smiles at his wife. She giggles.

"Tora, my mom," Kris nods to us,"she wondered how we'd make it. She'd shake her head and say, 'A Dutchman and an Italian, a Dutchman and an Italian? And they are the pragmatist and the romantic.'"

"I say we make it pretty good, don't you, Yarra?" Kris retorts. "Here we are."

One creak of the arched, wooden, castle door revealed a circular staircase, a crumbling banister, and ivy twirling through broken windows. Vacant for years, the place had surrendered itself to New Zealand's moisture, the walls molding and stained. Heaped, small piles of plaster dotted the baseboards. The cheery realtor prattled on with possibilities. Yarra nods her head, Kris watching her over his shoulder. *Was she really being taken in or being polite?* Chris and I rolled our eyes at the possibility of this disaster as a joint investment.

"We'll get back to you," Kris promises the realtor, as we silently pile into the car. There was a long pause. Yarra says, "I really would not be able to go up and down that staircase." Kris guffaws, then

Chris and I laugh and finally Yarra, realizing her understatement, giggles, too.

"I was holding back," Kris said. "I heard from Inez that her neighbor's house up the Brook is worth a look. It's not on the market yet. I'll check with my sister, Inez."

Up to "The Bach," 1999

Brother Hein's getting in touch with Annie, an old family friend and keeper of the Bach, to see if we can use it," Kris says. He looks pleased, and Yarra gave a thumbs-up and a nod.

I'd heard people at the B&B mention "Bach" as some kind of little vacation home. I play along with their excitement. "You've been there, Yarra?"

"Oh, yes, that was one of the first places we went as soon as we got here," Kris says. "Kolffs have gone there for years. Margaret and Pete were friends of Ma and Pa, very special." Kris and Yarra's eyes dance with delight. "It's in Golden Bay, right on the beach, lots of places to walk, and Pupu Springs, deep underground springs." Kris' eyes get dreamy.

"And a great café," Yarra adds. "The Old Schoolhouse Café; homemade New Zealand food, you'll love it."

"What kind of clothes shall we take?"

"Nothing fancy, just your swim togs and a jumper. It can be a bit fresh near the beach. It'll be warm mid-day. Hiking boots and jandals." (New Zealand for Japanese-made sandals.)

New Zealand life flashes by the car windows. Swirling spikes of scarlet penstemon grace the roadsides. Farm fields, delineated here and there along the fencerows by tropical palms, which seem out of place to me, yet obviously not to the cows lying beneath them in the shade. Unusual cows, too; black with a broad white bellyband. Wooden clapboard or stucco houses, white or an occasional pale cream, their porch ledges popping with containers of brilliant flowers, rose bushes and tall dahlias. People bike along the roads with plastic store bags dangling from the handlebars.

"Nice fruit stand here, shall we stop?" Kris gets out of the car and goes immediately to inspect the baskets. Chris comes around to help Yarra. In the car, she sits on a flat pillow mounted on a revolving base, very handy for swinging her legs out. As we approach the stand, we hear Kris humming as he mulls tomatoes, cucumbers, peppers, lettuce, arugula, avocados, plums, spinach, all the summer vegetables and fruit.

Yarra laughs, "He loves his fresh veggies—me, too."

I say, "I'll get enough for a few big salads while you pick out some fruit. How's that?"

After two more hours of driving, Kris pulls over at a low wooden bridge. "Here we are at Pupu Springs." With a flip of his arm, he disappears under his Australian sun hat. He turns for Yarra. She takes his arm, wobbles over the gravel to lean on the bridge rail. I can't see Kris' face. He is very quiet, his head turned to look out over a bluish-green stream that broadens into a tranquil, wide pool fringed with tall grasses. Near the bridge, a central, dark swirl of celestial blue floats under the surface.

Kris extends his hand, "This is the largest freshwater spring in New Zealand, perfect clarity."

The sun's warmth eases my shoulders. Bees and water bugs zoom around. Peaceful. It reminds me of going back to a childhood haunt in Pennsylvania. We kids thought it so magnificent we called it Creek's Kingdom. When I returned years later, it was only a trickle of water seeping down a gravel slope.

Kris continues his silent reverie.

Chris breaks the silence, "Can you swim in there?"

Kris turns. "I guess you could, but nobody does. You'd need a wetsuit."

"How come?"

"It's the coldest spring water in the southern hemisphere or something, been studying it for years. Sacred to the Maori."

None of us has more to say about Pupu Springs. We gaze. Kris pats the rail, turns. "Love this place, lots of memories."

He takes off his hat. "The Old Schoolhouse Café is next on the docket. You ready?"

I feel I've missed something of importance. Guess I have a lot to learn in this new country. *Better watch my p's and q's.*

Inside the spacious one-room Old Schoolhouse Café, sunlight streams through ceiling-high windows. After being in the car for two hours, it feels as if we've walked into open space. On a long wooden table, piles of greens practically spring from burnished, steel-compartmented trays. Heaps of multigrain breads and fresh fruit and mounds of cookies in woven linen-lined baskets cover the table. Pedestaled glass cake dishes display interesting chocolate, coconut, mango, orange, and cornmeal offerings.

"Fresh daily from the garden, farm, or sea" is printed in bright colors across the top of a portable, wood-framed chalkboard followed by lists of all the selections, Kris points out and suggests his favorites. We pile food on our trays. Yarra chooses a dense slab of chocolate cake for us to share, and we make short work of it all.

"Hey, this even feels like school lunch," Yarra says. "Hurry up and eat, so we can go play."

Back in the car, we turn into a gravel lane. "Watch for the painted mailboxes," says Yarra.

It's like an art contest. Who can design their mailbox to be the cleverest or paint it the brightest colors? We get a closer look at the yards with rotating clothes lines, kids, dogs, and cats. A tethered goat trims the edges of the lawn; bikes, wheelbarrows, flowering bushes, grapevines, pots of flowers, lemon trees, and parked cars are everywhere. We drive slowly until enormous dark pines replace the homes and small cabins shaded by twenty-foot drooping pine branches peek from the dense bush. Slashes of dark waves and white caps flash on the left side of the car.

"Oh, look," Kris points out the front window. "There's a good view of a Tui right there on the lower branch. See his bow tie?"

A large black bird with two very white curved tufts at his neck sits upright, silhouetted by rust-colored bark.

"It really looks like a bow tie. A rather formal bird, isn't he? My "binocs" are in the suitcase; I hope he's here tomorrow."

Kris rolls down the window. A moisture-laden draft swirls into the car with scents of pines, the forest carpet, a whiff of mushrooms, perhaps, and sea salt.

"Smells like New Zealand, Kris—fresh."

The lane narrows into a path and finally ends at a traditional, miniature white-clapboard home perched on the very edge of a rocky shore.

A glassed-in porch turns out to be the kitchen. We squeeze between a water heater and an open-shelved cupboard, stacked with assorted crockery, to deposit our grocery bags of fresh produce, cheese, crackers, tea, and milk on a bench counter underneath. Kris turns on the water heater then reaches into a tiny, chipped-enamel stove on a patch of trodden linoleum. He pulls out a saucepan and sets the bag with the whole grains for his cooked gruel inside. He and Yarra live by a concoction of soaked mixed grains that Kris soaks every evening and stirs like a magician's brew every morning. He swears it sets him up for the day and strengthens Yarra.

I set out a box of corn flakes from the market, "You don't mind, do you, Kris?"

"Ah, you just don't know the good stuff."

Heavy curtains hang over one wall in a square living room. Kris steps forward like a carnival maestro and flings back sun-faded blue fabric. Right there, twenty feet away, the endless sea, dancing waves, a strip of golden beach, and not a man-made object in sight.

Worn, overstuffed couch and chairs, their cushions grooved into deep divots by the readers of a wall of floor-to-ceiling shelves crammed with books, are inviting. Kris points to a wicker hamper overflowing with magazines that bulges on the floor near the couch.

"There you go, Joanne," says Kris, "Read the North-South magazines, you'll find out all about us."

"But Kris, to see this many books, in this tiny place…we've been hearing about the afternoon radio book readings…we don't have those in the US, you know? New Zealanders are great readers. I've never been in a little cabin with so many books."

"Pick a bedroom, one on either side. Don't think it matters much. Here's the bathroom." He pushes open a door to a small room fully occupied by an enormous tub and a small stool. "All liquids just drain down on the sand under the house; for other business, we'll make a run to the gas station."

The guys go out for a walk. Kris describing the options for which way they might go.

I turn to Yarra. "How you feeling? Are you up for that hair wash I promised you?"

She grins and raises her eyebrows, "I'd love to get into that tub." It is the largest, deepest claw-foot tub I've ever seen, easily six-feet long and three-feet deep. "How'd they ever get this thing in here? I saw Kris turn on the water heater, but I'll put a couple buckets of water on the stove, too."

Six buckets of warm water from the tank just cover the bottom of the tub. I get another bucket for shampooing Yarra's hair. Yarra undresses. I see her body for the first time in years: her tiny boobs, the same, her belly and buttocks, the rounded and heaviest part of her body, pear-shaped, as usual. But the muscles of her legs are thin; her olive skin is pale. She sits on the tub edge. I lift her legs over the side and lower her into the water. The tub sides are above her shoulders. She splashes water over herself like play.

I pour water over her head. Strands of hair separate to reveal pimples in her hairline and heavy flakes of oily dandruff. She's had this a long time. Her head needs to be washed every week with special shampoo. *Guess she can't ask people to do that.*

"How 'bout a back scrub?"

"Yeah, that'd be great; haven't had one of those in a while."

I hand her the oval pink bar of soap, but it slips from her fingers. I soap up the rag and she rubs her arms and upper legs. She can't reach her lower legs and feet. I crunch the washcloth around the soap, rub her lower legs, and run the cloth between her toes.

"Gotta' be careful, or I'll be in the tub with you. I'm practically standing on my head now."

Her leg muscles are straight, no rounded calves. She's lost muscle. Compared with her tan arms, the black hair on her white legs stands out. She's not running around in shorts these days.

I rinse the washcloth, soap it up again, stand to un-kink my back, and hand her the cloth so she can finish her bath. I take two steps toward the door when I realize I've slipped into "nursey" mode. I would walk out so the patient could have privacy to wash their genitals. I almost laugh out loud. Yarra wouldn't give a hill of beans if I watched her scrub her crotch, or am I trying to shield myself from seeing those sickly-looking legs?

I grab a towel from the stack on a chair and come back to the tub.

She looks up with a silly grin, "Mom, I don't think I can get out of this tub."

Oh, my gosh.

"How do you usually get out of the tub?" *I hear the lame question. Stalling for time. Joanne think...think.*

She giggles, "Mom I haven't been in a tub in years."

My heart drops. *Oh, Joanne...you should have thought...SHE... can't balance on a slippery surface, can't push up. YOU...can't lift her 160 pounds. No telling how long the guys'll be gone.*

Two years ago in Longmont, she fell face down on the floor and lay there until Kris got home.

Now what're you going to do? She could fall and cut herself. You could sprain your back. Oh, God.

"What do you want to do, Yarra?"

You should know what to do, not her. What can you do? What can she do?

"Do you want to wait for Dad and Kris? I don't know how much strength you have. I know I can't lift you." I snicker. "It's not like we can call on the neighbors." We laugh.

"I'd wait, but I'm really cold now." Unusual for Yarra. She's always warm. It's chilly in here now, though, since the sun has moved around the house.

"Plenty of heavy towels in the cupboard. I'll dry your hair, then dry the tub and see if you can get a footing. I can help you."

Then I remember "the fireman's carry" from nurses training. Spread the weight over your body. God, where did that ancient stuff come from? Or did it come from God? Either way, it might be the ticket.

"I'm going to put my arms under your armpits, Yarra." I get behind her, bend my knees, spread my feet, hunch beside the tub and thrust my arms under her armpits." *I hear Chiara telling me "Set your 'scaps,' Mom, set your 'scaps.'"*

"Now I'm going to pull you over. Push if you can. Ready?" I

crunch my shoulder blades.

"Push" comes out in a puff of air and a grunt. I pull her towards me. I feel her pushing against the far side of the tub.

"Nggghu," she laughs. She's having an adventure.

"That's good." But I'm envisioning the next step…up.

"OK, here we go, I hope. I'm going to try to lift you up the side of the tub to the top. Use your knees if you can." I set my shoulder muscles, pull her weight across the floor of the tub.

My God, it's working.

"Good, Yarra, good, can you feel yourself sliding? There. Push your hips back. OK, we made it. Just sit there a minute and catch your breath."

I see her falling, I see me falling into the tub with her. I imagine a slash of blood. This is crazy, I wish the guys would come, but we're this far now.

"Now we go to the top, up. Press back against my chest when you feel my shoulders behind you, that'll help me lift you. Ready?"

I set my leg and back muscles. Pull…push against the floor. I re-set my feet and knees; curve my shoulders over hers.

A thick strand of Yarra's wet hair slides over my face.

I see myself hunched over her on a slippery rock in a cave, behind a thunderous waterfall in Supai, Arizona. She's eleven, determined to dive after me through the falls, out into the turquoise pool. The local boys, with wide-open dark eyes and sad faces, made a point to give our kids repeated warnings of "the kid who drowned because he dove straight down instead of straight out, and the water held him down."

Ange shivers in the center of the mind-deadening roar. We jerk our bare skin away from the cascade of waters stinging us on all sides. A sopping strand of her wet hair falls across my face. I put my mouth close to her ear. I yell, "Are you all right, Ange?"

She squints up through the black veil of soaked hair, and yells back, "If this is all right."

I stand, poised to dive, look back. She's pressing her hands together, arms straight forward. I push off. As soon as I surface, I look back. Ange's slender body shoots straight as an arrow through the roiling, glistening white torrent and slips beneath a serenely blue and sunny surface.

I glance down at Yarra now huddled in the tub. Tears well up in my eyes. Stop it. You've got to think of what goes where next.

"Are you all right, Yarra?" I take a breath to stop the tightness in my throat. I set my shoulder blades and bend my knees.

"Yah, I'm OK."

"All right, I'll put my shoulder under your left side, your strong side. Put your arm around my neck. OK, good. Hold on." I take a big breath.

We hear shoes clomp on the porch stairs, and the door creaks open. Kris' deep voice calls out, "Hey, where is everybody? What's going on in there?"

I nearly collapse in relief. Kris appears in the doorway. He looks startled, "What's going on in here?"

Yarra turns to the doorway, and calls out, "Tub wrestling, come see."

Has she got a surprise for Kris.

I breathe a long, audible sigh. Yarra turns her head, looks up into my face. She knows. I know. We just don't say.

"Tub wrestling, is it? Send Chris in, Joanne."

I rush from the room and call, "Kris needs some help with Yarra, to lift her out of the tub, Chris. I didn't know she doesn't do tubs. Whew."

Chris hurries to the bathroom. I push open the back door. A windy, cold, blast smacks me alert. I go out for some air. Only a sliver of the setting sun sits on the horizon. Football-sized stones form the beach here, *not good footing for me.* I stand waiting for calmness, some reframing of the experience I had with Yarra. My mind is empty. The sharp air keeps me present. I shiver and turn to the little "Bach" under the pines. I'll feel better inside, but my mind is turning over a thousand questions about this enigmatic disease and my daughter's future.

We were packing to return to a new home in the US, a small condo in Arizona, when we received a phone call from my brother, Joe. My mom, Lucy, has had a fall. She can no longer be cared for in the personal care facility and has been moved to a nursing home. Joe and Judy are raising a family of five, and they are both working. Chris and I change our travel plans and go to Pennsylvania to assist my mother.

We tell Kris and Yarra about Mom's fall. Yarra is close to Lucy, and it saddens her. I remind her of the day we visited Mom and went through her closet. Yarra tried on a new, pink fleece bunny suit that fit her perfectly. Mom gave it to her to wear on cold nights in Vermont. We're laughing at those memories. Yarra's smiling as we promise to return as soon as possible.

FAX TO: 1-520-625 1022
(Busy Bee Printers)
Attention: CHRIS AMOROSO
520-625 3855

AMOROSO
AMOROSO
AMOROSO
Angela
Hey Dad I love you!

April 9, 1999 Chris received a call from Busy Bee in Green Valley, Arizona, about "a surprise fax" waiting to be picked up.

The Right Question

In late 1999, Kris calls while we are staying in my mom's home in Pennsylvania. We've been here for eight months, tending Mom, who is in a nursing home half a mile away. We have airplane tickets for New Zealand for January 26, 2000. Kris sounds happy.

"We found a house we thought would be good for us. Inez, my sister, told me about it. It's right around the corner from her house. We went over to see it this morning. It's not far from our place at Silverbirch Grove, just up to 'The Brook.' Remember?"

"Good location, Kris," Chris says. "How's the house?"

"It's the ranch house of the original farm. The ranch owner, Jean, lives right next door. We like it, but it's a big decision. She's asking $60,000. I don't know if we can manage that.

"We'll be able to help you, Kris. We've talked about the possibility of you finding a house more suitable for Yarra. That means a lot for all of us."

"Ahh, Chris…that's very generous of you, ah, you too, Joanne. Yep, Yarra likes it, ah, yep, might just think about it for a while."

A silent moment passes. I imagine Chris is thinking as I am. He breaks the silence. "Kris, I'm going to ask you the question Uncle Carmen asked me when I was having trouble making the decision about closing my Longmont practice and going to work at Kodak. How will you feel if they called and said the job is no longer available?"

I am so grateful Chris broached the stall. He's the one who better relates to Kris.

"Ah-ha, ah," silence. "That's it." Kris' voice is suddenly firm, certain. "That's the right question. We need to buy this house. You're right. I'll contact the city council guys to see if it's suitable for remodel for Yarra. I think it will be. "Thanks, thanks again. I'll let you know."

Kris calls back in a few days. I can hear pleasure and excitement in his voice. "Good news. I went to talk to the government guys the very next day. They said the house was doable for renovation for handicapped. Yarra is very happy. Me too, of course, and for you helping us pay for it. We wouldn't have been able to afford it."

"You're welcome, Kris. We're getting excited about it, too."

"Yeah, and Yarra and I have another surprise for you when you come."

"OK, see you soon."

Sharing from Grandma Lucy

We return to Nelson in 2000, twelve days after my mom, Lucy's, death in Pennsylvania. Yarra and I are in the kitchen. She looks beautiful, as always, dark, thick hair tied in a deep purple ribbon, white shell earrings dangling.

She looks at me and says, "I cried and cried for you and Daddy, being with Grandma for so long, and then coming right here. My Father and Mom…to get off a plane…to see me like this? Well," she pauses and throws her hands up, then turns them inwards, towards herself, seated in the wheelchair. "My life is not exactly happy now, and to be parents and come and see your daughter like this…." Tears fill our eyes; I reach over and squeeze her hand.

She continues, "I'm sorry for all you went through with Grandma, but it has made you more understanding of me."

I sit on the chair beside her, lean toward her and rest my head on her shoulder. We hold hands and breathe. I lift my face to hers; tears roll down our cheeks.

The House Itself is Perfect

The house itself is perfect. Typical of other homes I'd seen in Nelson: one story, low rectangles or squares with angled clapboard, shingled rooftops with a shade overhang, angled and push-out windows—always open and no screens—"island houses."

This house had been moved to a different spot on the land and turned around. The approach to the back-entry door is up a separate, three concrete-block step set on the ground, not attached to the house. The screen door swings out. The inside door swings in. No way Yarra can balance on the cement stoop and safely get herself in. My hand gripping the door, I pull myself into the house's small entry room. The kitchen door swings open into a very large, sun-filled room with a wall of floor-to-ceiling wooden cabinets. Along another wall is a sink, refrigerator, and wood burning stove, all well lit by ceiling-high, north-facing windows looking out onto the pine-covered hills and an adjoining sunroom. As I pass the refrigerator, I see a small cartoon, which I've seen on Kris and Yarra's refrigerators in their previous rentals. I smile, grateful for their intention. They have adopted the words of an Australian poet, Michael Leunig, for their watch words. I am hopeful they will be sufficient for the path upon which they are walking.

The carpeting throughout the house is thick nylon, chocolate brown. Yarra comes down a hallway. She is using a walker. The wheels sink into the carpet. As she enters the kitchen, she slides the walker easily over a linoleum surface.

That's better, so much less effort. Don't think the carpet is good for Yarra, but it's going to be a tough call.

A long hall, the walls covered with forest and mountain scenes, divides the remaining rectangle of the house. Chris asks, "What's this? Was this here when you bought the house? It looks like Colorado."

"No, that's Chiara's work. It is Colorado. She put it up when she came to see us."

"Remarkable, she thinks of everything," Chris says.

The remainder of the house is a long living room, one wall of which is windows. There are two bedrooms, plus a laundry, and a recently remodeled bathroom, the floor coated with water-repellent covering, a toilet, shower and sink, all accessible for Yarra.

"Wow, this is wonderful," Chris says. "You say the government provided all the remodeling for you?"

"Yes, just about everything," Kris replies.

"Amazing."

"Even the mirror?" I see the long, narrow framed mirror has been lowered so Yarra can see herself. "Is that New Zealand ingenuity, too?"

"No," Kris laughs, "That was Chiara. It was up high, and she asked them to move it down. The councilmen saw she was right."

Everything is accessible to Yarra except the entrance. Kris assures us the councilmen already have plans for a wooden track going from the garage to the front porch for Yarra's wheelchair. He looks pleased or proud whenever he mentions the councilmen. I wonder if he may enjoy planning and working with competent men, in work he understands, and seeing it get done efficiently. So much of his daily planning for Yarra involves endless discussions regarding unproven attempts to manage the caprices of an unfamiliar, unrelenting, incurable disease.

Kris and Yarra have moved their beds and clothing and their kitchen things to 20 Karaka Street. A row of boxes lines the living room. Kris says, "We have seven months to be out of the rental, we want to move in slowly."

Viewing the unpacked boxes, I think it will be "forever" for them to "move in slowly."

I walk into the living room. There are hallway doors at two corners and windows along the whole north wall, which is the sunny side in New Zealand. An old overstuffed chair and one small wooden chair sit in the spacious room. On the fireplace, a spot of red catches my eye. A red geranium in a black, thick, pottery pitcher is placed beside a framed drawing of the same vase with a red flower.

Kris sees me looking at it. "That's Ma's vase and Yarra's drawing."

"Oh, that's beautiful, Kris."

"Tora gave it to Yarra."

"They must have been good friends."

"Yes, they were. The community members always wanted to hear Tora's opinions on issues. Yarra could walk her back and forth to those meetings. They got to know each other very well."

"I'm happy to hear that. I've read your mother's book more than once. I'm grateful to have it. She was an interesting, strong woman, wasn't she? I'd like to have met her."

"Yeah, Yarra made sure you got to read that book before we were married. She wanted you to know…you've got to thank her for that."

Kris and Yarra came from Australia to assist Tora, so she could die in her home at Riverside, New Zealand. She saw their differences. It's a family story. Tora would look at Kris and Yarra, slowly shake her head and murmur softly, "A Dutchman and an Italian?"

Yarra is using a walker on the thick rug. As she comes up the hall, I see her lifting, shakily balancing on two legs, and moving her walker forward with each step. The wheels sink into the thick, chocolate brown carpeting.

She comes to the kitchen entry and the linoleum floor. In one movement, she slides forward with ease. "The penny drops" as the New Zealander's say. I realize she is wasting energy she can't spare on trying to cross the plush carpet.

"The rug is beautiful, Kris, but as thick as it is, I think it will have to go."

He shoots back, "Why should I have to get rid of it? It's better than anything Pa had?" Before I can answer, I see Yarra's expression change; her eyes are panicked. She extends her arm "I need to sit, Mom."

I grab Yarra's hand as she leans to one side. I stretch my other hand back to grasp a wooden chair. Kris rushes to her and grabs her just as my fingers tug on the chair and pieces of it fly through the air, clattering around us.

Kris shouts, "What are you doing?"

"I'm trying to get a seat for Yarra. She needs to sit down."

He reprimands, "That's…Pa's…. chair."

"What's it doing here? What if Yarra grabbed it?"

Kris is bristling as he walks Yarra away toward the cot in the corner.

His voice calls back with stern emphasis, "Pa had that chair 'specially built when he came here, so he could take it on the boat."

"Oh, dear, I've bad-mouthed a family treasure, something of "Pa's." My first day back, and I'm already in the doghouse."

Living in the Neighborhood

When the neighbors learn we are returning, we are offered one of the student rentals across the street, a one-level bungalow, with spacious kitchen, and living room and rooms for single beds, plus a private backyard. Vikki and Cheryl, a neighbor, have been busy. We find cleaned rugs, nicely arranged furniture, and bouquets of garden flowers on the tables and in front of the fireplace in our rental. To our delight, Ralph, Inez's husband, has built a wooden ramp, so Yarra can use her walker to come over to our place.

In the morning, we have juice while Yarra eats her breakfast. She looks beautiful, her thick, dark hair tied back in a deep purple ribbon. I sit next to her, lean and rest my head on her shoulder. Once more we hold hands and breathe. I lift my face to hers; we both have tears.

It's more difficult now for Yarra to get food from her spoon and fork into her mouth. She dribbles liquid when she raises her glass to her lips. I dab a napkin at her mouth. It's awkward, uncomfortable. She's using her left hand. I see her right hand lying in her lap, claw-shaped. "Oh, God, no." I stifle a gasp. *What's happened? Has she had a mild stroke; Or is it the MS? Most likely the MS. Kris has not mentioned it.*

I try for conversation, some normalcy. I take a breath, "I love the guava juice, don't you? We didn't have that at home, or fresh farm eggs, either, huh?"

Yarra knows I'm trying to cover my sadness.

No good, no good.

I peek in the sunroom off the kitchen and see a big wooden table, and shelves with art paper and pencils, brushes, and paints.

"Oh? Someone's already started an art room. Who did all this, Kris?"

"Chiara, first. She bought the table and shelves for art paper. Then my sister Inez and my brother Hein and Chrissy, Lou's wife, got involved. She's a teacher. She's been taking Yarra to a place downtown for an art course. And our helper, Vikki; they've all had a hand in it."

I'm excited with the pieces Yarra has been working on. She has designed shells, twigs, and feathers she and Kris have collected on the beach into strong, graceful lines. I finger the broken bits of jewelry, dried flowers, and cutouts from cards and magazines. "You can create something out of anything, Yarra. It pleases you, doesn't it?"

Yarra joins me. She smiles and nods.

A box sits to one side of the table. Small rubber balls, sponges. Someone has devised holders for the brushes so Yarra can hold the brushes in her hands.

"Who arranged these for you, Yarra?"

"Vikki. She's good, Mom. She even took a class on intuitive art so she can help me."

I'm so happy for Yarra.

Kris may have had visions of the sunroom becoming a place of quiet for himself. He needs his quiet and treasures solitude. When it is quiet in the house, or he feels alone, he hums and sings. Yarra and I both love it. It's soothing to hear his deep voice and see him peaceful and "puttering." The art room may be beneficial for both her and Kris.

"Shall we go outside for a walk? Do you need to go the bathroom?"

"No, Mom, I'm wearing diapers now, easier for all of us. I'll wait for Vikki to come back."

I stay with Yarra a while. When I come back to the rental, Chris is in his bedroom. I'm sad, seeing Yarra's condition so deteriorated. I'm exhausted and wide-awake. I take my pillow and go to Chris' room.

"Honey, can I squeeze in with you, I need to be near you…seeing Yarra…I just can't sleep."

He slides to the side of the single, wire-spring bed and lifts the covers. I climb in. The bed sags and creaks. I keep losing the covers, trying not to toss. I pray, and finally I will myself to sleep. I awaken toward morning feeling lost.

I scrunch up close to him. He reaches for my hand. "I just needed to be near you, Honey." I murmur. I turn to him; we share the greatest gift of ourselves, our love and comfort. It is so good we have each other.

Trying the Nelson Art Scene

The phone rings. "Hey, Mom, you want to go with me to the Artists Guild meeting? I've been trying to get there. Wednesday morning. I can drive. It's at someone's house. I've got the address."

"Sounds good to me, Ange, ah, Yarra. I'll ask Dad to drive me to your house, OK?

What time?"

"Ten o'clock."

Wednesday morning, nine o'clock, I'm dressed for the occasion in my artsy, full-length purple tee shirt with Kokopelli designs. I call in the door at Silverbirch Grove, "I'm here." *Remember, not Ange, Yarra.* She is straddled over the commode, a diaper end between her legs.

She blurts out, "I was walking down the ramp when I started to pee. I was all ready!" Her hair is clean and curly, she's wearing our favorite earrings, the ones I had made for her in Mexico with long wires that are easier to put on.

She's disgusted. "Let me hold on to your shoulders. See if you can get this thing on."

I'll have to hold her skirt up, wrap the diaper around her, release the adhesive tabs on each side and strap them closed. "Gosh, Yarra, I need six hands." We both break out laughing. "How can we do this?"

"It works best when I'm lying on the bed, but that will take too long. Do what you can, OK?"

Yarra hangs on, and we do a little dance, she on her wobbly legs, me dipping and flipping the drooping yardage of her skirt, pulling the edges of the diaper around her, and trying not to stick the adhesive tabs on anything but the diaper. I imagine her walking in the artist's home, losing her diaper on the floor.

"OK, Yarra, plan for success, right?" We keep it light, but we both know we're late already, and we're not even out the door.

Yarra drives us down to town from The Brook, through center city traffic and up the steep hills across town.

"Boy, Yarra, you're doing great with the driving, so many twists and turns."

"It isn't easy, it's really a quirky layout, as if they've never heard of city planning."

Cars are parked along the street. "I guess we're here." We see cars parked around a tall Victorian home as we pass by. I see a long flight of entry stairs. "This is what happens when you're late. I'll see if there's a space along the street."

There isn't. The street just narrows to an unpaved drive at the edge of a field. Yarra lurches around, between the gleaming fenders of parked cars. I hold my breath. How must she be feeling? This is a lot already. "Good thing you decided to ship this car over, Yarra." She pulls up to the front of the house.

Yarra slings her purse over her shoulder, grabs the wooden railing with one hand.

"Can you manage your cane Yarra? Shall I take your purse?"

"No, I'm OK."

Her cane thumps on each step and across the wooden porch. The door swings open. A woman in a white ruffled blouse and narrow black skirt smiles, "Hello, I'm Zoe, can I help you? The speaker has started her talk, but there are two seats near the back. I think you can slip in."

Once seated, we're served full cups of tea on saucers. It's a game of rattle and balance. Yarra says, "Put this under your seat for me. I have to go to the bathroom." Women move their legs for her to pass and return. We are distracting others from the speaker. I, myself, have hardly registered a word of what the speaker is saying. Yarra looks at the crowd; I finish my tea. The speaker ends her talk. Yarra tips her head, "Ready to go?"

"I'll make a quick stop at the bathroom. Can you wait by the door?" Yarra nods.

In the bathroom, I see Yarra has left her wet diaper in a gilt and peach colored waste container. *She hasn't figured out how to handle that item yet.*

A few women standing near the door smile and raise their eyebrows.

We say, "Thank you, thank you."

On the porch, Yarra pauses to straighten up. She looks out over the long walk to the car. She advances to the top of the steps as if she's not sure they are manageable. "Walk down beside me, Mom, OK?"

"Not exactly our cuppa' tea, was it?"

"No, but we tried."

Yarra drives down the hillside silently. Suddenly she asks, "What are you going to do?"

"When?" I respond, "Today? This afternoon?"

"No," she replies, "with your life…you and Dad?"

Where did this come from?

Startled, I pause, "Well, Dad and I have decisions to make."

Should I say more? She's driving.

"What decisions?"

"I think our decisions partly will depend on what's going on with you."

"No," she says. "I want you and Dad to live your life."

Kris, Your incredible courageous wife
Took the bull by the horns tonight and asked
to talk about all the issues we have been
tip toeing around. Huge hurdle. She said,
"I want to talk to you about your
future. I need to know what you are
going to do." And that led to her saying we
need to make decisions for ourselves not
based on her needs + she has to make her
decisions etc. etc. She was very clear, did
not cry — very incredible. It was a
blessed discussion. All from her. Chris and
I had just had the same discussion and
he had some advance directive forms so
we even went over them a bit. She
acknowledged it would be too hard for you
to make all the decisions alone + wants to
make them for herself. Wow! 8–8:30
Cheryl very wisely got busy elsewhere, then we went into the art room. It
is a privilege to be able to go through this
with her + be able to be here in your home.
You must have felt some of this in your
singing tonight — did you?
Love,
Joanne + Chris

After we arrive at Karaka, I print a note to Kris and leave it on his bedroom nightstand.

Backyard Pow Wow and Peace Pipe

Chris, Yarra, and Kris spent 90 minutes visiting with neurologist, Dr. Malcolm Clark. Chris reports he is a wonderful doctor, addresses everything to Yarra, listens to her responses, responds to her or then includes Kris and him in the conversation. Chris has gotten permission to have the medication for Multiple Sclerosis which Yarra was receiving in the United States mailed here. Our son Joe will help with the arrangements for transit.

Chris has been suffering from increasingly intense neck pain. Yarra's neurologist was able to confirm an acute ruptured disc. Chris leaves shortly after to have his orthopedist in Longmont, Dr. Jim Britton, perform the surgery.

I have more time now to work with Kris. I want to share some of the observations I've made since we arrived, some as mom, some as nurse. My observations lead to lists and requests. Today, I've invited Kris over for a chat, hoping we can work together and learn from our varying viewpoints about what's happening with Yarra's MS, the household, and our relationships.

I review my list for most important, where to start, what's easiest? They're all tough. We'll start with a cup of tea; that should make it much easier. Who am I kidding?

I hear Kris' sandals on the wooden ramp, "You in there, Joanne?"

"Come on in, I'm making myself some Rooibos tea. Would you like a cup?"

"Rooibos? You bought some?"

"Sure, you said it was your favorite when you served it to me. Pick a cup…pretty motley selection."

"Same big door cabinets, must have been the same builder, huh?" Kris notices.

"Great, lots of space, I feel right at home in this kitchen. Love looking at the hillside through the back window. Yesterday, I saw some commotion in the grape arbor behind the house. Your nephew and his buddy…their heads and arms kept popping up through the leaves. I finally figured it out…they were having a grape fight. Very New Zealand, don't you think, zinging each other with blobs of juicy sweetness?"

I hear myself stalling. Maybe Kris does, too.

"Joanne, you can make a story out of anything."

"Everything's new here for me, Kris. I love it. Take our tea outside? Sit in the shade of the lemon tree?"

"Nah, the sandflies are less likely to bite you if you're in the sun. They won't bother me. I hear they prefer tourists, 'fresh blood.'"

We sit carefully in the prickly plastic chairs. Songbirds, raised by our landlord next door, provide the music. Kris takes his ease, lifting his cup and breathing in the warm aroma. He knows how to savor tea. I'm just learning. It may be the best part of any day when he has a moment to enjoy a cup of tea. I'll follow his lead, settle, and sit in silence.

"Good you bought the Rooibos, eh?" He lifts the cup and smiles. "Shall we get to work? He lifts his eyebrows, remembers something, "Ah but first…good…that you set aside some separate time for this. It's just too much at one time, at the house."

"Yes, I have something to add, Kris. The other morning, when Yarra was coming for breakfast, you had a bouquet of flowers on the table…you were lighting a candle. I took it as a strong reminder to Yarra of who she is, maybe part of who you are, and who you are as a couple. Very beautiful."

Kris laughs, "You were part of that, remember? I didn't think we needed two tables in the kitchen. That little one works just fine for candles, flowers and meals. 'Good on ya.' We really do stash all the other stuff that comes in on the other one."

"Kris, I met a couple at church, nice folks. She works at a women's clothing shop downtown. He was formerly a carpenter, now a taxi driver. He offered to drive me around so I can do errands for you and Yarra. I thought of something you might want to try when I saw you were having a tough time getting Yarra down in the bed. I think if you put sturdy wooden blocks with holes, like cups, under the legs to raise the bed a bit, it will shorten the distance from her chair to the bed. Easier on your back and hers, too. Marley says he would do that for us. It wouldn't cost much for the wood. Want to try it?"

"I'll give it a think. It might save my back."

"That's what I thought. Let me know, and I'll call him. My turn now? This is a tough one, Kris." I take a breath. "I mentioned it last year. I think the thick rug has to go."

He wrinkles his brow and frowns. "That again? Why do we have to get rid of it? We both like it."

"It is a good rug, but the walker wheels sink into its thickness. Yarra is lifting the walker with each step. She has to balance on her legs with no support as she moves the walker forward. Think about it. She's using up her energy, just to move the walker around."

"Makes her stronger, I think. I'll talk to her, see what she says."

I take a big breath. "There's something else about the rug for me, Kris. Remember back in Longmont when you were shifting house, and Yarra fell while you were gone with a load of furniture? She couldn't get up. She had to lie face down for an hour. That 'beautiful rug' has been on the floor here for fourteen years, while young guys lived in the house. Who knows what's on this rug? Yarra knows all this. Cheryl even found a hypo needle in the carpet."

Kris' eyes widen. He listens attentively.

"I can't stand the thought of Yarra lying on that dirty rug, helpless to move herself. It was devastating to her last time."

Kris is sober. "That is a tough one." He scribbles in his notebook. "This next one we can both agree on—Yarra's closet. Packed full. Her friends bring her things she loves, but she can't use them. I can't find anything in there. Can you cull the closet?"

"Done. I've got time with Chris gone. I'll sort it out with Yarra, a little at a time."

"There's something else, Kris, about the clothes. Are you having trouble dressing her in things that go over her head? And tight pants? I am. Too much rolling her back and forth and pulling and tugging?"

"Yeah, it wears us both out just getting her dressed."

"I'll find out about where to get easy-on clothes. My Aunt Jo lived in a wheelchair most of her life. There's a catalogue in the States. Maybe we can find a seamstress here, too. I'll let you know what I find out."

"While we're talking about changing clothes, Kris, I'm feeling some reticence from Yarra when we change her diapers; do you know what it's about? Do you have any ideas?"

"Yes, she did say something to me, we talked about it; are you sure you want to hear?"

What's this? Am I ready?

"Might not feel good, but I think I better be in on it."

Kris says, "Yarra says she's uncomfortable with you being a nurse and mom and changing her diapers."

"Ahh…I didn't think of that. I'm accustomed to that task from nursing. Sure, I can see that. It's about Yarra's feelings. That must be difficult for her. As a mom, I want to help her. As a nurse, I honor her right to privacy. It's her body. I won't attempt to change the diapers. There are plenty other things we can do together. Thanks for telling me."

The next time I go to Karaka, I size up Yarra's closet. A curtain on a wire spring covers the opening to a pocket-sized closet. It is just deep enough for wire hangers. Interspersed with heavy t-shirts and sports pants are some beautiful, colorful, dresses. Ah, these are the colorful, glitzy performance dresses of Anita and Debby, Yarra's musician girlfriends. Yarra loves to dress-up, but frothy and voluminous fabrics aren't for tugging her into wheelchairs and lifting her into a bed. They are as impractical for Yarra as butterfly wings.

But she DOES wear butterfly wings. PINK! WITH SEQUINS. Chiara and her five-year-old daughter, Ruby, brought them when they came to visit. Yarra wears them downtown and to market. People identify Yarra by her long dark hair, the purple wheelchair, and her butterfly wings.

I find a t-shirt in Yarra's closet that I've been admiring in a Trafalgar Street shop window. It's designed with red poppies. Anita and Debby must have bought it for her. I put it on and walk into the living room where Yarra is resting. I twirl around for her, "What do you think, Yarra?" Yarra is smiling right off the bat.

Wow, it must be really bad. "OK, tell me I look like a can of tomatoes, go ahead." We both burst out laughing and snorting. "A can of tomatoes, right?"

We find a seamstress to help make clothing for Yarra. She makes two button-up-the-front skirts, which are much easier to put on. Yarra and I shop for some button-up blouses. Irma shows me some funky print, wrap-waisted, soft fabric pants, which she wore during pregnancy. Perfect. Yarra and I both get a pair in wild print. Yarra's are purple; mine are green.

Into the Unknown Again

Chris and I decide to do a long hike. The trailhead is just across from Yarra's bedroom window and looks out on the original pasture land. The familiar pull of my leg muscles feels good, like starting up the trail from our cabin in the Colorado Rockies. Kris showed us the path over the Grampians. It will take three hours to make a round trip. As we climb, we pass through second-growth trees; they are tall, slender, mostly grey-barked. I watch my footing and plant my feet. We are surrounded in still, silent shade. With dappled sunspots filtering through the small-leafed trees, it's kind of spooky…no, not spooky, more like serene.

Perhaps these trees are silver birch, that's the name of the trees on the street where Yarra and Kris rented. Most of the mosses, ferns, the grasses, and bushes are fascinating and unknown to me…a daily reminder that…I'm a stranger here.

Chris and I are stepping into the unknown again, willing to risk. Chris, at 22, asked me to marry him after a first date. I'd met him in the hospital, when he visited one of my patients, Carmen, who was Chris' best friend. At that time, I wanted nothing to do with dating med students or doctors. I was wary, having heard too many stories of brokenhearted nurses, who, after supporting young medical students for years, were divorced or "dumped" when their husbands became successful.

Chris gently persisted, and I agreed to date for the summer to "see how we got along." So many times in our life together we've been willing to try.

The summer before his senior year of medical school, Chris took his first step away from Pennsylvania. He applied for a preceptorship with a practicing physician. He left me working at St. Vincent Hospital in Erie, Pennsylvania. His parting gift—an arrangement of pink sweetheart roses in a white ceramic vase of Mother Mary which he'd made as a camp counselor at Lake Chautauqua. With a tilt of his head and wistful eyes he said, "I'll be back."

Looking at the delicate buds, I thought, "He really doesn't know me well, and he's very sweetly trying."

Never before had he been any farther west than Detroit. He boarded a bus and arrived in Boulder, Montana at five in the morning to see a boy on a horse delivering newspapers on a dirt street. There he met his powerful, influential mentor, Dr. Phil Pallister, who stopped his car on the way to work to shoot game to feed his family.

Dr. Pallister lived BIG in all ways. Medical Director of Montana State Hospital, superb physician, diligent father of 12 children, husband, educator, humanitarian, ethicist, victim advocate, social activist, and woodsman. Chris came home with a broader understanding of the world and a whole new world to explore. His experiences with Dr. Pallister influenced our future life decisions. Thanks to Willie, his wife, Chris brought home a small bouquet of sage, with Willie's words, "Tell Joanne to tuck these under her pillow so you'll both come back someday."

The loving partnership I saw in Chris' parents, Alberta and Joe, and the love they showed for their son, encouraged me to marry Chris in 1958. After he finished an internship at Philadelphia General Hospital and a residency at the Philadelphia Veterans Administration hospital in 1962, we promised both sets of Pennsylvania parents we would always come when they needed us. Then, with our toddler, Chiara, and newborn, Joseph, we made our move to "try Colorado."

Chris completed a residency in rheumatology at Denver General, during which he visited internal medicine practices in Western states, also looking for an "eastern-looking town, with tall trees," on my behalf. He joined the Longmont Clinic in Colorado, and we moved to an old Victorian across from a beautiful park with tall trees.

Angela, Chris Jr., and John were born within the next five years as Chris began a new internal medicine career. Both endeavors left us happy in our new surroundings, exhausted, and physically out of shape.

One evening watching television, we decided we had to do something, or "We are just going to be roly-poly, old people, someday." We decided to get healthy through exercise.

A woman Olympian, Jean Bocci, introduced me to race walking during the pre-Olympic demonstrations in Boulder, Colorado in 1970. Toddler John was at my side. Both Chris and I enjoyed the sport, and, with the assistance of some local race walkers, Floyd Godwin and Jerry Brown, we became competitive race walkers throughout our lives.

In 1964, we had a small cabin built in Big Elk Meadows, Colorado, and spent many happy days hiking in the Rocky Mountains. I followed son John into Amigos de las Americas volunteer program in an eyeglass program in Ecuador in 1984, as a reward for having completed my B.A. in Nursing. Later, Chris and I took part in a private volunteer group, "Health Treks." We went twice to the same village in Nepal. For our 60th birthdays in 1994, we hiked the 475 miles of The Colorado Trail. We risked the unknown, became healthy, and felt rewarded.

Now, many years later, a wooded setting is the perfect place to ask the really tough question, "Can we stay in New Zealand to help Yarra and Kris?"

Oh, God, how can I even think it. Chris is having neck pain. He has plans to do consulting now that he's retired. We just bought a small home in Arizona. We want to sell the cabin. How can I dare to ask this?

I can hear the voice of our nurse friend, Lou. Her husband, Joseph Fennelly, is an internist and a specialist in end-of-life care. Chris talks with Joe all the time. They know exactly what we are going through, showing signs of stress. I have a rising blood pressure and weight gain. Chris has a persistent body rash, plus neck and back pain and injuries, and one neck surgery already. They listen to our misgivings and encourage us.

Lou's voice over the phone is clear and firm, "Absolutely, Joanne, it's your moral obligation to see them through this."

And I hear Yarra's voice clearly, "I want you and Dad to live your own life." *Will it be part of our own life to be with Yarra? Chris and I will decide.*

We thread our way through warm afternoon air, shaded, silvery white tree trunks, and silence. Chris' footsteps halt when we hear a deep thrumming whistle from behind us. He looks back over his shoulder and freezes. I look up. A hefty bird—part hen, part pigeon—labors to lift itself over our heads. My birder mind goes into check mode; brilliant bits of red: eyes and beak and a white breast and belly, and a back that looks like a purple, green, and grey velvet cape. Its broad lustrous wings beat the air with slow, forceful strokes, producing deep vibrating "whooshing" sounds. Gliding on powerful compressions of air, it tilts in elegant angles between tree trunks. "Whosssh," it levels. "Whosssh," it rises and disappears, eerily enfolded in the foliage.

I'm stunned. Tears flow over my cheeks.

"Joanne, what's wrong? What happened? What was that?"

I drag my fingers over my face. "A New Zealand pigeon…I think…a kereru. We first saw them with Yarra near the Milford trek." I dig in my pocket for tissue.

"But why are you crying?" Chris steps closer. I wipe my tears again.

"I don't know why I'm crying. The bird scared me, I guess. The noise startled me." I shake my head. "No, that's not it. It looked so heavy, yet the way it tilted, slid away so effortlessly and disappeared. Yarra…it reminded me of Angela, I guess. Angela…I can't get her out of my mind; the sight of Yarra waiting, standing on the sidewalk, telling me she couldn't get up the step…calling me to the tub, telling me she couldn't get out of the bathtub." I press my lips together and sob. "What's her life going to be?"

Chris stands silent, brow furrowed, his eyes on me, pondering.

"She's…they're going to need help, Chris. Yarra asked me what we were going to do with our lives. She said, 'I want you to have your own life.' What will that be, Chris? What can we do…help them? Can we stay?"

Chris' face blurs in my tears. He reaches out to touch my arm. "I've been thinking a lot about them too, and us, both of us carrying this around." He enfolds me in his arms. We hug each other, pat each other's shoulders.

He looks around, "Let's find a place where we can sit down, OK? A log or a grassy place, OK?"

His voice steadies me. I nod. He leads the way through the trees to a clearing. Below, all the streets of Nelson downtown are spread out under a brilliant blue sky. Nelson's unique windmill shapes of city hall raise blades to the sun. It stops us both.

In the distance, a horizon of a turquoise-green ocean, framed in a dark blue line, adds an accent of serenity. Breathtaking beauty and captivating newness, it clears my mind. I gather my thoughts. I relax. We find a fallen tree and a flat rock for seats.

"How's this?" Chris puts his arm over my shoulder. "Pretty 'gob-smacking gorgeous' view, no?" His smile is wistful, encouraging.

"Balcony seats. Remember, Chris, like the first time you took me to hear Segovia?

"We could use some of that classical guitar now, Honey. What's best for you? Do you just want to talk here?

"My feelings are…so close to spilling over. I think I'd just ramble on, let off steam. I don't know what's best to do.

"What about a Marriage Encounter dialogue?

"Yeah, that sounds good. I like that."

I don't want to move. This feels like sacred ground. "It's so peaceful here and beautiful. If we go back to our place, other stuff will come crowding in. Here, I feel far away from everything else. Can we try it here, without writing?"

"Why not? We'll spend ten minutes and see what comes up and share. Does that sound good?"

I nod. "I think that will help me. There's so much going on with me, right now."

Chris replies, "I'm glad it happened…the bird…you crying...it's time we talk. It's important, Joanne. Let's try." He pauses. "What's the question? 'How do you feel about staying to try to help Yarra and Kris?' Is that it? Feelings, not thoughts, right? Is that it?"

I nod.

I'm grateful we have this tool from early in our married life where our first halting letters were written in a motel room at a weekend workshop. It was billed, "Marriage Encounter, to help already good marriages become better." It strengthened our marriage by teaching us how to be open in our communication. Now we are here, halfway across the world, thrown into the vortex of our grown daughter's disease, looking out on an endless ocean, trying to get to the heart of our distress.

I hear Father Bakewell's words, "Anything is permissible in marriage, as long as you both agree, and it doesn't harm the relationship." Those words puzzled me at the time. Over and over, they have proven true. We'll see what we bring about this time.

We sit in silence, concentrate. Ten minutes pass. "Who goes first?" Chris looks up.

I say, "Me. I'm so ready. I'm grateful we're doing this now."

I take a deep, slow breath. "I feel fearful. I feel worried about how much stress this will put on our relationship and our physical health. I feel a strong sense of certainty that it's the right thing to do. We've helped our moms, my dad, and Betty Lou and the kids when Tom died, and you were with your sister Esther when she died and your aunt Josephine and your uncle John. I feel a loss of our new post-retirement freedom. I feel willing. I feel hopeful. I feel anxious. I feel intrusive."

Chris shares, "I'm alarmed, too, at what we have been observing in Yarra and Kris. I feel fearful, anxious, and worried about what lies ahead for them and us. My gut tells me we need to stay and offer help to Yarra and Kris. I only pray we have the strength and wits to do so. Will we be able to learn what to do as we move along?"

I ponder a moment, "Do you feel worried like when she was first diagnosed?"

"Oh, no, Joanne, we're well beyond that. We're well beyond the fear of the disease. What we're facing now are the day-to-day challenges of managing and living with it. That was a medical crisis, with the medical team to guide us. My concern is about our threading our way with Kris and Yarra, as we go along. Will we have the capability to manage that?

"Yes, that's what my anxiety is about, too. We're at odds with Kris and Yarra on so many things. We don't understand each other. We don't know this adult Yarra and all she's been through, nor where she is with her MS. Will we do or say something that offends Kris? He loves his privacy. I feel we're intruding in their space so often. He's frustrated and gets angry. Then there's all the energy that dissipates in discussions and disagreements. Will our staying be more draining than helpful?"

Chris nods, "Exactly. It seems too much to process." He pauses, "Are you as exhausted as I am?"

I nod.

"How about a walk home, *in silence?"*

"Good idea. Thank you, Chris." I turn to Chris for a hug and relax into his arms. *He's so willing to be open, how fortunate I...we, are.*

He steps back, his arms still about my waist, looks into my eyes. "We've done enough for today, don't you agree? Tomorrow we'll talk again, but I think in our hearts we know we're in this for the long haul."

Our walk home is a sidewalk tour of old Nelson. Tall shade trees, well-tended flowering gardens and an occasional newly-built brick apartment building, set off with great glass and balconies. Back in the neighborhood of The Brook, we shuffle into The Dairy, a one-in-every-neighborhood convenience store. We grin, and Chris cocks an eyebrow and heads for the freezer case. I lick my lips.

A dark skinned, sari-clothed shopkeeper catches our exchange, tilts her head and grins to herself. Chris lifts out two Memphis Meltdowns, our latest "New Zealand find," frozen heaven-on-a-wooden-stick. Creamy vanilla ice cream wrapped in gooey caramel and covered with thick chocolate. It is the perfect antidote for any emotional meltdown. We rarely indulge, but surely today's a day for indulgence. We "yum" and "umm" our last few blocks home.

Tea and Tears

Kris and I will start with a cup of tea; that should make it much easier.

Who am I kidding?

It's true what Yarra says, "He's beautiful." In many ways. How she must have fallen for him. Kris told me when he went to Australia he had a tarot reading. He'd "never done that before nor believed any of it." The reader told Kris he would meet a woman who would change his life. He had arranged for a room at the commune. When he arrived, he found Yarra living in his room "temporarily," he said. "I paid attention." Well, she certainly has changed his life.

Kris straightens, "Shall I get us a refill before we begin?"

I nod, "Thanks," and glance down at my list:

Yarra wearing sweats
Not given choice of clothes
Need for dandruff shampoo
Foaming perineal cleanser
Nail care & polish
Tampons
No sunbathing

"Kris, I've noticed Yarra is wearing sweats a lot these days. Is that a choice?"

"It's a necessity, Joanne." Kris continued, "Do you have any idea how many times a day we change her?

"I believe that's going to continue as she gets less able. Again, it has to do with who Yarra is. She told me no one asks her opinion anymore. I don't think she would have told me if she didn't feel it somehow."

"It ties into something else I noticed, Kris. I'm hearing, 'She this and she that.' People speaking about Yarra in third person, not addressing her directly as 'Yarra.' That can't feel good. I'd like to request everyone speaks of her and to her by "Yarra." We've got to keep Yarra in the picture. Agree?"

Kris lowers his head, purses his lips, "Yes, I think that's happening." He breathes out a long sigh.

"And wearing colorless sweats is not Yarra. Color is part of her day.

"Joanne, she's wetting herself." Exasperated, Kris exclaims, "Vikki can't keep up with the wash. If it's a rainy spell, we're wiped out.

"Here's what I know: she spent so much time picking out her clothes, her jewelry. I think it's a part of who she is. I think it's important. Can we think of some ways to better manage the clothes? She's losing so much of her independence. What can we do to give her choices?"

Kris lifts his head, says, "That's why I take her out. It's more important we get that in every day than the clothes."

"You're right, Kris. I love that you take her to the Buddhist functions—the "Possibilities Fair," to the beach. We've got to keep Yarra in the picture. Agree?"

Can I keep going on this?

Am I pushing too hard?

They're not using the dandruff shampoo or the "too expensive" foaming perineal cleanser, the nail polish she loves, or tampons.

She's still "sunbathing."

So many issues not understood or rejected...how will we get to peaceful agreement?

"Kris," I take a big breath.

Here goes.

"As long as I'm here, I'm going to stand up for Yarra. I promised her I would be her advocate. If I see something I believe is detrimental to her well-being, then I'm going to bring it up with you. She's your wife, and she's my daughter. Anything you want to say to me, I'm open. I want to try to get through this as best we can."

Kris' face disappears. I'm squinting into a bright light. What's happening? Is the sun peeking up over the roof? I see Yarra sitting in front of me, her arms resting on the black kitchen table. My hands are reaching out to grasp her hands. I cover my eyes as I see a thick sheet of glass crash down entrapping my wrists. I gasp, flinch. I can't move my hands…I can't reach Yarra's hands. Warm tears flood my face. My nose runs.

"Joanne, Joanne, what's happening?" Kris' voice, urgent and concerned, pierces my transfixed state.

"Oh, Kris, a…a…

What to say?

"Are you all right?" His voice again. "Sit down." He slides a chair under me, and I collapse.

"I saw something…so real. I only know the Italian word a… 'presentire'…I don't know…a vision…maybe. I saw Yarra sitting at the table. I'm trying to reach her…I see my hands reach for hers. A thick sheet of glass, like a mirror…the glass came down, trapped my wrists."

I tremble, gulp for air. I taste salty tears. I choke.

"I can't reach her. I see my own reflection in the glass. It's so very scary."

I shake my head, utter a feeble moan, scratch in my pocket for a tissue. I look at Kris, his blue, tear-filled eyes steady on mine and his cheeks wet. We sit silent for a moment.

Kris stands, "Are you going to be OK, Joanne?"

"I don't know…never happened before. I don't know what to say."

He mutters, "Enough for today, right? Shall we go inside?"

"Yes, …feels very warm." I stand.

"Mind your step." Kris takes my elbow.

I take a deep breath, wipe my eyes, "Thanks, Kris, I'll call you if I need you."

He puts a hand on my shoulder, looks at me quizzically. "Yes, do."

I stand in the kitchen. It's warm and still. I want to go back to the yard, to the space where it happened…that "presentire."

I feel something remains in the air.

Something for me here, seeing my face in the glass…

There is some remnant here for me to learn.

Seeing my own version of not letting go…trying to control what can't be controlled?

The self-closing door that Yarra couldn't use.

The closet that Yarra couldn't reach.

The foam pads that didn't support her in the wheelchair.

The neck brace that she wouldn't wear.

The nursing care notebooks that got lost.

You can love her, support her. You can't fix her.

The sun is bright and still and very hot; there is nothing more to see. I amble into the house, exhausted.

I walk to our place from Yarra's.

I find Chris on the phone. He smiles when he sees me and waves me over, grabs an envelope, and scribbles "Carmen." Carmen, his best, childhood buddy from "the old neighborhood."

Chris continues his conversation. "Yeah, we're hanging in there. But we love being in New Zealand."

He listens for a while, then motions me over and hurridley writes, "Come here?"

I nod vigorously. It would be so good for all of us if Carmen came.

"Oh, Carm that would be great." Chris listens... "No, Carm, forget it, don't come. A week's not worth it."

Chris begins a salespitch; "If you can't stay for a month or more it's not worth it. You want to be here long enough to taste and feel the beauty of this country; really meet the lovely people who live here. We have plenty of room.

Chris voice softens, " Don't forget, "Gumbah," we'd love to have you here. Yarra would love it. She'd think you came just for her. She's gotta crush on you, you know."

Chris laughs, "Yeah. I just asked Joanne. She walked in the room; she's smiling and nodding. "Great, we'll be looking for you."

How to Get Things Done

I have discussed with my counselor, Mary Jaksch, the troubled communication between Kris and me, the many assumptions and perceptions taken as truth, by all of us. Mary is an immigrant from England, and she understands the complexity of the situation, the various cultural norms, the anxiety, fatigue, and desires of all of us. I take notes as we talk of what she has learned through her experience of immigrating to New Zealand. I'm going to try to learn it and use it.

1. First, tell all that is good.
2. Say "and" not "but" because "but" negates all the previous good accounts.
3. "And I have some concerns," a phrase that works well in an egalitarian society. It implies you care for the good of all.
4. Invite your audience into the discussion; ask for their input. "And I would like to ask how you see it?"
6. Ask for suggestions to improve the situation.
7. Make your suggestions.
8. Ask for comment.
9. Decide on possible action.
10. Thanks, and plan follow up.

The Art Therapist's Gift of Wholeness

Kris and Yarra are looking at some paintings on the table in her "art room." She sees me and calls out with a smile, "My art therapist is coming today. Her name is Isobel. I've been painting all week because she came last week."

I nod, "good." I'd heard from Kris that he and the new helper, Vikki, had searched to find someone doing art therapy in the Nelson area.

"Mom," Yarra calls for my attention, "I picked a creature out of her box of sand and plastic toys, and, "wow," you'd think I would have put it together, but I didn't."

She looks at me as if I should understand.

She explains, "A mermaid doesn't have a crotch; she has a tail."

Again, she waits for my response. "Well, as I was working, my teacher was laughing, not out loud, but just giggling, because she knew I didn't get the significance. She was waiting for me to get it."

And so am I. It must be important to Yarra.

She explains. "A mermaid is a sexless creature," I hear the therapist's words in Yarra's, "but she can still be sexual…attractive."

Yarra is being so open.

This is so intimate.

I keep my eyes on her, afraid that if I look at Kris, we may all get terribly distracted.

I want Yarra to have this rare moment of expressing herself. She's excited and open.

"Now I'm in love with the idea." She lowers her voice. "Not that I wanted to become a sexless person. It's to value how I can be beautiful, and what it takes to be a beautiful person."

I nod and smile, but she has more to share. She hurries on, unabashed, "My crotch doesn't get the care it used to, because my legs don't work, but just because I don't have signs of sexuality doesn't mean I'm not…whoops, what's that same word that means 'sexual?'"

A few moments pass. We wait for Yarra to produce the right word. Silence, and then Kris softly volunteers, "passionate."

"Passionate…yeah." Yarra breathes. She turns to the pile of watercolor pieces, picks one up, studies it and nods, "Yeah, I can still be passionate."

Months later, Chiara and our granddaughter Ruby, back in Colorado, receive a large package from New Zealand. It's an eight-foot tempera and watercolor mermaid, her tail flipping jauntily upward, her hair streaming out behind her. Her arms stretch out in a powerful stroke.

We were filled with gratitude and marvel at the hours of detailed attention of Yarra and, perhaps, helpers who created it, but, more so, the joy Yarra must have felt as she saw her art completed. It hung for years on Ruby's bedroom wall.

Ruby left for college; the mermaid frolicked on her wall. Some sunny days her scales shimmered in the sunshine, reminders to me that it was the creative, compassionate mind of Isobel, the art therapist, who saw the green plastic mermaid in the sand play tray. It was she who realized and initiated the healing connection, allowing Yarra to envision herself still as a still beautiful, passionate woman.

Now "The Mermaid" is landlocked on the wall in Chiara's storeroom, still visible every time the garage door goes up.

Finding an Angel

I'm seated at the kitchen table watching Yarra try to fill her spoon. It's difficult for her to twist the spoon against the edge of the dish and lift it. *It would be helpful to have some dishes with partitions. Maybe we can get a local potter to make one.*

There's a light tap at the glass window of the kitchen door. A young woman cracks open the door, sees Yarra and me at the table. She steps in a few inches.

Her clear blue eyes are remarkable, wide open to the world. "Good Morning, I'm Vikki." She nods. "You must be Joanne." She drops her voice, "Yarra's mum."

I assume she is Yarra and Kris' household helper, but her silky blouse, wrap skirt, and the startling knee boots give me pause. So much so, I forget to speak. "Oh, yes, of course, come in, welcome. Yarra's already at breakfast. Would you like something?"

"No, thanks. I'm fine." She sets a bag on the small, extra "hold things" table and drifts towards Yarra. "Mum finally here, Yarra?" She places a hand on Yarra's arm. They share a knowing smile.

She watches Yarra push the cereal around the bowl, trying to capture a spoonful. "Need anything?"

Yarra shakes her head, indicating no.

"I'll get the laundry going and come back." Yarra nods and returns to her cereal.

Vikki slides toward the hallway like a breeze.

In gumboots? How does she do that?

I'm mesmerized. I stare after her and smile to myself. *"Vikki is going to bring a different tempo to the order here. The room feels calm...Thank you, God."*

The HE-ART-RY

Chrissy has been taking Yarra to lessons at "The HE-ART-RY." Tonight, she is not able. *Would I like to take Yarra?* I'm excited to share the experience with my daughter, see another side of the Nelson art scene.

The aged brick and dark metal building looks like a heavy equipment factory. There are extremely wide docks, staircases, ramps and very large elevators. Heavy black chains hang from the ceiling.

We go up in a platform elevator, which opens onto a large room with high windows on all sides. Students stand around chatting until the teacher arrives. She explains tonight's class on "quick sketching," five minutes each period to draw with charcoal, each of three nude models who will pose before us. *Five minutes for each model? How's Yarra going to manage?*

Tonight, Yarra will wear an apron with large pockets across the bottom edge. It's a well-used apron of Betty Franco's, the mom of my childhood friend, Betty Lou. Covered with sunflowers and now splashed over with Yarra's bold paint colors, the large pockets work well for her. She stashes her supplies in the pockets. They save her time and energy.

Yarra sits until it is time to draw. I stand silently beside her during the lesson. I'm engrossed in watching her concentrate and move as quickly and adroitly as she can. She draws in long strokes. The charcoals break or drop from her grasp. She fumbles in the pockets for another piece. Even when she drops her chalk, she keeps her eyes on the model. I retrieve pieces as they fall to the floor. I replace them in her pockets.

"Time's up, new paper, new model."

Yarra sighs and sits until the next model is posed. She is totally absorbed and amazes me.

After the next session, the teacher calls "break." Yarra sits and looks over her drawings. "I'm pretty proud of myself, Mom."

"Your concentration and the way you capture the essence of the models in a few lines is…your favorite word, "amazing." She smiles. "You love it, don't you?"

"I do, Mom. I do. I'm so glad we found this place. I can do good work here."

"Wait until I tell Betty Lou. She'll be pleased her mom's apron is working well for you."

Being Crippled

We take Yarra out in the wheelchair to visit the horse corral. One day when we pass the two-story house next door, I ask, "Who lives here?"

Yarra says, "A crippled girl and her parents. We only see them when she goes out in a cab. We tried to visit with them. She doesn't want anyone to see her."

It's strange to hear Yarra describe anyone as "crippled," a word she disdains. Yarra wears the t-shirt she made with the dancing woman, the shirt, which is printed with "Dance Spirit Dance." She says, "Don't 'dis' my ability. I have MS, it doesn't have me." She espouses Dawna Markova's creed, "I will not die an unlived life."

I will not die an unlived life.
I will not live in fear
of falling or catching fire.
I choose to inhabit my days,
to allow my living to open me,
to make me less afraid,
more accessible,
to loosen my heart
until it becomes a wing,
a torch, a promise.

I choose to risk my significance;
to live so that which came to me as seed
goes to the next as blossom
and that which came to me as blossom,
goes on as fruit.

c Dawna Markova, www.ptpinc.org.

Is it because the neighbor woman doesn't "go outside" that Yarra describes her as "a cripple?" Is that why Yarra pleads, "Get someone to take me out every day"? To Yarra, does "being connected, being with people" mean "not crippled?" Wow, she is pushing us, pushing herself "not to be crippled."

It takes so much effort to enable Yarra to be out and about. Yet it happens. Some comes from her desire, spirit, and willingness to engage, and much from the willingness and energy of those in her family circle or those drawn to her. There are different ways of being crippled.

As we roll past the house, a loud fart from a tuba, or trumpet, blasts from an open window. Yarra, Vikki, and I break out into a fit of laughter. I move to see Yarra's happy face.

She blurts, "That's the father."

We laugh out loud again.

Yarra raises her head up when she hears what she has said, "No… not that," she snorts. "I mean," she pushes the words out, "he's a music teacher."

We laugh harder, together. It feels so good.

Yarra is a light. People are drawn to her. They want to spend time with her. Irma takes her to riding lessons. She wants her children to learn about people with disabilities. Erika, a physical therapist who treated Yarra in the hospital, lives nearby and has become a friend. She has donated hours of physical therapy. Kris' family members are doing art with Yarra, taking her to the art classes. Vikki works tirelessly. Kris is forever managing, planning, doing. It takes a cadre of willing people with endless energy to keep Yarra connected to life…that, and a generous health care system.

Those People

"Yarra's going to see the Lipizzaner horses when they come to Nelson. We'll take the new van. Want to go with us?" Kris asks.

"Of course. You know she rode Arabians for a while, don't you, in junior high? A woman in Hygiene, Colorado, invited her to help exercise her horses."

"Oh yes, she talks about it sometimes. She really enjoyed that. I didn't put it together before, but now I think that's a reason she took to riding therapy horses so easily after her MS."

"Yeah, she'd ridden those spirited Arabians."

When we enter the large auditorium, Kris wheels Yarra's chair up close and on the side of the performance arena. It's customary in New Zealand to make special arrangements for the less-abled. They are seated together at the best vantage point. It is very accommodating and thoughtful, though it places Yarra away from us. I won't get to watch her joy and share her excitement.

After the performance, we approach the van. Kris put Yarra in the front seat. He turns to us, stern looking and in a low voice says, "Yarra said she was not happy to sit with 'those people.' She wants to sit with her family."

Yarra's Van Remodel

Yarra's new van is wonderful. It has a cot on one side with a mattress where Yarra can have a "lay down." It works especially well on days when she has no energy but can be out of the house as she wishes. Kris can play Kubb, a favorite Dutch game of the brothers, or they visit, and Yarra listens and enjoys being outdoors. A lift opens down from the back door to raise and lower Yarra in her wheelchair into the left front-seat position.

"Kris, this is so well designed. Tell me about it. Did you have someone help you or was it the man who did the remodel?" Kris gets a silly, pondering look, that says, 'Am I going to tell this story or not?'"

He decides to tell me. "It didn't come like this at first. The guy did a lot of work to get room for the lift and the cot. I was all excited; we'd waited for so long, and then I could see Yarra wasn't pleased.

I didn't know what was wrong."

He laughs. "Yarra was meant to sit in the back..." He pauses; questions by raising his eyebrows..."in her wheelchair. They didn't know Yarra, and I didn't think of it. Ahh." He lets out a long sigh. "We needed some form of transportation for so long, but Yarra took one look inside and flat-out said, 'I'm not going to sit in the back like a piece of meat.' I was surprised. That was it, no arguments. We called the guy, and he saw she was right."

Kris rolled his eyes, expressing surprise at their accomplishment. "He did it over."

The next day, Kris handed me a typed letter, "Joanne, I thought you might like this application written by Yarra for funding the wheelchair van. We were given about $21,000 from the government."

Dear Sirs and Madams,

I am only 36, and I desperately want to continue living, to experience more of Life! This MS body is a huge challenge to me. But I still have so much to discover that I still can do, and I need a vehicle to help me with this discovery.

Every time I go out is a brand-new experience. Without a vehicle, I feel stuck. I can't get to the sea, the mountains, the bush—to be in Nature, which is such a blessing to me.

Please give me this opportunity. Yarra Amoroso

Bee Surprised

One evening, Kris phones from across the street. There's a chuckle in his voice when he asks, "Are you ready for our surprise? Come on over."

"Come in," yells Kris, hidden in the dark behind a bright spotlight focused on Yarra.

I can't see her face. Vikki is at the side of the bed next to Yarra. Vikki's eyes focus to a point of the shiny, narrow instrument she holds. Kris' arm moves forward. He opens a jar lid just a crack and holds the jar out to Vikki. An angry buzz fills the air. Bees! It's bee sting treatment.

Oh God! No! ...the big surprise. Oh no! I feel myself getting very warm and nauseous.

Vikki holds long metal tweezers and is trying to capture a bee in the jar. She pulls one forward towards Yarra's belly. Angry zings in fits and starts fill the space over the bed. Vikki's eyes are intent on the bee. She's focused and determined. She gently lowers the squirming insect.

I'm shivering. How can I be warm and shivering at the same time? Oh, dear God, she wants the bee to sting Yarra. She loves Yarra. She wants Yarra to get better. Oh, this must be so hard.

Sudden quiet, then I see a red swelling begin to form on Yarra's pale belly around the bee. *Oh, oh, I think I'm going to collapse.* Kris' voice drifts from the darkness behind the glare of the spotlight. "Would you two like to help us?"

I part my lips in a partial gasp. Careful, careful, Joanne. This is "the big surprise" they were excited to share. Any rejection is going to hurt. Oh, what to say? I look at Chris, his face sober and his eyes cast down.

I watch him closely as I murmur, "No...no, I don't think I can... sorry."

Chris and I turn, slink out of the room, through the kitchen, as silent as snakes. Chris puts both hands up to steady me on the broken steps. Pale yellow light glows from neighboring house windows. I raise my eyes to the dark sky. Chris slips an arm around my waist. We walk to our house and fall into chairs. We stare at each other. I cross the floor to Chris and kneel at his feet, putting my head in his lap. He slides his fingers into my hair and gently pats my head.

When six-year-old Joseph walked down our neighbor Pat Meade's front porch steps and bees flew up his pant legs and stung him, he howled for hours afterwards. I can't think of what it must be like for Yarra to subject herself to that pain, twice a week.

We have heard of this treatment for years. It's billed as a natural steroid as the body reacts to the stinging. It hasn't been recommended by any of our doctors or at the Heuga Center. Some people believe it helps, give rave reviews, and others said, "It helps for a while, sometimes." There's incidental, personal evidence, but nothing proven that it's sustainable. I hate to see Yarra go through the pain and Kris, the arduous task, only to be disappointed. *It's their dream. Maybe it will work for them.*

Chris sighs. "It's inhumane, looks like torture. I feel angry, but it also shows how desperate they are. We're so far apart. We want to talk with their doctor about bringing some medicine from the states. This means a manufactured chemical injectable. And they want us to try something natural, which makes sense to them, bee stings."

I shiver, "I feel so helpless. I don't want to dash their hopes. I want to support them, but I can't support this."

The New Doctor

I press into the stain of Yarra's red cotton underpants with cold knuckles. I hear the thump of a car door being closed over the clap, clump, and splash of the washing machine in the corner of the laundry room. I lift my eyes to a steamy window. A man in a tan cord jacket with sturdy shoes is crossing the lawn. He carries a black bag straight-armed at his side. *Ah, it's the new doctor. Hmm, will he be "too English" for Yarra's liking?* Just then, he skips over a deep crack of broken concrete in the sidewalk. Atop his head bounces a mass of "little boy curls." He leaps up the steps like a kid. Yep, this would be our man.

He sticks out his free hand and grasps mine firmly, "Dr. Williams. I'm here to meet Yarra." He knows her name. I like him already. I hope Yarra does. He introduces himself to Yarra and pulls up a chair, asking, "May I sit down?"

I move to a chair across the room. Yarra watches Dr. Williams as he speaks to her as easily as if he were a neighbor in for a visit. "I can come to your home if you like, or you can come to the office. It's not too far from here." Yarra nods.

"I received your history from Dr. Malcolm Clark. I would do an exam today if you feel up to it." Again, Yarra, nods, smiles. I think she would jump over the moon if he asked.

I could see she was rapt with this very non-officious male doctor who retained, it seemed to me, the disarming charm of the child he had been. I was pleased myself with such respect.

Kris enters from the kitchen and puts his hand out to greet the doctor. That evening, I return to 9 Karaka. Kris greets me, "Well, we have another special doctor, don't we? Yarra thinks so."

"I do too, Kris. How lucky can we be? Now she can have two special doctors, no three, counting her dad. Pretty special, yourself, Yarra." I give her shoulders a squeeze.

Handicap Access – Not!

The next two days we stay at 20 Karaka with Yarra while Kris stays with his grandsons. I hear a local photographer has an interesting exhibit, and neither Yarra nor I have been to the art gallery. Should we go? She nods affirmative. So, Yarra in her wheelchair, her nurse, and I trundle in the van to The Sutter Gallery.

An entry attendant gives a slight lip smack of regret and says, "There is no easily accessible entrance, but we can open a back door around the side." We all get grumpy. Helene bristles as she wheels Yarra's chair down a ramp to the gallery floor. Yarra knows the Spanish saying, "No vale la pena" (not worth the pain). I'm wondering if that's what she is thinking. I'm angry with the City of Nelson Council. *Public buildings should have access for all.*

The exhibit room is warm and stuffy. Small, framed photos of old Nelson are difficult to see, especially from a wheelchair distance. We've wasted precious energy, and I feel to blame.

Outside, we find that someone has parked too close to the back of the van. We need to open the doors to lower the hoist for the wheelchair. I push Yarra under a shady tree. We wait for Helene to go in the gallery to try to find the owner of the car.

Helene has her own running battle over the lack of handicap-designated parking spaces. She groans over cars without handicap tickets hanging in their windows that park in those few designated spaces available. She reciprocates by not hanging a handicap sign in the back of our van, not even the one I brought from the states, the silhouette of a cowgirl in hat and boots, seated in a wheelchair. She parks bumper-to-bumper with the offending car—makes sense to her.

"Hey, Yarra, want to hear that story about when the Fennelly family from New Jersey came to visit? Young Chris went with you, and you brought them down from where you were camping at Kenny Mountain for the night?"

Yarra might have lifted her face a bit. I'll try it.

"Remember, Chris thought he was having an appendicitis attack 'cause he had a bellyache?" She turns her head toward me.

"You brought them two miles down that steep mountainside in the dark. You said you saw that star, the planet Venus that always came up over the cliff, so you knew which way to head back to the cabin. Dad and I and Lou and Joe couldn't believe you could do it! I don't think I ever told you, but that has stayed in my heart ever after, on all your long explores: New Guinea, India, all those years in Australia. It reminded me you once came home by the light of a star."

Yarra's not responding. I think she's heard. I'm content to have shared that story, but today is definitely not our standard normal.

Helene comes ruffling across the sidewalk toward us, the sun illuminating her red hair, followed by a man rattling his keys.

We tell Kris about our day. He shoots back, "That wasn't the exhibit Yarra wanted to go to, Joanne. It was a big Maori display in the main gallery. I told you it was 'local' people."

The photographer was a local person. Misunderstanding words again. I'm not going to touch that one.

I look at Yarra. We're both disappointed and very tired. I don't want to talk more about it. I shrug my shoulders and turn up my open hands in the Italian "boh?"

"No Sweet Sorrow"

Joanne T. Pisoni Amoroso

"When are you leaving?"
Her voice…sudden clarity
suspends every word.
Each reverberates like
distant thunder in a canyon.

She asks the unspeakable,
"When are you leaving?"
Does she hear it?
Catch her misperception?

In her purple wheelchair,
head drooping to one side,
she waits for my answer.
She reads my mind, always.
Her topaz eyes, parallel stop signs,
halt my thinking.

My fingers wrap hers.
"Oh…" falls from her lips.
"No one said you were leaving,
did they?"
I have no breath
no response.

"Well, I think you will leave
two months from now
when the rains begin."
A hazy thread
reminds me,
yesterday,
we applied for residency.

"Being Spoken To" in Nelson

Kris and I are in the kitchen. He's cooking. Smells like butter and onions so far. I'm sorting Yarra's laundry on the small table. He says, "There's some rough stuff going on at the ablution blocks. The police might close them."

I hear what he says. I have no idea what it means, and I'm not sure I want to engage in a discussion. I'm tired.

Since Kris usually only tells me things that matter, I think over what I heard. *"Ablution?" Sounds like Holy Water being poured over someone...like...the forgiveness of sin...no, that's absolution? But "ablution blocks?"*

"Hmm, the ablution blocks?"

"Oh...yah, you call them "toilets," the public toilets…the ablution blocks in the car park."*OK, but why is he telling me?*

"Some ruffians are going to be spoken to by the police."

"Spoken to? That's all?"

"Well, if they don't straighten up, they'll get their names printed in the paper."

Kris is sounding as if he's wished he hadn't brought it up. We get into such convoluted discussions. *What does what's happening in the ablution blocks have to do with us?*

"Kris, I'm not sure why you want me to know this."

He turns his head, stares at me and blurts out, "It's about Yarra. She won't have a place to go to the toilet in the market."

"Ohhh, OK. I understand." I nod.

So many times, I don't understand what's going on. I don't catch the drift of a conversation, the assumed and usual for those around me. For me, so many unknowns, unfamiliar people and place make it challenging.

I wonder if it's like this for Yarra. I stop asking. I wait, and the pieces gradually fall together, but it's like walking on ice most of the time, except with Chris. With Yarra, trying to figure out what she would say if she could, that's a constant. She looks at me with those soulful dark eyes, and I wish, I wish....

Kris has gone gardening. Yarra is napping. I'm tidying up the kitchen. As I swipe the counter, a yellow sticky note in Kris' handwriting catches my eye. *Is this here for me?*

"She has eyes that go
straight through you.
You into the essence
of me
Take away the
bullshit
Show the Buddha
within
The river is flowing."

They Might As Well Be Speaking Dutch

Kris says, "The Kolffs are getting together. Will's coming to town. It'll be a good chance for you to get to know everyone."

"Will?"

"He's our younger brother who lives in Denmark. He brings tour groups every so often." A look of mischief crosses his face. "You'll probably like him. He's the good-looking one."

"Ahh, better looking than you, Kris? I don't believe it."

"You'll see."

And I do. Will arrives first. He steps into the kitchen entrance, head up and smiling. He's dressed in creased trousers, matching blue silk shirt and jacket, which is much different than the casual attire the New Zealand men I've met would choose for a house party. That makes Will different—more like an American—more like Yarra and me. Yarra likes to dress up. I remember Will had to scramble over the unstable, stacked cement blocks to get to the door. Did he notice or hop right up like his brothers, all experienced trampers?

The Kolff kin I've met have blonde hair, soft loopy curls, or straight, stiff, shiny black hair, lively blue eyes and square white teeth that form toothpaste-ad smiles. Short and compact, they are strikingly handsome people. Animated and gathered together, they are eye-catching. But, Kris was right. Will, the youngest, his hand around mine and smiling, seems to be the perfection of the brood.

"Yarra's mother? Yes, I can see the resemblance. He bends low, drops his left hand into Yarra's lap to touch her red-polished fingers, curved and resting in her lap. "Well, Yarra, do you remember me… Will…the brother from Denmark?"

Will watches her face. She stares.

"You look very festive this evening, Yarra. I hope you enjoy the party."

Kris comes in from the hallway, "Brother Will!" He and Will throw their arms around each other and thump on each other's necks and shoulders. Big smiles and a tumble of incomprehensible syllables spill from their mouths.

Kris' sister, Inez, and her husband, Ralph, enter in New Zealand casual, woolly sweaters and slacks. Inez is tiny and wiry. Her round, tanned face is elfin-like, the perfect foil for her crown of short blonde spikes. Inez and Ralph carry paper-wrapped trays and their son, Nicholas, lugs a bulging plastic bag of dark grapes.

Mark, Kris' son, comes in the back entrance carrying a beautiful, large, round chocolate cake. The noise level rises as everyone moves toward the cake. Mark grins proudly. His two young sons, their hands gripping spatulas and knives, are surrounded by the Kolffs, who gather to look with eager eyes at the cake and say, "Yummy" and "Ahh, it's been too long," and "Mark's Dutch chocolate cake, wonderful!"

I look to see if Yarra notices it. Nothing. She is really low if she doesn't see chocolate.

The party's on as Walt, the oldest brother, white curls and serene, arrives alone. I learn from the others asking, "How's Julia?" that Walt's wife is very ill, and he will return to Christchurch early in the morning. There are multiple offers of lodging from all the siblings.

Yarra's chair is by the door. She wears her favorite Monet color-splashed chiffon skirt from India and a lavender top. Black onyx and silver earrings I'd brought her from Mexico dangle at her jaw line. Her dark curls hang gracefully across her shoulders. Vikki is wonderful at getting Yarra dressed, and they have fun picking out matching clothes and jewelry.

We are engaged briefly with handshakes and relatives greeting Yarra and me. They bend over to say a few sentences to Yarra or put a hand on her arm and then disappear into a whirl of "Kolff-ness," chatting, hugging, laughing, arguing, joshing, moving constantly to position themselves directly in front of whomever is speaking at the time.

I keep hearing, "Where are Hein and Johanna?" and "Oh, they'll be along soon." They arrive with trays of crackers, cheese with bits of fresh herbs and green peas from their garden. Yarra and I see them disappear into a wall of silhouettes which is gradually moving to the center of the room.

Overhead a dangling, conical, dark green, shaded light creates bright halos in their full heads of hair and deep shadows under their thick eyebrows and sculpted facial features. Their eyes glisten and dart from face to face, reading reactions. We hear "Ya, ya," a back slap, tones of disbelief, "Naah," giggles, then a resounding rapid retort and a guffaw. It is a noisy beehive of motion and guttural sounds pierced with snickers, exclamations, all of them touching. Thirteen in a circle press toward whoever is speaking, talking over each other, interrupt, and all in Dutch. They are children again, holding plates of goodies, pushing bites into their mouths quickly between bits of conversation. I can relate to their joy of being together and speaking in their native tongue, having fun.

It is Yarra and I who are "out of place" in her own home. We cannot understand a word, nor is anyone attempting the impossible of including us. It's a social conundrum I've never faced before. In Ecuador, Nepal, Italy, Germany, Mexico, there was someone who tried to translate, to help include me in the conversation.

Time passes. Yarra and I sit by the wall like two brooms in a corner. What shall I do? It's too noisy to talk with Yarra. She wouldn't hear unless I stood up in front of her…with my back to the crowd. At least if they were speaking English, we could hear the stories and laugh at the jokes. Well, it's not so easy for them to talk to Yarra, either. Best make our own plans. I reach over to pat her hand.

I say, "Yarra, one time Dad and I were at a weekend fiddling contest in Colorado. It was a lot of the same-sounding music. They even told a joke…'How can you tell one fiddle song from the other?' Can you guess?"

"No? You can tell them apart by their title. It did get pretty repetitive. Late in the afternoon, about three o'clock, Dad turned and said 'Joanne, I think I've had as much fun as I can stand.'"

Amazingly, Yarra blurts out her laugh. She caught it. Laughter is one of Yarra's remaining signs of self-expression. It tickles her nurses. She hears what is said; she understands. We laugh together.

"What do you think? Have you had as much fun as you can stand?" She nods. "Me too, shall we go back to your room?"

Mark winds through the crowd, holding his delectable Dutch chocolate cake before him. He's slicing the cake. We'll wait. Yarra will want a crumb to taste, and I'll treat myself, too. Mark sends his boys to serve us first. With shy smiles, they offer a tray of cake pieces and napkins.

I hold a piece to Yarra's nose, "Smell, Yarra, the chocolate's so rich." She gives a faint nod. "Want to try a taste?" She nods again.

As soon as the crumbs are in her mouth she begins to cough and gag. I wipe her lips. She coughs again and again. The noise around us drowns out her coughing.

I say, "Maybe another time? Would you like a sip of water? She nods.

I check her urine bag. "Time to empty your bag. How about we go back to your room and read a book?"

Gone Beyond Beautiful

I found a note on which Yarra wrote, speaking of Kris,

"He loves me so much, but it has gone beyond beautiful.
He needs to toddle off in the morning…get back to his gardening…and know that I will be all right."

If You Don't Think I'm Brave

Yarra and I are going to rest and read. I settle her in bed and pull up a chair for myself. "I have a couple of books here. This one is about an Alaskan woman who goes with some explorers to an Arctic island for the winter. You might be thinking, 'When do the polar bears show up?' Well, they do. Pretty scary. I don't know if you want me to read it?"

She seems to stop breathing and looks at me in disbelief. "If you don't think I'm brave…?"

Brave? Yes, brave, every day, I see her make decisions to do, to go, to create…I don't see her as brave? I can't speak for a moment. My sadness is overpowering her spirit, "Mom cries too much," she told Chiara. I don't think I've been crying, just sad. But sad is not helpful. Yarra needs me to champion her bravery, her energy and find my own. Mary Jaksch told me, "She needs a strong mother." I'll try.

No Laughing at Bedtime

One evening I'm re-reading *Tisha* , by Robert Spect, a favorite book of Yarra's. A young schoolteacher from New England moves to Alaska. Yarra relives her own time in Alaska as we hear the story of a woman who falls in love with her students and later a Native American man. Then the cross-cultural troubles begin.

"Yarra, I'm just realizing now this may be the first book about cross-cultural issues you ever read. You read it so many times. Maybe this got you off to American Field Service and Peru and working in Alaska, and the School of International Training. What do you think?"

She looks at me, seems to be thinking, s then moves her thumb up.

"I'm pleased to think that about *Tisha*. Shall we start?"

As I read, I imagine Yarra's experiences in Alaska. She smiles and nods, and occasionally gives a thumbs-up for a remembrance and recognition of similar experiences when she lived in Alaska during her summer break from CSU. Soon we're both deeply engrossed in the story. I mispronounce the words "snow falling softly" and instead read "snow foftly salling."

We both burst out laughing. If there's ever anything for the two of us to laugh about, I milk it for all it's worth. Kris comes charging into the bedroom, startling us both.

"No laughing at bedtime!" he announces adamantly.

What? He isn't kidding.

"I don't want her to get wound up."

I just stare at him, "No laughing?"

Did he hear himself? He leaves.

The remnants of our peals of laughter shatter on the floor. The room feels empty. I reach for Yarra's hand, look at her. I sigh. "Shall we try to get back to Alaska?" Yarra looks at me with no sign of affirmation. The mood has changed.

"Yarra, I'll have to think about what Kris said. Maybe it's about you both getting the rest you need. What do you think?" She closes her eyes in a long blink. "I'll leave now. Maybe Kris and you can sort this out. She gives another long blink.

"I love ya.' I'll say some prayers, OK?"

Note from My Diary

Kris is reading *The Diving Bell and the Butterfly* by Jean-Dominique Bauby to Yarra. He told me about the book and that he thinks it will help me to understand how Yarra feels. The title alone is enough to terrify me. Bauby is a French actor, author and editor who suffered a stroke and is left with "Locked in Syndrome." Bauby is unable to speak or use any muscles of his body except his left eyelid, yet is able to comprehend and respond by blinking his eye. A friend, Claude Mendibil, devised a way for him to communicate by reciting the alphabet and enabled Bauby to write his book one letter at a time.

I read the book. In fact, the story so pertains to Yarra's limited ability to communicate that it's being read by many of our relatives. I am in awe of Kris and Yarra's courageous and intentional dedication to maintaining their relationship. Kris is selective, choosing books with topics useful to their situation and subjects they can read and "discuss" together.

Bauby's book is fascinating and helpful. It also brings home the need for persons who care for the ill to contribute to their well-being in as many ways as possible.

Falling Down

I'm entering the hallway. I hear Kris' voice booming from the kitchen, "Bloody hell! Use your legs. Press with your feet."

Oh my gosh, what's going on? Must be serious. Yarra told me "Bloody hell" is a real swear word in New Zealand. I've never heard Kris say it.

Yarra's legs are limp. She can't help Kris. He is trying to help her make a transfer from the wheelchair to a kitchen chair, and she's slumping down. On the flat rotating disc we call the "roundy-round," her feet and legs are lying sideways. Usually, when she stands firm, the disc rotates and turns her body, but not today. It's sliding away under her feet. Kris' arms are wrapped around Yarra's upper torso, but her body is sliding to the floor. He's trying to keep her upright, puffing and working hard.

When Yarra took a softball-umpiring course in college, she had the guts to referee male softball players. I went to watch her games. She was tough. She flung a stiff arm, finger extended, calling "Stee-rike."

Today, she is collapsing, her head facing down. She is not staring straight at Kris as she did when she faced down angry baseball players with her shoulders square and her jaw set. There's no intake of breath to shout out a retort. Her head is bent forward, her torso folded in Kris' arms.

She and Kris are both collapsing. She looks at me over his shoulder with wide eyes that say, "See this, Mom? This is not all right." Oh, God, it breaks my heart. Kris is exhausted.

She's his wife. He's her husband. I can't interfere. They've got to work out this whole issue.

Kris is overloaded and exhausted. They need more help. He doesn't want strangers in the house.

I want to extend a hand. I'm afraid if I do, Kris, at wit's end, will retort, "Do it yourself" and storm out. It's not my place. If I dare to offer a word or hand the whole scene could well explode.

I pause before I go down the steps. *Be careful, Joanne. You're upset.*

Slowly, I cross the street and find myself deep into a scene I witnessed two weeks ago, same scenario. I hear them in the bedroom and call out, "I'm here."

Kris is lowering Yarra from the wheelchair on the far side of the room to the bed, but she is slipping down. He heaves her and tosses her onto the bed. Kris keeps his arms around Yarra and they fall together, his arms taut to protect her from his weight. They land with his face directly over her and inches above her eyes.

She laughs a real laugh; she thinks it's funny. She is having fun. *Oh, God, when did they last have such a physically intimate moment?*

"Yes, you bloody well might as well laugh," Kris says with a flat tone of resignation and frustration. *There is nothing to laugh about for him.*

I cast my eyes to the floor where a bed sheet lays crumpled. I pick it up and place it on the corner of the bed. I walk out the door. "Call me if you need me, I'll be across the street."

Two years ago, we were trying to convince our daughter she should use her cane. Then later, would she consider a walker? Last year, we encouraged a wheelchair. This year, we tell them no need to keep trying to find foam pillows and wedges and neck supports to improve on the wonderful, electric, Australian-made, purple wheelchair.

It's difficult to say it's not the wheelchair that's inadequate. It's Yarra's musculature, losing tone, weakening and slumping. She needs to recline more now. For years, each time we came, it has been our sad task to hold up a mirror for Kris and Yarra so they can see a situation of which they are unaware or reluctant to see.

There have been so many systems, so many adaptations put into place with diligent detail only to be quickly found no longer adequate. It's like running to catch someone who is sliding in front of you down a slippery slope. You stretch to catch them, but they are always just out of reach.

How to ease whatever is the next normal or next moment? Who knows? This is what it is.

Up the Track

"Up the track" is what Kris announces when he needs to get off by himself. To lift his eyes to the skies, to spot the harrier perched in the top of a tall eucalyptus tree or scatter ahead of him a few of the sheep Jean keeps there. The city of Nelson made that concession to Jean after she donated the land to be used as a reserve for hikers and horse riders. Jean now lives next door in a small, modern home. The house we bought from her was the original ranch house, and her family was the former owner of the whole section.

Daily from Yarra's window, we see Jean's curly white head bobbing by, as she heads for the trail with Lars, her German Shepherd. The track is one of the attractions of the house on Blick Terrace for Kris and Yarra. They hoped they would enjoy the forest bush and flowers and the plump iridescent wood pigeon, the hawk, whose kee-ah, kee-ah call she could hear from her bedroom. They tried once. Grassy clumps, loose stones and ruts were too uneven a footing for Yarra, even with a walking stick. Too much energy expenditure, "exhaustion in paradise."

There is a new possibility in bright red enamel, displayed on the sidewalk in front of Pace Drugstore, an electric scooter, and it can be taken out on trial. Yes, it would be expensive, but it will be Yarra's freedom again and worth the price. She could go out of the house herself.

Her eyes dance in anticipation of going up the trail, which she can see from her bedroom window. Hawks, owls, horse riders, her neighbors and townspeople also frequent it.

Kris agrees. The day comes. Yarra is dressed in slacks for driving instead of a skirt. With great excitement, up she goes into the hoist, settles on the seat of the scooter and is guided out the front hall and down the porch ramp, giggling. Kris engages the handgrip starter, guides the scooter slowly, steadily up the sloping trail. "We'll turn around under the hawk tree. That's far enough."

"OK, now here's what you do, Yarra. You keep your hands on these metal grips and squeeze. If you want to stop, take your fingers off the grips. You can turn it just by pushing the way you want to go. Get it?"

Chris and I wait twenty feet below at the bottom of the slope. Delighted, Yarra looks down the path. Kris positions her hands on the grips. One lurch and down she comes, squealing, one speed—full ahead. I can see the three-year-old on the merry-go-round, her eyes glued into the corners, looking over her shoulder each time the colored horses whirled past, gripping the pole, no control, watching me. "Do you see me? Is it all right?"

Kris calls, "Yarra, slow down, slow down, take your fingers off the handles!" We laugh, then we gasp, as we realize she cannot release her grip. She rumbles pell-mell towards us. Her hands fall from the handles. She stops with a lurch

Kris, Chris, and I chortle. "Great! Was it fun, Yarra? What a ride, eh, Yarra?" But we read each other's eyes. *There hasn't been much control. No one speaks a negative word. We hide our disappointment.*

"Tomorrow, we'll try some on the sidewalk. OK, Yarra?" She gives a thumbs-up and a grin. Tomorrow, it becomes apparent that it tires her fingers to hold the handles for more than half a block. Once again, we learn we're too late.

The beautiful red enamel machine sits in the back yard for two days. When Chris sadly and slowly drives it back to Pace's, he notices how people avoid eye contact with someone in a scooter.

Changes

We return to Brockway, Pennsylvania in the fall and spend two months clearing Mom's home for sale with the help of my brother. We plan a week's tour of the North Island when we return to New Zealand in January 2001, for a summer vacation.

January arrives, and we take a cab from the Auckland Airport to Auckland harbor. On the dock, we see the man with the tuk-tuk cart who last year introduced us to Devenport, a small city across the harbor. We thank him and tell him we're again booked at Badger's B&B.

We arrive at the B&B, where our barefoot hostess, Heather, greets us with glasses of fresh guava juice. It's comfortably warm and shaded on the back porch, where we settle into a swing and chairs. She calls through the open door, "Badger, come greet the Amorosos from America."

Heather and Badger share an orientation on how things work, since there have been new renovations at the B&B since our last visit. Badger helps us with our bags to a long extension of rooms facing a shaded courtyard. We're not in the main house. It will be more private and maybe better for us.

We walk to "town Devenport" and a streetside shop to purchase red snapper, fresh from the sea, and chips. We sit looking out over Waitemata Harbor, relishing the superb snapper. Black-backed gulls circle and screech for scraps, and we oblige; never appreciated doing nothing so much.

Later, ten minutes' ferry ride away, we tour Auckland and eat seafood. A fish called pange is especially tasty, in a creamy, spicy sauce, plus delicate shrimp spring rolls. A shopkeeper suggests we stop at the library for visitor's information about a bird reserve in the Hauriki Gulf with a quickly alliterated Maori name that slips by my ears. "Oh, Chris, I'd love it."

Chris breathes out a long sigh, "I'd appreciate a day to myself. I'll race-walk around Devenport. Good for both of us."

We learn at the library that Tiritiri Matangi Island is one of the world's most successful volunteer projects, with much of the conservation work done by supervised school children. It has been re-vegetated with around 300,000 native trees and, consequently, twelve of New Zealand's endangered birds and three reptile species have been successfully reintroduced. A day tour on an island is irresistible, but they are booked.

Nan at the travel agency encourages me to call. There may be a cancellation. I tell Badger and Heather about my hopes, proudly rattling off, "Tir- e-tir-e -mi-tange-ee."

I get a phone call at 8:57 in the morning. "There's a cancellation!"

Maybe Badger or Heather intervened. In a flash, I'm up, dressed, grab my binoculars, and I'm ready to leave. Badger, all smiles, drives me to the harbor port, where I join a boatload of visitors of all ages and colors, most of them with backpacks, binoculars, sun hats, cameras and bird books, all hawk-eyed and chatting excitedly. We stand clinging to the rails for a short, exhilarating ride through salt spray and sunny breezes.

Although I've been a birder since 1974, when nine-year-old John and I joined the Longmont Birding Club, I've not encountered such an exciting opportunity as this. I'm not alone in my excitement. I meet Don, a US embassy worker from Washington D.C., who tells me he is retired and signed up on the spur of the moment. He is wearing his dark suit, white shirt and dress shoes, as if he just walked out of the office. As we disembark, our guide tells us he is hoping for "a spectacular day." It's his birthday.

I'm thrilled to be surrounded by nature and the opportunity to see rare and endemic birds. I grip my cane and remind myself to watch my footing, which is difficult to do as there are bird sounds coming from every direction. Our guide directs our eyes high into the sky, checking trees, limbs, feeders, down in the bush and streams. My friend, Don, is helpful and by day's end, I've spotted 27 bird species. Most of them are new or once-in-a-lifetime sightings for me. My heart is happy.

Sunday morning, Chris and I drive out of Auckland on an empty, wide-open, four-lane bridge. Chris says, "Joanne, do you notice, no traffic? We may have learned something. Sunday is the perfect time to get around in a big city, and look at this four-lane bridge."

I giggle, "Yes, I read in the tour book, the New Zealanders nicknamed the lanes 'the Nippon clip-ons' because a Japanese company designed and built them."

A whole sun-shot, blue sky opens over our heads. "We're on our way, yippee!"

We're soon driving through cone-shaped green hills, then farmland, to Miranda Bird Sanctuary. As we drive, we pray for Chiara; she's had some minor surgery. Our sons are keeping in touch with her, but we're not there.

The national park accommodation, set at the edge of sand and beach grass, is an open-door-and-window place. We walk into an empty facility—rough hewn timbers, wooden shutters, clean linens, bunk beds, and fully equipped kitchen. There is no attendant here. No park ranger. No other people, very unusual to us, and also, lovely—we are all to ourselves for the night. We awaken to soft grey morning light and the raucous varying calls of the birds. We move slowly down over the dunes toward the beach, where there are masses of head-bobbing, waddling, feeding birds which suddenly swoop up, circle and land, again and again, as they sense our presence. It's like a moving meditation, very absorbing and engaging.

We come back and forth to the shelter for meals and naps and book study. We return to the beach in the evening. The birds are settled, silent. There is only the soft whoosh of waves. We return to climb into our bunks and give our sun-soaked, brain-weary bodies a rest. As I drift off to sleep, I think of Yarra's saying, "If you live enough places, you can learn to love the whole world." Amen.

Two in Hospital

We enjoy the green forests and ocean views along the Coromandel Peninsula as we drive the curves and hills, but unaccustomed to driving on the left, we're dodging and wincing in our seats. When we round a curve, we see oncoming cars heading straight for our side of the car. By the time we arrive at our B&B, I have a sore hip and a toothache, both on my right side. I wonder why and realize that, all day long, I have been reflexively clenching my jaw and pressing my foot against the floor as if braking, even though Chris is driving. We decide that tomorrow the driver will drive only as long as the passenger can tolerate it, then we'll switch.

We call Chiara in Colorado. Her surgery went fine, but she's in pain and the meds aren't helping. We're sorry we're not there to help her.

Our B&B hosts are retired farmers who have welcomed "hundreds of travelers." Our meal is all from their farm, a roast, fresh vegetables, and apple pie. Two of the guests at the B&B are from

Fiji. The conversation is very Pacific-oriented, and we learn of concerns regarding a pending uprising.

The next morning, we leave and take turns driving along Lake Taupo, the largest lake in New Zealand, surrounded by mountains and 100-foot trees. We arrive at our next B&B, a comfortable, modest home in a neighborhood. Our hosts, Pauline and Allen, tell us there is a call from Kris. We are to hear that Yarra is "in hospital" and hasn't been able to swallow or eat. Dr. Clark is treating her. He's advising inserting a feeding tube. We call Chiara at the hospital in Colorado…no answer. The hospital says she has been discharged.

We explain our situation to Pauline and Allen, that we have two daughters in hospital, one in America, one here. They offer to help us cancel our ferry tickets from Wellington to Picton, but the computer system is down. We'll deal with it in the morning.

Pauline and Allen connect us to Link ANZ. For $59 each, we can get to Nelson. Because of the computer system being down last night, we'll get our tickets refunded. Despite a comfortable sleep, we are exhausted by our concern about Chiara and now this new concern about making difficult decisions with Kris and Yarra regarding a feeding tube.

We'll be traveling today and the conditions are uncertain. Pauline and Allen suggest a cooked breakfast. "Great," says Chris, "and while you're preparing, we'll walk to the beach for a wade."

We feel sad and grateful we can be here and healthy ourselves. As we talk, we come to a realization that we need to fit into our children's lives and not try to fix them. We want to be in their life with them. If we try to change everything, it sends a message that their lives are unacceptable, something is wrong, something needs fixed. We need to be supportive and accept what is. We'll try.

Allen and Pauline have prepared butterfish, steamed vegetables, and roast potatoes. We have a lovely drive to Wellington and a quick, rainy, flight to Nelson, where we find sunshine. At the airport, we get through to Chiara. With relief, we learn she is home from the hospital and able to care for herself. A cabbie takes us to 9 Karaka, across the street from Yarra's house.

He asks, "Coming home?"

I'm surprised to hear myself answer, "Almost."

We freshen up and get in the car to go to the hospital to see Yarra. We stop at Morrison's for great cappuccino. "Are we feeding our spirits?" Chris asks.

"Definitely," I reply, "and grateful for the opportunity."

The hospital looks old and poorly maintained, like the US hospitals in the 1940s, unlike the scrubbed clean, orderly hospitals run by Catholic nuns. It's grimy and depressing.

Yarra is surprised to see us. Her olive complexion has a rosy tint. Her glittering eyes spill tears as soon as Chris and I enter. She blurts out, "Oh, my dream, last night! Some dolphins swam up to me, a lot of them, in many colors—blue, gray, pink, and purple. They said, 'Hey, can you go for a swim? We know you like it, so we came to get you.' One raised his fin and said, 'Hook on!'

"They circled close to me; I even got to kiss them. One said, 'No, don't crowd her.' We just swam along and they said to me, 'We've just come to do you a favor. We've come to guide you to your death.'"

Until this moment, I've been enchanted. Yarra looks at us questioningly. I'm overwhelmed, silent, wondering what she sees on my face. My throat constricts. I feel tears and squeeze my eyes.

A year ago today, Mom died in Brockway.

Chris moves close to the bed. "What do you think, Yarra? You love those dolphins. Does it seem they came to tell you they would be here when you need them?"

Yarra's mouth is asymmetrical. She mumbles, "Isn't that beautiful? I have so many stories to tell you, important stories to me."

"Oh, God bless Chris." I feel my body relax. I'm so grateful for him.

Yarra smiles and nods; she seems more at peace.

Kris, Dr. Clark and Dr. Kleary, the radiologist, walk into the room. Dr. Clark nods to us, and Dr. Kleary goes to Yarra. "All ready for tomorrow, Yarra?"

We repeat the dream and her reaction. He grins. "Oh, Yarra, the Mic-key is simple, only twenty minutes, and you'll be done." She loves that the tube is called the Mic-key, like Mickey Mouse. She's already smiling up into his handsome face.

He swings his arm up and away, "If you don't like it, we can take it out, just like that." I think to myself, *will it be so easy, doctor, when the day comes that we must make that decision which will end her life?*

On the drive home, Chris and I discuss Yarra's upcoming surgery. We identify possibilities that may exhaust or increase anxiety for Yarra. She will have attendants unfamiliar with her and her limitations as she makes multiple transfers, from floor to floor and from the operating room to recovery.

We have some hesitation regarding interfering in an unfamiliar hospital system, but we both agree we must support Yarra as much as possible. We begin to plan.

Another hospital, but Yarra asks the same question, "Is this hospital normal? All I've been through, the pain in my body. I tried to tell the nurses I'm heavy. They don't believe me. Now, my neck is hurting again. Oooh, it took Gary so many years to get it right," She moans.

It doesn't do much good, but I do my best to connect with her. "I know, Yarra. I guess the nurses haven't had much experience with MS people, and you look so young and healthy. We've asked for the head nurse to meet with us to be sure someone who knows you, from this floor, will be with you in the OR. How's that for starters?"

She gives me a thumbs-up.

The meeting with the head nurse is not what I expected. His name is Michael. He was on duty when Yarra was admitted and off duty since we arrived. He shakes hands then lowers his voice and adds, "The only place for privacy is the sun porch. Do you mind?"

On my only visit to the sun porch, two sad-looking men in wheelchairs sit silently amid worn furniture covered with heaps of magazines. My image of meeting in a neat professional office is not to be. We enter a very shaded sunporch. Nurse Michael sits on the window ledge where dark pine branches crush against grimy windows. Chris and I push magazines aside and sit together on a couch facing him. He smiles. "You have some concerns regarding your daughter? About the procedure tomorrow?"

"Not so much the procedure. We're in accord with that," Chris says. "Our concern is about the possibility that as she is moved from her bed to the cart, to the operating room table, and in recovery afterwards, she will not have someone who knows her limitations and her physical needs."

Nurse Michael nods immediately. "I'll send one of the more experienced RNs to be with her for the whole day."

Done. Physically, I feel my heart lighten by his openhearted manner. My whole body releases in an internal sigh. He takes up a clipboard and writes. He looks up and sees me smiling and smiles back. I feel so grateful that someone in authority is responding positively. It is such a relief. "Anything else?"

I feel comfortable asking for more.

"Yes, there is. Yarra knows that the nurses don't realize how heavy her body is and how her muscles won't support her body. She has tried to tell them, with unhappy results. She falls or gets jerked around. She fell here. They caught her, but it aggravated an old injury in her neck."

"Does she use a lift at home?"

"I wish I could say yes; they use a transfer disc under her feet. At home, she moves quite easily with one helper most of the time, but not always. One of your nurses, Mrs. Kunce, brought up an interesting point. She told me, 'We often hear that. Our patients know and trust the person at home. Until she knows us and trusts us, it will be difficult.'"

Chris chimes in, "She's been on steroids, as you know. She's been having fearful dreams. She thinks she may die. She dreamt dolphins came to swim her to her death. Pretty scary."

"I'll make it a point to visit with her every day. Do you think that will help?" I want to hug him.

"Yes, she will feel more secure if she knows you are checking in with her." I chuckle, "She enjoys young, male energy. She'll be intrigued that you are a nurse. You'll see."

"It must be difficult for you to be here in a strange environment, facing these decisions. I have great respect for Dr. Malcolm. He will do his best for your daughter."

Again, my heart softens with a sigh. This man, too, is a healer.

Chris says, "People like you make it easier. Thank you for your time and for assigning a nurse to Yarra."

All goes well with surgery and Yarra. I pat her head and wait for her to recover from anesthesia. I am thinking like a nurse expecting her patient to be healthy again when she awakens; to be free of illness like an ordinary person. *Not so, Joanne.*

Yarra recovers quickly. Standing at the side of the bed, I press her cheek to my chest. She mumbles, "It's been a long time since I had a tit in my face. I remember…." She grins, "I'll have to tell my siblings."

Less and Less Able, More and More to Do

On the kitchen counter is a small mortar and pestle. Kris prepares food for Yarra daily. Previously she ate only organic food, the best Kris could find. For years Yarra took a vitamin formula by mouth, one which Kris used, thinking it the best and most necessary. Now he empties individual capsules, grinds the pills, and adds them to her canned formula, which he refers to as "the cans." It must be painful for him, such a believer in garden grown, naturally-fertilized vegetables and fruits, to be feeding his wife what he disdains. Kris is now giving Yarra her vitamin supplements and nutritional liquid via a baster into a new gastric tube, the Mic-key tube. Yarra is fed three to five times a day. It takes thirty to forty minutes, at minimum, and that is only if the baster does not slip off the tube and spray formula on their clothing or the floor. It often does.

Kris is still gardening, for his own solace as well as income. He does Yarra's personal care and medications, the cooking, and manages the household and Yarra's health care workers. Vikki brings companionship into the day, a joyous, gentle spirit, in addition to being a creative art assistant, a diligent housekeeper, and a competent caregiver.

She is bathing Yarra in a wheeled shower chair, dressing her and taking her out for rides in the wheelchair. She is also sharing household chores such as the cleaning and endless laundry. Yarra is now incontinent, which means even more laundry. During the rainy season, with New Zealand's mini-sized, super-efficient washers, but no dryers, it takes days upon days for clothes to drip dry on the line.

We came to help, but I feel as if I am adding to the problem. I want more for Yarra—safety and comfort and options. Each item I bring up, Kris needs to ponder and discuss with me; it takes so much energy. When he first hears my ideas, he thinks they are unnecessary, impractical. We have hours of discussions. It tires us out. In the end, we try some out; if they work, he's grateful and says so. Before we came, they went on their own way. I feel like a mosquito in the house.

I request the use of special medicinal shampoo for Yarra's hair, which takes more time to apply. I want her nails cleaned and polished as she would. I ask for her clothes to be colorful. I think she should have deodorant for her armpits. I tell Kris, "She smells."

"Ah," he responds with a dreamy look, "but I love her smell."

I want her pubic area cleaned with aerosol cleanser because it is more efficient and gentler on her skin than newspaper and repeated scrubbing with rags and soap. The cleanser comes from the US, with unfamiliar chemicals and costs $14 a can. Even when we offer to pay for it, Kris is slow to agree.

I ask him to consider getting Home Health Services, also advised by the district nurse. Kris' response comes with a long sigh. "More people in the house, Joanne."

Where are my boundaries? How much can a mother ask for? Fortunately, the district nurse also observes, makes recommendations, and follows through.

Dropping Yarra

Kris needs to get away for a few days to preserve his sanity. He wants to go this weekend with his three brothers and his son, Mark. Kris and 'the boys,' 36 to 70 years young, go tramping often. It's their favorite form of recreation. Anything involving family is worthwhile to me, and Kris sorely needs time away, which is the main reason Yarra, with trepidation, agrees to "respite care."

Twice previously, Kris placed Yarra in the Community Hospital. It's clean, small, understaffed, and, on the weekends, regular staff members are off duty. Yarra needs complete care. MS is such that there are times when she can walk with a walker or feed herself, but mostly now she is unable to move about in bed or be upright.

Yarra is unable to hold her own weight or use her arms and legs and needs to be hand-fed. Add to that her desire to be taken outside daily. "Get me out every day. The boredom is killing me."

The necessity to apply the hoist for lifting her up out of bed for seating properly in the wheelchair, then put her back to bed requires a trained, adequate staff. Her immobility and her request require knowledgeable, able assistants, and available equipment to lift and transport her.

We inquired of Kris' relatives and friends, "What do you know about such and such a place?" Either they didn't know or were reluctant to say. Kris and Yarra need a place where she can be safe and cared for on the precious few days when Kris can go off tramping. Kris and Yarra have tried a few places, with dismal results. We went to look about Nelson and even checked a few possibilities on the outskirts.

We hesitated to declare the long list of needs as soon as we entered the facility. We went around peeking into rooms and saying why this one wouldn't do…then the next one…gradually, someone would ask, "Well, just what is it you need?"

Her room must be large enough to store her lifting and transporting equipment, including the hoist, the swivel and the wheelchair. It must not be a sun-facing window, which would make the room too warm. We hoped for a facility where there were younger residents like Yarra.

The only places we found for younger people were veterans' hospitals. We started a list of places to call back later.

We looked at an older, larger place because the manager was the mother of a doctor friend and a nurse who understood Yarra's condition. She said, "The staff are wonderful. We just don't have the money to keep the place up." As the nurse manager alluded, the facility was so shabby it was depressing and just as, or more, important, Yarra would be the only young person in residence.

Finally, we found a newly built, American-owned, one-level facility with adequate-sized rooms to hold all Yarra's mobility aids. She could look out on green lawn with smooth paved sidewalks around the buildings, a rose garden entrance, stainless steel accoutrements and freshly painted rooms.

Kris and Yarra are “not so keen” on it. I think they would like less glass and stainless steel and more plants and greenery. But, it’s not the physical facility that is the issue. The most important question is, “Can they adequately care for Yarra?”

We meet with the director and the head nurse to plan a weekend trial.

They say, “Give us everything you’ve got that would help us.”

We have prepared a manual, now 18 pages, for the nursing staffs. It explains how MS has affected Yarra and how they can best help her.

But how can they study it while on duty? There are three pages of daily routine nursing care: details of all specific procedures, from how to communicate, feed, give her meds, clothe, transfer her, and care of her catheter tubes. We included long lists of everything we bring from home to the facility and a copy of standard doctor’s orders in case her doctors are out of town at the time of admission. The head nurse says she will take it home to read it and promises she will be there over the weekend.

I arrive noon on Saturday to find the head nurse is off today. She awakened with a bad cold; too much risk of contaminating Yarra. The instruction book for the staff is at her home.

Yarra says, “Mom, I need to tell you this place isn’t for me. They’re all crazy here.”

We witness well-intentioned, but unschooled, nursing personnel, especially regarding MS patients. It will probably be that way anyplace she goes temporarily, because her care is so demanding and detailed and staff members change schedules often. Staff members need time to learn how to care for Yarra. I hate to go to the next thought: Yarra needs to be permanently in an institution. All those years traveling about, temporary living, and now at last she’s living in a home of her own, and she will need to leave it.

The young aides come in to get Yarra out of bed. They set the six canvas hoist straps, hopefully, in the right position around her body.

Yarra jokes, “I call it my gorilla act.”

The ‘up’ button is pushed. The canvas basket of straps lifts her up and away from the bed towards her wheelchair. Yarra’s rear falls through the canvas webbing. The aides’ arms fly out to grasp her, but how can they safely stop a 140-pound plummeting body, and what harm do they do to Yarra's body themselves? I hastily push the bed under the hoist. Her bottom settles on the bed. Her head is turned sideways on her shoulder. She moans. She cannot recondition those painfully stretched muscles.

It's harmful, scary, humiliating and painful to be moved through the air, head thrown back, unsupported. It's unacceptable. Can we change it? How? If not, what next?

Sell-Buy-Swap

Kris reaches in his shirt pocket and retrieves a red spiral notebook.

Ah, he's got his list as well.

"I've got one for you if you're ready. I did try to get more people. It didn't work."

"Oh, you did? Where did you advertise?"

"Sell, Buy, Swap."

"What were you swapping, Kris?"

"What do you mean? I wasn't swapping anything." Exasperated he says, "I advertised for 'bedsitters.' The only people who showed up were old ladies who just expected to sit. Ask Vikki."

"Sell by swap? I never heard of it? What do you mean?" I ask.

"Oh, Jo-aanne, it's the Green Grocer ads," he yells. "Sell, Buy, Swap."

I feel like a crumb when he yells. I check Yarra. She's listening. She listens intently when Kris and I argue. Is it to garner support for her opinions, or only that sometimes I stand up to him? Or does it sadden her? Her head hangs down. I can't tell.

"Oh, I thought you meant "sell, b-y, by swap, sorry."

He shakes his head. *OK, Joanne, back to business.* "What did you write on the ad that brought Vikki here?"

"What did I say?" He casts his eyes down and shakes his head, "Huh! I think I just said 'I need help.'"

We both laugh, and Yarra's face brightens a bit. I say, "Boy, that was a miracle, huh, Yarra? Vikki's wonderful."

"You want these people to spend time with Yarra, right? Take her out for a stroll, a visit? How about something like, 'Adventuresome, young woman to spend casual visiting time, including outdoor wheelchair walks, with female, former world traveler.'"

"Ahh...." As Kris ponders, his face relaxes into a little smile. "I didn't think of that. What do you think, Yarra? Shall we give it a go?" Yarra smiles, gives a thumbs-up.

"OK. I'll write it up and get back to you. Now, my turn. When I first looked at my list, it looked impossible. Now, I see it boils down to one thing. *I pause for a breath, modulate my voice,* "The need for more help. Besides the visitors for Yarra, more qualified caregivers."

"Ah, Joanne," Kris turns away and sighs. "More people in the house, more confusion."

"I know, Kris. You treasure your solitude. I know you're trying to keep things calm for both of you. You're running a hospital for one patient whose needs are increasing. My opinion is that you and Vikki have done a huge and good job. But trying to do it all, as Yarra's needs increase, appears to be taking its toll on all of you. You and Vikki can't do all you do for running the house and meet all of Yarra's needs too.

"Yarra's feeding tube requires twenty minutes of your time six times a day. That's energy and time-consuming. You're exhausting yourselves. The proof of that is that Yarra has developed some small potential problem areas. They're not worrisome in themselves, but there are signs that she needs more constant vigilance. Do you want me to read them?"

Kris looks concerned and nods "yes." I try for a neutral voice and read my list.

"Small infected skin wound, upper thigh. Is the catheter not secured properly, or is the tape rubbing? Reddened skin, lower tailbone. Yarra's position not changed often enough?

"Pus around feeding-tube opening. Needs cleaned more often or carefully?

"Toenails ragged, skin on feet cracked. Needs nails tended, clipped. Cream for feet. Seborrhea dandruff. Use medicated shampoo. Nasal passages crusty with mucous. Ears—dirty inside; behind ears, smelly."

He reaches out his hand for my list. His face falls somber, and he tightens his lips. He looks up, sighs, presses his lips together, and nods, "I know. My family has been after me too."

"Sure, Kris, we all care for you as well as Yarra and Vikki. Would you be willing to meet with the district nurse and the Home Health Agency to explain what's going on here and see what they can provide?"

Kris looks sad, defeated. "It will mean big changes for both of us. Yeah, yep…Yarra and I need to talk this over more."

"Sure, Kris, think about it. Regarding Yarra's skin conditions, we could request an air mattress for the living room bed. It should relieve pressure. OK with that?"

"Yes, and I'll try to turn her more often at night," added Kris. "Sometimes when she's sleeping …well, I hate to move her…then she'll be awake."

"Yes, that's a toss-up, isn't it? Until those red spots go away, she'd better be moved at least twice a night. One more thing, Kris. I think when we meet with Home Health, Yarra also needs to be present. She's part of all the decisions here at home. It's her life."

Kris pauses only a few seconds, "Yes, I like that very much, Joanne. Good idea."

Good on us, I think. I say, "Good for Yarra, too. Thanks, Kris."

Joanne's Day in Town, Nelson, 2001

As Yarra's condition worsens, I'm finding it harder to maintain my equanimity. In the past, my remedy in tough times has been to give myself a challenge, something I can accomplish that reminds me of who I am and what I can do. I've talked to Chris about looking for a volunteer position that's not too complicated, and the Nelson volunteer office is near the women's center.

Today at the women's center, a favorite place of Yarra's, Georgina Beyer is visiting. She is a Maori woman and parliamentary representative of the New Zealand Labor Party—and the world's first openly transsexual person to hold a national office. I'm heading there to meet her and hopefully tell her how much my daughter admires the work she is doing for gender and racial equality. I am very curious to experience another cultural exchange and personally meet a Member of Parliament.

As I walk past the UNICEF store, I remember I need some stationery and go in. I peruse the offerings on the shelves. From behind the counter, the saleswoman asks, "You all right there?"

"Yes, thanks, just looking over your interesting stationery."

I bring my boxes to the counter and dig into my wallet to discover I'm short of New Zealand currency. "We're visiting here from the US, but I can write a check on my New Zealand bank account."

The volunteer is a white-haired woman wearing eyeglasses with bright blue plastic frames. She nods.

She studies my check for a long minute. *Something wrong?* "We're residing with relatives in Nelson. Would you like their address and names?"

She seems uncertain, shakes her head side to side, and hands me the purchases. I grasp the bag in my fingers, but the sales woman holds firm to the package. I look up to see what's happening.

Her clear blue eyes stare intently. "Please," she emphasizes, "tell your president we don't want war." She releases the package. I jerk back a step.

She thinks, as an American, I can talk with the president.

Touched by her courage, I breathe out. "Yes, I'll try."

Back on the sidewalk, I shake my head and check my directions. Yes, I still have time to go to the women's center.

Yarra loves the comfortable old house where any woman is welcome to ask for help of any sort, take classes, or hear speakers. Today the house is crowded.

"Just come on in," a woman greets me. "Georgina Beyer is not speaking today but is simply here to meet and hear from women in the community."

Perfect. It's very casual. I become absorbed in art projects on the walls. I turn, and there in front of me is a very beautiful woman in a stylish dress and hairdo. She's extending a hand to another woman and speaks to her. Then, I see them tilting their heads towards each other and....

Oh my gosh, they are doing the Hongi, and it looks likes she is heading my direction. Hongi is the Maori greeting of pressing foreheads and noses together, sharing the breath of life.

Gosh, I didn't prepare for this. Well, how would you prepare? Practice? Georgina moves toward me, leans toward me. I feel awkward. I stand still. So gracefully, she lifts her face toward mine. A subtle woodsy fragrance rises toward my face. I feel the warmth of her nose on mine, a slight pressure. *I should not be analyzing all that is going on, I should be honoring her person, her presence, or praying, whatever.*

She pulls away, extends her hand and straightens with a smile. I barely remember my main intention. I stutter, "Ah…I came for my daughter…no, I'm very pleased to meet you…. "

Do I say "your honor?" I'd like to address her, but I don't know how.

It all comes tumbling out. "I'm Joanne Amoroso, from America. My daughter, Yarra Amoroso, lives in Nelson and is ill. She asked me to come to greet you and tell you how much she admires you and the work you are doing for gender and racial equality."

Georgina smiles so pleasantly. "Thank you for coming, and thank your daughter for her kind words." She turns to the next woman in line. I feel I've met a great lady.

I float to the exit without looking left or right. My head is spinning. Musing, I go out onto the sidewalk.

Well, Joanne just shared a Hongi with a Member of Parliament. It's definitely not America. Shall I quit for the day? Wait 'til I tell Yarra.

I pass by the volunteer office, then stop and caution myself to wake up and watch the sidewalk before I stumble.

Just inside the door, in a small office, a woman asks, "May I help you?"

Almost before I can compose myself, she pulls out some notebooks and asks my interests.

I say, "I'm an English as a Second Language teacher, but I have many interests. I also am here with a very ill daughter, so I need something simple and orderly, regular daytime hours, if possible."

She has some suggestions, the most unusual being that since I am an ESL teacher, I might like teaching English to stranded sailors.

"Stranded sailors?" I ask. *Another New Zealand specialty?*

She explains, "The foreign sailors' boats have been impounded for various infractions of law, and the sailors must remain in New Zealand while the case is settled. Until then, they cannot live freely in New Zealand nor can they return to their homeland until the case is settled. Their lodging is here in the port."

All new to me, but, again, I put my spin on the fairness and compassion of New Zealand's government or citizens whose taxes provide housing and who want to provide activities for them.

"What are the hours?"

"Seven to nine in the evening," she replies, sounding somewhat dubious.

I imagine myself walking through the dark port beside the huge, building-sized stacks of raw tree trunks. *No, I don't think so, don't think I want to be wandering around the port at night. And what might Chris think?*

The woman quips, with a smirk, "It could be a little dodgy. Have you thought of trying the local schools? Maybe a reading assistant?"

"Perfect," I say. "I didn't think of that. I've even had some training in teaching reading." She suggests a few schools. When she mentions St. Joseph's, I say, "Yes, we go to the parish church, St. Mary's."

Sounds good—no stress, set hours, daytime activity.

When I see Yarra, I tell her about my day. She laughs at my befuddlement over the Hongi. I thank her for the excellent cross-cultural experience. I hesitate to tell about the woman in the UNI-CEF shop. There's a lot to absorb there, but it's 'up her alley,' so I do. She's touched. Her eyes tear up. She gives a big "thumbs-up."

The next day, Kris and Yarra have houseguests. Kris and the guests go out for dinner, and we stay with Yarra, which becomes an incredibly beautiful experience. Her condition, using the feeding tube, and hand feeding her goes well. We have a fiasco with her hoist and she, so fun-loving, says, "It happens to me all the time. Whatever you two do doesn't matter."

I reply, "I wish you were my mother, Yarra. My life would have been much easier."

After we get her ready for bed, she looks up lovingly and says, "Beautiful. I love it that you're here."

Yarra and Kris, parade watching with friends. Photo, *Living,* DeCino

Applying for Residency, April, 2001

Chris and I read the requirements for residency in the compassionate category. We must reside in New Zealand for 184 continuous days. We can do that. But there is more: We need a physical and psychological examination, a criminal records check by the police, fingerprints, proof of adequate financial funds to return to the US, all in addition to 14 approval points necessary for residency. We're in our 60s, which will diminish points. All the rest, education, medical professionals, local sponsorship, and our health should be points in our favor. We can prove our solvency through our local bank account.

First, we go to a square, brick, laboratory and medical clinic located in a parking lot in downtown Nelson. For twenty minutes, seated in the waiting room, I've been musing about the difference between medical practices in the United States vs New Zealand. Patients read to themselves or to their children. A nurse uniformed in white shoes, stockings, starched white cotton dress and a widely-winged hat appears in the doorway and announces a name. When called, people stand and follow her. A few minutes later, the nurse appears again for another patient.

When it's my turn, I follow her into the exam room. She prepares my arm with a tourniquet, an alcohol swipe, and says something I don't understand, "A small skritch?"

Oh, "scritch" instead of "scratch." That's different.

When she's finished withdrawing the needle, I say, "I'm a nurse from the US." I smile. "I've been watching for differences. I probably would have said, 'a small prick.'"

Pressing a bandaid over my forearm, she mildly responds, "I used to say that, until one day a man asked, 'How do you know?'" I laugh. She does not. She maintains her professional demeanor and turns away. "Next patient!"

Next, we drive across town to the police station for fingerprints and criminal record check. *What will I find different here?*

We push open a double glass door and face a cartoon-wall mural of a vicious shark leaping from high roiling waves, sharp-toothed jaws wide open and about to take a chunk out of a rapidly fleeing, brown-skinned man.

I'm slack-jawed as a policeman in pastel blue uniform passes by, sees my reaction, laughs, and says, "One of our 'regulars' offered to do that for us. You're here for fingerprints and records, right? Come with me."

I watch Chris as the officer rolls his finger over the ink pad. He looks so serious as a glossy, starkly-delineated black print appears on a piece of card. I feel this solemnness, too, a certification of self-identity and awareness of "otherness" at the same moment.

We sit as the young, freckle-faced officer asks us questions regarding our "criminal record," then places everything into a large envelope, saying, "We'll send these to the US. No telling how long it will be, but you'll be hearing from us as soon as everything is completed."

Finally, we visit a psychiatrist for our psychological exam. She is retired from practice and requests that we meet at her home on a Sunday afternoon. Not only is the appointment easy to make, it feels like a visit to our favorite "aunty" from the moment she opens the door. A woman with the most amazing long, thick, red hair, dressed in soft blue beach-combers and sandals, opens the door and greets us. "Come inside. The Amorosos, right?"

The rich aroma of something baking, something sweet and cinnamon-laden, floods the doorway.

Inside is actually outside, as the whole living room is filled with light from a wall of windows over the ocean. Pillows, comfy chairs, and stools are strewn about, and the inner walls are covered with books.

"I've got some cookies in the oven. Make yourselves comfortable, look over my library shelves. Coffee for both of you?"

She leaves the room. Chris and I smile, bemused…we're learning about New Zealand's "casual professionalism" on this trip through residency, enjoying our new fellow citizens already.

The slow pace of the afternoon conversation is so casual that I often feel we are interviewing her. Gerolyn excuses herself for periods of time, leaving us alone. I wonder if she is feeding her cats, peeking at us from a secret viewing spot, or looking up professional material in her manuals.

She advises, "Because of your age and because you will not be adding to the economy of the country by starting a business, you have slim chances of approval. Your approval would be based on points for the psychological exam, proof of adequate financial funds to return to the US, and fourteen approval points necessary for residence garnered from: age, education, profession, sponsorship, and health. That said," she pauses for emphasis, "New Zealand has a compassionate category, which states that a New Zealand resident's well-being depends on your presence. And why the 'petitioner,' that's you two, think you need to be in New Zealand.

"If you can prove that your family member's well-being depends on your presence, perhaps you will slip in. Your being a nurse and doctor is helpful, but we have many qualified nurses and doctors in New Zealand. Is there anything else which is special about your talents that might be persuasive?"

We weren't prepared for this question. After a few minutes thinking, Chris offers, "You know our daughter is unable to speak most of the time. She is unable to use her eyes much for communication or her facial expressions because her muscle control is diminished, and her hands are unable to hold a pencil to write. She does her painting with adapted rubber balls. Joanne is a teacher of English as a Second Language. She often works with native people, from Asia and Central America who are completely uneducated. She has a talent for being able to communicate with them through sign and photos, or acting out. She eventually has them speaking English. Since Yarra is unable to speak, Joanne has been devising ways to communicate through signs."

Gerolyn has her eyes on me as Chris speaks. *I'm surprised and so pleased Chris came up with this thought. I didn't think of communication as an entry point.*

Gerolyn drops her head, thinks a minute then asks, "What do you think of this, Joanne? True enough?"

"Yes. I didn't think of Yarra's non-communicative state as the significant, time-taking, frustrating problem it is. For example, her brother Joe spent two hours with her, convinced she was describing a toothache, then a few more people gathered round and finally discovered she was asking for some mascara.

"We used an eye blink system for a while, then she lost that ability, and we went to thumbs-up, thumbs-down. She signs her paintings with a lipstick kiss. I don't know what will be next, but it does take time, and I do try to help."

Gerolyn suggests we write a letter trying to prove "mental harm" for Yarra if we are not here. "I know that will be difficult, but do your best. There's a stickler over there at the immigration office. I'll walk my report over. You'll be hearing from them eventually. Good luck."

Those People Again

Kris calls, "Thought you might like to go to St. Patrick's Day at the music school. It's a big sell out. That woman, Theresa O'Conner, whose articles you read in the Nelson Mail, will be emcee."

"For sure, we want to go. Can Yarra go with us?"

At the event, Kris' brother Hein is ushering and greets each one of us personally.

Chris bends to me and whispers, "He's wearing my shirt, one I sent for Kris."

Hein grins at Chris, "How do you like my favorite new shirt? I like the blue palm fronds."

"Looks great on you." Chris nods his head.

"Hello all of you. Yarra, good to see you here for St. Patrick's Day." He steps in front of Yarra to talk with her. I hear something about a "special section." *I wonder how this will go.* Hein is compassionate. He is head of the Human Rights Council. I'm sure he thinks the special seating is a purposeful benefit for Yarra.

I don't hear what is being said. The look on Kris and Hein's faces tell me they have a problem. I'm glad I'm not involved in the conversation.

Chris steps into the conversation and returns to me, "Yarra wants to sit with us. The seats are small and the rows too narrow for a wheelchair. We'll have to take her outside, around to the back of the building, lift her up some steps so she can sit near the door in her wheelchair. You go over to the far side, near the door, and get a seat. Save two seats for Kris and me."

I see Hein is disappointed, but it's about Yarra and her desire to be included with family. I know he is also understanding and kind. He reaches down and touches Yarra's arm.

It's a music and laughter-filled evening. At intermission, Yarra needs to leave. We're ready.

Volunteering, Yes

At St. Joseph's School, I'm welcomed and assigned four third-grade readers, for two hours twice a week. The teacher laughs, "They are so excited to be with 'the American teacher.'"

I say to her, "I'm excited to be with them, too."

Elizabeth is so eager she sparkles. Harry is sweet and striving, talks lovingly about "My Mum and Da." Ken, the evader, opens our sessions with endless, wildly imaginative stories. He comes in with wet hair and clothes from swimming class. And there is Wally, who goes tramping with his dad at every opportunity it seems, "to give mum a rest." My time spent twice a week with the students is interesting, enjoyable, and routine.

One day after I've been there a few weeks, the principal calls to me as I pass by his office door.

"Joanne, do you have a moment? I want you to know the teachers have been talking with me. We don't know what you are doing with those students, but the teachers tell me they are thriving."

Principal Mike asks to be called by his first name. Though I'm uncomfortable with the informality, I say, "Mike, it's reciprocal. I'm thriving in the presence of those students."

When Chris comes home from surgery in the US, I request the students be told I will be absent. When I return to school two weeks later, Ken appears with wet patches on his T-shirt and shorts. With hair in dark, wet spikes, he looks like an angry mouse. Instead of his usual barrage of fanciful stories, he swipes water dripping down his neck and stares steadily at me. I am unable to focus his attention on any page, so I offer to read to him.

He turns sideways to watch me as I read. He interrupts and accuses, "You're not so old to be a grandma, and you have," he emphasizes, "apple cheeks and pink on your face."

Given his feisty attitude, I take Ken's words as disparaging; *Apple cheeks and pink on my face? Maybe my rouge and wrinkles? Is that the worst he can think of? Oh, I get it.*

"Didn't anyone tell you I was going to be absent from our reading time, Ken?"

He slips off his chair and points his elfin chin in the air. His face is filled with hurt. He turns away.

I lower my voice and address the back of his wet head. "Ken, I asked them to tell you. I'm so sorry if someone forgot to tell you. I asked them to. I had something very important to do for my family at my house. I needed to stay home for a few days to help."

He whirls around and gives me a spunky update: "Did you know my dad blew up a log with dynamite? We had a big fire!"

Is this forgiveness? He cared enough about our fragile new friendship to be angry. Probably I can't corral him back to reading today. Maybe we listen to each other for a while.

I walk away across the empty playground. I'm feeling myself again. I hear Mike's voice, "Don't know what you are doing....?"

Me either, Mike, but I love it. I smile.

Conversations with Yarra

All conversation with Yarra is modified by many varying factors, including her ability to control her energy level, speech, breathing, coughing, laryngeal spasms, and tears. Emotional lability is a side effect of her current steroid therapy. More often now, she is unable to recall and use the appropriate words accurately and realistically. Surprisingly, we notice a startlingly heightened awareness to the unspoken and perceptive responses to body language. I often feel she "reads me like a book."

Chris and I are unable to hear her frequently feeble voice or recognize the occasional New Zealand or Australian accent or phrase. We do our best to remain focused while we attempt to grasp, interpret, and fill in the meaning in all of the above.

We repeat what we think we understand. She signals thumbs-up or thumbs-down for verification. It's a painstaking and slow conversation.

Yarra's favorite words are "fantastic," "great," "beautiful," and "amazing." "Fantastic" comes out in a soft, three-syllable slur, after she's been lifted with an electric hoist instead of lugged and tugged from wheelchair to bed. "Great" is usually accompanied by a lopsided smile and a look of pleased accomplishment for having successfully maneuvered a teaspoon of water around the four sides of her mouth and dropping it down her throat without coughing, as per the speech therapist's instruction.

"Beautiful" is for any gift: a found shell from the seashore broken into the shape of an angel's wing, or a piece of raw cobalt sent by a neighbor "to heal the throat," or a day when she can taste three small scoops of her favorite flavors of ice cream sent by Irma, the shop owner, who is also the friend who drives her on "good days" to ride therapy horses, or the fun she had when her brother Chris came—"He's beautiful!"—and when she took him to Broccoli Row, her favorite restaurant, for a pre-arranged, spectacular pecan pie, just for him.

Things that are "amazing or fantastic" are when her doctor sits down to respectfully discuss her condition and acknowledge she is the main decision maker in our presence in New Zealand with her. Chris is her dad and the competent personal physician and gentle adviser, and I, Mom, nurse and female friend. Also "amazing" to Yarra and "fantastic," is Kris, her husband. In addition to being the responsible manager of all things in her regard, he reads to her every night before sleep, brings and prepares organic food from the market, collects the incoming mail filled with the letters, cards, email, photos, and other touching personal gifts which she receives from all over the world. "Amazing" and "fantastic" is also her opinion of most of her caregivers, who reciprocate and fall in love with her. Plus "thumbs-up," accompanied by eye contact, a grateful smile and head nodding when breath and energy are short, for any kindness, anything and anyone good, pleasant or beneficial.

When she has energy and the thoughts come to her at the same time, she announces, "I want to tell you something" or "I want to tell you a story." Her eyes shine steadily like two dark topaz stones.

Or, she tells a powerful dream that nails me to the illusionary scene in stunned silence.

I tell her, "Dad and I took a wonderful walk. We parked the car near the sidewalk along the bay and walked over to Tahunanui Beach." Her eyes light up. It is one of her favorite places.

"Do you like the café where you sit down or the little wheeled cart?" I ask.

Yarra indicates affirmative to "sit down" with her thumb.

"Oh, good, that's where we went. We watched the cutest little baby trying to pull himself up the steps. These babies in New Zealand learn to walk by toddling towards the water! Aren't they comical in bright, long-sleeved, long-legged bathing suits to protect them from the sun? They look like neon crabs crawling over the sand."

Yarra smiles in agreement.

I go on, "The coffee was delicious."

Yarra gives a "thumbs-up."

"We shared Asian fish—rock fish on basmati rice with peppers and tomatoes, delicious."

Yarra concentrates a bit to envision the food combination, then nods again.

"Dad and I want to thank you again for not marrying a man from Cleveland. New Zealand is a wonderful place to live."

We both smile. Yarra says, "Oh, yes, and my girls…." Yarra's face contorts as if she will cry loudly, but sound does not come out. I touch her hand and try to follow. She must be talking about the good fortune to have her caregivers. I wait for her to gain control.

"I'm sorry. I'm not tracking with you now. Would you like to talk about this after you rest? Was it about the young women who came in response to the ad, Nashi and Caroline? Do you mean you are fortunate to have good caregivers?"

"Yeah! And my men."

"You mean Dr. Clark and Kris?" She gives a firm thumbs-up and nods.

"And," she wails, "And…oh, my father!"

I pause to take it in. She's grateful. She's grateful that here in New Zealand she has found wonderful people to care for her.

"You know, I think they feel the same way about you, Yarra. Remember they call you 'that special lady.'" Yarra's eyes widen.

"Yes, it's true. It's a joy just to be with you."

Yarra closes her eyes a minute, breathes "Thank you." A few minutes go by, and I think she has fallen asleep.

Eyes closed, Yarra says, "I'll have to tell that to my sister."

I'm confused. I wait. Yarra opens her eyes, and they are full of merriment and mischief.

"I'll have to tell her, you recorded it as a joy." She giggles.

I am not on steroids, but my emotions also plunge and soar depending on my reaction to the immediacy of Yarra's awareness. I'm soaring.

Bewilderment

Kris is back from a few days of hiking. Yarra is home from the hospital. I find them in the kitchen seated side-by-side. They look up at me, Kris smiling and Yarra looking bright. Such a pleasure; I feel I am looking at a bright Christmas bauble hanging from a branch, beautiful and temporary.

Kris opens the tall cabinet doors.

"Copious," I tease. "Those cabinets are copious. Like that?" We both enjoy words.

"Just right, they are great, aren't they? My mother would have loved them." Kris swings open a long door. He's arranged all his colorful mixture of bottles, clear canning jars, metal boxes with lids, all labeled in his bold-curved lettering.

"Some of these boxes belonged to Tora," he grins. "The same brand of crackers I had as a kid. New Zealand's damp like Holland. Everything has to be kept airtight."

He pulls open all the doors and scans the contents. He tells me of new plants from New Zealand that he and Yarra are trying. "Plus, I've got Hein's garden and the Green Grocer for fresh vegetables and good advice."

He sure is excited about food. What's the advice he needs from Hein? They talk about food like medicine?

He pulls down an assortment of bottles for the concoction of supplements Yarra has taken daily for several years. I've heard of some of the ingredients including primrose, cranberry and garlic, which friends have used in hopes of building immunity. He shows me how to open the capsules and measure the oils into a small glass beaker to mix them. The oil and powders do not mix easily. He hands me a cardboard card in his handwriting:

Yarra's Supplement Mix

- *Efamarine from Health & Herbs Int. North Harbor, Auckland*
- *2 capsules daily am, contains Rigel*
- *Evening Primrose Oil 720 mg*
- *Fish oil 18:12 EPA:BHA 250 mg*
- *Docosahexaenoic Acid (DHA) 28 mg*
- *Di-alpha Tocopheryl acetate 15 mg*
- *Equivalent Vitamin E 14.9 units*
- *Kyolic Garlic-high Potency 1 BID*
- *Nature's Sunshine USWA 1 od am*
- *Cranberry and Buchu capsules 2 od am*
- *Ester C 1 od*

Yarra watches Kris as he works. They look so happy.

Again, I'm clueless about all these products he's so careful and intent about. Yarra gets them every morning, plus a little cup with seeds and flakes that he soaks overnight. Kris pours the supplements into a syringe and inserts them into Yarra's new Mic-Key tube. The oily liquids leak around the tubes. It's messy, but some goes into the tube.

I hope they will prevent infection. People with indwelling catheters often get urinary infections. Thus far, Yarra has not had one.

Kris reaches for a bowl of what looks like mashed vegetables. He picks up a large plastic baster and spoons in some mash.

Is he going to force that mixture into the feeding tube? Will it block the tube? Will it be enough nourishment for Yarra? How long would it take to force an adequate amount of food through the tiny tube?

My tender feelings plummet to bewilderment and disbelief.

They so believe in the value of natural foods. They've decided to do it their way. I'll ask Chris' opinion. This is too touchy for me to handle alone. Surely someone on the nursing team will see what's going on.

Losing Control

Yarra is wetting her underpants. Kris complained to me that the underpants weren't thick enough to hold the urine. Neither he nor Yarra would hear of absorbent pads. "What would we do with the used ones? We can't fill up the tip with plastic and paper waste," said Kris. The "tip" is a compost pile common in most backyards.

"I don't want to wear diapers, Mom," Yarra declares.

It's getting to be a lot of work for the caregivers and Kris, changing her over and over. The Fisher-Pakel washing machine, a small, plain, giant-of-a-machine gets overstuffed with every load, yet chugs away endlessly. Laundry is constantly hanging on the line. It gets half dry in a day and moistened again with the nighttime dew. If it rains, we wait for the sun.

When I explained I was looking for sturdy under panties, the clerk in the Nelson lingerie shop smiled brightly and said, "I think I have just the thing for you." She brought heavy cotton undies in six colors with ethnic, cactus, and stellar designs. Yarra will love them. She may have wet panties, but they would be classy panties. Of course, I know it's a stall. Tomorrow, I'll go over to help Vikki with Yarra's shower and show them the panties.

The next morning, as I walk down the hall toward the bathroom, I hear the shower beating against the floor. The door is standing open. Yarra is seated in a lightweight wheelchair, which has a seat with a hole and a minimal frame. It's expressly for shower and toilet. Yarra is not really seated. She is slumped. Her body has lost its musculature; her torso is pale and bloated, and she looks vulnerable.

Vikki smiles. "Good morning, Joanne. Yarra, here's your mum."

I come to the door. "You got started early. Can I help?"

Vikki has pinned her soft curls up off her shoulders. She offers a welcome smile. With the purple shorts and white gumboots, she looks like a benevolent character out of the Wizard of Oz.

I often think of her as a wizard. With her quiet manner, patience, and a watchful eye, she cast a spell over the frustration which was rising in the house. I admire her so much. I can't believe Kris found her in the Swap Meet magazine when he advertised for a housekeeper.

Vikki is now Yarra's confidant, guardian angel, best friend, art assistant, and nurse. She gently presses her fingers through Yarra's long hair, rinsing out the soap, lifting it from her face.

"Get me a few more towels from the closet for Yarra's hair, will ya?" *Vikki always uses Yarra's name. She never refers to her as "she."*

"I'll be right back." I grab the towels and return to the door to see Vikki fling aside the long shower curtain. She walks through the pelting shower to the left side of the bath wheelchair and vigorously begins to push Yarra toward the toilet.

The sudden movement shifts Yarra's flaccid body. Her arms dangle from her shoulders like puppet arms loose from their strings. It is the first time I have seen Yarra's totally naked body. Her wet, black hair forms black ribbons across her pale skin.

I am alerted by a thump on the floor, then more thumps. I see Vikki push harder, try to move faster. Both Yarra and Vikki look startled.

Vikki looks a bit panicked. Yarra looks at me with a wondering, expressionless face. "Yarra has to use the toilet," Vikki says as she flexes her arms for a final shove.

I see movement on the floor. Small hard balls of feces roll across the floor down towards the drain or bounce away in any direction.

My God, my daughter, what's going on?

Vikki's expression is urgent, grim.

It finally hits me—a sign as significant as the foot flap. Yarra is losing control of her bowel. Incontinence: "incapable of controlling excretory functions." One more sign of neurological loss of innervation.

Yarra keeps her eyes on me as Vikki pushes hard from the shower area, across the slippery floor, to the open toilet seat.

What is Yarra thinking? Does she realize what is going on?

I can't respond. I lower my eyes. I drop the towels on the bar next to the door, turn into the hall, reach my hand up to steady myself. I hear the shower steadily drumming against the floor. Tears flow across my cheeks. I walk away, out the door, steady myself on the crumbling steps, take the rough path, past the mailbox, cross the street to my neighbor's yard. Gigantic, surreal, purple artichoke blossoms reach out on long arms. I pass by and push open the door to 9 Karaka. I can't see anyone now. Breakfast aromas linger. Maybe Carmen is still in the house. I don't hear a sound. I slip thru the house into the shaded kitchen and collapse in a chair. A blue bowl I don't recognize sits on the table with small fresh artichokes. ...oh... the neighbor's purple flowers...artichokes...delicious...how nice.

I walked away. I didn't help Vikki.

I hurry to the bedroom door and plop on the side of my bed. The springs creak, the noon sun streams in the window. I sit, just sit. I see my daughter's body. I hear those hideous, ridiculous thumps.

I have just walked away; I left Vikki, left Yarra.

I didn't help. I just walked away.

Tears flow.

After breakfast the next day, I tell Chris what happened with Yarra and Vikki. He nods and responds, "I was wondering what happened, I'm glad you told me."

I glance at him. "How did you know?

"Carmen told me he saw you yesterday, walking across the street." He pauses, reads my face. "We can talk if you want to." He pauses, expectant, "He said you looked like you were carrying the weight of the world on your shoulders."

"Yes, we need to have a talk, but it's sad, and first I want to tell you something good…something happy…about Carmen, OK?"

"Nurse Helene had Yarra out in the van with Vikki. They saw Carmen walking on the sidewalk downtown and offered him a ride home. Well, you know Carm, he made a big deal about Yarra 'picking him up' and the others joined in."

Chris grins, "Yes, I can just see Carm doing that. Yarra must have loved it."

"Oh, she did." I think they turned a joke into a celebration. I was coming across the street when they drove up. I saw their beaming faces and Yarra in the center of it all." I feel a wave of gratitude. "So normal, Chris, and for Yarra so, so rare."

Diary Note, Joanne, 2001

I'm reading *Like Water for Chocolate* to Yarra. She's closing her eyes, not paying attention. "Have you had enough reading?"

She looks at me, says clearly, "I'm getting weaker. Things are happening to me that are hard to explain…to someone without MS. I need to read books, do art, and see sunsets."

I nod and wait.

Yarra says, "This country is so foreign to me."

I'm surprised. What's going on here? "Yarra, you are not foreign to other people."

"That's because I have a soft heart."

Ruminating

When I last saw Dr. Holt at home in Longmont, he told me that if I found myself ruminating at night, losing sleep, I should give him a call. Maybe the time has come.

Chris and I are not on the same page on several issues, and one is heavy on my mind. I know of no one except Chiara who is talking to Yarra about end-of-life issues. When Chiara was here three years ago, she talked laboriously with Yarra over a two-week period of time and wrote down Yarra's wishes. No one else is mentioning it, nor has anyone mentioned the written pages, nor their whereabouts.

I want Yarra to know her options under the New Zealand system, make her own decisions while she can and have them written and signed. With the time-consuming challenge of Yarra's daily care, it's a heavy subject to bring up.

Kris and Chris think it may be too soon and will disturb her. I think we should talk with her about it. Yarra must be thinking about it on her own. Chris and I have had endless discussions. We're being sharp with each other. I don't want to harm our relationship. We desperately need each other's support and understanding to do this work. There's a lot to ruminate about.

Email to Family and Friends

As I write this, Yarra is having an art exhibit in Nelson at our favorite, Morrison's Café. She wants to encourage others to use art, as she has all her life, as a way to understand life. Especially, she hopes to influence the parents of small children, teenagers, and people less able. What a girl! Her paintings are finger paint now, broad strokes of color, bold, evocative and full of movement. A dear singing companion of Kris' had the skills to prepare the pieces, hang them and volunteered to do so. I hear there was a fine crowd opening night, and she sold five paintings. Besides, now that her art is on display, she and Kris are going down every day, for a "cuppa," and just to look at the pieces. "Handicap access" in Nelson is rarely accessible. Yarra will be wheeled up the back delivery ramp.

Our youngest son, John, and Amy, his wife, arrive March 12, bringing their youthful energy. John's stated intention was "to spend as much time as possible with my sister" and he did. It was beautiful to see the bond between them.

Because John was with us, we planned to try to take Yarra and Kris on a vacation to a lovely health resort, at Kaiteriteri, a beautiful ocean community one and a half hours from Nelson. Chris and I had spent two days there previously and thought it would be perfect. A lovely setting, easy access, vegetarian, organic food as Kris and Yarra prefer. The pool at Kimi Ora Resort is cedar, tile, glass-walled, greenery enclosed; indoor and outdoor elegance. We thought and hoped it might be possible to get Yarra into the pool.

Once we presented the idea to Yarra, she was determined to go. She had not been away, overnight, from the house except for hospitalizations, for three years, and she had not been more than twenty minutes away in her wheelchair van.

It took two full days to prepare, but it was worth every minute. The view from our cabins, raised up out of the forest canopy, facing a lovely island in a sheltered bay, was idyllic.

Yarra was thrilled, and she told us so, "When I saw that beautiful bedroom and the views, I thought 'Oh, that my parents could do this for me. I am so grateful.'" In fact, we all were grateful. We told her our vacation was a treat from "Grandma Lucy's money" and how much my mother would have approved as her favorite thing was for "all of us to be together." Tomorrow is her birthday, so we're celebrating.

On Grandma Lucy's birthday, another of Yarra's wishes came true. She has been longing to get back to her swimming. We had investigated, planned and purchased patches from the pharmacy to make her tubes 'waterproof.' It was risky. Would we be able to do it physically? How would her body react? We were all uncertain and anxious.

Typically, Amoroso style, with Kris Kolff adding his part, we all started giving cautions and suggestions. The anxiety level was rising until we said, "No! Wait. Only one person will talk. Yarra, you decide who it will be."

"John," she replies. *So, that was it*. Of course she'd pick John, he was her baby brother, and she was little mother all through grade school, walking back and forth from school to home with the boys, Chris and John. It was John who drove her out of Big Elk in December of 1997 to the airport for New Zealand, despite a snowstorm and a flat tire.

Here we are now, holding Yarra, following John's careful directions, relying heavily on his strength to hold her, and cautiously maneuvering step by step, to lower her over and into the pool.

We support her, and she floats, smiling in delight. All too soon her muscles begin to cramp, her smile disappears. We cautiously lift her from the pool and wrap her in sun-warmed towels, all the while keeping a "Wasn't that wonderful?" grin on our own faces.

No one said a thing, but I was feeling a combination of gratitude and remorse…our sister and our daughter, whom I saw dive into Sydney harbor.

Breakfast followed as we lounged by the pool. We sat relaxed and happy, enjoying our food and each other. It was the most fun we all had together. This more relaxed time was very fruitful. Because we weren't totally responsible for the food preparation and household chores, we were able to sit, talk, and listen to Yarra. She was able to tell us this was a time when she could be heard. She was able to tell us she is often unable to be heard; for lack of voice or memory, or us being too involved in tasks, too noisy, or forgetting to give her time, or having too much to say ourselves. She was able to express some very important ideas. We were able to really hear her and let her know she was heard.

Meeting with Heaphy

Kris, Yarra, Chris, and I are ready when the district nurse comes bustling in. We ask if she has a few minutes to talk with us, and Kris offers her his chair. She smiles "thank you" to Kris, but declines the chair. "Yes." She looks at her watch. "What would you like to ask?"

Kris begins, his speech peppered with "uhs" and pauses. "Yeah, yeah, we realize we need more help for Yarra. We wonder if you can suggest something? Are there nurses who have had more experience with MS?"

She looks puzzled. "Well, yes, that's my main function, to evaluate and offer help when needed, so Yarra can stay at home."

Now, I'm surprised. I'd misread her as being too busy or too overworked to help us at home. That's why I thought she left the self-catheterizing kit. She just didn't make clear to me that she is a liaison person, not an in-home, active nurse. True, all the equipment so far came through her, but I didn't put two and two together.

The nurse replies, "Would you like to meet with Home Health Care? We have an excellent one here in Nelson."

I say, "Could they come here? We could go to their office, but we'd like Yarra to be part of the meeting."

The district nurse makes notes, smiles and says, "I'll give them a call, tell them, and you will be hearing from them to set up a meeting."

Chris smiles at me…"A ray of hope," he breathes out, "at last."

Kris, Chris, and I go to the home health office; they are very pleasant and ready for our request. Only a week later, the male manager of home health and a nurse come to meet with Yarra, who is seated front and center in her wheelchair. Kris, Chris, Vikki, and I are all there. We express freely all of our many concerns including Yarra's needs and our exhaustion. They listen. What's more, after they leave, we all pause to absorb what has taken place. Chris says, "They listened, they really listened. They really heard us."

The next day, they phone to say a nurse will be coming soon.

Nurse with Buckets

Yarra is in her wheelchair at the table. Kris is fixing porridge. We hear a metallic clatter on the porch. "Is that the nurse?" I say.

We're to have a new nurse today, according to Heaphy Home Health.

There she is. She walks right in carrying two metal buckets. Each filled with roses of various colors. She is a tall, broad-shouldered, long-boned woman with red hair. She smiles down on us with a smile that could melt a glacier.

"I'm Judy, your new nurse," she announces. "The flowers are from my garden to share with my friends." She puts the buckets down and sits down next to Yarra. "Are you Yarra? I've heard wonderful things about you from the other nurses."

Yarra's expression goes from bewilderment to awe. Judy is just her kind of person.

Judy grins and tells us about herself. "I'm captain of the Nelson netball team. I'm working so I can earn money to get myself new teeth. I grow my roses to share with my patients. I got sixty-five dollars for my birthday and spent it on fertilizer for my roses. My daughter said, 'Mom, you're the only person I know who would spend her birthday money on fertilizer.'" She gives a big laugh. "Of course, she didn't say fertilizer."

Yarra is riveted, her mouth happily agape. Kris stirs the cereal, grinning from ear to ear. A breath of energy and unabashed joy swirls around the room.

We're all looking at Judy and each other like the best thing in the world just happened. A jovial, lively, strong, "I AM Woman" nurse just walked into our life, and oh, do we need her right now.

Prayer Meeting

Sunday at church I see the Italian woman, Maria, whom I also see every other day at the swimming pool. I introduce myself, because Chris and I want to meet some of the Nelson Italian community. She invites me to her home for coffee in the Italian section, "the tomato flats" neighborhood. It is very close to St. Mary's, and Chris is off hiking, so I accept.

Maria's home has tall windows covered in lace and damask. The upholstered furniture is covered with protective plastic. Every polished wooden surface is peopled with photos of loved ones. Each photo sits on a crocheted doily. Maria introduces me to the relatives in the photos with stories of each. She is especially proud of her grandchild, who is the descendant from a Maori princess, Rurutu Elkington.

"You might meet her; she stops on her way home from school sometimes. Would you like to read about her in this book?"

Smiling proudly, she shows me the cover, "Angelina, from Stromboli to D'Urville Island" by Wetekia Rurutu Elkington.

"Maria, I think my daughter will be so pleased that I found a real live princess and her grandmother in Nelson. One Sunday morning when she was four, she walked into the kitchen to find me in a long wrap-around brunch coat. Her eyes lit up. She asked me "Mommy, were you always a princess lady, before?"

Maria laughs, "Then this book is perfect for her. I hope she likes it."

I'm pleased and intrigued after my visit to Maria's home. Though Maria's home is like my grandmother's home in Pennsylvania, this female Italian immigrant has developed in a different culture. She exercises at the swimming pool, is related to Maori, and knows the historical background of many nations who settled in New Zealand.

She is also proficient in English.

Maria and I sit on a large wooden patio under a tree burgeoning with ripening figs. The branches spread their thick, lobular-shaped leaves gracefully over the porch. As we chat, I tell Maria we are in New Zealand to help care for our daughter, and of her condition. She tells me of a prayer group meeting at her home Wednesday afternoons and invites me to come.

At the prayer meeting, I sit sad and silent. Five women are seated in the living room: two Italians, one Hungarian, one Irish woman and my American self. I hope for comfort. As we sit waiting for the session to begin, a woman asks, "Is there a hope your daughter will recover?"

I flinch, feel tense. *Maria must have told the women my daughter is ill.* "My daughter, Yarra, has MS."

She interrupts, "Oh, that can go on forever, my sister-in-law had it for twenty-two years." She began describing all the failed treatments, the falls, the infections. I feel my shoulders sag, the energy flowing out of my body, my throat constricting, my legs sinking deeper and deeper into the chair. *Oh, please stop. Don't you know how terrible this is for me to listen to you?*

I could not open my mouth. She went on and on, one disastrous incident after another. Seated in a circle, the other women watch my face, as I plead with my eyes for mercy. I thought they could see my discomfort, especially Maria, but no one stopped the babbler. I hated her now. Stop! You stupid woman, stop!

When she drew in a breath, Maria looked at her watch and said firmly, "It's time to start our prayer meeting, now." She sent a gentle glance toward me, "We go around the room and ask for prayers, then we spend a half hour in prayer."

I debated leaving, but I knew Maria was hopeful the prayers would help Yarra and me. Each time I heard another woman's prayer offering, I felt sadder. Each "miracle" included the anxiety preceding the recovery. I was afraid to speak for fear of crying or blurting out my feelings of anger. When I could compose myself, I prayed silently for myself that I could hold it together for another few minutes.

Maria stood at the door as we left. She asked, "Did you pray for your daughter tonight when we prayed?"

I smiled. "I'll see you at the pool tomorrow."

Tomorrow, I will tell Maria I haven't learned all my lessons about how to be with suffering yet. It's too overwhelming for me to hear about other people's problems now.

Stepping Up

Sunday morning is sunny with a slight breeze. Chris and I walk to St. Mary's church. I sit, musing, much on my mind. Midway through Mass, the congregation stands, moving us into the aisle to receive communion. A woman in bright, flowered slacks with yards of black, curly hair steps back into her pew. I recognize her. I've seen her photo accompanying her columns, which I've been enjoying reading in The Nelson Mail. Her articles on social justice perhaps present a more realistic picture to me than my dazzled crush on everything New Zealand. I admire her language skills, humor, forthrightness, and her courage to present current issues new to me.

As Mass ends, she comes down the aisle. I point in her direction and whisper to Chris, "Woman from the newspaper. I want to meet her."

Chris tosses his head "Go ahead."

As the center aisle people and the side aisle parishioners converge in back of the church, I position myself so I encounter Theresa O'Conner.

"Excuse me, Theresa. I recognize you from your photo in the paper. I want to thank you." I poke out my hand. She grasps it. She flashes a bright red, lipstick grin.

"I'm new here, from the US, and I'm finding your articles very interesting. I'm learning a lot about New Zealand."

Her eyes glisten, she's vibrant. "I'm glad to hear those kind words."

The crowd moves us apart, not the place or time for more. I feel lifted and energized by our brief connection.

The Rock Café

The Rock Café in downtown Nelson is the perfect place for us to go with Yarra. It's a large, open-sided building, a former warehouse, now graced with glass as only the New Zealanders do glass. Large angled sheets, suspended with sun-reflecting panels hanging between metal girders which curve up to the roof in smoky black and red. During business hours, all the walls of The Rock Café slide open.

It attracts "the greenies," of which there are many in Nelson, including Kris and Yarra, their relatives and most of their friends. The "Rock" in The Rock Café, is Earth, symbolized by a bar designed from a huge, round boulder and corrugated metal. Most wonderful for us, we simply stroll in from the sidewalk over the black cement floor, or in Yarra's case, roll in. Whether the restaurant is organic in any way other than décor, I don't know, but David, is the most kind and handsome manager in the entire world. His biblical name is significant to me, as I see him strong and well-spoken enough to stand up to any naysayers who might challenge us with, "What's a person like 'that' doing in here?"

David tells us, "It is an honor to have Yarra here."

We've called ahead for a reservation. The moment Kris and Yarra pass over the threshold, David smiles, nods his head to the corner where our table is positioned for privacy and space for the wheelchair. He picks up the place settings ready on one side of the bar. As we push Yarra's wheelchair across the floor, he sets our table, and ushers Yarra into her place.

"I've been saving a table for you all afternoon," David says as he drops to a squat at Yarra's side. He is so gorgeous. He turns his blue eyes to Yarra. Her chin rests on her shoulder, a ribbon of drool slides over her cheek.

David smiles, "Good to see you, Yarra. It's a special day for us all, right?" My whole being softens as I witness his compassion.

He remains at Yarra's side as he presents the specials. We order from a tempting selection of fresh ocean fish including Warehou, Garnard, Dory, green-shell mussels, all of them unfamiliar to me. David helps with the selection. Then the big question, "Shall we order chocolate cake?"

Dessert in New Zealand is a performance. Each piece is an art form. The slice is decorated in an artistic assortment of fresh fruits and a mound of artfully swirled, rich, New Zealand whipped cream. You must order ahead to allow a twenty-minute preparation at the end of the meal. For us, it's a question of Yarra's condition after the meal, and whether she should, again, try her favorite chocolate cake. It is very difficult for her to swallow chocolate crumbs. We all know it, but as usual, we concede, "Well, bring us a piece to share," knowing we may not eat it or regret we did.

David says, "We'll be back, Yarra, with your food, very soon."

This is when I begin to worry. Yarra is having a terrible time swallowing, but she wants to go out to the cafes with us. She told Chiara, who recorded her advanced directives "I no longer want to live when I can no longer go to the cafes." When she can no longer enjoy going out in public, her life and ours will change.

Going out takes energy, hers and ours, physically and emotionally. Although her energy is more elusive, variable and limited than ours, she knows she owes us something, too. So much energy is used in preparing to go out. Rolling, lifting, turning as we clean and dress her, and move her from bed to chair to street to restaurant. When she is tired, it affects her ability to swallow. She coughs, gags, and drools.

We see other patrons staring over their dinner plates. They are here for a special evening out. Is it ruined by the sight of a family trying to make things right for someone who can't help coughing, gagging, and drooling? That someone is my daughter. She has a right to enjoy going out to a café...but so do others. She is still her own highly intuitive therapist, who once could read a person's body language from across a park. My stomach churns.

I've just begun this familiar rumination when David's girlfriend Haley, an ethereal Nordic beauty, approaches our table with a basket of rolls and a water pitcher. She bends over the table. Her yard-long, satin-straight blonde hair glides back and forth in silvery cascade as she pauses and leans toward Yarra to whisper a personal welcome. I feel myself swooning. I imagine Yarra feeling similarly touched. More than incredible, that these two, beautiful people welcome us to their establishment.

Chapter 4—I Can't Be Me

The Truman Track

Flat roads over farmland and forests do nothing to improve my sour mood. Exhausted. That's why we decided to take a break. Hopefully, we can make it a break that suits us both. I'm craving something wild and wide open, something to shake me from my lethargy and my surliness. After we snipped at each other about where to stop for coffee in Murchison, we agreed to some quiet time in the car. It's going to be a long day...a long trip if we can't get ourselves turned around. *Poor Chris. I'm just so out of sorts.*

He threads his way through Westport then heads south on the Coastal Road, where glimpses of dark and frothy, churning water, along with amazing and unusual rock formations, are enough to absorb us both. We're keeping silent, and our intentional silence is gratifying. Lining the highway are slender green reeds topped with miniature scarlet flowers that nod gently as we pass.

"Chris, I think the Pancake Rocks are ahead. Let's stop."

Chris pulls into a parking spot. A wooden sign informs, *Punakaiki. "Puna" is Maori for blowholes, and "kaika" means to be in a heap.*

I ease out of the car and up to the cliff, hopeful. I'm not disappointed. A spectacular sun-filled ocean vista spreads to the horizon.

Blue-black waves arch in tall froths of silver droplets. Below the handrail, they smash like cannons against giant mounds of rubble. Strewn boulders and precariously stacked, giant-sized, pancake-shaped monoliths then cascade back to the sea in churning swirls. It's magnificent! I purposefully breathe it in again and again. My spirit, dull and empty, refuses to engage.

"Petulant," that's the word. I haven't used that since the kids were little.

Further along, at the Punakaiki Cafe, the fruit and whipped cream-topped pancakes don't please me. They're overcooked.

"Would you like to go over to the gift shop?" Chris asks.

I know he's trying to please me. "Sure, that sounds good."

Display cases of unique New Zealand artistry in bone, stone, paua, silver and flax weavings, which usually intrigue, today leave me wondering if the store has changed management.

Pfft, what am I going to do with myself? We'll find a hike, maybe.

We walk across the highway to a path over the top of Pancake Rocks to wait for the blowhole to erupt. Today turns out to be one of the few days when even the Blowhole doesn't blow.

A brown, wooden sign at the side of the road catches my eye, "Truman Track 2 km."

"Hey, let's try this one. It's a short walk, even sounds American." Chris pulls in. We grab our gear and my walking sticks. A gentle downhill path leads us into dense greenery shot through with sunshine, brilliant reflections off shiny leaves, and the darting shadows of birds. Soon, we hear rustling in the underbrush, soft grunts. We lift our chins to each other to signal, "What is it?" Before long, a loud, cackling "chi-ca-go" signals a bevy of California quail who scamper away across the path ahead of us. We stop to watch. Chris smiles back at me.

The track dumps us out on a small curve of amber beach.

I plop down to remove my boots and socks. "I'm going wading."

"I'll walk down the beach a-ways," Chris says as he strolls off.

The water is cold. My toes grip the coarse, orange sand and feel massaged. Ahh! Although the sun is beating down, a light breeze cools me with a refreshing salt spray. *Ah yes, this is it.*

The waves have washed a long, curved shelter from the cliff side above the beach. It looks like the red lands of Utah but in a lovely apricot color. As I plop through the water, I spy colored particles being carried in and out with each wave. I bend to scoop up a quick handful. Tiny stones, some smaller than an apple seed, some black. *Chert, maybe? White, maybe granite?* As I stand still, peering into my palm, the small stones tumble over my feet like a massage of minute fingers.

I try to snatch them with my fingertips. They disappear, sifted by the ebb and flow of each elusive wavelet. It's like trying to catch a fly. It's here, and it's gone.

I jump. I bend down. Splash, scoop with my hands, examine my catch of sand and one or two precious particles. I pinch them up one at a time, drop them wet into my tight pockets.

Here comes the next wave. I scoop for stones. *Here's a green one, not round, more like a fragment. Could it be jade?* From my rock hounding with Chiara in Colorado, I recognize two rusty-red pieces as jasper.

Chiara? Colorado? I'm jolted back to the present. *Chris? All this time I haven't seen Chris.* When I bend, I feel a crunch. My pockets are half-full of stones. *How long have I been at this? An hour? Two?* I look towards the beach. The washout is in shadow now. There sits Chris.

I have not even thought about him, and he's been there, patiently watching me, probably being tortured by sandflies yet allowing me the solitude to be lost in my own recovery.

Oh, precious man, precious friend. True-man Track, indeed.

Afternoon with Arvind

Kris and Yarra are going to Arvind's retreat center for a counseling session. Arvind lives there with his wife, June, who is a writer, a singer, and works very hard to keep up the retreat center. It's a long, low building in a sunny spot, high above the river, with large, house-sized rocks for its foundation. Below is a secluded spot for stream-side dips. I've been invited to go along to the session. I'm not sure why I am invited. Maybe to sit with Yarra while Kris has his session, or while Kris has a relaxing dip in the water. Or, perhaps, it's for Arvind to get acquainted with the woman who is causing Kris so much consternation these days.

Yarra looks festive, wearing a favorite skirt from India made of gauzy fabric dyed in splashes of blues, magenta, greens, and bits of black. She's wearing the black onyx and silver earrings I had made for her in Mexico. They complement her long dark hair, and she looks regal, despite the awkward foot drag and the clumping of her heavy branch cane. Kris and Yarra decided her walker would not fit on the narrow, twisty sidewalk and steps at the retreat center.

Yarra's increasing loss of function has ratcheted up the volatility of their emotions. Chris and I, though we want to help, have made it more difficult for Kris emotionally. He wants to keep his home life simple, peaceful. Yarra's illness has introduced strangers and caregivers into his home. Now, here we are, Yarra's parents, with questions and suggestions for changing their routine, the house, the way they live, all with the hope of improving life for our daughter. We are all learning that we cannot control this disease, but we are trying to control everything else. It makes for hours of tense discussion. He and Yarra are seeing Arvind more often for counseling, massage, and treatments.

"Welcome, welcome," Arvind ushers us in with an air of reassuring confidence. He's handsome. He has dark, expressive eyes, a tawny complexion and appears calmly elegant in a long-sleeved shirt of gold suede and trim black trousers. His appearance alone sets him apart from the casual Nelson crowd. We follow him through the kitchen, where a frosted chocolate cake sits on the counter.

"Yes," he smiles. "It's my birthday. Later, when the kids come home, we're going to have a family celebration." He extends his hand. "Pass through." He leads the way to his therapy rooms.

Arvind and Kris help lift Yarra onto a low treatment table. I perch on a padded folding chair, which I have moved to the wall, deliberately out of Yarra's sight, to give her at least the feeling of privacy.

Arvind speaks softly to Yarra and gives a gentle massage on her shoulders and neck. He asks her where she feels tension and then presses those trigger points. Kris stands at her side with his hands on her arm. His eyes are gentle. He looks to the side. The sunlight slants through three long, narrow windows. Willow branches sway over the river. It's peaceful.

Kris turns his face up sharply. He sniffs and looks down at Yarra, "What's going on? Oh, I think we have a problem, Arvind. Yes, we do…oh…ah…how can we take care of this?"

I can smell the problem now, and, by the concerned look on Arvind's face, I see he, too, is aware Yarra has had a bowel movement. He assures Kris, "We can take care of Yarra, right here. Would you like that, Yarra?"

Yarra looks to Kris. He says, "I think that's best. It wouldn't be good to try to move her."

"Yarra, do you want your mother to help?" Arvind asks. "No? Kris and I, then? And your mother can stay in the room? All right, let me get a basin and some cloths." Oh, he handled that so well. He turns, draws a chair up to the treatment table, and goes out a side door. He passes me but does not make eye contact. How calm he is, how composed.

Kris looks both relieved and concerned. He stares at Yarra and reaches for her hand. "It's OK, Yarra, it's going to be OK."

Arvind comes back with June, his trim wife, who is carrying a bundle of white towels. She goes to Yarra while Arvind sets a basin of water on a chair.

"Yarra, dear," June says, smiling. Her voice is soft, playful, a girlfriend talking, "You don't mind if I help Arvind, do you?" She must have winked or cocked an eyebrow, because Yarra smiles back.

The three of them, Arvind, June and Kris lift my daughter's skirt, pull down her underpants, and clean her bottom. Yarra steadily watches their faces, their eyes, all through their ministering. *What is she feeling, thinking?*

I sit tight, tight, on my stiff chair. I'm hardly breathing, trying to be invisible. I see the suede-cloth sleeves move back and forth slowly, dabbing. Kris' movements are more practiced. He wipes and scrubs. June wraps and folds soiled tissue paper. I am so grateful Yarra can't see me. I feel my jaw clenched. *Breathe. Breathe. Inhale slowly; breathe out all the way. "She needs a strong mum," Mary Jaksch once told me. No, you will not cry, I command myself. Breathe gratitude, gratitude, you are witnessing an act of compassion. Breathe in, breathe out. Slowly, evenly.*

Kris rolls Yarra on her side and removes a towel they have placed under her. June pats her dry. Together they pull the gauzy skirt under her. It's so old, please, please, don't let it rip. No more problems. They arrange the front of her skirt.

"There Yarra, all fresh and clean," says June. Arvind pats her leg, "All done now."

"I'll see you later, Yarra," June says as she gathers up the soiled linens and tissue to leave. She gives a non-committal nod my way as she passes. What expression does she see on my face? I'm having trouble naming my feelings. I could drop to the ground.

Arvind smiles down at Yarra, a gentle smile, but any smile on his face is charming, "Yarra, I am honored that you felt so comfortable that you could leave me a little present."

Oh, God, how did he come up with that? And does he mean it? It sounds like he does. What a man. Will Yarra buy it?

Yarra's face is pale. She looks up at Arvind, her dark eyes wide open, searching, "Now, what would you do if I was a horse?"

Stunned silence. I stop breathing. My throat constricts.

Arvind's words spill out on a deep sigh. "Ah, my dear Yarra…." His shoulders slide down. He interlaces his fingertips and leans over her. "I would love you…and stay beside you…for as long…as you wanted me to be there."

I feel as if my bones have melted. My fingers grab the chair seat.

Kris' eyes well with tears, his arms fall to his side, his whole frame seems to loosen. I hear myself exhale a very long, slow breath.

Check in with Yarra, 2001

We call Kris to ask him about going to see Yarra on our return from Arizona. Sadly, when we arrive, her head is hanging forward over her right shoulder. I wonder how long she's been in that position. Periodically, someone, usually Kris, lifts her head up to relieve the stress on her muscles. At least she is looking down on Aunt Esther's silver, squash blossom necklace. *Does she remember that Esther, Chris' sister, willed the necklace to her.* It lies over a bright cobalt T-shirt with cactus and birds; hopefully, her artist eye may glimpse a reminder of the American Southwest.

Yarra smiles when she hears our voices. Chris and Kris shake hands and thump each other's backs. I approach Yarra, but it's awkward trying to hug her in a wheelchair, especially with her head drooped down. I sidle up to the chair, but I can't see her face, so I drop to my knees on the side of the foot rests. I can't reach her shoulders, but I can look in her face, so I reach for her left hand and hold it and press my head against her knee.

"Oh, Yarra, you got all dressed up for us, didn't you? You look so pretty." She smiles. "Aunt Esther would be pleased to see you're wearing her necklace. It looks perfect on you. You remember what trouble you and Aunt Esther used to get into?"

"Here now!" Kris chides, "Yarra, getting into trouble? I don't believe it."

"Oh, Kris, they were a pair, what one didn't think of, the other one did. Aunt Esther was a dickens, wasn't she, Yarra? At Chiara's shower, do you remember, at Suzie's? When you sat at Suzie's fancy table with silver tea pots and lace and flowers and the pink crepe paper tricycle that Suzie made in the center?"

Yarra stares blankly.

"Oh, Kris, here we were at a spiffy lady's party for Chiara's shower. Everyone was 'gussied up.' Suzie was an artist. She decorated the whole house beautifully. She asked Yarra and Esther to sit at either end of the table to serve tea and coffee. I was standing behind them, talking, when out of the corner of my eye, I saw something fly through the air. I thought it was a big fuzzy bumblebee which came in the patio door."

Yarra looks at my face, focused now.

"Then I saw whatever it was, again. I turned just to see Esther, school teacher Esther." *I am really laying it on now for Yarra's sake*, "chuck a piece of frosted cake across the table."

Yarra's eyes begin to change, sparkle.

"Wait," Chris chimes in. "My sister did that?"

I tilted my head so I could look into Yarra's eyes. "Yes, your sister, a teacher and our children's aunt, chucked a piece of cake across the table." Yarra gives a little muscle spasm, the remnant of a laugh, her eyes come alive, "straight through the flowers and plop into Yarra's lap. I was mortified!"

Yarra is grinning now and fully present. We connected.

Kris says, "Oh, Joanne, you and your stories. You're not in the house two minutes and you're telling stories."

"That's OK, Kris, I can go now, huh Yarra? We had our laugh."

I see her left thumb twitch up a bit. Kris has told us she can't speak now, except for an occasional whispered word or mouthed "wow." She is able to move her right arm in thumbs-up for 'yes' and moves her eyes left right for "no" with questionable reliability. It takes hours of repeating the question, at different times, with lots of patience before Kris is sure he has the answer right. Then he checks with Vikki, and she tries it.

That's it, the extent of what she can communicate by herself.

Kris says, "Sometimes in the middle of the night or early in the morning she is able to say a few words clearly. Sometimes I press my hands carefully over her chest and push, and a few words come out."

I am stunned. Those are the saddest words I have ever heard. They slide around me like grey smoke.

Kris goes on talking. "I'm learning to keep my questions in a notebook in my pocket." He pulls out a 2" x 3" blue spiral notebook. "This one's for the nurses. I've got three of them going now, a red one, of course, for Yarra, a blue one for the nurses; and a green one for me and the house."

I look, listen, then say, "Excuse me," and walk into the hallway toward the bathroom to let the tears fall down my cheeks.

Kris calls after me, "Oh, here's something for you. I'm thinking you two might like to go along to Mosaic with me. Cheryl next door said she would be available for Yarra."

I hear Chris say, "Yes, I'd like that, Kris. Thursday, isn't it? We'll drive."

Entering Glynwood

For the past two years, Kris and Yarra have agreed, reluctantly, to short-time stays in various community nursing homes. Those days are barely enough for Kris to relax and maybe get a tramp in with his brothers. For Yarra, they are generally very difficult with unfamiliar nurses and her ever-diminishing voice. There are periods now where Yarra can't speak.

Very few homes are staffed with permanent personnel who know anything about Multiple Sclerosis patients. Weekends are terrible because they are usually staffed with part-time helpers. Originally, it was enough for her and Kris to make a cursory decision on which nursing home they thought had the best quality of care, but now unskilled staff cannot give Yarra the complete care she needs.

Appearance also is important to them. We thought one place was clean and modern. Kris and Yarra dismissed it as having too much glass and stainless steel. A natural environment is important to them. Other places were too old and dark or too cheerless. We tried for a place with younger persons. But, as was our experience in the US, we found none.

Glynwood, which Yarra visited several times and liked, also pleased us upon our return in 2003. With mostly glass window walls on all sides, it fills with light and lovely views of wide green lawns and mature shade trees with low-hanging branches. It is away from street noise.

From what I observed the time I had been there, it seemed the nursing staff was autonomous in managing their scheduling. I ask for a certain nurse, who I thought would be caring for Yarra one Saturday and was told, "Oh, she had a wedding today, so I traded with her." *I'm surprised at the casualness of this, but the nurses seem content. And this is New Zealand.*

The nurses and aides do seem happy to have a young woman for a patient, one who came with her nail polish and bright clothes and jewelry. Yarra, although she could not respond verbally, seems pleased with their cheery patter.

In March 2003, Yarra and Kris finally and reluctantly concede that it isn't the new wheelchair that is inadequate, it is Yarra's musculature losing strength. She is slumping in the chair. She needs to recline more. She needs constant care. They chose to try Glynwood Nursing Home.

When my mom moved to a nursing home in Brockway, we asked for permission to paint her walls the same blue as her bedroom at home. Kris and Yarra liked the idea of asking Glynwood for the same.

When asked, the nurse manager replied, "I'll need to call Christchurch for that." Thus, we learned that Glynwood had just been sold.

Yarra's room at Glynwood is as personal and cheery as a room can be. The Kolff relatives painted it a beautiful magenta like her room at home. They also brought colorful, floral, hanging baskets for the courtyard outside Yarra's sliding doors. Vikki hung Yarra's art on the walls.

There is also another new nurse manager. The staff is unhappy with lower wages and more restricted scheduling changes. That results in nurses leaving and new staff replacing them. It also means Yarra frequently has unfamiliar, poorly-informed caregivers.

Without someone to assist and speak for her, she can't welcome people into her room or show her art projects. She is uncomfortable sitting silently in a wheelchair with the other clients in the visiting room or yard.

Many of the residents asked us about our daughter, and we wanted Yarra to become acquainted with them. We offered to start a "Getting to Know You" program for the residents and staff where, one at a time, the residents and their families could be introduced.

We began with another artist who has a huge painting on one wall of her room, clearly visible from the hallway. She told her life story, and the residents listened attentively. The following month we scheduled to introduce Yarra.

It happened to be a day when Yarra had very low energy. She slumped in her wheelchair. We had hoped she could meet each person privately. Instead, Chris and I walked around showing the residents maps and photos of the places Yarra had lived. Some were delighted to recognize places they too had been. Everyone participated as best they could.

We showed the audience her art. They were very interested, which surprised and pleased us, as they were some of the very residents we had seen day-after-day mindlessly dozing. We reported their comments back to Yarra.

To us, they murmured their appreciation for our concerns by a tearful eye or murmuring, "Too young…."

One of the aides told us she met Yarra previously at a beauty parlor. The aide suggested she could prepare an art class, if Yarra could help her. It sounded hopeful. Yarra and a few residents came. Despite all good intentions, it was too much for Yarra. It was too taxing, too structured, and too tiring. The class continued without Yarra, and later the aide told us, "I've been here five years and now, only because of Yarra, we have art class."

Yarra has her own art class. Thanks to Vikki, who comes not only with art materials, but she brings herself—her gentle, encouraging self. It is a gift to Yarra each time she appears.

Yarra increasingly chose not to join the community outside her room. The nurses made friends and joked with her. They repeatedly told us, "I love to go into Yarra's room for a chat."

I asked, "How can that be? She can't talk." One aide giggled. "Oh, but she knows how to keep our secrets." They all grinned and nodded.

Without someone to speak for her, Yarra cannot welcome anyone into her room, tell them anything about herself, or ask for anything. In her room, she waits for the world to come to her.

We covered a notebook with photos of Yarra in many places around the world. We pasted a note on the front asking visitors and nurses to pass on notes of their visits so we would know who came, and so others would have a starting place when talking with Yarra.

As we visit Yarra I see some of my concerns are cultural norms, like doors and windows being constantly open, "beach style," which I consider a safety issue for Yarra.

Whenever there is a pile of green trimmings left beside Yarra's sliding door, it's explained, "Glen will be around to collect it later, when it has dried a bit." Anyone could come in the open sliding door.

Yarra likes to have her heavy drapes and the windows open. I ask Kris to close them when he leaves. I doubt he does, since Yarra wants them open. I say it's to keep the "mozzies" and sand flies out.

I ask for the sliding door to be locked. From the looks on the faces of the nurses and the aides, I know my request is very unusual. I doubt it's done.

There are a few younger patients here, close to Yarra's age, three young males and one woman. They walk freely about the facility and sometimes come into Yarra's room.

Glynwood is a designated center for Huntington's disease patients. (Huntington's disease is a progressive brain disorder which causes uncontrolled movements, emotional problems, and loss of thinking ability.)

One young woman, beautiful and friendly, comes to Yarra's room to visit after she is dressed up prettily to go out. Once she came by when I was there.

"Oh, you're going out by yourself today?" I ask.

She replies, "Yes, I'm like my father. I will stay here until they put me into a place where I can't hurt anyone." Her severe self-knowledge touches me deeply, but not enough to overshadow my fear.

On staff are a male nurse and male orderly. I told the nurse manager I was concerned for Yarra's safety. I asked her if the staff was vetted for sexual abuse charges. She assured me, "Yes, there is a thorough criminal record search on anyone who works here."

The janitors? The handymen? The constantly rotating "temporary" staff? *I doubt it.*

I'm in a country where I know young women who run for exercise alone, unafraid, in the parks or streets on hot summer nights. And some nurses bicycle home from evening shift at 12 a.m. Perhaps, in this country, the last thing nursing home managers would think about is someone molesting a young, woman patient.

Well, I do.

I asked that no males, neither orderlies nor the one male RN, enter Yarra's room without a female in attendance. I said she might be alarmed. The nurse manager stared at me quizzically, then widened her eyes and nodded, as if she suddenly thought of something she'd never thought of before. "Yes, I can do that."

Maybe she thought the request strange from an American woman. Cultural norms are different. Yes, well, other things are different.

Yarra can't speak or use the call bell. "Change the things you can." I must do what I can do.

We've responded to staff requests for information. We gave them the only books we found on MS: *Waist High in the World* by Nancy Mairs and *Women Living With MS*, by Judith Nichols. We typed an eighteen-page daily care plan specifying Yarra's individual needs and left it with the nurse manager.

Not enough. There are still so many mistakes, for which Yarra pays in energy loss, skin damage, infections, pain, depression, boredom, isolation, and sorrow.

We've had our first regular joint meeting with the staff and had a nice little teaching moment. There wasn't enough space in Yarra's room for chairs for all of us. I heard someone say, "We can move to the conference room."

I hesitated a moment, then said, "At home, she usually sits in her chair with all of us. Will the patio be all right, Dr. Williams?"

The nurses swiveled their heads. He nodded.

As I turned to push Yarra out into the patio, I saw Dr Williams, head down, smiling.

I Can't Be Me

I have been learning how to be with suffering, not to lean into it and lose myself. Not to try to fix it. Not to pull back from it, cold and objectively, but to stand compassionately present with an open heart and expansive mind.

I'm learning to treat myself with compassion, so I can be in sadness and be true to the grieving part of myself. It takes practice and strength. I discussed this when I talked with my fine counselor, Mary Jaksch, last Monday, after a day with Yarra.

Sunday, Yarra, Kris, and I went to a family picnic. Contrary to all my fretful negative expectations, Yarra was full of energy, enjoyed the company and joking long into the evening. *Best not make an assumption about MS based on past performance; it varies constantly. Her energy and ability can change from minimal to passable, from hour to hour. She also has whole good days and bad days, and it all depends on the heat, the stress, or the unknown.*

We were still enjoying the evening sunset as we drove back to the nursing home at nine o'clock. Kris and Yarra were delaying getting out of the van to come into her room. I went to the visitor's lounge and waited on the porch where I could check what was happening in the parking lot. Yarra is in her wheelchair at the back of the van. Kris is standing still in front of her, his shoulders drooped, waiting, staring.

I hear a loud wail! Yarra wails a mournful wail, desperate beyond sorrow, an alarmed, prolonged wail. My new learning disappears. My heart freezes.

Yarra is realizing she is not coming back home. Oh, my love, what sorrow.

A slight breeze ruffles a small-leafed green vine; it brushes my cheek. I focus on six tiny, exquisite petals, six yellow pistils, slender as an eyelash. The blubbery moment stops. Silence, then Yarra's pushed out, almost shouted words, enunciated painstakingly slowly, "I...can't...be meeee."

My knees feel weak. I grab the doorframe, swing into the visitor's lounge and slump into an armchair. I press my hands tightly together and begin to rock. I wait in there until Kris comes to find me.

He stares at my tear-filled eyes. I see his cheeks bathed in tears. He nods. We stand without speaking. He leads me to the van, remains silent, and so do I. Yarra still wails, "I can't be me!"

"Scan of Yarra's Diary Note"

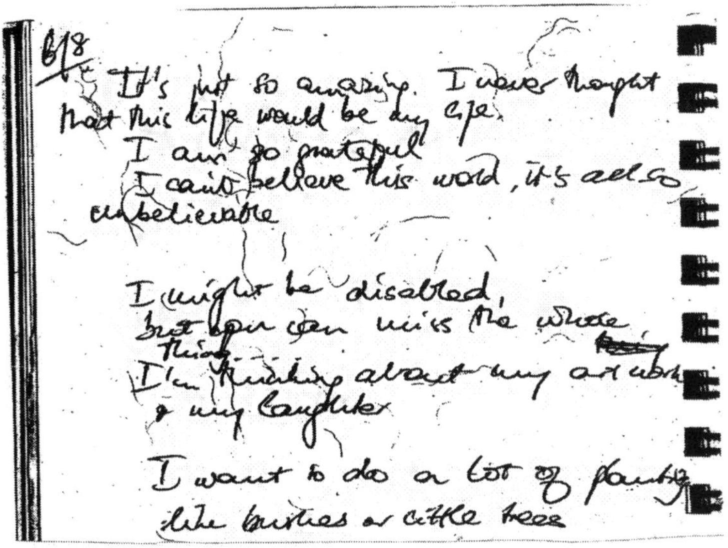

It's just so amazing. I never thought that this would be my life.

I am so grateful can't believe this world, it's all so unbelievable.

I might be disabled,

But you can miss the whole thing…

I'm thinking about my art work and my laughter

I want to do a lot of painting

like bushes and little trees

Return to Glynwood

Chris and I have been back in the US for eight months, tending to other family members. We are preparing to return to New Zealand. We receive a recorded, last-minute phone message from Kris, "Please bring some new t-shirts for Yarra. The nurses say size ten."

Size ten? Yarra has always been size 14 to 16. It must be confu-

sion with New Zealand to America sizing? I buy three size ten tees.

The morning after our arrival in Nelson, I go to Glynwood. I'm told Yarra's room is "just past the tub room." I hurry down the hall, carrying Yarra's new T-shirts, eager to see Yarra. Steam is rolling out into the hallway as I approach the tub room door. I glance in.

Yarra hangs suspended in the canvas basket straps of an electric hoist over a steaming tub. Her brown eyes are riveted on me, and they are wild.

Oh, God! I want to scream at her nurses...aides...whoever... Stop! What are you doing?

Three women are toweling Yarra. I can almost hear their voices, "There you go. A good hot bath will make you feel better."

Has no one gotten the message that heat is detrimental to Yarra? That even a slight rise in temperature can bring on the symptoms of MS? Has she been getting hot baths all this time? I'm frustrated... angry. Yarra's mother yelling at the nurses won't help Yarra.

I whirl around and head for the nursing station. No one is there. I look at the bookshelf above the desk, and neither of the books on MS nor the red plastic manual for Yarra's care is there. I check around for the nurse manager then go to Yarra's room. She is in her bed, and the nurses are pulling up her multicolored skirt.

I shift my mood to happy, "Good morning, Yarra. I'm here."

The nurses turn, "Your mum, Yarra?"

"Yes, I'm 'Mom Joanne.'" I move forward, and they stand aside so I can give her a kiss on the cheek. I snuggle against her very warm cheek for a moment, "Dad and I are back, Honey."

Her whole body is limp, curved in bed, exhausted, her chest bare and red from the shower, and for the first time in Yarra's life, I think she is "thin."

I press a smile onto my face, "Looks like I'm just in time, Honey. How about a new tee for today? Pretty turquoise?" *A charade. I'm faking, and she knows.*

I hand the t-shirt to the aides. Amazingly, it slips on easily over her stiff shoulders. *Size 10? What's going on? Chris and I will have more than hot baths to discuss.*

Chris and I go to Glynwood mid-morning. An aide tells us Kris has taken Yarra in the van to get weighed at the hospital.

"Why'd he take her to the hospital?" I ask Chris.

"Don't know, he must be concerned. It's not like Kris to jump into action like this."

When Yarra and Kris return, she's slumped in the wheelchair. Kris wears a somber face, "The nurses told you we went to get weighed, eh?" We nod. The aides come forward to push Yarra's chair. Kris says, "Yarra's ready for a lay down. She's worn out after all that moving around this morning."

He turns to us, "I'm going to grab a "cuppa" from the visitor's room. You two, OK?"

Chris says, "How about we pull some chairs out on the lawn. We'll talk there. Just had coffee, thanks."

We sit quietly for a while, during which I muse that a New Zealand "while" is purposefully longer than an American "while."

Finally, Kris says, "Well, as you can imagine, the news is not good. I asked the new nurse manager for Yarra's weight chart. She found none. Worse than that, she asked someone to check the scale and found that the scale is broken. Those same weekly weights were wrong. Unbelievable, how many months without anyone noticing the scale was broken."

I can't speak. It may have happened even if we were here we might not have noticed. *There's enough blame to go around. Blaming will not help Yarra. From the defeated look on Chris' face, I see that we have come to the same realization, there is no way Yarra can regain that lost muscle tissue. She will be even more challenged to support herself in an upright position, especially her head.*

Kris squares his shoulders and says, "That's why I took her to the hospital this morning…to weigh her, in her wheelchair, on the scale at the loading dock. I'll do it from now on." He pauses, "By my calculations she's roughly…38 pounds less than the last weight at the doctor's last year. I don't know how we all missed it."

Thirty-eight pounds! I remember how Yarra refused to be driven in the back of the van, "like a hunk of meat." What does she feel like being weighed on the loading dock? Like…what? Like what?

Change the Things I Can

Since we discovered Yarra's weight loss, her fluid intake is measured and administered through a syringe into her feeding tube, and recorded. Her nutrition is totally canned supplement these days, which seems dismal, especially when the food carts are rattling past in the hallways, but it has solved Yarra's coughing and choking.

Often, there is not a glass at her bedside. Today, I need a glass for myself. I have permission from the cooks to go to the kitchen anytime, to get whatever I need.

I head down the hall where a huge floral basket sits on the floor and passing the nurse's station, the visitors' room, with its set of proper tea cups and boxes of tea and Milo cocoa mix, on through the activity room where a few patients huddle over puzzles, sit quietly looking into the garden, or sleep.

The dining room and kitchen are quiet and shaded. I draw a glass of water and sit down for some quiet meditation. Shards of bright sun reflect the shiny foliage, interspersed by flashes of salmon-pink hibiscus or the deep green of tall trees. I'm facing out toward a small ravine in which a slow creek flows along one side of the property. I hear the squeals and laughter of children playing on another side. A grade school swimming pool and two sides lined with bushes, but open to the street. *That's a problem for me. Is it really safe for the patients? Their rooms are easily accessible to anyone. I think about Yarra alone in her room, unable to move or call out.*

It's been quiet in the dining room with the staff gone for mid-afternoon break. The sun has dropped below the treetops. The room is shaded, peaceful. I shake my head to bring myself out of my brooding. I walk toward the hall to Yarra's room.

Three old-style wooden wheelchairs, slanted open, almost flat, are lined up along the wall, piled with folded laundry. I stop mid-step. I gasp. No, it's not laundry. Oh, my God. It's three patients, all tidy and rolled up in white linen, like cocoons. *Am I seeing things? Why are they here? Maybe their rooms are being cleaned. They seem "put aside," like doll babies on a shelf. Oh God, this can't happen to Yarra.*

I rush in silent panic toward Yarra's room. We won't always be here. We've got to find someone right away to help us get advance directives, or whatever they call it here. We must talk with her doctor, a lawyer—someone. Oh, no, God, no. That can't happen to Yarra.

Windsurfing

I plop my weary body into the front seat of the car, turn on the motor, and slowly drive the short distance from Glynwood to Tahunanui Beach parking lot. I crawl out, face the sea, take a big breath and head for the water. I go left, down to the "back beach," where rough, soft, mounds of sand, and heavy, low-hanging pine branches prompt me to meander and muse, where Kris had warned me, "Joanne, don't swim at the 'back beach,' there's a strong vortex there."

Seeing my puzzled look, he continued, "A strong current, it can sweep you away."

I nodded. *Vortex; only thing Kris has ever warned me about; must be really strong.*

"Thanks, Kris."

Bright flashes of colors out in the bay catch my eye, three windsurfers. They glide so easily over the water, arching over the waves, circling in long swaths. I did that once…for about three minutes.

Years ago, our friends Roxie and Bruce invited us to spend a week sailing on their boat in the Bahamas. One of many new water experiences was trying to windsurf, or rather, trying to stay on the surfboard. I remember how difficult it was; you pull yourself onto the board, assume a kneeling position and tuck your feet under your bottom. You try to stand erect on a wet, plastic surface while clinging to the up rope, which is attached to the mast. A wave lifts the sailboard. You lose your balance. The sail rotates. You shift for balance. Whoosh! You swim to the now free-floating board, stretch your arms, and pull your body out of the water onto the board. You're exhausted. You start all over again.

Exactly right! I'm struggling for balance and control. That's what it is, this kind of care giving-windsurfing! Minus, of course, the thrill of breezes and an invigorating sea spray. I watch the three sails circle back across the bay. Breathe. Standing in deep shade, I delight in the dancing of sunny patches through the pines. I walk back to my car.

A flock of seagulls descends, with raucous squabbles, on the remains of an open lunch bag. Rude awakening. I am distracted by my thoughts as I step up onto a grassy circle in the parking lot. On the other side, I mindlessly step down. A car with bashed fenders roars by, dangerously close. I jump back up on the curb.

The male driver yells something indistinguishable as he leans out the window. He speeds, motor blasting, to the turn-around and heads back!

I've not heard any "rough talk" in New Zealand, but it looks like I'm about to receive a lacing. Rightly so, as I'm totally at fault. A sandy-haired driver tilts his jowled face out the window. Blond strands of hair swirl as he leans sunburned cheeks on a muscular upper arm. I cringe. Here it comes, booming across the parking lot, "Sorry, lady, I didn't see you!"

I stop mid-step. Hot sun beats down. The car's roar recedes. My whole body softens, "*Ah...New Zealand.*"

The Solicitor's Visit

Last year, before Yarra went to the nursing home, she prepared her advanced directives. Advanced directives are not common here, so we hired a solicitor. I must add a piece here about Yarra. She is a flirt, always was, hasn't changed. Doesn't matter if the man is a surgeon, lab tech or physical therapist. If he's young and good-looking, Yarra starts to have fun.

You can imagine the following scene. The hapless solicitor sits at the bedside of an unusual, beautiful, severely ill young woman who cannot speak. Her interpreters are her husband, who treats her with respect and questions her as if she can speak, pausing and reiterating to make sure he gets everything as close to her wishes as possible, and her father, a doctor, who knows all about advanced directives, but nothing about how they work in New Zealand, or if they are going to be useful and valid, while hoping patiently that the outcome will be worth the effort.

It takes over an hour to read through and agree on two sheets of paper documents dealing with the serious matters of life and death. Now comes the time for signing the papers. "Oh, she won't be able to sign her name?" the solicitor asks with surprise. "Can she make an X?"

Kris, Chris, and Yarra try to determine if she can really make an X, and it doesn't look like it's going to happen. The three men start a discussion on what might substitute for a signature. In the meantime, Yarra starts blowing kisses. Chris looks dumbfounded. Kris thinks she's up to her usual trick of flirting, until he realizes she's signaling a message, "I can do as I've done for years; sign my artwork and letters with lipstick kisses."

Kris runs into the bedroom and brings out dark lipstick and puts it on Yarra. The solicitor looks on in amazement and comments, "Of course, I'll have to check with the powers that be as to whether it will be acceptable."

Of course, and in the meantime, Kris has held the official papers up to Yarra's lips, and she has affixed a big red "smooch-y" lip print on the signature line.

Medical Durable Power of Attorney for Health Care Decisions

1. I Angela Yarra Amoroso. Declarant, being of sound mind hereby appoint:

Johannes Kris Kolff
20 Blick Terrace
Nelson, New Zealand
Telephone (03) 546-6477

As my agent to make health care decisions for me if and when I am unable to make my own health care decisions. This gives my agent the power to consent to giving, withholding or stopping any health care treatment, service or diagnostic procedure. My agent also has the authority to talk with health care personnel, get information and sign forms necessary to carry out those decisions. If the person named as my agent is not available or is unable act as my agent, then I appoint the following person(s) to serve in the order listed below.

2. Christian R. Amoroso
186 a Paseo Quinto
Green Valley, Arizona
85614 USA
Telephone (520) 625-3555

3. Joanne T. Amoroso
186 a Paseo Quinto
Green Valley, Arizona
85614 USA
Telephone (520) 625-3555

By this document I intend to create a Medical Durable Power of Attorney which shall take effect upon my incapacity to make my own health care decisions as shall continue during that capacity.

My agent shall make health care decisions as I may direct below or as I make known to him or her in some other way. If I have not expressed a choice about the health care in question, my agent shall base his/her decision on what he/she believes to be in my best interest.

I only desire life-prolonging care, treatment, services and procedures if there is a reasonable hope of maintaining my quality of life (spiritually, mentally, emotionally and physically). At the present that includes doing my artwork, seeing the sunset, occasional trips to a restaurant, meditating looking out the window at the trees, being free of sever and constant pain.

X 11.7.01

Angela Yarra Amoroso Date

I declare that Yarra/Angela Amoroso signed this document in my presence and appeared to be of sound mind, free of duress or undue influence.

11/7/01

Witness Date Witness Date

11.7.01

Smoochie lipstick kiss above

Living Will

Declaration as to Medical or Surgical Treatment

I Yarra Angela Amoroso, being of sound mind, direct that my life shall not be artificially prolonged under the following circumstances:

1. If at any time my attending physician and one other physician certify in writing that I have an injury, disease or illness which is not curable or reversible and which in their judgment, is a terminal condition.

2. For a period of 7 consecutive days or more, I have been unconscious, comatose or otherwise incompetent so as to be unable to make or communicate responsible decisions concerning my person then

I direct that, life saving procedures shall be withdrawn and withheld pursuant to the terms of this declaration, including artificial nourishment.

I would welcome efforts to comfort me and alleviate pain

* 11.7.01

Angela Yarra Amoroso Date

I declare that Yarra/Angela Amoroso signed this document in my presence and appeared to Be of sound mind, free of duress or undue influence.

11.7.01 11/7/2001

Witness Date Witness Date

Yarra has delineated her quality of life as "until such time that I cannot enjoy the sunsets, go out to the cafés, and do my artwork." Enjoying the sunsets is increasingly difficult, and two teaspoons of coffee is usually all Yarra can manage at a sitting, but her enjoyment of being able to do art continues to be immensely satisfying.

It is amazing what the tiniest amount of paint applied to paper can do. Once a week, if possible, Kris, his sister-in-law Chrissy, Vikki, or I will go to Yarra's room at the nursing home and "do art."

It takes time, and sometimes two helpers, to get Yarra in position in the bed. These are Yarra's choices: Which paper and size? Which brush? What color paint?

Next, the helper will wet the paper, then tape the paper to a cardboard for holding, offer color choices, and wait for Yarra's decisions. Choose a brush. Dip it in the paint. Place the brush in Yarra's fingers. Hold the cardboard to which the paper is taped so that Yarra can reach it. Give her a choice as to where she wants to place the paint. Wait until she has the energy to make a stroke. Repeat the process, or wash the brush, change colors, and make another stroke.

Conversation is only focused on Yarra's painting. "Do you want to add more color? Shall I re-wet the paper or leave it dry? Shall we let the paint run or should I hold the paper flat?" It is like watching something sacred as the forms and shapes take place. It is awesome to see Yarra's slight signs of satisfaction.

The papers are set to dry, then hung on the wall. Yarra spends hours gazing at them. Periodically, she signals that she wants to see one up close or send one to her siblings or friends. In the past, she habitually made cards of her artwork, so we still do that, or wrap them as gifts. Oh, how precious it is that the most minimal piece gives her choices and the feeling of satisfaction. Yarra's ability to share a gift or decorate her room with her individuality touches her caregivers and those who help her paint.

Kris' Handwritten Preparation Notes for Talking with Yarra about Dying:

Ask Yarra, while we can still communicate

Want to discuss about dying-one day

Who knows when

Want you to have freedom to talk about dying whenever you want to

**Cremating?*

**What needs to be completed?*

**Would you like parents to be there-or who?*

**Who at farewell... (who welcome)*

your dream of your dying...the boat going over the horizon

"Discussion" you know the quality of your life

Some winter pneumonia?

Enjoy life? Loving

Like to die?

Emergency room?

Could be cured + maybe worse

How much intervention?

Celebration?

"The Rose" song?

Radiant Coat?

Balloons?

How's "Miss Princess?"

Before I saw her, I heard her mocking, high nasal voice, "How is Miss Pr-riin-cesss today? All chuffed because mum is here with lots of "pressies?"

I tighten and draw back into my chair. She strides into the room, crossing the foot of the bed in one lanky stride.

Yarra no longer can do that.

She flicks a stringy blonde ponytail over her shoulder.

I imagine her tossing a hay bale into the back of a pick-up. Phew, get hold of yourself, Joanne. "I'm Joanne, Yarra's Mum." I offer a hand, but she passes by heading to yank the window curtain cord.

"Righti-o. We know who you are. Looks like we need some daylight in here, eh, Yarra?

Ow-wee! Look at the fancy new shirt Mum brought you. Going out to party later, are you?"

I hear my teeth click together. Yarra is zoned out. I walk to the side of the bed, turn down the covers.

"Yarra needs some help with her toe, if you could look at it." On her left foot, the nail on her big toe is torn away mid-way down her nail bed, like a bright red square. I checked Yarra. *She sees me wince.*

I look at Yarra, "It seems someone gave you new socks, Yarra, and didn't know they should clip the threads inside. That must have hurt." I stroke her foot gently. *Not that it would relieve any pain, I just want to do something.*

I envision someone pushing hard to get the shoe past her frozen ankle joint…while the nail was being ripped away. Could she feel it? Cry out? Or are the nerves to her foot dead? Her face doesn't show pain.

I nod and raise my eyebrows to keep the words from catching in my throat, "I think she needs it cleaned and a band-aid. Can you help?" The nurse bends over Yarra's foot, "Ow-ie. Nasty, Yarra, nasty. Back in a flash." She was gone.

Yarra is turned away, but she looks at me with her left eye. I stop myself from saying, "I'm sorry." I touch her ankle. "I'll check all your socks today and clip any threads that need it." My words hang in the air.

Change the things you can.

Painful Apology

Today, Tuesday, Kris and I thought we would take Yarra to the "World of Wearable Art Gallery" and Café. She has wanted to go for long time. The nurses dress her in a multicolored, long-sleeved tee with her Mexican silver and black onyx earrings, suitable for the World of Wearable Art Museum. When I arrive at Glynwood, Kris tells me we're going to their house instead…to talk.

Yarra shakes her head, "No." She doesn't want to go either place, nor stay in the nursing home. What to do? Kris tries to figure out what is going on in her head with questions. No clear responses. Finally, she agrees to go out, but with no enthusiasm, no energy. She looks very depressed to me. Our "big treat" is falling flat.

As we drive along, Kris says, "I think Yarra has a very sore toe, today. I have an apology to make to you, Joanne.

What's this, an apology?

"Remember when you asked me to tell the nurses to hold Yarra's toes when they spasm and curl up while they try to put on her socks and shoes?"

He pauses, so I respond, "Yes, I do remember that."

"I said I didn't want to overburden them with details? Well, you were right, Yarra's toenail did get caught in her shoe and ripped. I'm sorry." He puts his hand on Yarra's arm. "And I'm so sorry to you, Yarra, that I caused you pain because I didn't listen to your mum."

Vexation

One day after Mass, Father asks, "How are you managing?"

"Oh, Father, it's been hard. We're looking for a place for our daughter for respite care." I begin a long list of complaints.

"Oh, my dear." He shakes his head. "There are so many things in life to vex us."*Whoa. I stop for words. "Vexed?"*

He reads my face—waits.

I hear my Italian grandfather's voice muttering "brontolone" as Nonna grumbles in the kitchen.

I laugh, "Father, in all my life experience in the English language, I have never been vexed. You are always presenting something new for us to think about. It doesn't seem to carry quite as much dissatisfaction as angry, discouraged or frustrated." I pause and then say teasingly, "I may just try being "vexed" this week. Thanks for that."

"No thanks needed." He smiles. "Enjoy your vexation."

Monica Clark-Grill

Monica Clark-Grill is taking a course for a degree in bioethics at Otago University. She is home for a holiday in Nelson. She has come to meet me. She is pleasant and calm. I'm grateful she has come. I have two pages of topics and questions.

She doesn't know me from Adam, yet she was kind enough to come see me. She's a student, but we're talking ethics. I suspect she will be cautious. I think I'm the one to take the lead.

I look over my papers and take a deep breath.

"I have a long list of questions and topics…concerns. May I read them to you?"

Monica nods, "Of course."

"I would like to bring my questions up with Yarra, or with both her and Kris, her husband, and Chris, my husband, as time and energy permit. I'm a nurse and Chris is a doctor. We don't know the New Zealand system regarding end-of-life care. I would like to talk with you because I think you may understand where I'm coming from. I'd like to hear your opinions."

Again, Monica nods.

I continue, "I would want someone I trusted and who cared for me to talk with me about the quality of my present life and the end of life. I don't know whether Yarra also wants this. Should we ask these questions?

- Do you want to talk about end-of-life planning and then be free to go on living?
- Should we explain palliative care to Yarra, and what can be done to keep her comfortable? Ask her for her desires for end of life?
- Is Kris the sole designated patient advocate?
- Who does Yarra trust to help her with these decisions? Family: Kris, Chris, Joanne, Chiara, Joe? Friends: Vikki, Irma?
- Do you realize you are still the one making decisions regarding your treatment?
- Do you realize you can refuse any treatment, including intravenous and Mic-key tube feeding?
- Do you want to continue the feeding tube?
- Is your life with all its restrictions still worth living? If Yarra's answer is ambivalent on one or two times, let it go. If strong response, ask, "Do you want to die soon?
- Do you still feel as you said, "I hurt, and I love life?"
- If you get an infection, do you want antibiotic treatment?

- Do we need a witness to hear these questions? Should they be recorded?
- In New Zealand, what is ethical policy and procedure regarding end-of-life care?
- How legally binding are power of attorney and medical power of attorney?"

We were both silent for a few minutes as I end my long spiel.

Monica spoke first, "I think as a mother you have a right to talk about any of these topics with your daughter, Yarra, right? I don't know the quality of your relationship. Do you think she trusts you?"

"Yes, I think so. We were very close for years. For many years, we even felt that we had shared a past life. More recently, with a degree in International Living, she's been living her own life, mostly overseas. But I think that bond of trust, regarding advice seeking and giving, still exists. We love each other."

She pauses, gently asks, "Do you think it may be…that you are… both…trying to protect each other from grief?"

Spot on!

"Oh, yes, thank you, I feel that. I realize some of my reasons for wanting to talk with you, although I know I want to advocate for my daughter, may also be my attempt to protect myself from, or prepare myself for, witnessing my daughter's prolonged suffering.

"I want to protect her from seeing me witness her being disabled. I see her watching me do things she can no longer do. She sees my sorrow, and, though I don't think I've cried in front of her, she told her sister, Chiara, 'Mom cries too much.'"

We sit silently. Outside the wide windows, I watch tall wands of green flax gently moving side to side. In the distance, a dark swath of deep-blue ocean is highlighted by white waves and a brilliant blue sky. Sun-filled clouds are slowly drifting by. It is very calming. It feels appropriate to pause with our own thoughts.

"Chiara and Yarra have already discussed these things, and Chiara wrote them out. Kris has copies. Yarra has expressed her limits. Chiara asked her if she wanted to be put on life support when she could no longer respond to life within her parameters. According to Chiara, Yarra responded rather bluntly, 'What's the point?'"

After our meeting, Monica contacted Dr. Grant Gillett, neurosurgeon and bioethics physician, and her professor. He sent two pages, which explicate the "lack of benefit argument case," a landmark in New Zealand court (Gillett et al. 1995), and a second case (Peart and Gillett 1998) from "Medical Ethics," Third Edition, Campbell A., Gillett A. and Jones A., Oxford University Press 200, pages 202 –203.

Dr. Gillett stated that POA, Power of Attorney, and MPOA, Medical Power of Attorney, are not legally binding in New Zealand. At such time that a patient can no longer respond, a medical team takes over, along with a patient advocate. They decide, based on the reasonable practice consideration, the objective assessment of best interests, and a subjective consideration of best interests of those involved.

I wrote out my personal questions to discuss one-by-one with Yarra, when and if the opportunity arose:

- Do you know I love you and will be your advocate, no matter what happens?
- Do you know I will stand up for you if you no longer can communicate?
- Are you happy with the way we have been spending time with you?
- Do you enjoy doing art class here? Finger painting?
- Do you want to find other ways we can do art? Picking the colors for your calendar, find more varied colors?
- Do you see that the patients here at Glynwood are beautiful beyond their physical appearance?
- Do you want to try going to the HE-ART-RY? Parties?
- Do you prefer a more private setting for outings, especially involving eating? Visiting? Seeing nature? Art?
- Do you want me to read? Books, news clippings, and magazines?

Brookland

Chris has been struggling with back pain and rash. He has been thoroughly worked up by a good orthopedic physician here and is preparing for back surgery in the States.

He has gotten permission to have the medication for Multiple Sclerosis that Yarra was receiving in the United States mailed here. He's tended to everything he could, business and packing, but has been limited because of pain. I feel like momma bird flying out to get food for the chicks and then returning to the nest.

This afternoon when Chris relaxed into a chair at the airport, he seemed relieved. "All the things you got me worked out well: the backpack, the medicine containers…we've done a good job. We've taken care of me, moved—we're both exhausted, and we'll be all right."

I kissed him. He reached up to bless me on the forehead. I kissed him again, tenderly. "I hope you'll be OK, that all goes well. I'll be waiting for you. I'll be praying for you."

Friend Nancy came by this evening. We walked under a bright orange, purple and rose-colored sky. Afterwards, I went to Yarra's to finger paint a card in Yarra's art room for Kris and Yarra's anniversary. I set my purse down on the table, and when I picked it up, it was smeared with paint. Happy accident…I turned the purse so Yarra could see the sunset colors and said, "I go to the same art school you do." Her eyes sparkled. We both laughed. It felt so good.

Friendly Fire

May 7th, 1:20 a.m. I'm awakened with a start by a loud 'crack' and the hall light blinking off and on. Chris is away in Christchurch for X-rays. I'm alone in our new rental, on the third floor. I see pale grey through the balcony doors and feel my way out to the porch. On the hillside, I see flames. I don't have a flashlight, but I have a whistle on my car keys. I grope my way to the nightstand and finger around for the keys. Back on the balcony with a flashlight, I flash what I think may be S.O.S. I feel very silly; I don't remember if it's three shorts, three longs and three shorts or the other way around. I try both. Soon, I see a very bright light moving up through the dark.

The light falls on the balcony and a strong, formal male voice calls up, “Madam, is this the way you usually contact your neighbors?”

Are you kidding?

“No sir, but I can see a fire on the hillside. It seems to be spreading quickly our way. I want to report it to the police.”

“The police are aware of the fire, madam. Would you like to join your neighbors who have gathered in the street?”

“I sure would. It’s my first night here, and I’m not sure of the stairways. Don’t know if I can safely make it down.”

“I can flash my light into your main floor, perhaps that will be enough light for you to come down.”

“Thank you officer, I appreciate that very much.”

As soon as I step in the hallway, I see pale light on the pitched ceilings, enough to find the railings and slide my feet to the staircase. I sit on the steps and bump down, open the door, and thank the officer. He says, “I’ll give you a hand down the hill.”

I hear buzzing chatter as we descend the hill. The street is filled with people. *Hmfph. I was worried I wouldn’t be able to go safely up and down the steep drive, and here I am going down in the dark, assisted by the Nelson police and a huge flashlight.*

Many flashlights bobble in the dark street. Behind me the officer says, “I’ll leave you with your neighbors now, ma’am.”

The officer disappears into the crowd and darkness. Two lights come towards me. I recognize Terry and Elizabeth, already declared our “first angels” on Brookland Terrace.

“Where’s Chris? asks Elizabeth.

“Gone to Christchurch for some X-rays.”

“Oh, my dear, you must come home with us, we have lots of spare beds. Come along.”

As I turn to follow, I see other people standing nearby, smiling. A jovial-faced man pokes his hand out, “We’re your neighbors, too. I’m John, and this is Elizabeth. And here are Nancy and Bill…from just across your driveway. We don’t usually throw a welcome party with fireworks.” He laughs. “But welcome.”

I’m dazzled. *It seems nothing is usual here. Again, I’m bewildered and grateful.*

These neighbors become our walking partners and advisors. They welcome us for meals and into their homes and hearts. They had a "proper" farewell party when we left, and in the years to come, though we no longer lived in the neighborhood, they continued to host many joyous "welcomes and farewells."

Chris' surgery was successful. When we returned from Colorado in 2002, there were Poly-Tech students in the rental. Kris' family put out feelers, but we were fussy. We needed quiet and outdoor space, so that limited our options.

Temporarily, we checked in at a neat motel on the Maitai in downtown Nelson. It looked ideal, with our expectations of walking and sitting along the river. And we did—about twice, until the rains came down and never left. The ground was soaked, the skies grey. The temperature dropped.

For two weeks, cold, rainy and wet, we huddled over a small oil heater. We asked for a second heater for the bathroom. The receptionist paused. "Well, we've never had that request before, I'll ask the manager."

The second heater arrived. We froze at our motel on Maitai. When we hurried to Kris and Yarra's warm kitchen, Kris assured us, "It'll be fine soon."

We put an ad in the paper. "Reliable, retired, professional couple, caring for ill daughter, looking for furnished, temporary rental, home or apartment. Good references. Non-smokers."

Chris received a phone call. "They said we don't need references, just come see their place." Tony and Susan greeted us like old friends as they showed us through a one-level bungalow. We chatted and told our story. The location was interesting. High in the port hills overlooking a wooded valley dotted with white clapboard homes and old Victorians, all with gardens. We nodded to each other, and Chris said, "This will be fine for us."

"There is a cat to be fed. She's in and out."

We nodded. "We've learned that everyone in New Zealand has a pet."

Susan and Tony both smiled. Tony looked at Susan and asked, "Would you like to come next door and see our place?"

"Oh, you live next door? How nice." We tromped along a path of dense vegetation and scrambled by a sprawling, towering, bamboo plant and climbed onto a long porch which fronted two sides of a two-story Victorian. We entered downstairs to see a roomy living area with stocked bookshelves, a small and large bedroom, and a bath. Upstairs, there were fascinating views. A living room and office faced the port entry, a kitchen and bath overlooked a valley of homes nestled between gardens and masses of greenery, plus there were two long, outside balconies facing a landscaped yard and the port.

All the walls were covered with stylized, brightly colored art. "You have an interesting collection of art. Far Eastern? Indonesian?"

Tony looks again at Susan. "Yes, that's it," Tony begins. "We're going to Indonesia with VSA, a volunteer program, for a year. If you like this house better than the first one, it's yours. We'll rent the other one."

"Gob smacked." That's the New Zealand term for flummoxed or overwhelmed. I saw Chris' wide-open eyes, scanning the rooms and the views. Neither Chris nor I could respond…this beautiful home overlooking the port, being offered to us?

I stammered, "Oh, the house is wonderful…we can bring references."

They looked at each other and laughed, their eyes dancing. Tony says, "We knew the minute we read your ad in the paper that we wanted you."

Did my eyes fill with tears? Did I feel an intuitive connection with their compassion and their generous contrivance…as I do now, remembering?

Regardless of the exact feelings I had at the time, once we moved to the heights, with the ambient space of foliage and sea, the quiet of the neighborhood, and the tiny green-blue-grey cat, Silver Eyes, we paused and allowed ourselves time for self-awareness.

My major awareness comes when the sound of my own groaning awakens me at night. Once awake, I realize that my groan is not of physical pain, but the overwhelming awareness of how much I must let go.

For me, it seems the individual, introspective striving for this necessary human learning of letting go is equivalent to the amount of scientific study necessary to bring science from the age of Galileo to the development of the space shuttle.

Chris feels some of this, too. Once when we discussed how difficult and constant is the task we're about, he commented, "Just how much character do we have to develop in one lifetime?"

I feel Chris, in his gentle way, is farther along than I am. He reaches Yarra's stillness with tender humor and communicates calmly, while I still try to rearrange, improve, and change things.

Joe Visits Nelson, December, 2002

When our son Joe came in December 2002 for an extended visit to "help us with Yarra," he also added a new element into Yarra's life in the nursing home: play. They were born 18 months apart, so they were "little buddies" as toddlers. They rode a rubber rocking horse for hours with Angie's arms encircling Joe's waist. Her head pressed against his back, she hung on for dear life. He was her "big brother" through teen years.

When Joe walked into her room at the nursing home, Yarra's face lit up, as did the faces of the nurses. They also raved to Yarra about "that gobsmacking, gorgeous brother of yours," which tickled her no end and made her a co-conspirator in possible matchmaking.

Yarra could no longer use a call bell nor speak. Joe invented a game that he and Yarra played on new nurses. He rang her call bell, left it in Yarra's bed, and then hid behind the door. The new nurse would come, asking Yarra what she needed. Of course, Yarra couldn't answer, but she was smiling a lot, as unbeknownst, Joe peeked from behind the door. The perplexed nurse would leave the room. Joe rang the bell again and hid. Two nurses came, one, who knew Yarra couldn't ring the bell herself, quizzed Yarra to no avail and left again.

I don't know how long this ruse lasted, until Joe revealed himself from behind the door, or how many times they pulled the trick, but it empowered Yarra enough that once, after severe leg spasms, when she had fallen hard against the bedside rails and tumbled out of bed into a corner near the wall, she remained silent when a nurse came in and wondered aloud where she was.

The nurse came back with the nurse supervisor and found the

bed empty. In the re-telling, quite a fuss was described as aides and nurses were asked, "Do you know where Yarra is? Is she out in the yard in a wheelchair? Did Kris come to take her out?"

Finally, Yarra made a sound. They found her under the bed, delighted with herself.

Special Visitors

Chiara told Kris it was important to Yarra that she see "the horses" whenever she could. Irma drove Yarra to ride therapy horses with Vikki. Kris took her in the wheelchair to the corrals at the end of the street, and so did brother Joe when came for an extended visit. At times, when we were in Yarra's bedroom and heard the likes of heavy iron pans being clanged against the street outside her window, Yarra's eyes would light up. We knew what that sound meant, "The Percherons are coming!" All of us were in awe of the two huge, black animals, easily 6 feet tall. They came clomping by Yarra's bedroom window on their way up "the track" in The Reserve.

One day, Joe said, "Mom, I gotta tell you what happened today. I was at Yarra's while Kris was away. She woke from her nap, and I was helping her get up. We heard 'the big' coming up the street. I said, 'Wait, Yarra. Gotta check something.'

"I ran out and told the two riders how my sister always heard the horses going by and would love to see them. I asked if they would stop. They said they were going for an hour's ride but would come back if they had time.

"I said, 'That's OK, I'm just getting her up and she uses a wheelchair, so it will take us some time to get ready.'

"Kris came home, and I told him what was up. We pushed Yarra outside in the wheelchair, and when the horses and riders returned, she was waiting. They recognized Yarra because a year or two ago she came to ride horses at a place where they worked.

"Yarra was so excited. The horses came into the yard, very slowly, and man, they look so big—couple thousand pounds at least. They towered over Yarra, but she had a big smile and was so excited. No one said a word. Then one rider backed one of the horses away.

"The other rider loosened the reins down over her horse's mane.

The horse took a step forward, then looked at Yarra. He put his head down above the grass and brushed it with his nose, looking at the distance between his feet and Yarra's on the wheelchair pedals. He lifted his hoof back and forth very slowly, looking at Yarra's feet. It was so beautiful."

I have tears in my eyes and gratitude in my heart.

Joe continues, "I could hardly breathe; this giant horse, towering over Yarra, inches from where she was sitting. Her eyes were wide open in wow-ness. The horse kept its big black eyes on Yarra. Then he looked down and placed each huge hoof closer and closer to Yarra, so carefully. Then the next thing the horse did…ahh, mom."

Joe pauses, he has a catch in his throat, his voice softens. "The horse lowered its head…very slowly…straight down into Yarra's lap…as gently as a mother touches a child, and…" Joe swallows again. "held it there, as if the horse were giving itself to Yarra… like a gift…of kindness.

"The horse and Yarra stayed still, then the master gave the rein a little twitch, and the horse lifted its head, and, keeping his eyes on Yarra all the while, he backed up slowly. It was 'kinda' magic. It was really cool."

Breathless, I remember a phrase from a letter he sent to Yarra years ago, "It's a gift to walk by your side. May the spirit of angels always be blessed with your company."

Advice

Before Joe returned to Colorado, we met for lunch. We had a wonderful chat about all that went well, then Joe's face turned somber.

He said, "I had a talk with Yarra the other day. I told her I was leaving soon. I was very surprised." Joe paused. "She got angry, I could tell by her eyes and her face. I was surprised."

He looked unsure. "We'd had a big day. I did a lot of errands for her. I took her in the wheelchair up to see the horses at the corral. I was tired. Yarra asked me to make chocolate chip cookies after supper. I knew she couldn't eat them, but she still likes the smell and taste. I told her I was tired and she had a responsibility to take care of the people who help her, just as her caregivers are responsible for her care. It went well. Yarra understood."

"Thanks Joe, she could probably hear that from you more easily than from us or Kris. Valuable lesson for her to learn, and helpful for all of us."

"Yeah, just wanted you to know."

Get Me Out Everyday

"Oh, that mouth," Melissa says. They were pals from first grade to twelfth. She's heard all Ange's past zinging remarks. She knows all her secrets. When Ange went off traveling the world, Melissa also went to Africa, Ireland, and New York City. They kept in touch for the big things—heartbreak, marriage, divorce, new baby, and illness.

When Melissa, her husband, Javan, and child, Elijah, arrived in New Zealand in 2003, they found a Yarra who "could speak for fifteen minutes, sometimes" and was confined to bed or a wheelchair. Melissa knew Yarra was dying, but she also knew Yarra would wish to be engaged in life to the last breath. As a professional photojournalist, Melissa spent the next seven months at Yarra's side, photographing her life, honoring her, fully present in a book called *Living.*

When Chiara, who early on had recorded Yarra's wishes; "someone to get me out every day" and "to go to the beach" offered to help Kris, they devised a way to place pieces of plywood in front of Yarra's wheelchair, and Yarra, with help, could navigate the sand.

When Melissa and Javan arrived, they replaced the pieces of plywood, and spread a large roll of plastic as they walked ahead of the wheelchair, creating a "sand walk."

Both methods required a team of helpers, but it was very satisfying to see Yarra enjoy the ocean view at the beach.

Fairfield House Exhibit, June 7, 2003

"Come see what's been happening in the Art Room," says Kris.

I muse. *The Art Room? Kris is calling it the Art Room. How wonderful.*

Yarra's long table is filled with bottles of paint, glasses with brushes, and many paintings.

"Wow, you've really been busy. How wonderful Yarra can come home to work here."

"Yes, I finally made time for it," says Kris. Everyone helped me, and Yarra has put it to good use. With the help of Vikki, Inez, and Chrissy, she has done seventy paintings. Look at these."

Yarra sits where she can see as we stand sifting through her art pieces; they are mostly abstract designs and bold colors. We remark on the flow of colors and the moods of each piece. I'm thrilled to see how excited and involved Yarra is. Her sessions with her helpers are opportunities for her to make her own choices.

After Vikki started working with Yarra, she took a class in intuitive art, thinking it would be helpful for her in assisting Yarra. I see the evidence before me. The helpers offer choices: "Which brush? What color of paint? What size paper and shape?" and Yarra makes the decisions on what she will or won't put on the paper, often surprising her assistants. Vikki is constantly designing simple adaptations for holding her brushes, using rubber toys or balls and sponges.

As I compare this art to Yarra's previous work, I see her hands and fingers are less capable of control. I don't think that really is important to her. What happens accidentally or impulsively she accepts, even welcomes, as an opportunity for creativity.

"Yarra," Kris says, "is this a good time to ask your folks about our idea?"

She nods and smiles. "Yes."

Kris straightens his shoulders. "Vikki, would you like to start? It was your idea."

Vikki focuses on Yarra, then begins to speak, "Yarra's been so excited about her art lately. Right, Yarra?"

Yarra nods.

"She's keen on sharing with other people her belief that anyone can use art as therapy." As Vikki halts, she checks to see if Yarra agrees.

Vikki laughs, "Yarra has so much work now that we could have an exhibit, a big exhibit. It would take a lot of work, and we'd need to find a suitable place."

"Sounds good," Chris says. "I'm not an artist, but I can help with the organizing and run errands. I'd be glad to help do whatever."

Kris adds, "Sometimes Hein comes to paint with Yarra. He and the rest of the family are artists. Inez and Chrissy all like the idea and would help put it together. They may even include some of their work, and we could add some of Yarra's previous work in a 'retrospective.' If you like the idea, we'll sit down and have a talk about it."

I'm so pleased. I feel grateful, thinking of how this exhibit will bolster Yarra's feelings about her life and work, and provide her an additional avenue of communication to share who she is.

"Oh, there's another thing," Kris adds, "Yarra's friend Melissa from Longmont…is here with her husband, Javan, and boy, Elijah. Yarra loves having them around. They will be here for a few more months. Melissa is doing a photo journal of Yarra's life. They like the 'retrospective' exhibit idea and will help as well."

New Zealanders call certain events organic, meaning they evolve on their own. Our whole project took off with the declarations of many people who said, "We want to help; just tell us what we can do."

As ideas of an exhibit flow, I have an image of Vikki, bringing a flat balloon to Kris and saying, "What do you think?" Together, they agree to cautiously inflate the balloon. Then people commit to tie a string onto the balloon. The balloon then ascends farther than any of us ever dreamed possible.

Fairfield House, a beloved, appropriately-restored historic home which stands in beautiful woodlands and gardens, is the choice for the exhibit. It has large, light-filled rooms and spacious verandas. Kathryn, a pleasant, gracious and helpful hostess, does everything possible to assist us.

Phil Barnes, reporter for *The Leader*, the local newspaper, came to Yarra's room at the nursing home prior to the exhibit. Handsome, tall, brown dreadlocks, woolly Alpine sweater, cargo shorts and boots. Yarra approved; I could tell by her sparkling eyes.

Phil was totally focused on getting all the details right. Vikki and I did the best we could, checking every answer with Yarra during an interview at her bedside. Yarra responded through nods and blinks, as she hasn't been able to speak for months.

Phil's article was wonderful. He wrote about Yarra's perseverance and accomplishments, despite MS. Her photo was on the front page of the magazine section, entitled, *Still Painting On*.

I'd heard from Kris that when he read it to her, all the nurses were in her room "raving it up" with her. When I went to see her the next day, the newspaper clipping about the art exhibit dangled on her bulletin board. I tapped my fingers along the outside of her doors before I entered, to awaken her and announce myself. Still, she was in the semi-somnolent state in which I often find her.

I took her hand and said softly, "Hello, Miss Celebrity." Upon hearing those words, the most beautiful, pleased-to-the-core smile wreathed her face. *Oh, joy! It is so encouraging for her to receive this affirmation in her life.*

We learn that Nelson had assorted-sized frames available for loan just for artists to use for exhibits. I am surprised and encouraged that such an expensive and troublesome detail for new artists had been attended to by the city. We bring frames to the house and, from an artist friend, learn a special way of mounting the mats. We suss out mats for the paintings.

The only ones available at the art supply shop are pale colors and thin paper, not our first choice. I inquire when more supplies will be coming, and the shopkeeper replies impatiently, "They are on order."

I ask him if they will arrive by May 20th. I see a glint of irritation in his eyes, "They are coming by boat!"

His words impact me with the realization that I had slipped into American mode where such questions are normal and can be answered. New Zealand is a distant island country. New Zealanders would be creative and use what was available. So, we did as they would, we used the art paper available to make mats.

Kris came to our place one day, "Would you like to hear what's going on, Joanne? It'll take a while, but it's good news."

"Sounds good, it's time for good news, Kris. Shall we have some rooibos tea?"

"Yes, thanks. Every time I go to the nursing home, I remind her what's going on and all the hard work everyone is doing for the exhibit. All my family are collecting art pieces and helping prepare the exhibit. Nephew Ben is being an all-around helper, and Irma is preparing an appetizer table, which I'm sure will be yummy." He smiles. "Yarra's dental assistant will make 20 chocolate éclairs. Melissa and Javan are cutting, stringing and wrapping bundles of lavender for the table, and Javan is arranging extra lighting for the paintings. I told her you and Vikki are framing and matting, and so many friends have volunteered to do whatever needs done. I showed her the handbill."

Kris paused, "Yarra listened, took it all in." His voice softens, and his eyes glisten, "Then she spoke very clearly, 'I love it!'"

Please come celebrate YARRA and her ART with us!

Fairfield House, Upper Trafalgar
Friday June 6th from 7:00 to 9:00
View Yarra's Art Recent and Retrospective
Digital Camera/TV Presentation
Light Refreshment
7:30 Music by Mosaic
Visit with Yarra, family and friends
Saturday June 7th
12:00 noon to 5:00 pm
Viewing of art,
Digital Camera/TV Presentation
Light Refreshment

We invite you to a celebration of YARRA AMOROSO and her dedication to art as a tool for expression and healing. Yarra's desire to exhibit her work is to CELEBRATE AND ENCOURAGE OTHERS of all abilities to use art in their lives.

Our goal is to make visible the tremendous power of the CREATIVE SPIRIT over the debilitating effects of disease, in Yarra's case, multiple sclerosis.

It all happened. We did our work, hanging many of Yarra's college pieces; and a throng of people came. It was wonderful. All the relatives and close friends hosted: Irma with her newborn wrapped in her baby shawl hosted a lovely table of delicious appetizers; Javan and Melissa decorated the table with small bundles of rosemary tied in cord. Yarra was able to stay in her wheelchair all evening, enjoying the people who came to view her art and visit with her. I glanced over and saw some favorite people speaking to her. Arvind, her therapist, and Mike Ward, a Nelson artist, whom Yarra loved to visit with at his street-side booth downtown. Both knelt to be eye level with Yarra in her wheelchair. Theresa's eighty-year-old mom, "Big T," gently held Yarra's hand as she visited.

Afterward, I was unable to sleep. My mind was crowded with many images of people showing appreciation both for Yarra as an artist and for her art.

"Chris, are you awake?"

"I've been awake all night."

"Me too."

"No regrets, though. I keep seeing the beautiful faces."

"I've been naming all the beautiful faces I recognize. I reached 96 names!"

Well over 200 people came Friday evening 6:30 to 9:00, plus a steady stream Saturday from 12:00 to 5:00 p.m. An awesome gathering.

We have been swept away in the ripples of that glorious evening. It has been an emotion-filled week. Hearing personal reflections of so many people touched us deeply. We had to ponder, discuss, and process. I would say we reached Yarra's goal of making people aware that anyone can use art in their life, regardless of their ability. She and our whole team of helpers lifted the level of people's perception of how to live life fully with a disability. She, herself, exhibited how she has Multiple Sclerosis. It does not have her.

Invitation to Tui

Meandering the streets of Nelson one afternoon after a difficult week, Chris and I hear a male voice call out, "Seeing you two is like a breath of spring." *What delightful words.*

Coming toward us is Steve, the owner of the Sussex, which was our first B&B stay in Nelson. We chat, and he says, "We're inviting a few friends over for some music for a few days at our new place in Tui. We'd like you to come. It'll be over Christmas next year. Is your email the same? We'll send you the invite."

Chris and I glance at each other. A few friends? Tui? Music? Who knows? But anything with Steve and Carol sounds good.

We'll ask Kris.

"And we'd like you to see what we've done at the B&B. Come by. We've created a handicap access suite, the only one in Nelson… because of your daughter's visit."

I fold my hands to my lips in gratitude. "Oh…wait till I tell Yarra, she'll be "chuffed."

Kris tells us, "Sounds like a festival. I've never been, but people who have a big enough place invite friends and musicians for a few days. I hear you can stay in trailers, or maybe they have some rooms. You can use my tent if you want to go."

Come December, 2003, we get the email invitation. We want to go, and we will be tenting with New Zealanders. But we can't imagine what else it will be like or look like. We collect some sleeping bags and camping gear. I go over to Yarra's. Kris said he would check his tent. I see it is partly up in the back yard. Yarra is sitting in her wheelchair in the shade of the house, laughing and laughing. The tent is moving around. *What's happening?*

"What's going on, Yarra?"

The words barely leave my lips. Kris' muffled voice, angry or frustrated, emerges from inside the collapsed canvas. "Open the door! Hey! Open the door for me. I'm suffocating."

More laughing from Yarra; I haven't seen her so animated in years.

"I'm here, Kris." I yell.

I fumble in the canvas to find the door and the zipper. Kris is silent. It's so hot and sunny; he must really be distressed.

Yarra continues to giggle. Kris appears, exasperated, his face red, his hair a mess.

"You OK, Kris? Thanks for checking it out for us."

"Yeah, I'm not getting inside that again." He glances at Yarra, "You had a good morning, did you?"

She's grinning. I think she enjoyed herself very much, but I refrain from comment.

Packed for the festival, we drive outside Nelson into the country. The farther we go, the more obscure the directions become. "When you come to a gas station, take the dirt road…." We crest a hill.

Before us, we see a huge mown hay field and well over a hundred vehicles, caravans and tents, and even a little horse buggy. People are milling all over…"a few friends."

Some folks welcome us, tell us we have choices for sleeping, "There's the kids' section, 'early to bed, early to rise,' the derelicts' section, 'party all night,' and over there," he shakes his hand at a small rise at the edge of the field. "That's for people who want to go to sleep early."

One tent is set up on the crest of the hill, under a tree. That's where we head, wondering if the lone person there will be welcoming. The lone person, Eva, is a friend from Mosaic choir. She greets us with a smile, "This is a good spot, quiet at night and close to the river for swimming. Would you like a cup of tea? I've just boiled some water."

I'm so thrilled to be in another New Zealand wonderland. I take my tea and sit against the tree trunk and smile on it all. After tea and a visit with Eva, I'll help Chris with unpacking.

There's constant music and musicians at every turn: fiddles, guitars, violins, drums, wind instruments and singers. I recognize some wonderful women singers and musicians from a Nelson acoustic group, *Cairde*. I can hardly believe that we are here. We learn everyone is urged to contribute to the entertainment. There are sign-up sheets for various programs. The "Liars Club," "Story Time," and ukulele lessons among them. Chris signs up for ukulele lessons. I sign up for "Blind Date," where random people make up a performance piece or song.

The constant sounds, colors, and movement of kids playing and of people practicing music, dancing, eating, and swimming dazzle us. I'm overwhelmed and more than a little unsure of myself when I find that the other "Blind Date" participants are professionals, songwriters and singers, the very ones I listen to on my CDs. I signed up for singing because I like to sing, not because I'm especially good at it. Here is Theresa O'Conner, whose St. Pat's performances we've enjoyed, and Evie McAuliffe, a woman I know and respect from the Nelson Human Relations Council, and the Cairde singers, Yikes!

Our group writes a song, "Going to the Festival," and our turn comes to perform. I try to disappear, back up, and hide my voice.

The group members call to me, "Sing into your microphone."

Of course. I try. I survive. It's an experience I never expected and certainly a complete change from what I've been doing every day. More like me, I realize, and I'm grateful. I've always enjoyed performing, but it was a long time ago. I wish Yarra could be here with us.

We grab our "togs" and follow a trampled path through tall grass to the Tadmor River, a clear river which runs through a cove of tall shade trees. A crowd of people are laughing, playing, and swimming.

Chris, with sensitive feet, picks his way over the stones, walks into the water and waits. It's cold to us, but not to the New Zealanders. They are a hearty bunch. Some of our new friends yell, "Dive in, dive in." He stands, pale skin shivering, and waiting.

A shapely young woman stands twenty feet away. She dives into the water. Chris does, too. She comes up out of the water, shakes her wet hair across her shoulders. Chris surfaces with gusto a few feet in front of her. Someone yells. I think it was Theresa, "He's had an Ascension!" Around the pool, others call, laughing, "An Ascension, an Ascension, he's had an Ascension!"

We head back to Nelson after a totally enjoyable few days. New Year's Eve brings another New Zealand gift. Chris and I are seated around a kitchen table, listening and laughing as old friends tell their favorite, personal funny stories. We've been invited to Theresa and Ian's and introduced to relatives and older family friends, and still others who are friends of Theresa and Ian's. Here we are again, where everyone treats us with cordial ease, as if we, too, are old friends. I am awed by this openhearted kindness.

When Theresa takes a moment from serving, she tells about the first time she saw Chris and me. She was sitting in St. Mary's Church with her friend, Peter.

"They walked up the aisle, Chris dressed all in black and Joanne in a full-length, purple tee with a Kokopelli design. Peter nudged me with his elbow, saw I was staring, as he was, raised his eyebrows, lowered his head and muttered, 'Not from around here.'"

Everyone laughed. We no longer felt we were "not from around here."

Choosing to Make the Best of It—Nurse Carol

As we strolled Yarra around the neighborhoods and parks near the nursing home, only a few people would speak or respond to our smiles. Were we too sad a sight to see, no matter how gaily we dressed? Did people not want to get involved in a long story? Were we reminders of what could happen to them?

We looked at flowers, ponds, and birds…but it was a long soliloquy. No matter how interesting the subject, Yarra couldn't respond. Did she feel stifled, left out? We weren't a team anymore. I didn't know how to change the atmosphere. I felt lethargic and sad. I believed Yarra felt bored and tired, too, and that made it even more difficult.

As the weeks passed, we began to notice small adults in the park. On different days, we saw two men; both wore dark britches and embroidered shirts and vests. One wore a pointed hat with a feather, the other a pleated, brimmed cap.

One morning, a very small woman with flowing, wispy hair drifted by like a breeze in a brightly flower-printed, flowing dress and black patent shoes. I wondered if there was a family of "little people" in the neighborhood. Their stylish, colorful outfits accentuated their uniqueness. *Similarly, I mused, to the way Yarra chooses to wear her colorful clothes. Is there a lesson here?*

We asked at the nursing home. No one knew.

At our first encounter, we must have looked amazed. We passed and smiled to ourselves. The next time we saw them, I smiled at them. After that, we tried to engage them in conversation, but they looked at Yarra warily and silently passed by.

At the nursing home, we met a private duty nurse. She possessed a winsome smile, bright blue eyes and long, dark hair, fine and wavy. She had a spritely, pleasant New Zealand-Irish patter. Kris noted her, too, and the next thing I knew, she was taking Yarra out—even in the van.

Kris commented, "I asked around and had good reports."

Nurse Carol Best changed our lives and Yarra's life. She was an excellent nurse. She had a gift for creating gaiety. She also had a bag of tricks for engaging with people, and she made her strolls with Yarra a secretive game. Each time they went out, Yarra and Carol made it their goal, to "teach" at least one person "how to be" with a non-speaking person in a wheelchair.

She and Yarra would contrive, meaning Carol would include Yarra in "sussing out" a likely participant to tag for their game. Together, they decided what might be the best object to drop behind them on the sidewalk, to see if "the participant" would pick it up and return it. If the person complied, Carol would respond thankfully, introduce herself and Yarra, and explain, "Yarra can't speak, but she loves to hear other people's stories." Or "Have you seen the flowers blooming on the other side of the park? We're strolling over there right now? Care to join us?"

Carol told Yarra about her "almost run over the toes" trick. She would gauge how close she could get to the shoe of a newspaper reader on a bench without running over toes. Yarra watched as they drew closer to their subject and saw all the action when Carol apologized as if she had run over toes, then introduced Yarra, told her story and drew in the stranger.

Nurse Carol opened Yarra's world. They became partners in zany escapades. I describe them only through Carol's retelling, in her slightly Irish, impish way. I would see the joy on Yarra's face as she listened and relived the story.

One lazy, drizzly, humid day, Carol drove Yarra in the van down to a grassy open field near the ocean. A moist breeze wafted through the open windows. They decided to take a "little kip," a nap.

A sharp bump against the van jolted Carol awake. Looking across to Yarra from the driver's seat, she saw a cow with its head in the window, eyeing Yarra's loose, long hair. Carol hurriedly pushed open the high van door. She swung out with the door, fell, and slipped in mud, face down.

She ran around the van yelling, "Out…out, get out!" slapped and pushed the cow out of the window and replaced it with her own mud-splattered face, arms and hands, trying to see if Yarra was all right.

Yarra was shocked at first, then burst into her version of uncontrollable laughter. That story was a top hit. Nurses would stop in her room, as they did whenever there was something funny or wonderful to share, to hear Nurse Carol repeat it and laugh again and again with Yarra.

The Room, An Essay, by Carol Best, R.N.

There is a room unlike any other, a simple room of quiet and calm where all are welcome to enter. Within the simplicity of this room lies a quiet vibrancy where energy, colour, and growth exist, and nothing is too loud because the noise is always in the silence. Those who enter do so carefully.

They tread as if on silk, they speak with threads of muted tone, and they smile with gentleness. Even the spider from the outside violet basket asks to enter to create her world of frail silver, to stay quietly with privilege up in the corner simply wanting to belong. The room accommodates her as it does all others. Those who pass by often glance in, drawn, not so much by the seen as by the unseen, and not so much by invitation as by need. A place of laughter and music is also offered within sharing, and gifts here are given with serenity and dignity. There are wide and shining windows reflecting balance as the breeze fans the ebb and flow of the world, and expressions of a heart come to life on the walls, created from caressing hands and brushes flowing with life. A glow fills the room, and strangely, on leaving, it cannot be remembered whether it was seen, or grasped, or merely felt within the moment of time, where some come to laugh and talk and stay a while; others come in sadness because once sadness was known here.

The Room has held many tears and gives the invitation for them to be left behind where they are accepted and then gone, being gathered and understood. Time is given freely, and you will be blessed to hear the unspoken, and feel rejoicing; you will be touched by the colour of living and will feel the need to stay, but with your leaving, you will know an embracing. You will come in to give and leave having been given. You will visit within a place of balance and order, because here the fire of chaos has been replaced with the path of peace. You are welcome. It is in the room where you will celebrate the world, and you will be refreshed.

Florida Everglades

Late in our stay, I receive a phone call from Chris Jr. "Mom, how would you like to go kayaking for a week with me in the Florida Everglades?"

Wow, how's that for openers? "Chris, run that by me again?"

He laughs, "I wanted to do something special for your 70th birthday. How'd you like that, Mom? I'm going with my buddy Otto. He used to guide the Everglades and still knows people who could help us get set up." Chris Jr. owns a River Center in Colorado and taught our whole family to kayak. I love being on the water; whether rapids or still water, both revive and refresh me.

"What would I need to get ready, Chris? Brush up on my strokes? They teach kayaking right below our rental house. We live a five minute walk to the harbor."

I've wanted to get down there and paddle around the harbor; this is my chance.

"You'd have to be certified in the Capsize Drill, Mom. That means you'd have to be able to get back in the kayak if it capsized. I think you can do it."

"I'd love to go, Chris. Are we sleeping in tents? The Everglades—alligators, right?"

"Focus on the Capsize Drill, Mom. Call me when you pass. We'll plan for when you come home from New Zealand."

My musing comment on alligators brought a computer video of a whale leaping over a kayaker on the open water. I believed it and called Chris, "Is that real, Chris?"

He played me along for a while then said, "No, Mom, just settle down."

Settle down, Joanne...yes, you said you would go. Chris and Otto are in this with you; they are reliable guides. What more could you ask for?

I'm down on the dock for my kayak lesson. Daryl, the owner of Harbor Kayaks, sends me out with Jason, tall, hefty, and young. His thick black hair falls over his black wetsuit like a hood.

"The first thing I will do is put you through The Emergency Drill," he announces formally, though I am the only student.

I am a little dubious as he roots through a three-foot pile of boxes, papers, swimming togs, and wet suits in the back of a beat-up van upon which is hand-painted "Harbor Kayaks."

He swings around, pointing at me what looks like the prototype of the original tampon, and asks, "Do you know what this is?"

I am forced to say "no" and display my ignorance, in the very first moment of my kayak lesson in Nelson harbor.

"This is a flare." Most of the orange paint is washed away. Right-angled rusted wire is bent along the sides. It looks more like a relic floated up from the Titanic, but I nod in compliance.

"In case you get into trouble, this is what you do." Using two hands, he yanks down the rusted wire that forms a handle. He unscrews a small, rounded green knob from the top of the object, again using two hands. Well, I suppose if my life preserver is very adequate and the waves are not too high, I will have one hand to hold the flare up and one to remove the tiny, round, plastic, screw-off lid. As the lid is removed, a small green ball attached to a length of waxed ribbon pops off.

Jason grabs for the small green ball as he demonstrates, "This is what you hang onto as you…jerk," he grabs the now dangling ribbon, "up and out. Be sure you are pointing it away from you, because it will release a white-hot flame. It will burn for thirty seconds!"

He stares at me ominously, and I read, "After those thirty seconds, you will be taking your last watery gasp."

Visions come floating to mind of a short trip we took last year. Whilst on a pitching boat, with both feet planted firmly on the toilet floor, my cold, wet hands could not even zip and button my slacks. In my heart of hearts, I know that if my life depends on my being able to grasp, point, and jerk a small, wet plastic ball as I tread water in the sea, I am sunk already.

I hear my voice pleading as I ask, "Who will be watching for that flare?"

I look to the imposing watchtower-shaped building at the edge of the wharf. "Rescue Patrol," it boldly advises in large blue letters. The door on the inland side of the building hangs ajar. Five men are chatting casually, crouched in the shade, "having smoko." I see no movement in the circular windows above. Jason's eyes follow mine, “Well, the guys are not always in the tower. But,” he reassures me, “there are hundreds of people who live up on the port hills, who watch the harbor every minute. They will see it and call in to report it.”

This I know to be true. Last year, we were curious to see some police along the quay road looking out into the harbor. Later, in the newspaper, we read of “a person up in the port hills, who noticed a kayaker in the water over 30 minutes and reported it.” That instigated a rescue. Hurrah for the “sticky beaks!” (NZ for the “nosey people” who habitually peer out the window to keep an eye on the neighborhood.)

Jason and I are out for a two-hour double kayak lesson and tour of the port. The water is so clear I can see the rocks on the bottom, smooth as a pond, and the dribbles that slide down the paddle to my hands are warm. This is nothing like the frigid, wild pace of “dodge’m, don’t dump’m,” Colorado River kayaking.

Jason seems to be well versed in many local topics and is imparting vast sums of his knowledge to me as part of my lesson. I am thinking about my survival.

I interrupt him to ask, “Where is the flare kept? Will I have it on my person?”

“No, they’re kept here,” he slaps the top of the kayak, “under the elastic ropes.”

That’s good, I think. If I capsize, I will just reach up to the kayak while I’m still under water and search around among the cords to find the flare.

Reassured, I return to improving my strokes and listening to Jason’s recent history of the port, which heavily comprises his daring surfing adventures along Boulder Bank. We are headed for the deserted lighthouse to which Jason reveals he is “one of three persons who have a key.”

I am delighted to be going inside. For three years, I have observed the play of sunlight on this lighthouse, day and night, in dawn light, sunset, moonlight, in every kind of weather. I have photographed it and sketched it. It’s part of my daily life here in New Zealand since we moved above the port. As we approach Boulder Bank, I’m surprised to see, at the base of the tower, a small group of women in silky, colorful skirts lounging on a blanket, sipping from stemmed glasses, and sharing from picnic baskets. Jason and I swing our legs into the muck and I wonder, as we plop by the elegant women in our flat boat booties, our clownish kayak skirts noisily flopping around us with every step, if the women approached their blanket wearing their high heels, or in their bare feet. Maybe it's a bridal shower. The pretty, laughing women remind me of Yarra. They are raising their glasses in toasts. *She would love it. What are you doing here, anyhow? Your daughter is in the nursing home? Stop it, Joanne, you're saving yourself, that's what.*

"Coming?" Jason looks back with his foot on the ladder.

The lighthouse is very tiny, a slender wooden and stucco tube. I twist and tuck myself up the slick steps as Jason continues his historical commentary, now centering on the watchtower keepers.

When I arrive at the top of the steps, I pull myself forward onto a narrow landing. There is a momentary silence in Jason's patter as we find ourselves, suddenly—eye to eye—breast to chest, give or take a few inches of flailing neoprene, under the roof and squeezed between the now useless metal casing of the old light and the walls.

Jason recovers quickly, resumes his commentary regarding framed photos of the families of former lighthouse keepers, and points me toward an open book on an old wooden desk, indicating I should sign.

I take up the pencil on a string and read the previous entry note "There is too much trash around here. Look in the desk drawer." Sure enough, the writer has not only complained, but has also helpfully picked up some of the offending evidence and stashed it in the desk.

Jason and I paddle back to the harbor to "go over to touch the boat." I'm wary about this. A sea-faded red and cream freighter is docked at the pier. By its depth markings, we see 44 meters (133 feet) of its enormous hull curves awesomely above the water, and who knows how much is submerged below. I'm surprised that just any boat paddling around in Nelson Harbor can access these vessels. I'm wondering if we're allowed here, or is Jason "showboating"?

We round the end of the hull. Jason slips the kayak skillfully under the public wharf with one stroke, into green, sun-shot water, carefully stroking by vertical pilings, sliding over diagonal shadows. The tide is in, creating for us, under the pier boards, a dappled, watery cave. I imagine I am surrounded by silence. Jason's chatter turns into the sound of twittering bats. I see myself in this strange and wonderful place.

Yarra comes to mind again. *All the things I do which she can't. Sometimes I see her watching me open a bottle, lift something heavy, move quickly to catch something. I wonder what she thinks.*

Back on the wharf, lesson over. Daryl is a lovely young man with spectacular blue eyes. The sun and sea have salted and fried his body and hair. His fingers and toes and even an ankle have deep, dry sores, which he tells me won't heal due to his constant immersion in seawater.

I talk with Daryl about my next lesson a few days later. I say, "Jason knows his business, but I still have some concerns about my paddling strokes, and I would feel better if you would take me out for the capsize drill."

He thrusts his scruffy chin seaward and sighs "I know, I can't stand him myself sometimes."

I am eager to try the capsize test, but eagerness is not enough to enable me to right the kayak, then pull my water-soaked bottom out of the water and over the side of the bobbing kayak. Exhausted after a few tries, I look toward the dock, where I see Chris standing next to Daryl with a camera. *You can do this, Joanne. Float your legs up parallel with the kayak and roll yourself in.*

My legs fall in the kayak, followed by the rest of me; I twist around and sit upright on the seat, facing backwards. I look to Daryl. He laughs and yells from the dock, "Well, I've never seen that one before, but it works. Passed."

Birthday Surprise

On our return to the US in May of 2004, Chris and I parted ways in La Guardia Airport. He proceeded to Colorado. I met Chris Jr. and Otto in Florida, with my lightly packed duffle, as per Chris' requirements, for five days in a kayak.

On our drive across the state, I sit in the back seat watching a parade of boats and motorcycles lurch, clank, and roar by the window in a chrome-streaked parade. *Big Boys Toys, I muse. Not my style.* But I am on my way to an adventure with two energetic guides in the front seat. I feel the wonder of my being here at all and marvel at my good fortune.

More unaccustomed diversion as we turn on to 1-75, known as Alligator Alley, where, from my window, I see lolling, yawning alligators—big alligators.

"How many did we count, Mom? Thirteen?"

Now I really have something alive and real to ponder.

When we arrive at our "put in," Chris Jr. says, "OK, Mom, it'll be a squeeze to get our gear in the kayaks." He opens my duffle. "Let's see what you have in here."

I remembered the joke we told about a cub scout who got caught with an umbrella in his backpack. When asked, "What's this?" he replied, "Sir, did you ever have a mother?"

But Chris Jr. is serious. No joke telling. *I cringe, I know I have something on the no-no list, and there it is in Chris' hand: a medium-sized plastic bowl with lid.*

"What's this for Mom?"

"Ah, I thought I'd be more comfortable using that in the tent at night to pee. I did that when we hiked the Colorado Trail."

He looked at me with kind eyes, "Mom, if you have to get up in the night, just call me and I'll be there to help you. Let's pack our kayaks, and you'll see what I mean."

Chris Jr., Otto, and I spent five tranquil days, blessed with only the sound of the slip of our paddles, the ripple of water and the distant clatter of hundreds of roseate spoonbills and flamingos. Beautiful days spent gliding over still, green waters and under dense, overhanging bush. The only live creatures which gave us a fright were a Manatee, big as a bull, which shot up five feet over our heads as it leapt between our side-by-side kayaks, and the stinging hot "no see ums" that swarmed over my netted hat when I went outside the tent in the night. At the end of the first day of kayaking six hours, I felt the only muscle aches of the trip. They were worth it for the sound sleep I had on the sandy, soft hummocks where we pitched our tents. I felt very pleased with myself.

The evening after our trip, I walked into the bathroom in our motel room, for my first glance in days into bright lights and a large mirror. It reflected the face of a woman looking years younger and smiling broadly.

Pelorus Mass

We're celebrating Kris Kolff's birthday by going on a "bush walk," his favorite thing, at the Pelorus River Area. This morning at 6:00 a.m. it was dark and overcast, rain predicted for the afternoon. We drive an hour, chatting all the way. The sky has cleared, with just mild sun, which is a big change from the intense 90 degrees and higher we've been experiencing. We walk along a clear river through giant ferns and silver beech trees. Drops of honey exuding from a coal black fungus that grows on their dark bark fills the air with a sweet aroma. We tilt our heads to see the great heights of sequoia-sized remu trees. We hear the trickle of water and arrive at two secluded, moss-framed waterfalls. Enchanting.

We three stop as one, inhale the sweet air, and listen to the silence. We glance over the forest floor, spy three mossy stumps and lower ourselves down, without questioning. Golden shafts of light pierce the green darkness. Nothing moves. Time passes; we sit mesmerized, silent and peaceful. For the first time, I feel "us," not individuals pursuing our own quest, but a team for Yarra and for each other.

We barely get the car doors closed when the heavens open and splats of rain pelt the car roof. There is no talking over such fierce drumming, partly because we are tired, and for me, because I feel something new—Chris and Kris as brothers, the three of us standing together for the good of us all. By the time we turn into the drive, high winds whip sheets of rain across our path and bend the trees over the house. "Well, Happy Birthday, Kris! This is some gift… the heaviest rain we've ever seen."

Chris cancels a meeting with a friend, offers a plan for dinner and advises me, "Tonight I'm either going to get a video or go to bed early."

I start supper, go out on the balcony in my raincoat to pick some dill and chives for salmon and have trouble pulling the door closed behind me.

At six o'clock, Theresa calls, "Sorry, I should have called sooner, but it entered my mind and didn't stay there. Tonight, they are having a mass for married couples at seven o'clock, a Valentine's Day celebration. Ian and I are going."

As I set the table I notice rain running down the inside of the windows and puddling on the window seats. I muse that Theresa had probably called so she and Ian wouldn't be the only ones in church. It will be interesting to see how many Kiwis would turn up for mass in this kind of weather. Hmm…convincing Chris will be another thing.

He asks, "Do you need help, Joanne?"

"No, I'm fine."

"That's good, because I'll help you if you need help, but I'm enjoying just sitting here reading the paper." *Good, good, so far so good.*

I tend the salmon so it will be done "just right." I warm some corn and call Chris for supper. Suddenly, the wind dies down. *Good, good.*

When I propose going to mass over a video, Chris folds the newspaper with a sigh. "OK, if it's our Valentine celebration, but I want to read you my entry in the Lover's Day contest first. They printed it; how I knew when we held hands that you were the one."

"Congratulations, Chris. I feel as if we're celebrating our Valentine's Day already." We go out in the rain and reminisce on the way to church about how clearly we both remember the special warmth we felt holding hands on that first date.

We find many cars parked around the church. The place is packed, about 200 people. A table with champagne glasses is set in the foyer. Doffing their raincoats, nicely dressed couples greet each other and file into the church. Father Ed tells us the most visible sign of Christ's love on earth is the loving commitment of a man and woman in marriage. He leads us in a meditation, "I request that you hold each other's hands palm up and look at your hands. No, I won't ask you to look at each other, I know my limits," he chuckles. "Everyone holding hands?"

"These are the hands that..." Father reads of the traditional roles of husbands, the roles of wives, and the roles of a couple. Very touching.

After communion, we listen to a CD of Andrew Lloyd Webber's "Love Changes Everything." We're invited to share champagne or a sparkling drink in the foyer.

Chris kids Theresa, "Thanks, Theresa, for sparing me from an ordinary evening at home. This was very touching."

"I am grateful. It was very touching."

When we slide into the car seat, he reaches over and gives me a sweet kiss. "I almost missed that, thank you. It was a lovely experience."

Not the New Zealand Way

In the grocery line ahead of me, I listen to two young women wearing worker's boots and black, sleeveless tees, with "cut offs." One says, "Did you hear the space ship blew up?"

I glance at the newspaper stand, where I see a photo of the Columbia in flames and gasp.

"Good," yells the other girl. "I hope they all get blown to hell!" Stunned. I'm stunned at such vehemence. The first and only negative words I've heard toward…what? Americans? The United States? Our space programs? I'm not sure, but it is shocking. I walk away very sad.

Billy and Kathleen

I'm planning to go with Yarra to the rose gardens near Glynwood Nursing Home. It is only a block and a half away, but I am wary. I don't trust her energy to sustain her upright in the wheelchair, nor do I trust the fickle weather, nor my ability to cope in case something goes wrong.

Yarra is wearing a stiff polystyrene and Velcro collar, because her muscles no longer support her head. Did you know the head weighs ten pounds? She's dressed in a jean skirt and a striped, spaghetti-strap top. Maybe a little cool for today, though she prefers to be cooler than is comfortable for me.

We've come outside to discover the wind is still sharp, and it looks as if it may rain again. I leave Yarra in her wheelchair while I go back to retrieve my rain jacket to cover her. Hurrying, I return to find a man standing with his back to me in the foyer.

I'm not sure if he is a resident or a visitor. He is slender and tall. His jeans hang straight from a wide black belt. His shoulder-length, dark brown curls seem to have been growing out from under a thick woolly cap undisturbed for a long time. Is he a wooden toy soldier who has marched into the Hippie era and gotten lost? He clicks his heels, and it seems I see sparks. How did he do that?

"What time is it?" he asks a nurse, "and what day is it? I don't even know what day it is."

He laughs, a little boozy, I think. He finishes his conversation with the nurse. "Well," he clicks his heels again, "We're off to the rose gardens."

He dance steps out the door, stopping for a moment to reach for the handles of a new wheelchair in which is seated a small woman with a short white bob, wearing a baby-blue dress. He turns back to loop his hand through a plastic bag he has left behind the door. He holds it high, swinging it to someone inside the lounge behind us.

"Look, Tony," he calls, a huge, teasing smile wreathing his ruddy face. "Never go out for a walk without a few cans." He looks over his shoulder at Yarra and me and calls, "Come on, we'll have a race." Yarra is loving it. Her eyes are glued to this lively creature.

I ask, "Are you going to the rose gardens, too?"

He smiles, reaches his hands down across his mother's collar and pats her as he replies "Yes, by and by, but first we're going to…the pub. Come on, Mum, we're off to the pub."

He clicks his heels. Does he have metal taps on his shoes? He bounces away like Gene Kelly.

Yarra and I follow down the tree-shaded lane at a slower pace, maneuvering over the bumps to minimize jostling. The lane is lined with six-foot agapanthus leaning their bright blue globes toward the sun. They are above Yarra's line of sight.

"Can you see the long line of blue flowers, Yarra? Aren't they wonderful? Cobalt blue, your favorite. Do you hear the school kids squealing? They are in the swimming pool. Isn't it great to have swimming for playground time? You would have loved that in Longmont. At St. Mary's school, where I listen to kids read, some don't even dry off after swimming. They come in for reading with their hair wet and clothes dripping."

On the other side of the lane, a small creek flashes in the sunlight. Birds pop around in the brush. "Those birds, the ones hopping like black robins, are called blackbirds. Not like Colorado blackbirds, are they? Remember how the blackbirds used to swoop over the track at the junior high? So graceful, playing in the wind on sunny days." I can't tell if Yarra sees, hears, or understands any of it.

We turn on the sidewalk past a combination neighborhood store and post office. I can tell now which pedestrians live in the neighborhood. They are the kids and adults who look us in the eye or say "hello" with intentional warmth. They are accustomed to seeing the patients from Glynwood out for a walk, and perhaps have come to peace with their differences.

Others, especially the teenage girls, lower their eyes, stop talking and look away. Are they frightened to see a beautiful young woman, distorted, helpless? I push a smile if I catch their eyes.

We bump across the road to Broadgreen Home and Rose Garden. It's an historical home surrounded by lovely old trees and a rose garden the size of a football field. The bushes are drooping with blooms in all colors. Brilliant reds and pinks, as one might expect, but also flame orange and wine red, blackish purple, white, peach, lemon yellow, salmon, bronze, and gold.

The fragrance is heavenly. I stop and look into Yarra's face. "Can you smell the roses, Yarra? I'm sorry they are too high for you to see." No response, she seems so far away today.

"Oh, oh, here comes a sprinkle. We better head for home."

I spread my rain jacket over Yarra, put her arms outside to hold it down, and for her comfort. I hope the skies don't open in sheets as they did yesterday. I hurry as fast as I can without causing Yarra's head to bob.

When I get back to the entryway, Judy and Irene, her nurses, are waiting to put Yarra back in bed with the electric hoist before they begin serving "tea." I feed her a few sips of pumpkin soup. It's bland, even with added salt, which I found in the kitchen. She doesn't want it.

Tonight is sandwich night, so there is nothing nutritious for Yarra. She can't eat the bread or the cold beef or the beets and onion, or lettuce. She eats a sponge cake and pink pudding dessert, tiny morsels at a time. When I think of how careful she and Kris are to eat only nutritious, organic foods, I cringe. I remember what a good cook Yarra was and how she enjoyed having fresh vegetables. When she phoned from Australia, I'd ask her, "What are you going to have for supper?" She'd reply, "I'll have to go out in the garden to see what's ready." *I can't let myself think thoughts like this. They come up constantly, and if followed, they lead to comparisons of her life then and now, or comparisons of her life and mine.*

Later, as I am leaving, the tall dancing man and his mum are returning.

"Did you go to the Rose Gardens?" I ask. Mum grins, and, as if to offer me proof, waves a small yellow rose.

"We also went to the pub," smiles the son. "We lost $50.00, but never mind. We won $200.00 a while back, and we're still living on the winnings."

"Good for you!" I say. "I'm Joanne, I'm Yarra's mum."

Sadness immediately fills the woman's soft blue eyes. "So sad," she breathes. She looks up, her eyes glistening, "So sad. Too young."

The man catches his breath, straightens and shifts into action to change the mood. I sense he doesn't want his mom to lose her happy feeling. He reaches his hands down to touch the woman's shoulders and presents her. "This is Kathleen. She was born in the bogs of Ireland and never had a pair of shoes until she was fourteen. She wouldn't wear shoes now, if she had a choice." He squeezes her and puts his cheek near hers. "Why do I spend money to keep you in shoes?"

His mother crinkles in a laugh and presses against his cheek.

"I...am Billy. Well, Robert William Casey, but Billy. We lived in Golden Bay, the most beautiful place on earth. She lived on her own, said she 'had to have her independence.' Oh, yes. We had a great time, didn't we Mum?" We're all smiling as he pulls the wheelchair back, and I start towards the door.

I say, "So nice to meet you, Kathleen, and you, Billy. Good night." I walk into the parking lot. *I wish Yarra and I had gone to the pub with Billy and Kathleen.*

"Being Spoken To" in Stewart Island

Chris and I take a bus trip from Christchurch to Invercargill, the southernmost city in the world and the southern tip of New Zealand. We are looking forward to visiting Stewart Island, New Zealand's southernmost island. It will be the closest we have ever been to Antarctica.

My first impression of the small plane is that I am sitting in my parents' living room on their wide, wine-colored, mohair-upholstered sofa. The cordial conversation offered by the pilot and the familiarity of the surroundings causes the fifteen-minute flight to pass quickly. In spite of being jarred by the high winds over the ocean, we are landing almost before I have time to become worried.

It is raining when we arrive at our B&B. Our hosts inform us the rain is normal. The annual rainfall of 50 to 60 inches is harvested on the flat roofs of public buildings and processed for drinking water. Instead of walking into town, we have tea.

Cups in hand, we stand with our hosts at their wide, high, front windows. They give us a "locals" view of life in their community. They point out a two-mile, recently constructed, asphalt road; the only paved road on the island. They are pleased to have it because it traverses the central village area, very helpful given the heavy rainfall.

They giggle and say, "There had been a problem when it was first installed. A teenager with a gas-guzzling vehicle couldn't resist using the roadway for constantly 'hooning' back and forth. The folks living alongside the road were being annoyed. The police called him in, and he was 'spoken to,' but that didn't turn him around."

There it is again, the New Zealand bad behavior deterrent—"being spoken to."

"One day, the young man found his car missing. He went to the police. Our hosts grin, "The police played innocent, claimed to have 'heard about something metal reflecting light from a small island off shore, but hadn't investigated, since no one had inquired.' It wasn't long before everyone knew where the car was "parked" and who had ferried it out to the island."

Chapter 5—Transformation

Fly Away

In January of 2007, Kris phoned, "Is Chris there, Joanne? Yeah, would be good to have you both on the phone, if he's there."

"He's here. He's picking up the other handset now."

"Hi, Chris, yeah, doing well...doing well. Ahh...it's Yarra who's not doing well. She had a bladder infection a while back that kinda' wiped her out. Now, her doctor called to say she may be developing a slight pneumonia. We're not going to give her antibiotics."

Oh, dear God, we've come to this time.

Silence on the line. Kris says, "Yeah, you remember, don't you? We had a big discussion with Yarra when this new doctor came on board."

"Yes, I do remember that."

"We decided then that we wouldn't treat a pneumonia if it came along...and Yarra's OK with that, too, remember?"

"Yes, yes, I do," Chris says.

"Her body is not accepting food supplement either. She's pretty uncomfortable. I thought you two might like to come now. She really enjoyed the visit with Joe and Chris when they were here in December."

I need to affirm that, I think. I say, "Yes, the boys told us they had a good time with her and everybody there. We saw the photos of Christmas with Black Peter and all."

But why are we talking about having a good time? We're talking about Yarra preparing to die.

"Irma and Jan are thinking about taking the kids for a trip, so you could stay here on the farm."

I say, "Gee, we're just thinking of going to help Amy and John in Oregon for a few weeks. They're having a heck of a time finding milk that suits their baby, Marco. He cries a lot, and they're all exhausted. Since we're on the West coast, we might just come on to New Zealand. How would that be time wise? Get back to us, OK?" We hang up the phones and turn to give each other a soft, long hug.

"Joanne, I think we better go to help now," says Chris.

"That's just what I said to myself. Since you had stents put in, we've concentrated on other things like the Heart Healthy classes, exercising…the time has gone by."

"Well, it's two years. We're both doing better. We could go. I think it's significant Kris called to invite us, don't you?"

"Yes, I agree. Kris always thinks things through before he moves. Could be he's thinking of us as well as Yarra. We don't know how much she's deteriorated. I do want to see her while we can still connect."

We arrive at the airport in Eugene. John greets us, "Hey, how's this for good news? The neighbor couple came to tell us they're moving. They agreed to let us rent their place for a month so you could be nearby…couch, bed, table and chairs, fully furnished kitchen." He smiles, "Amy and I looked at it. It's clean and seems OK to us."

"Wow, convenient," I say. "So thoughtful of them. Isn't that an incredible coincidence? Good things keep happening to us."

The house is perfect; it's clean, comfortable and warm.

Amy is home for her last week of maternity leave. Amy and John have talked with doctors and therapists and changed Marco's formulas many times. We're learning the ropes: bouncing, singing, walking, talking, doing anything we can to soothe Marco. Beginning next week, we'll have him alone all day.

Next door, we meet our warm, round and darling new grandson. He's chubby with wide blue eyes and a fuzzy bit of reddish, curly hair. He hangs in the bouncy chair in the doorway while we dig into an appetizing buffet; Amy has prepared healthy, low-fat veggie burritos.

"Joanne, I have a new vegetarian cookbook that I like. You and Chris can flip through it, and we can prepare anything that looks good."

"If this meal is a good example, let's do it." says Chris. "Thanks for thinking of us."

Amy and John look tired. Midway through the meal, Marco starts to cry, and they take turns holding him and trying to soothe him.

Our first morning in Roseburg, the radio awakens us with news that the first snow in twenty years has fallen overnight. We push back the ruffled curtains and see tips of grass poking through light, fluffy snow. That's all we can see. A four-foot-high dense blanket of fog closes out the neighborhood.

"I guess fog doesn't make the news here," says Chris.

We watch the window. By ten o'clock, while we have been singing and rocking Marco, the fog lifts.

"Ready to go bye-bye, baby?" I ask Marco.

The walk around the neighborhood is eerie. The constant humming, undertone of rushing river water and high, white, fluffy caps tip boulders and stones askew in the dark streambed. The underbrush crackles as moisture drips and snow plops from laden branches. Dark, thick foliage glistens under infrequent shafts of light. Marco's whimpers crescendo to a wail.

Chris lifts him up into the fresh air, but nothing soothes, nothing improves his demeanor. Chris cradles Marco's head, gathers him closer in his arms, and begins to sing "Figlio mi…" *son of mine*. Our family lullaby opens a scene in my mind. I'm sitting at Yarra's bedside, holding her hand, humming "Figlia me…" *daughter of mine*.

I reach out to Chris. "Here, let me have him for a while." Chris passes Marco over. I think, *Marco may sense my discomfort; I need to change my song.* I begin to march, chanting another of the kids' favorites, "Hush, little baby, don't say a word…."

Chris pushes the empty stroller.

"Hey, Chris, it's a new baby parade. I wonder if the neighbors are watching."

Later in the day, the sky clears over Roseburg, and we see a distant mountain. John tells us, it's named "The Nebo," after a mountain in the Bible. We made up a new song, "The Knee-bone Mountain," to sing to Marco as we bounce him on our knees. Chris sings, "I'm going riding on the Knee-bone Mountain, I'm going riding on the Knee-bone Mountain today." Many similar verses evolve over the days as we sit bouncing Marco.

On the third day, after supper, Chris says, "You do realize we're putting in 12-hour days, don't you? I didn't know we had it in us."

"Yes, I'm beginning to appreciate what Amy and John have been going through. Imagine four months of doing this. If we have enough energy after we pack, let's offer them a night out."

I'm sitting near Chris, cradling Marco on my lap, as Chris pecks away on the keyboard in the living room. Marco has been fussy for several hours, but now we are just "hanging out" for as long as this peaceful period might last. Marco reaches out, encircles his tiny fingers around my right thumb, lifts my hand to his cheek and keeps it there. I melt.

"Chris, Chris," I whisper. He looks over. We exchange glances and both move our heads from side to side in wonder.

Midway through the month, Kris calls with a message, "Yarra is holding her own; she didn't develop the pneumonia. The days you picked to come work well with Irma and Jan's departure."

"Wow, Kris, Yarra is amazing, isn't she? She seems able to resist everything."

"Well, I gave her some grapefruit seed capsules into her feeding tube. Maybe that had something to do with it," he chortles. "Grapefruit extract is a strong natural antibiotic."

Speechless, Chris and I each hold our individual phone receivers to our ears and share a baffled look.

"Oh, and...yeah, you'll need to shift someplace for the first week's lodging, Chris. I'll look around in Motueka, see what I can find."

We're relieved to hear Kris' opinion that Yarra is holding her own.

We spend all evening discussing the call. In the morning, Chris emails the family:

Email Regarding Conversation with Kris Kolff about Advanced Directives

Hi loved ones, Kris Kolff and I were reviewing what they and we have just been through with Yarra. It may well have been a good awakening for us to prepare for the future. Kris decided not to give antibiotics when Yarra developed her pneumonia. His thinking was that this is what she wanted and she was at peace with this decision. He reviewed this with Vikki and other trusted friends. Inadvertently, or by the hand of a higher power, he did give her a grapefruit seed extract, which is an antibiotic, and may or may not have contributed to her recovery.

Yesterday, Kris reread her living will. Yarra very clearly stated if she had a terminal illness and had no hope of surviving, she would not want her life prolonged by extraordinary means (these aren't the exact words but close). By the way, MS by itself is not considered a terminal illness. People with MS usually die of complications or other causes, so she was referring to other circumstances, not just her MS.

He also read her advanced directives asking him to make medical decisions for her if and when she was unable to do so. She also mentioned her quality of life in the will. (Chiara spent a lengthy time helping her express and write this some years ago). It was revised annually when Yarra was more able to communicate, it included trips to a coffee shop where she could smell the coffee, seeing green vegetation from her window, painting, seeing the sunsets, and I'm not sure what else). If and when her quality of life were severely lacking in those things, she or Kris, as her agent, had the right to have her feeding tube removed.

This is, of course, a very difficult decision to make. Stopping antibiotics and accepting the results is a much easier decision. Kris told me this is a decision

> he hopes he will not have to make and, at the present time, is not contemplating it. He has had discussions with her doctors, and, if at any time he would suggest this to them, they would have at least two doctors involved plus the staff that is caring for her and a representative of her family involved in the decision making.
>
> If it were agreed to remove the feeding tube, there would be sufficient time for one or more family members to be with her during the time she was without feeding. Please feel free to discuss this with me or Kris, if you so desire. Love, Dad

Chris then spent hours hunched over the computer conjuring up a week's R&R on the very northern tip of New Zealand. We've never seen that historic, semi-tropical part of the country and anticipate it will be warm, wonderful, and relaxing.

Suitcases wait at the door. Amy arrives with Marco in her arms and hands him to us one at a time for a goodbye hug. He lays his little head on each of our shoulders and keeps it there quietly. We four stand gazing into each other's eyes over Marco's warm round head, awed. In our Heart Health Class we learned, "The heart responds positively to appreciation and gratitude." In that moment, I knew it was true for our own hearts.

John drives us to Eugene for the shuttle to the airport. He assures us, "I know the driver. He's a good guy. He'll take care of everything for you."

We board our plane to New Zealand. Sinking into our seats, we buckle seat belts over blankets. I say, "Hope you can get some sleep."

"See you in Auckland," responds Chris.

We push in earplugs and snap on eye masks.

The stewardesses' voices, "Would you like warm washcloths?" and the aroma of breakfast warming stir us from our rest. In the Air New Zealand's Boeing 777, with comfortable wide seats, it's been a good 18 hours of napping, and wakeful resting and reading. The flight crew provides courteous service, from lowered lights to lowered voices.

Our plan has us arriving in Auckland on Sunday, a low traffic day, for the drive out of the city. We are well rested when we hear the pilot's "Welcome to Auckland, New Zealand, on this balmy morning. The temperature outside is 16 degrees Celsius. It's 5:15 a.m. New Zealand-time. Reset your watches, and reset your calendars ahead one day. Today is Monday, the 26th of February."

Monday? Not Sunday? Whoops, we forgot to allow for a lost day. The car rental agent assures us the traffic will be light for a while yet. He hands us a map saying, "Most people prefer to drive up the east side of the island on Highway 1 and down the west side on 12."

"Hey, looks easy," Chris says, showing me the long, straight, red line on the map. "Ready for some left-hand driving, or would you rather navigate this morning?"

"I'm your navigator today, if you don't mind. I'll get used to it a bit before I drive, OK?"

Auckland's good motorways speed us past the combination of conventional, English-style public buildings and cozy bungalows. Soon, we are out into rolling green fields spiked with occasional nikau palms. Atop their trunks, they raise swaying fronds that reach to the sky. It is incongruous to see a cluster of cattle gathered at the base of a nikau palm, where there is no shade. I count them.

"Hey, Chris, I see at least twenty cows all crowded on a knoll over there. Twenty cows on the head of a knoll instead of twenty angels on the head of a pin."

Chris shoots back, "No, you mean, 'knoll cowherd,' don't you?"

"Oh, funny, you just can't miss a pun can you? Hey, let's see who spots a Welcome Swallow first."

"They're blue and white, aren't they?"

"Yes, with a long, forked tail and orange breast. They should be here."

Not the Kiwi Norm

On Monday afternoon, though it's almost evening, the sun is still high in the sky. Usually it would be the time we are flying from Auckland to Nelson. Instead, we're driving through north Auckland and skimming along the almost empty streets to The Beachside Hotel, a hotel where Chris Jr. stayed in December. The Internet promised it to be "efficient, quiet, a convenient home away from home." It was right-priced and near the airport. Other than that, we had no expectations.

"There's the number, 3591 Beach Road," I say.

"Sure looks strange—like business offices, don't you think?" Chris says. We pull alongside a towering, glass-walled monolith surrounded by stairs and a cement dais.

"Here's a parking ramp," Chris says. "I'll go down, see what we can find."

We descend, park in guest parking and follow the sign, "Elevator to The Beachside Hotel Entrance." The elevator doors open, and we look through glass walls into a ground floor of highly-polished, golden tile and burnished steel. No one is standing behind the long, black counter. No one is in sight at all. We look for buttons, sliding doors, slots, and we finally find a speaker-audio box inserted in the wall, covered by a heavy glass door.

We open the door and hear a New Zealand accented woman's voice "Welcome to The Beachside Hotel. Please tell us your name, address and telephone number so we may confirm your registration."

Chris speaks into a screened black box attached to the wall. Silence. We wait.

The woman's voice resumes. "We hope you enjoy your stay. You may approach the doorway to your right. Your room is 345 on the third floor. Repeat your details into the floor phone for entry to your room. In case of any emergency or questions, pick up any phone. We hope you have a pleasant stay. Cheerio."

Chris and I look blankly at each other.

"Flummoxed," I announce. "That's the word I'd choose. Wouldn't you say flummoxed?"

"It's so not New Zealand," Chris murmurs. As we walk to the right of a section of glass, it slowly slides open. *A motion sensor or a sound sensor? It's weird.*

The lobby is utterly silent, stainless, sterile, odorless, and modern to an extreme—in metal, dark wood, granite tile and glass, and efficient. We enter room 345 by telephone message, as we were advised.

Our room is designed in tidy, straight lines. There is comfortable black leather furniture and a narrow balcony window screened by glimmering, sand-colored, gauze drapes. Beyond the window, we see a portion of magnificent sunset sky reflected on Auckland Bay. I walk toward the window. There is nothing to distract us from a good night's sleep.

A flicker of movement and color distracts me as I unpack my necessities for tonight and tomorrow. I walk toward the window.

"Look, Chris." My voice slips out in a whisper. Outside, above the privacy wall dividing the balcony from the neighboring apartment, a bit of color flips in the breeze. I angle closer to the window edge and peek out. Ragged strips of red cotton rag tie a cascade of green tomato leaves to a bamboo stake.

I grin and point my finger. "All is well, Chris. The New Zealand organic resistance is alive and living next door to us in The Shore Tower."

In the morning, Chris leaves for breakfast. I'm rested and anxious. I'm anxious, period. This place, where all night long, not a sound was heard, where no trace of human activity was spotted except the rogue tomato plant, is too quiet, spooky.

Yarra listens to what occurs in the hallway, the nurses say. She listens to decipher sounds that will clue her to what's going on outside her door. She hears the conversations of the nurses, cooks serving trays of food, aides wheeling patients, the tapping of maintenance personnel, and chatting visitors. Inside her room, the walls are covered with reminders that she is loved. But for much of her life, unless someone comes, the phone rings, or mail arrives, she's alone, listening, waiting.

One day she was physically sagging. Nothing I said or showed her caught her interest or lifted her spirits. I sat in a chair beside the bed. I heard the sound of heavy shoes in the hallway. Yarra's eyes shifted so slightly. The door swung in, slowly. Kris' white curls appeared first, then his bright smile, blue eyes and a sincere, steady, "Hello, Beauty."

The kindest, sweetest words—my heart melted. Yarra heard those words. Did I see a bit of a twinkle? Never mind, she surely heard them, bless this man.

In Auckland, we pull out of the dark, underground car park, heading toward the airport. Bright and low on the horizon, the rising winter sun blasts light across the flat surface of the marina straight into our windshield. Chris slows and reaches for his sunglasses. I squint, my eyes watering. I can see swaths of sidewalks, deserted, except for a few neatly-dressed walkers, perhaps going to a nearby church.

"There it is, St. Thomas Catholic Church."

"We're on time." Chris glances at the car clock, "and we have time. Shall we?" Inside a modern, white stucco church, colored glass window designs combine nautical and liturgical elements. The service has begun. The priest is speaking. It can't be the gospel already? I can't hear what the priest is saying, but the people laugh.

"What is it, Chris?"

Chris whispers, "He told a joke, I didn't hear it all." We settle into our pew, and I cast my eyes about to see a variety of parishioners of various dress and skin tones: Maori, Asians, and a family group of Cook Islanders; the females, young and older, wear traditional, long, pastel dresses and large, intricately-woven, white straw hats They sit side by side with New Zealanders in sun dresses or Bermuda shorts with knee socks.

During the Lord's Prayer, the congregation recites, "save us from the time of trial." That line, which New Zealand Catholics say, instead of "deliver us from evil," always causes me to ponder. *In the New Zealand culture is trial preferable to evil? Is trial more akin to their expression, "going through a rough patch," a time to be endured rather than a concrete force? God, give me the courage and resilience of these hardy people."*

We drive away through a restaurant district. Over an open doorway, two muscular gilded dragons breathe flame-colored letters blazing, "Yummy Tummy." We laugh, and Chris says, "Looks like the Asian immigrants are adopting the New Zealand sense of humor."

"Or it's their best attempt with the English language and their own sense of humor? Remember 'Chippen' Nails' in Colorado?"

"Actually, it looks like an ad for antacids," Chris says. I giggle, aware that I suddenly feel less tense, and I'm grateful. Chris makes another turn, and we see a sign for a restaurant on a corner called "Thai D Up." We both burst out laughing.

"Oh, isn't that great? 'Tidy' is high praise in New Zealand; we hear that all the time—'a tidy lot...garden...outfit...shop...even a tidy person.'"

"They got that one right. Let's stop, shall we? We have time, and I'm hungry, are you?"

We munch tidy spring rolls, fresh and crunchy. "Can we talk about something?" Chris asks.

"Yes," I say "but it depends on the topic…I'm feeling pretty apprehensive." My words tumble out. "Yarra's probably changed a lot in two years. She might not know us. We've changed, too; we're thinner, older. I think it's going to be hard. I don't know how I'll react. I'm scared."

Chris says, "That's just what I want to ask you about. I'm thinking we're both tired. If Yarra doesn't come to the airport to meet us, let's go right to the B&B, and then go see her tomorrow at the new place."

"Good thinking, but she may be expecting us. Let's see how it goes."

We return to the car. Chris glances over, tilts his head and asks, "How'd you like to take a beach walk before we head to the airport?"

"Oh, yes, yes, I would. That's a wonderful idea." He pulls up along a slip of deserted beach.

"Want to walk alone? We have about fifteen minutes."

I nod. "Perfect."

The weather today is what New Zealanders call "settled," no wind, mild, and with morning sun. We attempt to stroll silently, but we scatter the ferreting gulls. They scream at us, threaten us with sturdy, yellow-hooked bills, and flap their wings to chase off fellow foragers who have rushed in to snatch scraps in the discarded food wrappers.

I turn away, looking for flotsam and shells, "a Yarra thing." Her art is filled with bits and pieces from the beach. Pips and cockleshells; that's all there are on this beach, but they are different shades than Tahunanui Beach shells. They're the same shape, but more pastel colors: salmon, pink, lavender, grey, tan. I scoop up a few I think are especially lovely. Yarra will like these. An image comes to mind. *I see myself tucking the shells into her hand.*

Mirror Image

Floor-to-ceiling glass walls usher a sun-filled sky into Auckland Airport. We wheel our carry-on luggage through the streams of travelers and pass a ten-foot-high, free-standing, carved and glossy-painted fun-house mirror framed on two sides with wooden palm trees. Across the top, pink seashells bounce above aqua waves. A kiddie pool-sized yellow sun perches on a corner of the frame and beams down with large red letters, **"YOU, IN NEW ZEALAND!"**

Do they really need the capital letters? They caught me. Newly arrived, travel weary, misshapen and wobbly, re-entering their playful society. My long nose is longer, my small eyes smaller. My treasured New Zealand woolly, black, no-waistband, pull-on trousers reflect as a long swath of pleated, s-shaped, hip-to-toe drapes. *Oh, yikes.* My vest of possum fur balloons my chest to wheelbarrow size. The arms of my black knit sweater hang down to my knees. *Yikes, again.* I'm walking on water above the wooden waves. Me, in New Zealand, wildly askew. *Too right!*

My hair shoots out in auburn shreds, no longer the experimental blond streaks the New Zealand beauticians insisted on. My shoulders are stooped, and I look tired. No distortions there. I pull my shoulders back. The slight shift zooms my whole body up ten feet, skinny as a pole with enormous feet. Well, I have lost weight, but not that much in two years, with our new vegan diet. I move an inch to the right…there it is…my real smile, the best part of my face. *Thanks for the fun, New Zealand, and whoever that whimsical Kiwi is, in the Art in Public Places department, or the talented student from a Poly-Tech who thought up this little game…just for us, just for fun.*

Chris walks ahead of me; his white curls catch the light. His athletic body and medium frame have been kept fit by years of keeping a promise to himself to live a healthier life than his beloved dad, Joe.

Grandpa Joe Amoroso was a kindly philosopher, loving father and husband, and an excellent butcher. A connoisseur of aged steaks, cold cuts, and cheeses. He was proud of his life in America. He enjoyed his family, good food, his store, and his customers. He smoked, had an occasional beer, played the French horn, treated himself to a game of golf and opera whenever he could find it. He died suddenly at fifty-five of a heart attack.

Chris has modified his lifestyle in every way possible. He's race-walked thousands of miles, the equivalent of more than twice the circumference of the world. He doesn't smoke and controls his diet.

Despite that, we've been away from Yarra for two years because he "felt a little winded" while competing in a mountain marathon in Colorado. He's had stents put in his heart twice. We've attended Heart Healthy classes and modified our diets. He's half-guarded, half-joking when he says, "At 72, I've come successfully to an age where I don't need to worry about 'dying prematurely.'"

He waits, looking back for me; composed, patient, his handsome Italian features lined with fatigue. Under his bushy, grey eyebrows and above his full lips, his soft grey-green eyes reflect tenderness.

"Coming?" He smiles. His face comes alive. "Next stop, Nelson." My "joy boy" for fifty plus years.

I relax on the flight to Nelson. I can't help but notice that the stewardesses' uniforms have changed dramatically. Gone are the military deep blues and the cocked flight hat. Our stewardess wears a stylish, feminine, aqua-green suit, which is no doubt made of New Zealand wool. It's draped by a blue-green scarf, glamorous, but impractical, its loveliness being constantly flipped out of her way.

As we near Nelson, she passes up the aisle of the small plane. She turns from side to side, offering a small basket of cellophane-wrapped, colored candy. Just as we were first charmed to hear on our first visit, she asks, "Would you care for a lolly?"

We see Kris standing on the platform roof of Nelson Airport. As we enter the terminal, he is coming down the steps, smiling. He is looking lively in his favorite US western shirt, now worn to a soft, sunset pink. He has a fresh haircut, probably in preparation for his brother Walter's wedding in Christchurch. We spend minutes just holding each other, hugs full of compassion and knowing.

"How are you feeling?" he asks. "Would you like a 'cuppa' or tea before we take the drive?"

"Oh, yes, one of those New Zealand cuppas would be great," I say. And then murmur, "I had half expected to see Yarra here today."

"No, no. She can't take the long ride anymore." Kris' blue eyes focus on mine, "It's two years, Joanne, and she's gone down quite a bit."

He's trying to prepare me. I hate and appreciate it at the same time. Crockery bowls of aromatic coffee arrive with designs of the New Zealand fern floating in creamy froth. "Oh, wonderful, Kris, look at this. I've missed this."

We relax as Kris gathers our luggage. We settle into the old Nissan we've left with Kris.

"How's the car doing?" Chris asks.

"No problems. We still haven't gotten that back window fixed; don't think we will. The garage bloke says it will cost too much to fix it, have to take the whole door apart."

"Well, that makes sense. It's mostly for your use, isn't it?" Chris said.

"But you know I'm leaving it here for you, don't you—when I go to Christchurch?"

"Oh, that's great; it's working out, isn't it?"

"Yeah, when I come back…say, you know I am leaving tomorrow for Wally and Judy's wedding, don't you?"

We nod.

"I'll just use the van when I come back. You can keep the car." We pull onto the highway.

"Say, are you two up to a welcome picnic at the farm?" Kris asks. "We wouldn't have it tonight, but I leave tomorrow, then Irma and Jan, Albert, and the kids leave next Monday. It's the only time we can have a get-together. Yarra's waiting at the farm."

Walking on Shells

We have a few minutes to rest as Kris drives us to the farm that Irma and Jan own. Kris lives there, as does Vikki, Yarra's longtime aide, confidant, and trusted friend. Mesmerized, I watch the scenes flashing by the window. People are poking around in estuaries with a hoe in one hand and a plastic bag in the other, to gather a meal of pipis and mussels, anise seed bushes along the roads, and tall, drooping, shaggy-barked eucalyptus trees. I catch the occasional whiff of manure, see kayaks on the rivers, and people fishing. Waddling paradise shelducks are flashing coppery brown and white. The Maori names on road signs: Riwaka, Kaiteriteri, Pokororo…things I would have exclaimed about years ago, or asked questions about, all seem normal, comforting.

At last we turn up a gravel lane, pass some pungent sheep pastures onto Irma and Jan's crushed-seashell driveway. We park at a low ranch house with many windows. I go to use the loo. In the hallway, a six-foot-high vertical white board is covered with words in Irma's even script. She is tall, but even she had to use a ladder for this. What new learning are they up to now?

Outside, Kris is waiting, "Yarra's out under the tree with the family. Let me show you the yurt first."

The scent of a wood fire wafts from the back of the yard as we walk around the house and past Vikki's caravan on a dirt path, through some tall bushes. A 25-foot-wide, tan canvas yurt sits at the edge of the yard, at the edge of a forest. Kris has built a small landing and ramp for the wheelchair. He has also arranged a sitting area under a red-leafed tupelo tree, a gift from my brother Joe and his wife Judy. I stop in my tracks. Tears spring to my eyes to see this extraordinary version of "home."

Chris asks, "How did you decide to get this yurt? Have you lived in one before?"

"Oh, I've seen them, and Yarra and I always talked about living in one. I knew this fellow who had one for sale. I went to see it and liked it. He taught me all about how to put it up and helped me move it. We did the work, and here it is."

I look down to an ankle-bending pile of stones and pieces of cement block stacked to form three steps. I cling to the canvas wall, no doorframe, yet. We enter a warm, well-lit, and pleasant space about twenty feet in diameter. It feels spacious with its circular, creamy-white canvas walls and wooden struts. Most welcoming, with treasures of Yarra's art, photos, and postcards tacked about on the wood. Light streams in through large, clear vinyl windows bringing views of the bush directly into the room. Piled on the old family furniture are woven woolen blankets in the patterns of many cultures, reminders of Kris and Yarra's travels.

Kris and Yarra's round, dark wood table, complete with candle and flowers, various chairs, and a bed and dresser we once bought for our rental complete Kris' home.

"Feels very cozy, Kris," Chris says.

Grinning impishly, Kris points up to the vent hole to a splash of new paint. A magenta round frame, with gold crescents, encircles a spot of blue sky directly over the bed. "What do you think of that?"

"That's beautiful," I say. "How'd you come by that?"

Kris giggles and shrugs, "I kept asking Vikki to do it. When she didn't get around to it, I did it myself. Yarra can look up at it while she's lying here resting."

I envision Kris carefully applying the magenta.

"I'm sure Yarra appreciated you did it, Kris, very thoughtful." I look up again. "And just the color she likes."

"Yeah, she loves it." He looks at the vent hole and admires it himself.

"Come see my kitchen." Outside, Kris has organized a long wooden table with a gas burner, a dishpan, a drainer, and a hose for water. He grins. "We're playing house again, under the trees, like Oz, remember?"

"I certainly do, and you and Yarra love the whole bit."

Outside, I see Yarra in her wheelchair reclining almost horizontal. *I didn't know it would go back that far.* I feel sad; she's lost the muscle strength to sit up. I breathe in and take a few minutes to center myself. I look at Chris; he, too, is staring and solemn.

Yarra's head is resting down on her shoulder, eyes cast to the side. But she is dressed for a party in an elegant black, red and cream skirt and a vibrant red sweater. We bend down and forward to touch her feet and hands, to hug her shoulders, stroke her hair.

"Oh, Yarra, you look so pretty. Your hair is curly and beautiful and..." I move in front of her eyes, "you're wearing such dramatic colors today. I bet you helped pick them out, didn't you? Did you remember black and red are my favorites?" Yarra remains still; she seems to be someplace else...waiting.

On the other side of the yard, a table has been set up near where Jan is tending a bonfire and a big, boiling, kettle of corn on the cob. Jan and Irma's toddlers, Cella and Yiba, hop around peeking through the drooping tree branches, waving and calling to us, "See you. See you." They are pale complexioned with straight blond hair, like white silk banners in the breeze.

We watch Vikki and Irma carry platters of sausages and salads from the kitchen. A World Wide Organic Farm Volunteer, or "woofer," as they're called, named Mary, receives cheers when she brings out a large watermelon. A few minutes later, more cheers go up as she and Irma return with two frosty metal buckets of homemade ice cream.

Chris and I stand near Yarra with our hands on her as the kids come over to greet us. Vikki, Irma, and Jan leave the fire and join us.

"Oh, yes, Yarra's been waiting all day," Vikki says. "And she picked out the clothes she wanted to wear, didn't you, Yarra?" She looks into Yarra's face and touches her hand. "She wanted to look nice for mum and dad." Yarra remains unresponsive.

"Come over to the table when you're ready. It's all from the farm—sausages and corn on the cob and garden salads," says Irma.

We stand with Yarra for ten minutes. "Your friends really love you dearly, don't they Yarra? Do you remember the day Irma was sitting with you and me in the kitchen? She said to me, 'We want them here, Kris and Yarra…both of them. We have room for them here.' Irma looked into my eyes with such meaning. I knew then how much she loved you and Kris."

When Irma looked at Yarra, I saw total acceptance, not sorrow—something I still have not been able to do. It's one thing to provide comfort, but am I still resisting reality, hoping she will be cured? Still trying to make it all better? I think of Vikki and how long she has been with Yarra. She and Irma, both here on the farm with Kris and still helping Yarra. What an enduring friendship. What a gift.

I turn to Yarra, "How good that Vikki has come to live here on the farm, too. Aren't we lucky? Remember when she first came walking into the house, with her long hair, looking like a little fairy in gumboots? We were so surprised."

Yarra's face is expressionless, and her eyes are far away.

"Here we are, Yarra, all together, with a bonfire and little kids popping around to make us laugh. Who would have dreamed it?" There's no perceptible response. *Maybe she doesn't hear any more.*

Kris would have said something. M*aybe not, maybe he doesn't see the change…or, given MS, he sees it all the time.*

Chris looks up, gives a little shrug and shakes his head. He touches Yarra's hand. "I'm getting hungry, Yarra. I'll go get something to eat." He looks up at me, "I'll be back, OK?" I nod.

Yarra's head is turned to one side. I can't see both eyes. Her right eye is out of alignment and hidden. *Can she see? Has she had a stroke? It's been two years since we've been here. Maybe she really doesn't know us this time.* My chest tightens. I look across to the bonfire and see the kids playing. I take a breath, look down at Yarra, still and beautiful. I reposition her head and pat her hair. Her black curls frame her face, her dark eyes stare, empty as marbles. My throat tightens. I swallow hard. My back is aching. I stretch. *What to do? Just stand here? Get a chair? Keep talking?*

I slip a hand in my pocket and find the shells. *Oh good, I forgot about the shells.* My eyes fill with tears. *Breathe. Settle yourself.* I dig the shells from my pocket, lift them, rattle and click them purposefully. I sift them from palm to palm. I bring them close to Yarra's face.

"Dad and I went to the beach this morning, Yarra, in Auckland. We stayed there last night and walked on the beach this morning. I remembered how you loved to walk on the beach. I thought of you when I saw these shells. Look, the shells in Auckland Harbor are a different color than the shells at Tahunanui, softer colors, more pastel."

I hold my hands in front of her eyes. *Can she see?*

"See the pinky salmon, the deeper lavender, the orangey tan… the sunset tones?" I hold them before her eyes, tumble them rattling into my other hand, tiny castanets. *Did I see a glimmer of recognition?* Hoping to create movement as well as sound, I lift her left hand and drop in the brittle pieces. I fold her fingers gently around the crackling shards, watching her eyes.

"Can you feel them, those pretty shells from the beach? I brought them from Auckland just for you."

Slowly, slowly her lips start to lengthen. I catch my breath. A gentle smile curves across her lips, as if she's remembering something. Her smile broadens; her eyes come to focus from far away.

She blinks. Her eyes look amazed. We're connected. I know she sees me. *Oh, joy! A hand full of little shells…who knows…whatever… she's in the present for now…we're connected again.*

"Hello, Yarra, oh, hello…Mom and Dad are here, Yarra. We love you. We're going to stay with you awhile. Just a minute, I'll get Dad."

Thank you, thank you, God, again.

We bring Yarra over to the party. Irma listens intently as I tell her in front of Yarra a modified version of showing Yarra the shells.

Irma's face lights up, and she leans over Yarra, "Oh, Yarra knows you, don't you Yarra? Oh, you should see how she responds to your voice on the phone. I always try to be at the phone when I know you are calling, huh Yarra? We answer the phone together, don't we, Yarra…just so I can see her eyes, so alert, so focused. Oh, yes, how she responds. Right, Yarra?"

As the afternoon winds down, we walk toward the car. I'm deep in my thoughts of Yarra.

Kris says, "Oh, I just remembered, I met your friend Mike at the airport. He and his wife, Annie, are going to WOMAD in Taranaki next week. Thought you two ought to consider going. He'll call Irma to get a message to you if there's still room on the plane."

"Whoa, wait a minute. What's WOMAD? Where's Taranaki? What are you talking about?" I shake my head in bewilderment. I'm bushed.

Kris says, "Yeah, too much for now. It's a music festival on the North Island. Irma will tell you all about it. It'll be good for you two."

Until our room is vacant at the farm, we're staying a day or two at a B&B in Motuweka, very close to the hospital. Our spacious room is on the second floor, with a great view, overlooking a bay. Our gentle hosts are a father and a young son who carries in our luggage.

The father says, "I'll send my son, Brian, up with milk and the newspaper." He smiles, "I hope you don't mind, I'm teaching him to have a polite and brief conversation with our guests."

Approaching Silence

In the morning, Chris asks, "Does this look all right?" He opens his arms. He's trim and handsome in black jeans and a dark-striped shirt. His hair stands up in white ringlets.

"Black looks good on you. Your hair looks nice. I want to wear something special for Yarra, too. Think she'll like this? I'm wearing an ocean-scene pullover and turquoise slacks.

"She'll like that," Chris says. "Looks good on you. Do you mind if I walk? I'll meet you there."

I'm behind the wheel of our New Zealand car for the first time in two years. I adjust the seat back and drop my sunglasses in the well beside the gearshift. A glint of gold from deep in the cup holder catches my eye.

My bracelet – solid gold, handmade, the links are replicas of various New Zealand's port chains. My big splurge, lost, gone for two years. Tooling around in a car with a door that doesn't lock. A car that has been parked beside the highway at various beaches; in the midst of the throng of cars at The Bin, the huge used clothing warehouse; in town squares, bus parking lots…everyplace. And no person has peeked in the window, shone a flashlight, or tried a door. I thought my loss was just one of the consequences of the life I was leading now. I didn't remember New Zealanders were part of that life.

Chris is waiting in front of the Motueka Community Hospital. The orange and bright yellow of mums and deep red roses brighten the circular cinder driveway in front of a one-level, green-roofed building. A Maori-style, long porch and roof extend the entire length of the building. Hanging from the soffit over the steps we see shells, strung on parallel cords, attached to a driftwood branch. "That looks like the wind chime Vikki made for Yarra. I bet she brought it over here from Glynwood." Chris glances up and nods.

Across the wooden porch, inside the double doors, a huge bouquet of tropical ferns and bird of paradise flowers welcome us, as does a young woman in the hallway.

A small blond nurse comes forward. "Yarra? You must be her mum and dad. I'm Crista. I took care of Yarra this morning. She's been waiting for you."

"Oh, thanks, which way to her room?" Chris asks.

"Best to go out and walk down the porch to the end, I'd say. Yarra has a nice big room in the corner, to the left. The only one that's big enough for her bed, the wheelchair and the hoist, specially for her."

Yarra has been here more than a year and a half. I don't know any of the personnel. Certainly, they don't know us. How much do they know Yarra? Joe and Chris Jr. visited in December. They thought it was "a good place" for Yarra.

Our footsteps resound "scrape-clunk, scrape-clunk, scrape-clunk," on the suspended wooden planks of the porch.

The sound unleashes images of a Maori marae, a ceremonial wooden porch which requires a formal request to approach and a response. I remember hearing the shell horn sound and the high-pitched chant of welcome. Crista welcomed us.... Then I see a flash of Chris and me driving a curving, winding road through towering kauri trees. Next, we are still, reverent, standing silently at the base of a fifteen-hundred-year-old tree, named by the Maori "Tane Mahuta," the god of the forest. The feeling of awe and respect we felt when we stood at the base of that ancient, silent, living organism calms me.

I remember, also, what Chris discovered a few years ago, that we have to slow down before we approach Yarra...try to match our energy level with hers.

Chris turns around, sees me stopped. "What's wrong?"

"Nothing wrong," I say. "I just remembered that we slow down before we enter Yarra's living space. Let's stop a minute."

"Yes...we've been running around like crazy, better get centered."

We pause, look over the greenery in the yard. Breathe.

Inside the entry, we are surrounded with a comfortable pale, peach color. Two chairs are placed beside the door. Perfect. We quietly sit, close our eyes, and breathe. It is pleasantly warm, and the air smells fresh, my initial test for good nursing care.

I see the founders' framed photos on the wall. From their clothes, it looks like "the thirties." The facility has twelve general admission beds and a small maternity wing with four beds. When Kris came to inquire about admission, the administrator remembered his mother, Tora, had stayed here for a while, before he and Yarra came from Australia to care for her at Riverside community.

Chris looks at me, raises his eyebrows, "Ready?"

I nod. We walk toward double doors in the corner, where peach curtains hang over high, square windows, "Yarra, Yarra, do you hear us out here in the hall?" I rattle my fingernails across the door. We sing-song softly, "Yarra, we're here; Mom and Dad are here." Chris taps, and we enter. Yarra is turned toward the door

Yarra seems to recognize us more readily today. We take her hands, stand by the bed, waiting for Yarra to come to the present.

On the bedside table is another book made by Chiara, a book for all visitors and caregivers to write notes. It's spiral bound, with a white, sculptured-paper cover and thick black calligraphy. "You recognize that handwriting, don't you?" I show Yarra the cover. "Your sister has made you another visitor's book. She sends her love to you today, as well."

We begin taking turns speaking to Yarra with long pauses. "Your room is lovely, Yarra…lively, too. All your artwork on the walls makes it "your space," for sure. Yarra blinks. *Wow, was that a 'Yes?' Maybe.*

Chris says, "We're early today, honey. We're going to Hein and Johanna's in Nelson, later. You probably heard them talking about "Compassionate Communication," the new thing Irma and the folks are doing out at the farm?" Yarra's eyes are focused; she seems to understand.

Yarra blinks.

"We want to learn more about it."

We lower Yarra's bedside rails. We pull two chairs up beside her.

I pick up Chiara's book…turn to Yarra. "So many nurses and visitors have written in here. I'd like to read some. Would you like to hear them, too?"

Yarra's face seems more alive, though her eyes are far away.

Chris sits down, holds her hand. "I'll read. Here's what Brenda writes: 'I love to come into Yarra's room after all the patients are put to bed. She is always wide-awake. We have a nice chat.'"

"Here's one from Annie. 'Yarra is high energy today. There was a ruckus in the hall. Yarra and I laughed and laughed.'"

Yarra makes a long sound. "Ahnnnn."

"You remember that?"

"Oh, hear this one Crista wrote, "Mum, you write like your sons, Joe and Chris, talk...about the colors, about the flowers and the birds." Crista must have read you one of my letters. She must have met your brothers when they were here, right?"

Yarra's lower lip drops, a smile? Or is she getting tired? "I can see the boys hamming it up for you and Crista. Bet that was fun." I touch her hand and hold it.

Getting to Know the Neighbors

Chris and I will take turns visiting Yarra. I'll go this morning; he'll go this afternoon.

Jerrold, the B&B owner, says, "No problem getting to the hospital; just go three blocks down the sidewalk, follow the gravel path through the cemetery, pass through the gate, cross the street, and you're there...easy peas-y."

But it is getting to be a problem, and it isn't easy. Midway through the gravestones and vases of flowers, the low, green-roofed buildings I assume are the hospital come into view through locked iron gates.... The sky's still overcast...no signs of sun peeking out... rain maybe. *I'd better find a short cut.*

A dry, mud-rutted track cuts diagonally across a field next to the cemetery. It looks like it's going in the right direction. I pick my way carefully. *Is Yarra waiting?*

A screen door slams. I pop back to the present. I am surprised to find myself in a backyard, gaping at a woman, who is squinting at me. She stands on her porch with her cat in her arms. She calls out, "Are you right there, dearie?"

Half an hour later, I tap and scratch my fingers on Yarra's door. She's propped on her right side, facing the door, all washed, hair styled and wearing her favorite colors, purple and red. She is waiting.

I greet her. "Good morning, love." I pat her hair. "The nurses got you ready for company early, didn't they? Hey, that's the galloping horses t-shirt Chiara sent you from Colorado. Looks great."

I stick out my chest, "See what I'm wearing today? Your "Wild Woman" tee, and it's a good thing. I pulled a Yarra today."

I see in her eyes a look of clarity.

"Are you ready for a story? I…got lost—locked gates, muddy tracks, I got turned around and walked right into a sweet little old lady's backyard."

"Ahhgaa." Yarra vocalizes a happy sound.

"Like you, when the bus driver dropped you off in the middle of nowhere in Peru. Or like the story you told me when you were in Alaska, about sitting on the little bridge over a stream and a gigantic moose and her calf moseyed up for a drink and hanging around." Yarra's listening, her eye focused on me.

"This little biddy comes mincing down the steps in a man's raggedy sweater and house slippers." I pitch my voice in a certain high, nasal New Zealand accent, "Are you right there, dearie?"

Yarra gives a spasm-laugh. "And I'm standing at the foot of her steps."

"Mona, that's her name, and, of course, she's got a cat. I told her I was walking to the hospital.

"She says, all concerned 'The Motueka Hospital? Oh, dearie, you've gotten yourself all catawampus. Won't you come in for a wee spot of tea and rest yourself up a bit?'"

I primp a little-finger-in-the-air-cup-a-tea.

Yarra's eyes glisten. *So, good, so good, feel connected.*

Tears sting. It hits me. This is what Yarra loved to do…go away… then come back to tell stories about the people she met. I swallow hard.

I see my counselor's eyes looking at me intently. I hear Mary's voice, *"Joanne, Yarra needs a strong mother now."* I raise my wristwatch to shield the tears in my eyes. I blink them away. *Did she see?* I go on.

"Mona's cat started winding around and through my ankles, like he was trying to get me to stay. Remember? Chocolate used to do that to you when he wanted you to pick him up? I knew I'd be answering questions all morning about how and why I'm here. I told her my daughter was waiting at the hospital." Yarra's eyes liven.

"Yes, Mona sent you lots of 'God Blesses.'"

"She led me to the front sidewalk, pointed me in the right direction, and then asked where I was from. When I told her Arizona, she stopped short and just looked at me. 'Oh, my, that's the far West…the land of Indians and cow…boys, is it? I hear about it on the tellie, you see.'"

The connected look in Yarra's eyes has disappeared. *Can she see me? Is she just turned toward my voice—hard to tell?*

"Mona grabbed up the cat like this," I scooped an imaginary cat as if to protect it in my arms as I watch Yarra's eyes. No movement, but her lips are parted in a weak smile. Maybe it's too much, I better wind it down.

"Mona asked me, 'But you don't still have cowboys, do you?' You should have seen Mona's face, so worried."

"I told her, 'Yes, we have cowboys and Indians, too, but it's not like the movies, you know. They're real people, just like anybody else.' She was relieved to hear that."

Yarra is fading.

I lower the bedside rail, drag up a chair, and sit. I lower my head on her arm. We're still, resting. I feel her breathing. I lift my head to look at her, "Fun story, wasn't it? When your social studies teachers at college dropped you off with two dollars and said, 'Find your way home,' you found your way back by getting to know the locals, right? Today, I tried to do what you did."

At home, Chris greets me, asks, "Would you like a cuppa? I set the jug." He grins at using New Zealand phrases. "Got us some nice Tarakihi to grill, too. This is 'linner,' OK?" Linner is Chris' pun-ny word for a late afternoon meal.

"Oh, that's great, thanks, honey. Yeah, I'll have some of that Redbush tea, that box with the lion on it." I let myself down and sigh.

"How'd it go? Tired?"

"No, not really. It was a good day. I got lost, and that made a Yarra-kind of story. She was interested and had the energy to enjoy it. I'm happy, but I'll tell you later, OK?"

"Sure, I just wondered how you are."

He says, "A lady I met told me you can spot the hospital grounds by those three telephone poles behind the buildings."

Chris is carrying my cup of steaming tea. He stops and sits down. His sparkling eyes have turned soft. "When I sit there with Yarra, I see those poles, just the cross arms sticking up above the bushes." He gazes off to the side, "I think of them as the crosses of Calvary."

The Walls Don't Tell All

On the wall are photos of the donor of the hospital and a plaque stating he was a local mercantile owner who saw the need for maternity service for mothers and newborns, and for the elderly of the community. Another photo honors the first matrons, white-haired women with shelf-like bosoms encased in stiff, white fabric.

"Imagine, Chris, our American daughter benefits from the generosity of these people, how fortunate we are."

"Yes, Kris told me they still have four maternity beds, and only 12 rooms in all. Yarra is the youngest long-term care patient.

"You know Irma found this place, don't you, Yarra?"

"Irma told me, 'Just fifteen minutes from the farm, so I can visit Yarra anytime I come into town, even with the kids. Remember when you went to the opening of Penguinos, Irma and Jan's Gelato Shop in Nelson?" I put on a kidding face. "Dressed like a penguin? The photo of you is over here on the bulletin board." I go to the board and carry the photo to Yarra. I giggle.

"Irma loved that you did that. Do you remember?" Yarra looks up.

"To hear Irma tell it, she was swamped, madly taking ice cream orders for the masses of squirming school kids going crazy and crowding the front counter. Irma was dipping her arm into the vats as fast as she could, scooping up gelato, but each time she lifted her head, she could see something big, black and wobbly from the corner of her eye. Preoccupied with the many little children about, she finally paused to see what the dark moving object was. There you were, in your long black coat, white swim goggles, the pointy yellow paper beak you made, bright blue swim flippers, and wobbling on your heavy wooden cane. That's just the way she rattles it off—so excited—in her Dutch accent."

I hope Yarra is getting it; I'm having a good time. *My Italian grandfather used to put on a heavy black coat on the fourth of July and walk two miles to town, in Pennsylvania humidity, just to make people laugh. Here is my daughter, doing the same thing.*

"I think that's what started your friendship. You two were just getting acquainted at the time. Irma volunteered to drive you to the stables to ride Chief every week, remember? But when you did that…dressed up like a penguin…that did it." I laugh. I see Yarra's attentive look. She "gets it."

"Irma knew how much effort it was for you to get your outfit together. How heavy that long black coat was. She knew your leg muscles were getting weak."

When Irma tells the story, she says, "She was even walking kind of like a penguin, but much more, in those floppy flippers. How did she ever get them on? Do something so zany?"

In the heat of the conversation, I mimic Irma's clipped tones, "I knew I wanted that woman to be in my life." That's what she said. That's what really cemented your friendship. Yarra seems relaxed, listening, alert.

"No wonder she noticed you, a five-foot penguin! Not your everyday Nelson sight." Yarra gives her spasm laugh. "Yeah, pretty funny, you were."

"You had already moved out to Glynwood when they sold Penguino's and went to the farm. Then Kris decided to move to the farm. He was driving in to see you, and it was too much for him, remember? Irma went on a search. This place was so unusual. They call it a hospital, but no one knew if it would be OK for you. Dad and I had come to Motueka years ago, to check out the nursing homes. This one, we heard, was so small, and you had to wait, sometimes for years, for a room, so we passed it over—didn't even look at it. The rooms in the other places were all small. Not suitable at all for all your stuff."

I check Yarra, and she is still listening. "Irma went to see it and liked it, then Kris went to check it out and when they got done telling them your story, you were on the waiting list, and here you are. You're here because of your silliness and people who appreciate you."

Compassionate Communication

Kris is waiting for us at Irma and Jan's farm, named Wanto Wanto. He hurriedly carries in our luggage. He's off to his brother Walter's wedding in Christchurch.

"Need anything else? Vikki will be here most days. Here's a list of the chores." He hands Chris a scrap of tablet paper. "Not much, just watch the garden. Pick things that are ripe and eat them. You can store extras in the baskets on the porch. Vikki will show you. Feed the chooks every evening. There's a bag of seed in the shed. You'll have fun herding them into the hen house. If you can't find them, Colleen, down below, will help you. I'm ready to go."

I see a big, office-sized white board hanging in the hallway. Irma's fine handwritten script covers it in columns of feeling words: joy, happiness, fear, hurt or loss, anger, guilt, depression, curious, disturbed, depression, hundreds of words.

"What's this about?" I ask.

"Oh, this is NVC (nonviolent communication). I forgot to tell you. It's a new thing we're trying, "Compassionate Communication." A fellow from the US, Marshall Rosenberg—have you heard of him?"

"No, don't think so, but I like the idea of compassionate anything."

"Irma was hoping you would be willing to let a few people meet here Wednesday after tea. They've been meeting here with Irma and Jan."

"Sure, it's their house." I look at Chris. He nods his head.

"You can just sit in, if you don't mind. Those words on the board are words about feelings. Marshall's book is on the counter. Take a read, but you don't have to know anything. We'll tell you more about it when we get back."

We don't have to wait. Johanna, Hein's wife, calls. "An American woman, an NVC person, is coming to speak at Fairfield House. We're having a practice session at our house before the meeting on Friday. We like it…thought you'd like to hear about it."

"Always something new when we come to New Zealand," I reply. Some of the farm friends had a meeting here last night. We're interested. Thanks, we'll come."

We stop by to see Yarra in the morning. She's had her bath and is sound asleep.

I go to find Crista.

"We're going into Nelson for the day. We came by to tell Yarra."

"Oh, I doubt she'll even notice you're gone. I'll tell her, though, when I turn her. Enjoy yourselves."

The curving drive along the bay, through farmland, is relaxing. I doze off. Closer to Nelson, I hear the whoosh, whoosh, whoosh as we pass the tall pines, and wake up.

I say, "Mind talking? Something I've been thinking about?"

"No, go ahead," Chris returns.

"Do you feel different this time…about how we're acting… regarding the time we spend with Yarra? It seems freer somehow."

"I don't know if I feel a change about how we are with Yarra," says Chris.

"Well, today we came by to tell her we're leaving her for the day. We're packing to go away for a weekend in Taranaki. Before, we were at the nursing home all the time and trying to manage her care. I don't feel the need for that now."

Chris pauses. "Maybe we feel more trusting. It's a much smaller place. All the staff are RNs. She's the only medical case as far as I know; the rest, all geriatric and four obstetric beds." Chris looks out into the distance ahead. "Remember way back when we first came? She said, 'I want my parents to live their own life?' Maybe that's what's different. We've been away two years. She's survived without us. And we've come to a place with her where we're not trying to stem the disease, or cure her, or fix anything."

It's true. It's easier now because we've let go…we're still here, and she's leaving, but we've let go.

"Yarra's World" ---from Chris' Journal

> "Yarra's room is like a poem and a prayer. It is full of her art, prayer flags, photos, flowers, branches, and lovely views of nature. An aura exudes from her serene, connected space. It feels like a magnetic

field inviting you to take a refreshing, healing break. Silence is spoken beautifully here. In her motionless, speechless, soul-full, spirit-filled room, serenity fills the spaces. Creativity is alive in her surroundings. Anyone who looks and listens and allows their spirit to connect with hers feels the joy and wonder of being fully alive.

Yarra says in silence, "OK, life, give me what you've got. I can take it, and I can make it mine. I will make it my beautiful world, thank you, thank you, thank you."

If you come into her world and bring peace and pause, she will share it with you, and you won't want to leave. You walk away marveling at the life challenges that she's been given, and you are awed by what she has chosen to make of them. You are grateful to be part of her world.

Yarra's life has been a revelation of miracles for me, and she is part of the life challenges that have been given to me. I, too, must accept my challenges and make my world beautiful. I have, at times, been too entangled in the details, and that's not where the magic and the miracles reside. They are in the spaces. Like the pauses between the notes, they are what make the music. Yarra's space is full of the miraculous music of life, and I am privileged to play in her orchestra.

You ask me, "How is Yarra doing?" It reminds me of when she could still speak. With a hearty laugh she'd say, "Disabled, who's disabled? I'm accepting what I have been given and making the most of it. How are you doing with your 'gifts'?"

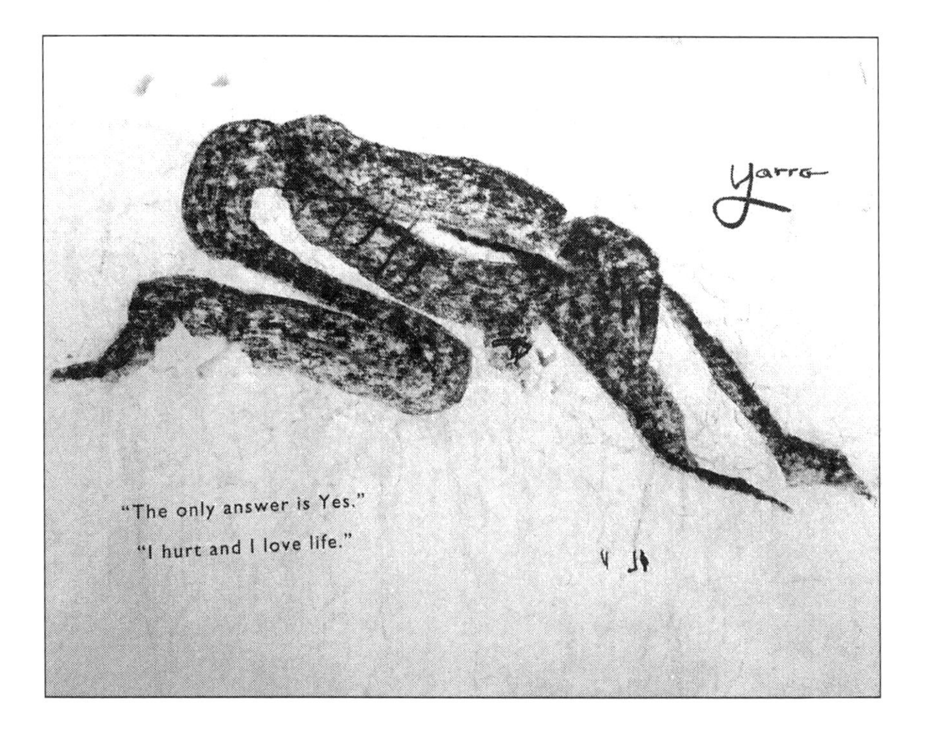

On the Farm

I've phoned Yarra. Crista is holding the receiver to Yarra's ear. "Kris and Chris have gone off tramping for the day to Abel Tasman. I'm sure they'll have a good time, hiking to their hearts' content." I hear an "ah" sound. *Yarra hears me.*

"We are learning a new way to talk, 'Compassionate Communication.' Hein and Johanna took us to hear an American woman speak at Fairfield. Today, I'm studying the book. You know we have so many green salads out here on the farm. I'm trying to find in the book how to tell Kris, in a compassionate way, that he has spinach on his teeth."

In the distance, I hear "agggh," Yarra's laugh sound.

Crista's giggling voice says, "She had a spasm with her laugh, and I dropped the phone. Whatever you said, she really liked it."

"I told her I'm studying how to talk compassionately to Kris. How to tell him kindly he has spinach on his teeth. I'm sure you've seen it. He's such a veggie." Crista breaks into laughter, and I hear

Yarra growling her laughter again.

"Tell her I love that she enjoyed the spinach story. I hear a vehicle coming up the drive. I'll call her later."

Out of the vehicle came Erika, Rene, Yarren, and our friends from The Brook. Erika was Yarra's physical therapist, and one of the family who lived here at the farm for several years. Yarren was a newborn and Shauna, a little girl when we lived at Karaka.

"Hello, welcome, I'm the only one here today. Kris and Chris are off tramping, and Vikki is gone for the day."

"That's fine. We're glad to visit with you, and we'll only stay a few minutes," Rene says. "I brought some fresh coffee beans. I'll brew you a cup of coffee if you'll share with us."

"Oh, that sounds good. I didn't want to risk trying the new coffee machine."

We sit at the kitchen table. Yarren shows me how he can make origami figures. I have a T-shirt for Shauna. Erika tells me how pleased they are living in Golden Bay and starting her new physical therapy practice.

"I'm so glad to see you and that you came by. I feel I live here, and my friends have come to visit."

"So, they have." Rene smiles, serving a fresh cup of aromatic coffee. He presents it like a gift, and it is.

"We'll stop for a short visit with Yarra, either now or on the way back home. It's a good place, don't you think?"

"Oh, absolutely. We're so fortunate to have you all as friends."

I begin the next day by going for a walk along Ferring Stream Road. Cows, goats and sheep graze in the fields. Hidden by the bush along the stream, twenty feet tall in places, the houses and yards are either meticulously tidy or invisible.

Over the stream, I see the New Zealand flycatcher swooping from a bare branch in a flash of turquoise, black, and cream. The sun is warm. I head up the road for a stretch.

Returning to the farmhouse, I enter from bright sunlight into a shaded kitchen. I spy a white tablet sheet on the corner of the counter. It's covered with Kris' distinctive handwriting:

Could you please let the chooks out about 2-3 p.m. Open the wooden door of the run and put the stone there so it doesn't shut. If we're not back by 6:30, please scatter the big container of wheat in the laundry in the chook run. Just leave the door open. The smaller amount of wheat in the laundry is for the three in the veg garden. Just lift net at the top and throw the wheat in. Kris

On the back, Chris has scratched, "Kris said if it doesn't happen for any reason it's not the end of the world, it's OK. Love, Chris."

When I look at "the three in the garden" I see they are the roosters. If I open this door, they will be three free roosters. Nope, not a good thing. *Kris must mean the "chooks" over the hill and down a steep, grassy slope.* I'm not sure if those chooks are ours.

I go down the road to find assistance from the neighbor who lives near the field where the chooks are foraging in the grass. She introduces herself as Colleen. She looks like an Irish lass in a long, soft dress, though her curls are turning white. She says, "Yes, those are your chooks. I'll show you where the gate is and the stone."

When I go back at 6:30 to feed the chooks, Colleen invites me in for a cup of tea. "It isn't often I get a visitor out here on the farm." A harp stands in the corner of her room and many of her paintings. She had met Yarra on her visits to the farm. We share a little of our lives. I'm sure Yarra was charmed by her. I am. *Another story for Yarra.*

When I get up the hill, I see Vikki getting out of her car. "Hi, Joanne, I brought some rockfish for tea. There are cukes ready in the garden for raita. Have you had purple potatoes?"

"Yarra introduced us to them and raita. She had the purple potatoes in Peru."

"I know. She loves them."

I chopped fresh greens, onions, and carrots for a salad. Vikki grated cucumbers. We boiled the potatoes. By the time we finished, we heard a car crackling over the shell driveway. Kris and Chris were home. We sat on the porch, exchanging stories about their pleasant hike in Abel Tasman National Park, my morning visitors, and feeding the chooks. We sank into relaxed silence over rooibos tea.

The milk cow came to the fence. "Rip, rip." Long grass hung from her mouth as she chewed and kept her eyes steadily on Kris. We all laughed.

Kris says, "She won't be leaving. She knows who's going to milk her. See you tomorrow. Good day, Chris. Good tea, ladies. Thanks."

Sorting Yarra's Art

Vikki, Chris, and I are the only ones on the farm. It is very quiet, peaceful. Birds chirp, an occasional cow moos, hens scurry around, scratching and clucking. Vikki has chores to do. Chris and I are walking the farm paths and side roads. We take turns being with Yarra.

Yarra's eyes are far away these days. I feel sad on the days when she is not present. I sit with her. Sometimes, I read to her. Sometimes, I think I talk too much.

Yarra's where she is, and I'm uncomfortable with silence. I want to engage her in my words, in my world. Am I wearing her out? I'm disappointed to find I still haven't learned the lesson of "let it be." I'm also uncomfortable with the fact that I still am not able to remember which direction to turn when leaving the small hospital parking lot. It's simple. I'd like to believe it's because directionally, this location is across the bay from our rental in Nelson, so everything is turned around for me. But it's so simple...disconcerting, probably stress.

Kris returns from his visit with his older brother. He seems relaxed. He offers, "There is some artwork down in the storage sheds. Would you like to look at it?"

What? I've been passing Yarra's art every day at the bottom of the hill, in the barn? I just never envisioned it. I never thought to ask. Kris lives so minimally. I never thought of Kris helping Yarra cart her art pieces around from place to place. I imagine them standing side-by-side, looking at stacks of canvases, discussing the project: the time, the effort, the money. She couldn't help him much.

Her early college pieces had been kept in our storage rental in Colorado for fourteen years. I forgot that. When they moved back to Australia, Kris and John packed and loaded them into the old truck, and John drove them to the airport in a snowstorm. Then they moved back and forth in Australia three or four places. She wasn't well. He did this for her. How did they ever manage? Four living places in New Zealand, and her artwork is right here? Why not? I feel I've been awakened to another part of their life.

I look up to see Kris' eyes, soft and wondering, "Maybe you're not up to it, eh? I thought the family would want to have it. I found a place in town that packs for mailing. I could take them there."

I pick up something different in his voice: calm, composure, no fractured phrases. *Completion, that's what it is, it's about completion. He wants to get this done. Don't blame him. He's waited to share the photos and art with me, when we could both "take it." Is that it?*

I breathe. "Yes, I'd like to see them. I'm just surprised to realize they're here," I murmur. "Yes, it probably will be easier for us to do it now than later, right?" *I see myself in tears.* "Let me talk with Chris."

In the morning, we walk to the barn to find Kris rooting through a cardboard box. He comes to the car window. "Morning. You two all right? Are you going to look at these, Chris?"

"We had a good night's rest. I'm thinking I could use a little walk. Joanne's OK with that. Can I drive anything up to the yurt?"

"Good, yes." Kris is already moving the boxes toward the car. "This will help."

Kris has stacked many brightly colored canvases and folders of drawings and paintings in front of the shed. Stunned, I stop, gaze, and absorb her work of years.

Kris turns his hand up over a box of early work, "I'm not ready to give these up yet."

A simple declaration, those he's ready to give up and those he wants to keep. That helps me. No angst about the quality of the work, the setting or situation, which would tie us to Yarra's story. Simply, "Are you ready to let it go?"

For Chris and me, it translates to which paintings do we want to take home for ourselves and Yarra's siblings?

"That's helpful Kris. Simple and very helpful."

A few large paintings lean against sawhorses and boxes. I recognize the Adam and Eve one from Yarra's college days.

Kris sees me looking at the Adam and Eve and smiles. "Ah, that's a good one, no?

I'm thinking, *I'm going to keep that one for myself.*

Sunlight glares on bright clear colors: a brilliant green Eden and a red apple with a white tooth bite fills the canvas. A fat, yellow python winds round the trunk of a spreading tree. A nude couple stands facing each other under the branches. She holds an apple to his mouth.

Kris and I gaze, and he smiles. "You know, Kris, of all Yarra's pieces, this is a fine example of the precise drawing Yarra could do before the MS."

He nods. "The pencil-feathered partridge, the one in the art exhibit?"

"Oh, yes, wasn't that perfect in every way, even the way his head was cocked, listening, and his foot poised to run?"

"She sold that one. Don't know who has it."

We walk up the hill to the yurt. Kris makes a "cuppa" for us. He has boxes of photos, some which she brought with her from her younger days. I love them and offer them to Kris.

He glances. "No, those are from before I knew her."

That's good. He's saying, "I am only keeping the part of her life we shared."

There are photos of Kris and Yarra's life together. *I don't need those...I can say that to myself, I have enough of Yarra's things.* But I pull from the box a set of photos of Kris' birthday in Australia when they first met. A crowd of smiling people encircle close by.

Yarra's face is radiant in the light of flaming candles as she presents a cake. In the second photo, she is pointing to the cake and watching him intently; the patient teacher look, "Is he understanding?" Her little finger is cocked. She instructs him on how to cut his birthday cake in portion-sized pieces for the crowd.

The next shot we see is Kris looking ravenous. He crashes his knife into the cake. She stares at him in disbelief as he drags a ragged chunk out of the cake. Yarra snarls in the next photo, in her famous version of the "Amoroso sneer."

I hear Kris laughing. I look up to see him smiling into the photos, or a precious memory. He is laughing at Yarra, and with her, and for himself—and so am I.

His eyes glisten, "It's who we were."

Up the Garden Path

Kris is back from Christchurch. Chris and I will meet him at "Up the Garden Path," a café located conveniently across the street from the hospital. It's Yarra's bath day. The bath and moving around required to dress and groom her drain her energy, so she doesn't come with us.

At the garden entry, a rusted bike leans on the fence with its baskets and worn leather panniers planted with sedum and cascading vines and flowers. Outside, stone, wooden and metal statuary created by local artists, and pots of succulents, grasses and flowers are interspersed amid half a dozen wooden picnic tables.

Kris is waiting on the wide porch. It's fun for me to go anyplace with these two fellows; they are both trim and handsome. Heads turn. They appear to be brothers, but up close Kris' rosy complexion and blue eyes are much different than Chris' olive-toned Mediterranean features and grey-green eyes.

We cross over glistening cork floors. Their bronze color reflects a warm background for the bright island paintings and photographs hanging in the dining room. High on the entry wall hangs a "knock-your-socks-off" six-by-eight-foot Rococo gold-colored frame, matted in red velvet.

It holds a Rococo, gold-colored water faucet installed in the center of the frame. Aqua-tinted water streams into a semi-circular, equally elaborate gold basin just above the bottom of the frame.

We order at the counter. Polenta cake glistens in the glass case. It's made of cornmeal, honey, and orange juice. It is my favorite choice. Kris and Chris order their favorite blueberry scones, four inches high, tender, fresh-baked, and chock full of local blueberries. The host hands us a stiff plastic card with a number. "Just put this card in the hand holder on your table, so the server will find you."

Kris spends a few minutes talking about his trip to Wally and Judith's wedding, but he quickly asks, "How did you find Yarra?"

"Up and down, but we've had more good days," Chris says. "The staff really love her and take good care of her."

"And they're on to her, aren't they?" I add. "I knew that the moment I saw that book, *Walter, the Farting Dog,* on her bedside table."

Kris' face relaxes, and he shakes his head. "Oh, they've had lots of fun with that. One of her favorite nurses, an older one, gave it to her. They get along so well. She knows Yarra like a sister."

"We have been wondering about her eyes, though, Kris," says Chris. "Do you notice any changes?"

"Yeah, I guess I didn't tell you. I noticed, too. She doesn't look at things like she used to, and the nurses asked if she could see."

"That's our question, too."

"I took her to an optometrist in Nelson. Irma helped me find a good one. She said she really couldn't test Yarra's eyesight, but her eyes look fine. That's the best she could do."

"There is a blinding condition called retrobulbar neuritis, which is not visible by exam," says Chris. "There is a simple instrument which can be used, an old-fashioned whirling black and white wheel that attracts the eye. Very few offices have them now. Too antiquated, I suppose."

Kris says, "The nurses think Yarra has limited energy. They say, 'She sees what she wants to see.'"

"Do you buy that, Kris?" Chris asks.

"Some days I can, other times I think something else is going on. I heard the new doctor wants to meet with us. We'll mention it to her. Want to plan for our meeting with her now? It's two weeks from now. That will give us more time to work on it." Kris pulls a small notebook and a pen out of his shirt pocket.

"Still using the five-colored ball points?" I ask with a grin.

"Yeah, but I don't need all the five-colored pens now that Yarra's at Motueka. Don't need to keep track of all the nurses and Yarra's special materials."

"I asked one of the nurses yesterday if Yarra's advanced directives are on the chart. She said she couldn't find them," Chris said. "I would have thought they would be transferred from Glynwood."

Kris looks puzzled. "Me, too, though I didn't check that. I'll ask Jill, the nurse manager, if she saw them. You mean the stuff we signed with the lawyer?"

"Yes, that's pretty important," says Chris, "Especially the DNR order."

"Well, you know they would call me before they do anything. That's the way we do it here," Kris says.

"Let's talk to the new doctor about those directives, especially the DNR," Chris says. "What else is on the agenda?"

Kris is recording everything. We spend an hour listing topics to discuss and papers we need to gather.

Kris says, "Hey, have you two decided about going to "WOMAD?"

Chris replies, "It sounds like a big deal. World Music. I heard they're expecting 30,000 people from all over. Have you ever gone?"

"I went donkey's ages ago, with Mark. The Dell, the park where it's held, is magic." His face lights up.

Chris nods, "We think we would like to go, especially since we can go with Mosaic people who know us."

"And sleeping 'marae style'...only in New Zealand," I say. "Forty people sleeping side by side on mattresses on the floor. That'll be something to write home about."

"Hold on there." Kris tosses back his white curls. "Forty of your friends, that's not so bad, is it? Naah."

"Well, maybe," I say. "I guess we did it on a smaller scale at Jessica and Bruce's music programs, but I didn't know it was, like...a culturally accepted thing, sleeping in the auditorium, like a grownup slumber party."

Chris says, "If you're OK with it, Kris, I think we'll sign up. Annie and Mike are going to help us get registered. Last time we heard, there was still space available."

"Go for it then. Enjoy."

WOMAD (World of Music and Dance)

Kris comes by the B&B. He hands Chris a handful of orange canvas and black wires. "Mark asked me to give you these for your trip. I'm on my way to see Yarra, so I swung by."

"Gosh, what's this?" Chris asks.

"Slings, seats to sit on." He unfolds the black cross-wires with attached canvas, hardly bigger than a rectangular mailing envelope.

"Seats? Look pretty small," Chris says, laughing.

I stare in disbelief.

Kris looks at my face and laughs. "Oh, you've never seen these? These are Chinese camp seats. They're great. You'll need some kind of seats, unless it's changed. Chairs are limited at some venues, and there's only grass for sitting at most of them."

"Your tiny butt may fit on that postage stamp," I say. "I can't imagine mine will."

"Well, try it," says Kris. He opens the sling and sets it on the floor. It's about nine inches high.

I lower myself to the floor and aim for the bright orange target. "My gosh, it's comfortable," I admit, folding my legs crossways in front of me. I wiggle back and forth. "Try it, Chris. What else could we ask for? Hey, tell Mark thanks for thinking of us."

In a small charter plane, we fly over the blue-green Tasman Sea with our Mosaic Choir friends. It's a ninety-minute flight to the North Island, in the middle of which, the passengers pop up from their seats and lean left to peek out the small oval windows. Sounds of "ooo" and "ahaa" fill the cabin. Below us in the midst of miles of flat green farmland jutting skyward is a gaping black hole—Mount Taranaki. It appears like an abandoned monument to forgotten gods. I imagine farmers looking up from bowls of porridge every morning to view a volcano at the end of their field.

The captain requests we return to our seats as we begin our descent into New Plymouth. A shuttle takes us through the city to "The Dell," an amusement park, but not one with electronic, flashing rides.

We arrive at a huge, crowded, and sunny parking area. Campers have set up tables, stacked food coolers, suitcases, and plastic bags alongside small vans, tents, and trucks. On one side of the park is a racecourse and field restaurant. A sidewalk leads us into the shade, where giant ferns of many shapes and drooping vines intertwine with colored lights that dangle from dark tree trunks. Flashes of sun identify a flat, slow-moving, winding path meandering through a jungle world of towering trees and deep, verdant bush. We follow our group leaders over the asphalt path, up steep hills toward our lodging. Set back from the path, on either side, are performers' tents, small shelters, and various-sized stages.

Ukulele chords float across our path. A Polynesian quartet in bright-patterned tops and grass skirts sway and sing for a group of jean-clad dancers. Puffing, we pull our suitcases up a steep, short hill accompanied by chanting, rattles, and stomping. On a resounding stage, a Maori group performs the "haka."

Tents with handcrafted gifts and food kiosks surround us. The melancholy melody of Peruvian panpipes throws me back to Yarra's days in Peru and mine in Ecuador. My eyes tear up.

Chris sees, and says, "Yes, it gets me, too."

"Remember what she said when she came home? 'If you lived in enough places, you could learn to love the whole world.' She'd love this."

Chris nods, "What do you say we pick up something to eat now and skip the evening program. He points to a Chinese food cart. "Their moo goo gai pan smells good."

I agree. On the cart, there is a poster advertising a Chinese flute player. Our Chinese chef, handsome and tall, turns. He has popped an apron over his satin performance robes. He ladles glistening, fragrant vegetables and chicken over fluffy rice. Hands folded, he bows and smiles. Extending his arms, he offers us our take-away boxes like gifts. I stand enchanted, looking into his eyes. "Oh." I recover. "Thank you." I take my box.

Squeezed onto the paved paths, we thread our way, pressing our elbows to our sides and twisting to pass by people of every nation communing with eyes and grins. The performers and audiences are playing, interacting, childlike. Fairy lights are strung throughout the stands of tall trees. Stages and performance tents of various sizes are spread throughout the park, in shaded groves, beside ponds, on grassy parks and on the tops of hills. Dense bush softens the sounds. It's peaceful and exciting at the same time. Park attendants look like kangaroos with their hands clenched on chest-high handles of two-wheeled "Ezy-Goes," as they slowly and silently roll over the hilly asphalt paths. Our group walks slower and slower as we hear the deep drone of robed Mongolian throat singers, the high wailing chant of Jewish folk songs, and the rat-a-tat-tat of Irish tap dancers.

Across a grassy hillside, a woman's voice announces on a microphone, "Gustavo and I invite you all to free tango lessons. FREE—we want you all to come tomorrow at two o'clock, right here on the lawn." A stunning couple stand on a small stage: slender bodies, he in a slim tuxedo and she in a single-shoulder, silver sheath.

"Let's go," Chris says. "Just to watch them, if nothing else."

"We've been wanting to try tango. Let's do it."

Finally, we arrive at a standard, yellow brick, glass and aluminum auditorium. It seems oddly conventional compared to the mélange of color and culture we have just walked through.

We study the large auditorium. Some people are dropping their duffels.

Chris looks around. "What do we do now, just find a spot?"

"Look, Chris. Some people are looking up at the windows. I think they're checking where the floodlights are. They'll probably be on all night."

"Smart people. Let's try to find a good spot and…drop our duffels." We select a mattress from a stack. We look at each other and giggle…forty single mattresses, end-to-end and side-to-side.

"Toto, we're not in Kansas anymore." I mutter Dorothy's words from *The Wizard of Oz*, our mantra in lots of tougher, cross-cultural situations.

"Actually, we may be closer to Kansas than we've been in a long time." My trusted travel companion grins and cocks an eyebrow. He grabs his toilet kit. "I'll find the bathrooms."

Chris and I are the only ones who choose to rest instead of attending the evening's performances. We stash our luggage as close as we can get to home base. We flop on our mattresses, pull up our sheets and blankets, grab each other's hand and give a squeeze.

"Good Night."

"Good Luck."

"We made it."

I awaken at the sound of some rustling. I peer at my watch. It's 11:30. I raise my head; most of the mats already have people lying on them. They all returned without disturbing us. A half dozen others are very slowly and quietly filling in empty spots. *It's the New Zealand way.* My heart wells up. Chris is asleep beside me. *He was right. We are closer to Kansas.*

In the morning, the hush continues. Forty people rise quietly from their places, gather up their toilet necessities and clothing and softly walk to the bathrooms.

Chris cracks an eye open. His hair is mussed. His eyes are puffy.

"Did you sleep well?" I whisper.

He looks over his shoulder at the adjoining mat. It's empty. He shakes his head. "No."

"What was wrong?" I ask.

He shakes his head.

"What? What?"

He sneaks close to me, giggles, and whispers, "I heard a light snoring; I thought it was you. I nudged you, but the snoring kept up. It was the woman on my left side." He presses his fingers to his mouth. "I couldn't sleep the rest of the night. I kept waking up, afraid that I would reach out to…p-put…my arm over…someone…." He breaks into muffled laughter. "Who was not…Joanne." He puts his face in my shoulder and holds in a laugh.

We enjoy a day of visiting the whole world in the morning. Just strolling from venue to venue, we see every kind and size and color of people, instruments, and style of music. We lunch at the cafeteria in the racetrack at the far side of the park. Light drizzle has fallen all morning. Puddles are forming, and the grass is getting slick. We sit comfortably at the next performances, a few inches above the wet grass, on our Chinese slings, with only the slightest of smugness in our smiles.

By two o'clock at the top of the grassy knoll, the tango teachers are sheltered on a small, covered stage. A crowd of chattering people in slickers, raincoats, and New Zealand gumboots, carrying umbrellas, is gathering. Claudia, the instructor, says, "Welcome, everyone. Such a big crowd. Do you have room to dance?"

The crowd calls out, "Yes."

"Is the grass slippery?"

Again, the crowd chants an enthusiastic, "No."

"Let's tango!" Music fills the air.

"Hey, it's fun, and it's free. New Zealanders are all for that."

Claudia is a knockout in a body-hugging, tawny grey, snakeskin patterned sheath. She and Gustavo demonstrate from the stage with elegance and grace. The drizzle has increased to drops.

The crowd looks less elegant, with water dripping from rain hats, noses, eyeglasses and umbrellas, yet they continue dancing. Chris and I, in our heavy sneakers and with Chris holding our umbrella, clomp and whirl on the thick grass. The crowd takes it seriously. We are half-laughing and half-holding each other in a vise grip to keep our balance.

Claudia calls out, “Ladies, are you ready?” In one sexy move, she slides her right leg high, over her partner’s left thigh and draws him close. He encircles her waist with his right hand and twirls the couple to the left. I feel my right sneaker hang like a brick as I attempt to fling it over Chris’ thigh. My left sneak feels stuck on a clump and is simultaneously slipping down over the grass.

“Hold me, Chris!” I clutch his shoulder, “I’m going down!” But we don’t fall. Like everyone else, we keep on kicking, clomping, twirling, and giggling.

“Hey, look, they’ve stopped dancing,” Chris says.

Our instructors stand side by side, peering from behind the mike, open-mouthed, at the crowd. He nods to her. “New Zealand, what can I say? Never before have we seen such participation, such a willing crowd…or had so much fun. Thank you. Thank you.”

Sodden, we stand smiling in the rain. Umbrellas and arms go up in a cheer. *I can’t wait to describe this moment to Yarra, to remind her of her saying, “learn to love the whole world.” I can’t wait to tell her all about WOMAD. Especially, I can’t wait to see her face.*

The Eye Test

“Hey, Yarra, you and Mum going out in style!” calls Crista. “Woo-wee, look at Yarra, her fancy pants even match her wheelchair.”

We both wear floppy straw sun hats and wrap-around New Zealand slacks. Yarra’s are purple and black, and mine, green and black. We are quite a sight dolled up. Yarra is in a reclined position in her purple wheelchair as we trundle across the street to Up the Garden Path cafe.

“We’re our own little parade, Yarra. Remember when you kids got dressed up on Saturday mornings for the Pet and Doll Parade?”

Yarra is listless, her expression attentive. She's here, but no response. I'm so grateful Garden Path is close by. I maneuver the wheelchair through the wooden tables and large pots of greenery and flowers, up a ramp to another Maori-style veranda. I scan the dining area. There's room for the wheelchair near an empty table in the far corner. I turn to the waitress, "Just a decaf and a blueberry scone, please."

Two servers hurry ahead to move our chairs out of the way. *Such lovely people.*

The waitress hands me a stiff plastic card with a number. "Just put this card in the hand holder on your table. The server will find you."

Hand holder? On each table, I see a small bouquet of flowers and an upright wooden, jointed artist's model of a hand and forearm. The fingers all arranged to hold our table number card. *Clever.*

"Thank you, thank you," I call.

"No worries."

Yarra is limp and distant. Even as we pass the magic flowing faucet framed in gold and matted in red velvet or the startling red-and-black Maori masks. Nothing draws her interest. If there is anyplace she would enjoy, this is it. But today she can't.

Is it her eyes? Is the MS attacking her optic nerves? Heck, I used to teach ophthalmology at St. Vincent's School of Nursing. And, as an Amigos volunteer in Ecuador, we performed eye exams in stucco-walled school rooms illuminated only by slanted sun rays or the pale light of a single, dangling bulb. I could coax responses out of Quechua and Spanish-speaking kids. They would indicate which way the 'E' went with their fingers. Why can't I figure out a way to check Yarra's eyes?

Fear enters my mind as I recall a line from her advance directives. "Yarra does not want to be kept alive if she can no longer participate in life." *Is that what's going on?*

I position Yarra so she can look out into the room. I move the cardholder on the table, the wooden model reaching its fingers up to me. *Fingers…that's it, fingers.* I look to see if anyone can see me. I slip behind the next table, slide my arm around the wooden arm, slip it off the table into my torso, and turn to face her.

I look sideways to guard from any customer's eyes. I fashion the fingers of the hand with the outer fingers folded down and the central finger extended in that easily recognizable insult. *Perfect, something naughty. The nurse said, "She sees what she wants to see."*

I lift the arm high on my chest, lower my voice to a deep pitch and bark a two-syllable, "Yar- ra!"

Her eyes blink open. *She hears me. Does she see me? Oh, look, that face! Her mouth dropped open...wide, in a crooked, gaping grin. She sees me, she sees me. Her eyes are bright. She vocalizes "Ahhha." Her eyes, alive, look amazed. Oh, my God, look at her. At the distance of twelve feet, she sees something she thinks is very funny. Oh, joy.*

I'm laughing. I replace the arm on the table and rush to her. We're both crazy happy now. Connected, connected! "You saw it, didn't you? You saw it? The 'Mom invented—Yarra demonstrated, finger flippin' eye test.'"

Yarra looks into my face, grinning. What joy!

"Wait 'til we tell the guys what we came up with, eh, Yarra?"

Dr. Claudette Meets Yarra

"Look, Chris, that's got to be the doctor." Her blue-black hair is rolled in an upswept chignon. She carries a very large, postal-style, black leather bag with belts and silver-colored buckles. She's wearing a voluminous, cream-colored coat with enormous roses.

"I've never seen a doctor dressed like that," says Chris.

"I hope she is the doctor. Yarra will love it." Kris' van pulls in.

"Hey, Kris, good timing. You can help us arrange the furniture in Yarra's room."

Yarra's dressed in a deep turquoise tee and red print slacks. I'm pleased, but she's not responding. *Her hair looks wet. She probably had a shower this morning. Darn, I should have told the nurses no shower today. Her head is off to the side, her eyes staring. We'll have to go through with the doctor conference, regardless. I hope she perks up.*

Kris lifts Yarra's hand, "Yarra, you want to be part of this conversation, I know you do. The new doctor will be here in a few minutes."

The doctor knocks and pushes open the door. Under the cream

coat, now hanging open, are layers of black chiffon. Her blue eyes are large and round. She has creamy cheeks, a full, downward-curving nose and flawless skin. A floral fragrance trails into the room. *Ah, yes, roses. Yarra blinks her eyelids and moves her eyes a bit. I look at the guys. They are rapt.*

Dr. Claudette introduces herself, extends a hand to each of us, goes to the bedside and speaks softly and privately to Yarra.

She turns, "I asked Yarra for permission to talk with you about her. I want to learn all I can so I can understand her needs and give her the best care possible."

I hear a sigh from Chris and Kris as Dr. Colette sits down facing Yarra. Kris goes to his wife's side. "Yarra, we're going to talk about you now, right?" He sits on the stool, holds her hand, and strokes her hair. *Her head is drooping, but she seems to be listening.*

Chris hands the doctor a page. "Here's an agenda we prepared."

Kris asks, "How much time do you have, doctor, so we can pace ourselves?" He grins. "Some of us are storytellers."

She takes the paper in her well-manicured hands, reads it, looks at her watch and says, "I have two hours until I need to leave for my next appointment. Do you think we can cover everything?"

"I think so," Chris said. "If there's anything you'd like to add, just mention it. We've been doing this for quite a while. It's been helpful for all of us to talk to Yarra's caregivers with Yarra present." Dr. Claudette looks at Yarra and smiles approval.

Agenda for Yarra Amoroso's Care, 2007

- Living Will and legal power of attorney prominent on chart.
- Do Not Resuscitate order (DNR) prominent on chart.
- No antibiotic if infection occurs.
- Removing the feeding tube.
- We feel we would treat every scenario individually.
- Call Kris first. If he wishes, he will call us.
- If a doctor believes her death is imminent, we would like to be called as soon as possible so we can be here to support her.
- During the time preceding her death, or after the feeding tube is removed, we request pain relievers and palliative care.

For discussion:

- The vitamin supplement bladder cocktail Yarra currently gets in her feeding tube.
- What do you think about a mucolytic medication to help Yarra breathe? The nurses think using suction is irritating to the mucous membrane.
- Can or what can Yarra see?
- Yarra wants to go outside every day possible.

Dr. Claudette looks up at Yarra and says, “This is very helpful. Shall we begin?”

Chris says, “First, we want to check if the Living Will and the Legal Power of Attorney are on the chart. They should have been transferred from Glynwood Nursing Home in Stoke, but staff doesn’t seem able to find them.”

“I’ll talk with nurse manager Jill about that,” Dr. Claudette says.

“Also, we would like the Do Not Resuscitate order to be prominent on the chart, not lost in the back pages. Can you arrange that?” She nods her head and asks, “All of this is with Yarra’s approval?”

Kris says, “Yes. Here are Yarra’s wishes.” He hands two pages to the doctor.

(62)

Yarra's Life Celebration
"A Happy Party" ✓
Red dress – any lovely one will do
Burgundy Velvet Skirt + Top
Daisies – white, purple
Chocolate cake

Songs – The Rose, On Eagle's Wings, + music by B.B. King ✓ – or whatever

Family and Friends to tell stories about moments with Yarra

Let balloons go (maybe with messages to Yarra) Butterflies, if poss.

Rainbow colours piñata for kids – filled with chocolates

Would like to be cremated and family members each fling a few ashes to the heavens from Eagle's Head in Big Elk – or do with astros who

She does not wish to be kept alive if she can no longer participate in life – (see, hear, communicate, breathe, eat, etc)

program – ~~picture~~ drawing of dance spirit dance
black + white photo of Yarra

Readings for program and who to read them
maybe quoted from diary – ask her or think of some for her

Yarra's wishes –

- Trips to beach (bring along pad of paper and drawing supplies so she can draw)
- Boat ride
- Be around horses more – there are horses up the street at OK corral
- Art time with John
- Massages on neck and shoulders, gentle caresses on hands and arms – hair brushing
- Combination art projects with family and friends
- Tactile objects of interest or importance rather than letters, or stories (can't hold lots of words – looses train of thought) from family and friends – One or two photos okay overwhelmed by lots of photos
- Says "the day she can't do art anymore is the day she doesn't want to live." so please help her create things – even the simplest lines on paper will thrill her
- Chocolate cake and chocolate chip cookies
- Visit market
- Go out to dinner / lunch / coffee

"These are personal notes her sister made in 2003 when Yarra could still talk. It took a week working with Yarra to get them as complete as possible. A lawyer, quite a proper young fellow, witnessed the legal papers. When he requested a signature, I told him Yarra couldn't do it. He said an X would do, but I told him Yarra couldn't do that either. He doubted they would be legal without some kind of mark. Yarra figured it out." He grins at her, "but it took us a while to understand. She started blowing kisses in the air."

Kris' eyes roll up, envisioning the scene. He laughs and drawls, "We all thought she was flirting with the lawyer. Yarra often did that—eh, Yarra? When there was a good-looking bloke around? It was quite a hoot until we remembered Yarra signs all her paintings with a lipstick kiss. We were so surprised and proud of Yarra for thinking of a solution. The lawyer just stood there, clueless. We explained how Yarra could sign the papers with a lipstick kiss. Then he was really undone. He muttered about non-conventional and that he doubted he could get official approval. We thought what he'd say back in the law office. We couldn't stop giggling."

Yarra's totally with it, her face alert. She's smiling a gaped-mouth grin.

The doctor, too, is smiling and says in a serious tone, "It is so good to work with a family who have discussed the issues and agreed on their wishes. As a physician, it's so much better for me when I know I will not be the only one to address the difficult decisions. I congratulate you all, and you, Yarra, for the preparation you have done. Kris, I admire you so much for your caring of Yarra."

We continue discussing our concerns, line by line, and Chris says, "If you still have time, doctor, we'd like to tell you a little about our daughter. We think it will help when it comes to decision-making." Dr. Claudette nods and relaxes in her chair.

I begin telling Yarra's amazing life story. Yarra is listening intently, vocalizing short sounds. *Is she remembering, enjoying?*

I go to her bed and whisper, "Can I tell the 'washing their pits' story?"

She makes a loud "aggh." Her face lights up.

Dr. Claudette says, "From the look on Yarra's face, I can see she enjoyed whatever you said. I think this is a story I must hear."

As I relate the story, Dr. Claudette's lips are parted. She's sitting up in her chair, mesmerized, her eyes flitting back and forth from Yarra's to mine. I follow the doctor's gaze to Yarra's sparkling eyes and glowing skin. I haven't seen that in years.

Chris looks proud, wearing an "only Yarra" grin. "When Yarra worked at Kodak, the Mexican workers called her 'the gringa with the lingua,' the American with the tongue, because she wasn't afraid to speak up for their causes."

Kris' chin is raised, reading the glances. *He's hearing about our daughter before she became his wife.*

Something in the room has shifted; there is energy. *It's happening. Yarra's silenced voice is being heard; the woman she was is reappearing.* It's palpable, visceral. I'm thrilled.

We pause. Dr. Claudette slowly rises and walks to Yarra, "Thank you, Yarra. I hope you and I will be friends." She presses Yarra's hand. Yarra looks into her face.

She turns to us, "This has been a most enlightening and pleasurable afternoon. I thank you all. Keep up your excellent work. Call me if you need me."

My Guardian Angels

We're staying at a B&B in town until our room is ready at the farm. Karena and Theresa come by to take me for a swim. We talk and laugh all the way to the beach, which is far below the parking area, down a steep cement sidewalk. I didn't expect this, and I don't have on shoes that support my weak ankle. I'm going gingerly, as Theresa and Karena walk along as if this is what they always do, and that's exactly right. They've been scooting around on all kinds footing for years.

For goodness sake, Joanne, so have you. What's wrong? I don't know. I feel frail, old, and vulnerable today.

Down on the golden beach, it's glorious, and very secluded. A sheltered cove under a cliff wall holds deep blue water. Theresa and Karena are already swimming back to me.

I slather on sun lotion. My skin starts to burn immediately. What's happening? I splash water over my arms and face. *Oh, no, a rash is appearing all over my arms, and my face is burning. The sunscreen. I must be having a reaction to the sunscreen. We just got here and I will have to ask them to take me home. I get in the water and try to wash the lotion off. It hurts to rub my skin. Might as well tell them what's going on.*

"Hate to be a spoil sport. I'm having a reaction to the new sunscreen." I show them my arms. "Not sure what to do."

They stare for a moment, then both say, "Better get you home."

I'm disappointed with myself. No resiliency. Feeling weak and no fun at all.

"Sorry, it wasn't the day we hoped for. Thanks for coming to get me. Let's hope we get another chance."

Two days later, at the B&B, I got a surprise phone call from Theresa's mother, "Big T." "I'm going for a dip in the river up the Aniseed Valley. "Would you like to go along?"

I'm so surprised, and I would love to be in her company, swim or not. She's so positive and matter of fact. She makes me laugh.

"Oh, it's just the perfect thing. I'd love to go."

"I'll park my car along the Aniseed Valley Drive. Can you find that?"

"I'll get directions, T."

So here I am, dressed in my bathing suit, watching an 80-year-old woman dive into the river, hands clasped and extended, swiftly as a fish, no hesitation.

I wade in and paddle around. It's cold. I'm a wimp. I push myself into deeper water and take a real swim. That feels better. "Big T" pays me no mind; she has swimming to do. I love it.

The Beginning of the End—March 2007

"Ah, hello, Joanne, are you ready for this?" It's Kris calling from New Zealand. I hear a long "whoosh" sound over the phone line. *It must be something important.*

"Try me," I shoot back. We both giggle; whatever it is he's proposing will go easier now.

I see him sitting beside the yurt, near the eucalyptus tree. I wonder if the plump, iridescent blue-green wood pigeons are perched overhead.

"Yeah, well…Yarra has been talking, well at least…we've been talking with Yarra…Vikki and me…ah, about ah, a red-lace skirt."

"A red lace skirt?" I ask.

"Yeah, ah, she wants to wear a red lace skirt…ah…yeah…to her funeral."

Funeral? In February, when Chris and I were there, Kris handed us a book to read about a natural burial in a wooded area, complete with biodegradable cardboard coffin. It sounded like just what Kris and Yarra would like.

We discussed that with Kris and Yarra, then a friend offered to make a pine box which could be hand painted by all the friends and the kids. Everyone was enthusiastic about that idea until Kris remembered that Yarra had expressed, in the advance directives she dictated to Chiara in 2005, that she wanted her ashes to be sprinkled off Eagle Head in Colorado, and that was it. At least I came home believing that.

"Do you mean there will be a viewing, Kris? I thought you'd decided on cremation. Isn't that so?" My question echoes on the line.

"Yeah, I know…well, maybe she means…ah…yep, to wear at hospital…the last days. Ulrika, that young woman you met here in January, already made a felt skirt for her to spread on top of the blankets. Maybe she means something like that."

It's been a very long time since we could rely on Yarra's response to our asking her to blink "yes" or "no." Talking with Yarra now means posing a question to her, spending hours sitting with her, holding her hand, repeating the question in different ways, trying to read her eyes, watching for a nod, asking the question again the next day, and the next, trying to ascertain her wishes. Kris spends hours and hours patiently trying to honor her barely discernible wishes.

"That's the best I could make of it." Kris continues, "Vikki tried too. What we can definitely come up with is she wants a long, red-lace skirt."

"Well, it's March, spring here in the US, mostly pastel colors in clothing. Long red-lace skirts may be hard to find, but I'll see what I can do."

"Yeah, you see what you can do there. I'll tell Yarra you're looking for a red-lace skirt. She'll like that. Good on ya', Mum."

I made a few cursory phone calls, checked the catalogues and perused the second-hand shops. No red skirts. I think I'll have better luck when we go to New Zealand in July, their winter. Yarra seems to be holding her own now; who knows when we'll be going.

In May, Kris phones, "Good morning, Joanne. It's still morning, isn't it? What time is it, about eleven? Is Chris there with you? Maybe you better sit down for this."

"We're both here, Kris. It's ten o'clock. We're just having a "cuppa" and sitting down. How about you?"

"Well…we've spent a long time, the past months, Yarra and I, Vikki and Irma, even Hein, and I've talked with Anna, the neighbor lady who lives in Rene's. You don't know her. She enjoyed spending time with Yarra at Karaka, they got close…ah…yeah…and a woman from Christchurch who does readings over the phone. She doesn't know Yarra, ah…yeap…they're all getting the same message…. "Yarra's ready to go"...yep…yeah…."

There's a long pause, I'm struggling to grasp what he is saying, where he's going with this conversation.

"Everyone feels she is definitely ready to go. Vikki feels it very strongly; Yarra is trying to leave her body. We're going to close the feeding tube."

This isn't the phone call I expected and dreaded; the one where I would hear Yarra has developed pneumonia, a fulminating bladder infection, a high fever, and is dying. Or that she has aspirated on her fluid and is dead.

That phone call I am prepared for. I'm familiar with the common medical crises to which people with chronic wasting diseases succumb. There is no sudden crisis here.

Why not? Yarra's had her advance directives since 2001. This is the anticipated difficult moment I perceived when the Mic-key tube was first inserted, and after all these years…I'm the one who's not ready. No urgent medical problem, no doctor's input. Not even a mention of Burke, their trusted counselor, a psychologist from the United States, who sat gently, often silently, with them for hours, processing in a way Yarra and Kris appreciate.

This is the assessment of Kris, her husband and soul mate, Vikki and Irma, her closest friends and Anna, who is "very spiritual," according to Kris.

Vikki and Kris both spend many hours purposefully alone in nature meditating and listening for wisdom. They walk and wander in the bush, or at the beach, going for a swim, to silently search for guidance. Vikki's been so intimately involved with Yarra for so many years, she understands Yarra's every breath and flutter. Kris and Vikki are both perceptively communicating, often silently, with Yarra, both with intuition and patience.

Just like Kris and Yarra to "suss-out" someone to check out the spirit world, "...a woman from Christchurch who does readings." That's a clincher, all right.

Kris and Yarra are ready for her death. We have been given notice. "Do as you wish." *How could they?* A snake of anger and deep sorrow slides up my innards. I'm nauseated, fearful and confused. I thought I would be ready. Kris calls and announces he and Yarra, and other perceptive people, have decided Yarra is ready to go. Yarra is giving them strong, sensory messages. Kris is calling to tell us Yarra is ready to go. *I'm not there yet. They are.*

Here I am again, uncomfortable, resisting something I don't understand, nor resonate with. How can I be so sanctimonious about their bee treatments when I disparage how they feel about ours?

I challenge in my medical mode, "Have you talked to Burke?"

How dare I throw out his name as a trump card. Why? Because he has a degree in psychology? Because of my own need to have some degreed expert verify the situation? Someone with accreditation? How manipulative, conjuring up Burke as a litmus test to suit your need to stall, because you're not ready for Yarra to die. Think of your daughter and Kris.

"Yes, he feels it, too." Kris has great respect for Burke, who knows Kris and Yarra very well.

"What about another doctor?" We know Doctor Colette is gone. What's her name? *Nicole, yes, Nicole. She was the doctor who examined Yarra last June. Think of your daughter, Joanne, think of Kris.* "Have you talked with Dr. Nicole, Kris?"

"Yes, she says she'll close the tube anytime we're ready."

It shocked me last year when Kris reported that after her first exam for admission to Motuweka Hospital, Nicole said she would give the feeding tube six weeks.

It's almost a year since Nicole said she'd try it for six weeks. *What did I expect...that Yarra would go on forever? No...I need to think about this. Kris and Yarra trust her. Breathe, Joanne. Breathe. Leunig's Poem? "Let it go, let it out...." Kris and Yarra's mantra for years... "a path on which to travel."*

Kris told us long ago, phone calls go better for him when only one of us does the talking, or we take turns. My need to know all the details can become bombarding.

I've been reading Chris' face all through the phone call as we both listen on speaker. He's been running his fingers over his chin, listening. He looks compassionate, thoughtful.

Chris nods his head to me and raises his eyebrows. "Shall we go?" My eyes fill with tears. I nod in return, "Yes."

"We'll come, Kris. We'll be there," Chris says on speaker and takes the phone. When he speaks, I hear in his voice that he perceives all this commitment entails. "Thanks for the phone call, Kris. I'll email you the plane schedule, to see if it works for you, OK?"

Kris' voice is gentle and patient. "That's why I called...you and Joanne. I thought you might want to be here."

Chapter 6—Come Be with Yarra

Blessings, 2007

We've been vacationing in Durango, near Chiara and Ruby's. Today, we are working diligently to get our business accounts in order and get our rental house in Colorado empty and cleaned. We are preparing to return to New Zealand. Sunday morning I call our landlady, Meg, with thanks and tell her we are leaving. Chris enters from the garage. "Let me talk to Meg."

I hand him the phone.

"Meg, I just discovered the garage door won't close. You'll have to send the repairman back." He rolls his eyes at me and continues his phone conversation. "No, our flight leaves at noon. We can't be here for him."

Chris has packed the car. As we get seated, he says, "Let's spare Chiara the details. We want to get to Mass on time." We drive around the corner to pick up Chiara and her luggage. She scoots into the back seat.

Morning sunlight illumines the antique, pastel-colored glass windows of St. Columba's. Daubs of green and cream, purple, brown, and olive float over the pews and create a silent sense of calm. The gospel reader drones on. I zone out, start ruminating about the 18-hour trip ahead, but I hear random words from the bible story about pregnant Mary's journey to visit her also pregnant, cousin, Elizabeth, to help her during the birth of Jesus.

Casting his eyes over the parishioners, Father Jim approaches the podium. His sandy hair is getting a dusting of grey, but he still looks like the modest Ohio farm boy he was. He has advised us wisely regarding end-of-life issues for Yarra. His sermon is about how the gospel enters your life. His first words are, "Mary left in haste…."

Well, there you go. I suppose Mary had her own version of last-minute difficult decisions, and she was pregnant. She traveled on foot or on a donkey and chose a long journey to travel to help Elizabeth. She stayed three months.

We've been visiting with Chiara over the years. Father knows Chiara wants to be with us and wants to be with her sister. He talks about Mary setting aside her own concerns to help others, the strength of relationships, and the healing power of love. He knows we're going to New Zealand. I hear in his words a parallel for us. I take it as his blessing. I let it all in. Chris reaches for my hand, gives it a squeeze. I look at Chiara. She gives a little smile and nods. We'll make it.

Almost Home, June, 2007

Flying in from Auckland to the South Island, I search from my window for the Tasman Sea and the first glimpse of cone-shaped, verdant hills surrounding Marlborough Sounds.

Chiara is seated in the row ahead of me. I say, "There's the Tasman Sea, Chiara, and Nelson." The plane veers right, heading into brilliant sun. Tears form in my eyes and trickle down my cheek. I let them fall.

Silently, I tick off the familiar sites of the coastal community of Atawhai and the climb up into forested hills and between concrete cemetery pillars where we often walked among crumbling headstones.

"There's city hall, Chiara, with the windmill clock tower."

Our plane lifts over a dark wall of mature pines and slows. There it is, the runway of Nelson airport sticking out into the harbor. A small crowd of greeters wave welcome from the rooftop viewing deck. I feel the joy of arrival and the sorrow of our reason for coming. I squeeze my eyelids to clear the view.

Walking into the reception area, I'm looking around for Kris. I feel something is different. *What? What is it?*

"What's different about the airport, you guys?" I ask Chris and Chiara.

Both of them look sleepy and travel weary. They stare ahead.

Chiara engages her artist's eye, shifts her shoulder bag and looks around. "I don't know, but who is supposed to be here to pick us up?"

"Well, Kris has always come to meet us before," I say.

A courteous crowd moves carefully, no jostling. The café's shiny windows display two-handed, blocky sandwiches, their crusty edges fringed with greens, meats and cheeses. Chunks of dessert cakes dwarf white ceramic plates, the aroma of fresh brewed coffee, the bowl-sized latte cups and rows of white teapots. It all says, "Welcome." Yet it seems different somehow. What is it?

Sea-colored pottery and glimmering, brightly-colored, blown-glass pieces, sophisticated original jewelry, some embedded with bits of paua shell and jade, beckon us from a signature, tall, glass showcase. The exit wall is a rectangle of red-and-black Maori symbols above an ocean scene in the same bold New Zealand style.

There it is, at my feet. Nelson Airport finally has a new carpet. Appropriately, it is two shades of sea blue. Wow, they finally sprang for it. After all those years of that awful burnt gold flooring with the various sizes of bicycle tire shaped, black circles with off-red triangles tossed over it. The first time I saw it, I was slightly airsick. Walking over it distorted my vision so much I felt that last urge to upchuck on the spot. Seeing that awful carpet each year when we returned, I wondered why and how it came to be selected. New Zealand is known for its beautiful rugs. The best I could say for it was that it declared, "New Zealand is different."

I scan the room. I don't spot Kris' white curls. He isn't here. That means he must be very tired, or he needed to stay with Yarra. It's the first time he hasn't come.

"There's Mark!" Chris says, interrupting my inspection. Beautiful Mark, Kris' tall, blonde, handsome son strides toward us, welcoming us with a wide grin and sparkling eyes.

"Hi, everyone. Hi, Chris. Hi, Chiara." He shakes their hands.

"Good to see you, Joanne. I didn't know you. How long has it been since I saw you folks?"

"It's two-and-a-half years, Mark. We didn't see you in February when we were here."

He bends down to hug me. Looking over his shoulder, I see in the corner of the reception room a tall, black pole. Fashioned from the old, hideous carpet is a king-sized top hat, tipped askew. A horizontal bar with round knob ends extends at shoulder height and supports a yard-long piece of the same carpet cut into a pointed vest and an extra-long cravat. I laugh aloud.

Mark stands back, "What is it? What's funny?"

"Look, Mark, look, everyone. See? They got new carpet. There's the old one in the corner. Probably the staff at the Wearable Art Museum or the students at Nelson Poly-tech thought to save pieces of the old carpet to make a funky in-house joke. Isn't it great?"

Chiara laughs, "I remember that old carpet. It looked like a carpet that said 'Go away' instead of 'Welcome.'" It feels good to laugh. We needed a laugh. I'm rapt to be back in New Zealand again. That's what the New Zealanders say—"rapt." I say "wrapped" as well; I'm enfolded in the presence of people who revel in poking fun at themselves and making sly jokes of anything. I'm so grateful.

Along the harbor shore, we drive through towering, forested hills until the land flattens out to the farming plane of Motueka and the small hospital where Yarra resides. Chiara and I are collapsed in the back seat of the car, but I feel anxious. Chris is up front, listening to the Kolff family news. Mark is living in Kris and Yarra's place at 20 Karaka now. He plans to refurbish the house and the yard, which Kris never had the time or energy to do. Yarra and Kris dreamed about improving the yard, and gardening is his delight. He and Mark may work on it together one day.

Arriving at the Motueka Community Hospital, I notice the garden offers only a few wilted roses and scrawny asters on brown-leafed stems. They've had a hard frost. Cold air smacks me alert. Once again, our shoes clomp over the mare, a passage which has become sacred to us also, as we come to assist Yarra on her final journey into the unknown.

A waft of warmth hits us when we enter. A white cat paws the carpet beside Yarra's door, waiting for it to be opened. Reflexively, I jerk alert, *No, you won't go in.*

"Scat," I hiss, softly and stomp my foot. The cat slinks off.

Chris asks, bewildered, "What are you doing?"

He has good reason to ask. What am I doing? I'm going to greet my daughter after two years' absence, and I'm fussing at a cat... because I don't want him to go in my daughter's bedroom? Because I don't want Yarra to see him? It's a new cat, does he know? The old cat did, the nurses told me; it always knew when a patient was dying; spent days hanging around the room.

Yarra knows that, too. Someone would have mentioned it to her in the two years she's been here. Well, she knows she's dying, too. They've been spending lots of time talking with her about dying. It's her wishes they are following. She used to love having the old cat snuggle up against her back. How would she react now, comforted or fearful? It's me. I don't want a cat telling me my daughter is dying. I'll keep the door shut for now.

"Tell you later, Chris. It's OK, it's just me."

Yarra's room is a whirl of color, paints, photographs, paper, and a stack of multicolored blankets lays on her bed. Soft, salmon-colored light radiates from a salt-stone lamp, soothing and calm. Kris sits in a chair next to the bed. He stands to greet us with a broad smile. White stubble covers his jaw; his clothes are rumpled. He looks tired.

He turns to Yarra, "Oh, look who's here, Yarra. It's your mum and dad and your beautiful sister, Chiara." He comes around the bed, hugs me and thumps Chris on the shoulders. He looks into our eyes with joy.

"Ah, yeah, it's good you're here, all of you, yep, Yarra's been waiting." He stands back and looks us over, nodding his head. He turns to Chris, "You doing all right, Chris? Yep, yep. It's good you're here. Yep."

Chiara smiles, but her eyes are on Yarra, and she quickly moves to the bed, sits down and puts her face in front of Yarra. Chiara's thick brown hair hangs down long, over her shoulders. She's wearing one of her hand-knit scarves around her neck, a purple one, for Yarra.

She talks softly to Yarra, reaches out for her hand between the rails. "We're here, Yarra. Have you been waiting for us? We're here. I'm so glad to be here."

Kris comes around the bed to hug Chiara.

"I'm glad you made it," Kris says. "Hope you didn't mind I didn't come to the airport. Mark's a pretty good driver, no? Where is he?"

"He's parking the car," Chris says. "Just dropped us off out front. Here he comes now."

"Thanks, Mark," Kris says. "Saved me a long drive."

"It was just fine," Mark replies. "Happy to do it. I'll just say good-bye to Yarra now and get back with the boys." He goes to the bedside, puts his arm on Yarra's shoulder, and says, "Brought your mum and dad and sister from the airport, Yarra. Now I'm going home to the boys." He gives her hand a pat. Yarra's eyes are closed. After a moment, Mark turns aside.

Yarra is sedated, her complexion sallow, her face puffy, her eyes closed. Her hair is short now, still black and curly around her face, easier to care for. She looks weary.

I breathe out. *Yes, it's time for her to go.*

I move to the bedside. Attached high on the top corner of the mattress is a home-sewn cloth box fashioned from pastel flowered upholstery fabric. I assume it contains the dispenser for medication Yarra is receiving to keep her comfortable. I imagine a local white-haired seamstress getting this order…hearing the story…how very New Zealand. I assume the nurses would choose not to have a plastic syringe and noisy regulator clicking away, in plain view, expensive and perhaps not even available.

I place myself in front of Yarra's face, next to Chiara, and put my arm across Chiara's shoulders. It feels good to be "the three of us."

I see us bent with laughter in Chiara's Santa Fe bathroom when Yarra lived with her, after Yarra's graduation in 1986. The morning before I drove down to visit them from Colorado, I found a stick-on tattoo in a cereal box. I tucked it in my make-up kit.

In Chiara's Santa Fe apartment, we three crowded in the bathroom, getting ready to go out. The girls had showered and were toweling off their olive skinned, tan bodies, shaking out their long, dark, water-soaked hair. Beautiful as they were; Chiara small, slender and Yarra rounded and Rubenesque, I was seeing them doubled, close up, in vivo, and reflected in the large, brightly lit mirror over the sink. It felt like a lot of moving, naked body parts to me.

I had pasted the fake tattoo above my bra line. I waited for one of them to spot the discreet little rose. I stepped in closer to the mirror and spread my arms to reach high up to brush my hair.

Yarra started to scream, really scream, filling the small, steamy room.

"Big sister," Chiara cried, "What, what? What's the matter?"

Yarra was dancing now, her bare feet flapping on the vinyl floor. "Oh! Oh!...Mom's...Mom's...Mom's," she choked..."got a tattoo!" She pointed, "Look, look!"

Chiara screamed. I started laughing. Chiara and Yarra howled.

The restricting bedside rails bring me back to present. They are between us. How she resisted those confining side rails and the pads that blocked the precious view of her space. She set her jaw, cast her eyes down, and turned her nose up to tell me, "No." I saw her spunk. I wanted to cheer her on, fighting for her rights. I also knew she was falling out of bed when her legs went into spasm, getting bruised and cut. Does she remember?

"Hello, Yarra," I say. "We're here, Mom and Dad, and here's Chiara."

Chiara reaches for Yarra's hand, massages it lightly, touches her hair. "Pretty Yarra, your hair looks so pretty."

There is no response from Yarra.

Chris moves to the bedside, I stand aside. "Hi, Yarra. How do you like it? The Amorosos are here, and we're bringing love from all the rest." Chris speaks slowly, "Ruby, Joe and Kelly...Kelly is Joe's girlfriend, remember...and Christian...John and Amy, little Marco, they all send their love." He reaches out with his usual blessing, a sign of the cross, on her forehead.

Yarra's face remains impassive, waxy. She is piled under layers of blankets; they cover her bed and are tucked in tightly on the sides. She can't move; does she feel cocooned and overheated? It is bitter cold outside. Her room is very warm. Some caregiver wants her to be warm and cozy.

Here's the old ignorance of Multiple Sclerosis again. If she is dying, does she still feel the distress of being overheated? She may feel she's on fire, or suffocating, losing her strength…who knows?

Chiara knows. She begins to loosen the blankets. She takes off a few layers and drops them in their plastic basket.

"Is that better, Yarra?" Chiara leans her face down to Yarra. Her long, dark, golden-tipped hair reflects soft light. She glows. She and Yarra together are so beautiful. I'm so glad she came. Yarra opens her eyes and sees Chiara. She stares.

"It's me, Yarra, big sister is here." A tiny smile forms on Yarra's lips. Chiara's face breaks into a pleased, tender smile. "Oh, Yarra, hello. I'm here. We're all here for you. We love you, you know that don't you?" She puts down the rail and folds her body over the bed to hug her sister.

A new piece of art hangs over Yarra's bed, a linear piece of tan art board, with handwritten lines over daubs of color. I move in closer. Yarra is watching.

"You have a new piece of art from Denise, your art therapy teacher in Sydney." No response. "It's been years…It's you, Yarra, vibrant. I pluck the painting from the wall and turn it to Yarra. "And a poem." *I want to share this with Yarra.* "Shall I read it?" Chiara, Chris, and Kris are listening, watching. Yarra remains motionless. I take a breath; I can do this. I nod to Yarra. I read slowly:

"earth may be emerald
wind may be umber
rivers may be scarlet
fire may be cobalt
Yarra may be a rainbow"

I pause between the lines and gaze into Yarra's eyes. It's what we can do. "Denise writes, 'The words above somehow express how I see you, Yarra…colors…and their trick of turning up where you least expect them! Much love flows across the sea—Denise.'"

I look down into Yarra's searching eyes. "Denise's words…the poem is all you, Yarra. So powerful, and this painting of colors. Denise knows you."

Only silence in the room, a few sniffs, we come back to center. Kris asks, "Irma has lunch ready at the farm, if you're up to it, and you can pick up the car before you go to the B&B. Does that sound all right?"

Chiara faces her sister, "I'll stay here with you, OK, Yarra?"

"Good," I smile. "I'm hoping we won't be long. We'll bring you some food from Irma's." I turn to Yarra. "We're here to stay, Yarra. Our B&B is just a block away."

At the doorway, Chris turns. "You coming back in, Kris?"

"Yeah, I come in afternoons and stay through the night." He points to a bulging, white-sheeted mattress and blankets folded into a metal frame in the corner. "The nurses have made a comfy bed for us…whoever stays the night."

I feel my shoulders relax. *They welcome us here. "Whoever is staying with Yarra, we are caring for you."*

Chris says, "Good, we'll work out some shifts."

Kris turns and leans over Yarra. "Did you hear that, Yarra? Your mum and dad and Chiara will be here to stay with us now. We're going to get our car for your folks, then I'll be back."

"Come in, come in." Irma spreads her arms toward the kitchen table. "Cella and Yiba have been helping make soup for you." She smiles at two little blond-haired girls and lifts the lid on a huge stainless steel pot; a steamy aroma escapes into the cool air.

"Smells good, Irma," Jan says as he walks into the kitchen and extends his hands to us. The girls watch. Kyle comes smiling into the kitchen. "Joanne, Chris, Irma ground whole wheat to make bread for you. See?" He lifts the towel covering a basket to reveal two brown, crusty loaves of bread.

"I'll bet you helped, did you?"

"Yes, he did," says Irma with a smile.

Irma cooks in as healthy a way as possible, and everything she makes tastes amazingly fresh and wholesome. I realize I'm really hungry.

Yiba has come to sit on the bench between us, while Cella watches from across the table, snuggled close to her mom.

"I know you're ready to rest, we'll have time to chat later," Irma says. The "B&B looks OK from the outside. I've heard people like it there. I hope it works out fine, but call me if you need anything. You have my number, no?"

"Oh, thank you again, Irma, for everything." I nod, "We'll be seeing you. And Vikki? She's gone to see her children in Australia, right?"

"Yes, Yarra's known that trip was planned for a long time. We hear Melissa and Nurse Carol are coming some time."

On the way to the car, Kris asks, "How did it go for you…seeing Yarra."

"I was surprised to see her looking so healthy," I say. *How dumb, why did you say that? He can see. Her face looks puffy, and so tired.*

Kris interrupts my thoughts. "Oh, Joanne, there is something you can do. When you're in town you can pick up some frankincense and myrrh. We've decided to anoint her body Jill, one of the nurses talked to me about it."

"Frankincense and myrrh…where do you think I can find those, Kris?" I imagine myself walking into any store in the US asking for frankincense and myrrh.

"Oh, any of the vitamin shops, yeah, good luck. I'm too tired to talk about it now."

An old wooden bench with small, brown paper bags stacked in a basket stands on the sidewalk as we drive by. On the white pickets behind the bench is a hand-printed sign, "Feijoa $1.00 a bag." That wakes me up.

"Oh, good, Feijoa are in season. I hope you like them, Chiara. They're one of my favorite New Zealand fruits. Kinda' like a tart pear, huh, Chris?"

"Yeah, I guess so," says Chris, as he concentrates on making a tight turn at the corner of a picket fence. A windbreak of towering dark pines and drooping magnolia branches shelters the gravel circle drive. The lance-shaped, dark, shiny leaves of the magnolia hang low. Brown crumpled plants cover the garden area in the center of the lawn. We drive up to a tall Victorian set with black pillars and long colonial windows. A high, white sun glares off wavering glass, reflecting fragments of deep red curtains and grey clouds.

Chiara and I climb out, followed by Chris. On the porch, a jumbled collection of gum-boots sit together, black, red and white, a couple pair of plastic jandals, half a dozen women's and men's shoes, plus chewed tennis balls, and a small red wagon with two big sacks of apples. A fat cat sleeps under the wagon with his tail over his face.

"This porch says, 'We're family here,'" I say, and shiver as Chris cranks the old-fashioned brass doorbell.

Kris had heard that Becky was "nice." And she is; a smiling woman in a heavy knit cardy swings open the door. "Welcome. You must be the Amoroso family. Chris, is it? I'm Becky. Pass through." She extends her hand to a spacious, high-ceilinged entry, a dark wood staircase.

"You must be Yarra's sister. Welcome."

"Yes, I'm Chiara, and this is Joanne, my mom."

"Kris just called to say you were on your way. The strong young man, Kris' son, is he? He carried your luggage up for you—and for me." She chuckles.

"Kris said you probably were ready for a rest, just coming from a long flight. Just as well with you, if I show you to your rooms and the toilets now, and save the rest of the house tour for tomorrow?"

"Fine with me, how about it, you two?" Chris asks.

Chiara and I both nod. "Oh yes."

At the foot of the staircase, a bushel-sized, glazed pot spills long stems of seed pods of deep purple and cream orchids in every direction. How can they survive in the frigid blast every time the front door is opened? *Just like New Zealanders, Joann. Hearty.*

I puff as I trudge up the steep staircase. *Good thing Mark "uplifted" the suitcases.*

In a long hallway, Becky opens the door to Chiara's room, which is across from ours.

"If you feel a bit cool, there are electric heaters in all the rooms." We see a familiar electric, white-enamel oil heater on wheels. "I know you're used to heated homes, right? Your folks will be right across the hall, Chiara, but your toilet is up here."

We follow Becky down the hall to a short flight of steps. "During the day, I'm often out; you'll be here by yourselves. My rooms are behind the kitchen. I'll show you the rest of the house tomorrow morning. Sleep well." Her farewell "Taaa" hangs in the air as Becky turns away, then returns to add, "Oh, yes, the two other guests: one is an aviation student and the other a fruit worker. They leave very early in the morning. I'm sure you'll hear them, but after they leave it will be quiet."

We open our door to a room crowded with our luggage, antique furniture, a double bed, and a private bathroom. We shed our coats and drop our handbags. Chris is already sitting on the bed, taking off his shoes.

"I've had it. Let's just sleep now," Chris says. "If we wake up, we can get comfortable, put on our pajamas."

I'm slipping under the covers as he talks. "Good night, Honey. We 'did good.' I bend over to kiss him on the cheek, then slide my back down against his for warmth.

"Yeah, I know we 'did good.' G'night."

Near morning, we stir. Chris sits up and reaches out for the bathroom door. A blast of cold air engulfs the bed. "Holy cow, it's like unlatching a meat freezer," he says. "Go quick, if you can. I'm putting on my coat."

Chris comes out in seconds, dives under the covers, and shivers. "Whew! Your turn."

The bathroom is a stunning renovation of warm peach, lovely glass and chrome, a full mirror and a glass shower. The moon is still visible in the skylight. No heat, no insulation. I have waited for the last possible moment to expose my skin to the cold. I hop quickly to the toilet, careful not to touch any of the beautiful, frigid fixtures. It's "fresh" in here, all right; no organism could survive in these temperatures. We're off schedule, so we decide to postpone breakfast.

Chris has errands and drops me at the hospital. The door to Yarra's room is cracked open. I hear Irma's crisp, lively Dutch accent. I'm delighted. Yarra is on her left side, facing Irma. I see the head of her bed is raised high enough so she and Yarra can look into each other's faces. Soft grey light from the window backlights Irma's sturdy, straight form. Irma's arms and fingers flutter like shadow puppets behind a screen, animating her dialogue. Yarra is so focused on Irma's face that I expect to hear her respond. Of course, she can't. Instead, Irma's blue eyes flash up to greet me.

"Oh, Yarra, your mum's here."

I walk in and touch Yarra's leg, lean over the bed, say, "Hi, Honey, so good to be here."

Irma rattles off in her clipped, clear voice, "I was just telling Yarra, I dropped Kyle off. He's skating down High Street on his roller blades, on his way to Big World. He bought a microscope a month ago, with money he earned—twenty dollars, but the thing hasn't worked properly. So, he's going to have a go at trying to get his money back."

Irma flashes a wide smile to Yarra, "Huh, Yarra? You know he's pretty good at expressing himself, getting what he needs? So, I thought while I'm waiting for him, I'd just pop in to see Yarra. We'll see how it goes. He's coming back here to meet me."

I envision Kyle's earnest expression, his precise adult-like speech emitting from his child's face. I see the surprised expression on the manager's face as he listens to a young man articulate the exact problem of a non-functioning microscope and his request for a refund.

I press my hand on Yarra's leg. "Yarra, can't you just see Kyle giving his spiel to the manager?"

Yarra opens her mouth. I take it for a "Yes."

Irma laughs, "Yeah, I can hear it, too."

I see the corner of Yarra's lips curling. I slide forward along the bed rail to press my hand on Yarra's hip, and place my other hand on Irma's shoulder.

Irma and Jan's gift, the salt lamp, casts a welcome pink glow in the grayness of the day. The faint heat of the lamp is said to release healing salt ions into the air.

Only a bit of amber iris is visible at the corner of Yarra's eyelashes. She's waiting, listening, watching.

Outside, the bank of grey clouds must have cracked open. Clear, pale light flows through the window, across the bed, over our shoulders and bathes us in gentle light. We rest in the silence.

Becky's Wry Smirk

The following morning, as Becky predicted, I hear thumping footsteps in the hallway, the screeching of plumbing, and most annoying, the running of water through the pipes installed in the wall behind my head. Chris spent the night at the hospital to relieve Kris. I turn over and go back to sleep.

I smell toast. Chiara must be up. I come downstairs, pass the spent fireplace, notice an egg-smeared plate on the dining table and teacup sitting askew on piles of puzzle boxes. I follow my nose into the kitchen, a small green and cream-colored space made cozy by an oil heater. The over-hanging light is on. The windows over the sink are dark. Outside, it's raining. Dirty dishes are piled in the sink.

Chiara's bent over, her head inside the refrigerator. "Chiara, don't jump. I'm behind you. You starting breakfast?"

"Yes, I found some eggs, and I'm looking for jelly for the toast. The bread is whole grain. Do you want butter?"

"Sounds good. Becky's supposed to be here soon."

We hear the back-door crunch closed. Becky appears in a heavy jacket, gloves, and a scarf wrapped round her very rosy cheeks.

"I'm glad you're making yourselves at home. You can use anything in the refrigerator or shelves. Put your name on anything you want to keep for yourselves."

As she talks, she reaches for a skillet strewn with egg particles and plunges it into a pan of water. "I do ask that you clean up after yourselves," she said with a wry smirk. "But as you can see, some people get the message quicker than others. Eat whatever fruit is in the bags in the hallway." She points to paper bags of apples and feijoa.

"You can cook whatever you want in the kitchen. I'm not very good at it. Let me show you the laundry tubs out here." She leads the way into a long hall. "Here are the baskets and soap you can use. This door is my room when I'm here. You can knock on the door if you need anything. Here's the phone, so your friends can call in, but, as I told you, I'm often gone. If you see a fellow around the yard, that's my boyfriend, Roger. He chops the wood and brings it into the living room.

"I ask that you be responsible for your own spaces. That is why I call it "B&B Light." I'm here if you need help, but you're basically on your own. Bring your linen down here to the washer. The dryer takes so much energy, I prefer you hang your sheets on the line, but with the rain you'll have to watch for an opening. With the others away during the day working, the machines are free. Come out here, I'll show you the lines."

Under tall leafless trees, we walk into the cold of a damp, rain-soaked yard. Wooden boards crisscross the patchy grass under low-hanging lines. Sheets hang sopping wet on the back lines. "If it's rainy," Becky says, "it can take a few days. Just leave your clothes on the line until they get dry."

"It's like Italy, Mom, remember when you visited me. We had clothes hanging everywhere, all the time."

Becky chimes in, "Rightie-o. Then maybe you won't find it so annoying."

Becky pointed, "See over there, the white-and-green buildings? That's the hospital. You're not very far."

"That's an easy walk to the hospital then, isn't it?"

"Yes, I do it often."

I bundle up for my walk to the hospital. I pass a smooth macadam driveway which angles through a few green Department of Conservation "DOC" office buildings. Specimens of native bush, complete with identification tags surround the buildings. There are no cars in the parking spaces yet. I enjoy a mini-meditation as I study the plants, and it shortens my walk to the hospital by two blocks. Lovely.

At the hospital, Chris is sitting outside Yarra's room. "She had a good night, and so did I. She's sleeping now. My bed is really comfortable, and it's nice and warm. Don't feel sorry for me."

"You know you have the warmest place to sleep."

"It's great. I'll check with you to see what time you want to come back to the B&B."

"You know, I think the B&B is going to be fine. Becky calls it

B&B Light, meaning we have to take care of our own stuff, but that's perfect for us. We're free to come and go as we please and are not expected to take part in anything."

"I had a feeling it was going like that. She is certainly not hovering over us, or wanting to chat. She has her life, and we have ours."

"I think Chiara will want to come around two. I'd like to go to Mass. Let's see how it goes today. We can eat together, before you come for the night. If you're hungry, you can eat anything in the kitchen or the refrigerator, unless it has a name written on it."

"Sound's good. Love you. Hope you both have a good day."

Disruption

Chiara looks concerned as I walk toward her outside Yarra's room. "Oh Mom, there's a nurse here making trouble, maybe upsetting Yarra."

"What do you mean?"

"She came in the room. She complained about not being able to do her work. I don't know what she meant. She stormed out of the room. I went down to the room to report it and heard her saying something about 'what those people are doing in that room.'"

"I wondered if it was all going to be smooth sailing. Jill, the nurse manager, told us they had never before given palliative care, withholding fluids and food, giving sedation and comfort care. It would be new to some of the nurses.

I went out in the hall just as a nurse came stomping out of the office and across the hall with her head down. She did not see me. A little while later, Jill came to the room and motioned me outside. "I hope you will not have any more trouble with that nurse. I told her she must stay out of your room or leave."

Re-entering the room, I hear piano notes lilting, slowly, softly, one note at a time.

"Joe?" I ask Chiara. She nods.

My heart melts. I'd heard Joe had written a song for his Yarra. He'd composed a gentle piano CD to be played in her room. It is as gentle as the tapping of raindrops in a summer breeze or the soothing, gentle clatter of dried Australian seedpods woven into a wind chime. I know, because years ago, Yarra sent us one from Australia, writing, "Now that the children have grown and gone, you two deserve a new wind chime."

How appropriate that Joe, who traveled around Australia with Yarra, camping in the jungle and on the beaches, sent her a melody that sounds like the rustling of leaves, the clicks and smacks of native tongues ranging high and low, and the soft clinks of stones rolling with the tide.

Joe once told us he and Yarra tented on the beach and watched the sunset and the stars come out. Hours later, they woke to find themselves surrounded by the incoming tide. How they must have shrieked, jumped, and run laughing.

When she heard the tune was written and played for her by Joe, she blinked purposefully. On this rare occasion, she was able to let us know; she understood it was from Joe, that it was Joe sending her his love.

We played it constantly for the next weeks. It sustained us all and maintained a peaceful atmosphere in the room.

Red Skirt, Ready to Go

Hanging by Yarra's bed on a clip hanger is a long, funky skirt in many tones and patterns of grey and black bits and pieces. It is the New Zealand design, with felted flowers, pockets and buttons. *It's very au courant. Did someone decide it too stylish for a bed cover or maybe they decided Yarra could see it, rather than wear it, or Yarra didn't like the grey? I open her small closet. No red skirt. I'll look for a red skirt.*

Chris and Chiara are going to be with Yarra. I'm going alone to Sunday Mass at St. Peter Chanel, in Motueka. I'm sitting and waiting for the service to begin. Feeling empty, observing the parishioners as they walk into church, I have no prayers.

The parishioners' clothes don't look so quirky to me as they once did. *Is it the winter clothes, a different social level, or have I gotten accustomed to the casual island style?* No, these parishioners are dressed more upscale. Look, coming up the aisle is a woman with a fitted jacket, a hat, and a red skirt. A red-lace skirt, I can't believe it. *Perfect. It's perfect for Yarra. The woman is even the right size.* I wonder where she got the skirt.

My Mass is much distracted by my musing whether I can ask a perfect stranger for her clothing. When the woman walks up for communion, I check her size again. Perfect for Yarra, I decide. Yes, I can ask a stranger for her clothing. I plan: *first, I will make her acquaintance, then chat a bit. Then, I'll say my daughter is looking for a red-lace skirt, and that I'd like to find one. Next, I will politely ask if she purchased it locally, and this season.* I practice my comments and hope to remain calm.

I hear the priest sing out, "The Mass is ended, go forth to serve the Lord." He blesses the congregation; I cross myself and pray for courage. I search for the lady with the red skirt. *OK, I'm "going forth."*

I wait in the aisle as she visits with a friend. I hear their farewell, "Cheerio." The woman steps toward me. I know she will immediately recognize my American accent. *I'm a stranger, and that could be an advantage.*

"Hello, excuse me. Are you in a hurry? May I speak with you a few minutes?"

"No, I'm not in a hurry, my name is Liz. How can I help you? Are you a visitor here?"

Oh, this is going better than I hoped. "Yes, I'm Joanne Amoroso. I'm visiting my daughter here in Motueka. I was admiring your skirt. I wonder if you bought it locally, or recently?

"Oh, this old thing, no, I bought it long ago. I only wear it once in a blue moon. I looked in the closet this morning and thought I'd wear it today." Liz smiles dismissively, end of conversation. I gather my courage.

I begin, "Well, I wonder would you know where I could buy a red skirt this time of year around here. You see...." I pause and adjust my voice, trying to erase the pleading tone I hear. How pitiful.

Joanne, this is cheeky. You know you've heard it said about those cheeky Americans. I push on. "My daughter is in the nursing home around the corner. She's been wanting a red lace skirt."

The woman focuses her hazel eyes on mine, trying to read my face. I feel she knows my intentions, but I am flabbergasted to hear, "Do you want it? You can have it." *Did I want it? Just like that? Yes, but can I say so, standing in the church aisle begging from a stranger? Even a generous, openhearted New Zealand stranger who is immediately willing to give me her clothing? I am unable to speak.*

"Look." She grins. "I won't take it off right here in the aisle, but I know Ann, a nurse who works over there. I'll send it over to her in a parcel, and you can pick it up from her. I have lots of clothes, really. I'm happy to give it to you."

Singing My Grief, June 13, 2007

"Hey, Tony Backhouse is here for a gospel singing weekend," Kris says. I hear a touch of hope and possibility in his voice.

"You mean he's here now? At Riverside? For a workshop?"

Tony is our favorite singing teacher, ever. He is an internationally known, itinerant, master choir leader and gospel-singing teacher. And now, incredibly, he's here, just fifteen minutes from Yarra's bedside.

"Yes, lots of the Mosaic people are going. Irma sings now, and she's going. Chris will need to sleep, but Chiara can stay with Yarra while you and I go. It's only fifteen minutes from the hospital."

"Oh, yes, Kris, yes." My heart is full. Another New Zealand blessing at a time when we need it most.

The tall, clear-glass windows of the main Riverside Church Hall let in plenty of light and a dust-filtered view of leafless apple trees beyond. We walk past a wall of hooks holding coats, jackets, and long, knit scarves. About 30 people in wool, winter slacks, and heavy shoes cluster around, holding music sheets. As Kris and I walk in, some of the males tip their chins in greeting, some gaze and look away and some whisper to their neighbors. Many know Kris' wife is dying. Some recognize me as her mother.

Jessica, the first transplanted American friend we made in New

Zealand, sails across the floor in her long skirts. She smiles broadly and reaches her arms up to give us each a tender "welcome home" hug. "Oh, it is so good to see you."

It's been a long time since she and her husband Bruce came into our lives, kindly inviting us to music classes and programs at their home. They understood our need for belonging, perhaps more than we did, and welcomed us in.

In black t-shirt and jeans, Tony steps into the crowd of chatting participants. Singers move into voice part groups. I slot myself in between altos; Kris sings bass.

Tony lifts his arms, drops his circled thumb and forefinger. Thirty singers fall silent. My jaw softens. *I'm back, I'm home.* I smile with pleasure.

Tony sings the first line. "Jesus, remember me, when you come into your kingdom." He nods, gives the pitches, signals the down beat…a blend of many voices rises. "Jesus remember me…." We're singing. We follow with "Yes, I's a Comin'" and the soulful, lilting, "Lord, I know I been changed…Lord, I know I've been cha-a-anged…Angels in the heaven b'in call my na-me." The thrum of our voices, the exhilaration of combined notes, gentle swaying to the rhythms makes me feel I have belonged with these people forever. For two glorious hours, I feel I have prayed for Yarra.

We sing and sing, every word bolstering my soul.

As I walk to the door to leave, Burke, Yarra's therapist, catches up to me, puts a hand on my arm, "Joanne, remember, all those who love you here are sure you are doing the right thing."

People hustle around us. I'm stunned to hear such an open and tender affirmation. "Burke, it's a comfort to hear your words. You know we are carrying out Yarra's wishes. I'll remind Kris."

We step out into the cold, where Kris is waiting in the van.

Thanks, Kris, for Taking Me

We are both quietly humming on the way home. As we reach the hospital, I gather up my purse and gloves and grasp the door handle. Sunlight is dropping into the treetops, slanting into the front window. Kris tilts his head. "See you tomorrow."

"Thanks for taking me, Kris. It was a good afternoon. I got a lot out of it."

"Me, too." Kris smiles. "Good to try some new songs. Good to see some people I haven't seen in a long time." He keeps the motor going, his foot on the brake. "Quite a coincidence that Tony Backhouse would be here at this time." He laughs and looks into my eyes, "But you don't believe in coincidences anymore, do you?"

"I keep telling you, Kris, this whole thing has been a guided tour, as far as I'm concerned."

"I better get to the farm, need to feed the chooks and see if Irma has anything for me to do."

"OK, thanks again. See you tomorrow."

I walk into Yarra's room. The blinds are open. The soft glow of the salt lamp on the bedside table fills the room with a rosy glow. Chiara is standing and staring at the foot of the bed. "She seems breathless. It's scary."

The head of the bed is rolled up. Yarra's eyes are closed; her face is blue. I hear two weak, rasping gasps. She opens her mouth in a wide, slow yawn. I see a dam of white mucous filling her whole mouth, blocking her throat. She's suffocating on her own secretions. I rush to the sink, reach out…for what?

"Washcloths, Chiara," I yell. "Two." I see wooden tongue blades sticking out of the dental care cup, grab a handful, and rush to the bed. I put my hand out, and Chiara pushes clean washcloths into my fingers.

Yarra's jaw is clenched tight in spasm. Crunching the washcloths over my fingers, I enclose her chin with steady pressure, pressing down. Her jaw opens just slightly, wide enough to slip a small stack of tongue blades between her teeth, above her tongue.

Pushing her chin down again with the cloths, I twist my wrist and pass the blades across her tongue and pull a thick covering of mucus out into the washcloth. "*Oh, God, please.*"

Yarra sucks in a long, slow deep breath and then two more, like huge yawns. Her skin loses its bluish tint.

Chiara calls out, "Mom, she looks better."

Yarra's pale olive, tan color returns to her skin. It's over so quickly. I feel my legs trembling.

How did I react like that? It was automatic and instantaneous. "Thank you, God, for Chiara's help."

Chiara's face is pale and fearful. "Oh, Mom, you came just at the right time."

I begin to shake. Chiara puts her arms around me. I feel her warmth, bury my face in her long hair. "You helped me, Chiara. Thank God you were here."

Over her shoulder, I see Yarra's complexion has returned to olive. Her eyes are closed. She's breathing normally and looks peaceful.

Dazed, I plunk down in the armchair.

"Are you OK, Chiara? Sit down."

"No, Mom, I think I better go now. Are you all right here?"

"Yes. We'll be all right now." I steady my voice. "I'll tell the nurses what happened."

Chiara puts on her coat and gathers up her gloves and scarf. She bends to give me a kiss and signs a blessing to Yarra.

I say, "Be careful walking home, OK?"

When I return to the B&B later, I stop at Chiara's room. She has the heater going full blast. She's bundled in gloves and scarves.

"Can you feel it, Mom? The air is warm in strips and cold in spots."

"Yes, it's crazy cold." I get into bed next to her and prop myself on two pillows. I sigh.

Chiara looks at me and waits for me to talk.

"We need to talk, Chiara. I talked with Dad. We think Yarra's leaving. The circulation in her extremities is closing down."

"I know. I felt her cold legs, too, and her icy cold feet. I wonder if she feels that, if she has pain?"

"I don't know. The morphine drip is for pain relief. I'm praying it won't be much longer for her."

Chiara gets out of bed. She pulls on another sweater, turns to me and says, "She looked so peaceful today when I brushed her hair."

"I am sure she loved that, Chiara." I pause, "How you doing, Hon?"

Chiara looks so small beneath the long, dark, windows. She stands resolutely and straightens as she turns to face me, "Mom, you know what happened back there, in Yarra's room? You're a nurse. You can do that." She takes a long breath. "I've decided I don't have to watch my sister die."

I'm rapt at her words, her resolve.

She looks at me for a few minutes. "I decided I can go home now."

I let her words sink in. "I don't have to watch my sister die."

She knows how deeply that would affect her. I feel a great relief. She's going to take care of herself. She knows she has done all she could. She knows her boundaries. She knows what Yarra would want. Her clear thinking and steadiness have been so helpful to us; we've been a good team. Her loving gestures and sisterly companionship have been a comfort.

"Good you called it, Chiara. I think you've made a wise decision. You have done all you could for her here. Time for you to go home to Ruby and take care of yourself, too."

I slip out of bed and nuzzle into her silky, long hair for a hug.

"Look, Mom." Chiara picks a bouquet of small knitted flowers from the nightstand. "Show these to Yarra. One of the nurses made these and brought them in. So sweet. I don't know if they are for Yarra or us, or just because she wanted to do something nice for us."

Another nosegay. I pick it up, settle into the armchair and examine the tiny, perfect, handmade stitches. I breathe out. "Good. It's good to receive a gift of kindness right now. It's been a rollercoaster day, hasn't it? "

Immediately after I speak, there is a loud "cra-ack." The room turns dark. Chiara bursts into laughter. "Oh, oh, we've done it again, flipped the breaker. I've got my flashlight. I'll go down and get Becky."

The Internet Café

From the snatches of conversation, sniffles and sighs in the Internet café, it could be the "lonely hearts club." So many workers are away from home. They sell food here, too. I've already had lunch, but the aromas wafting from the kitchen make me wonder what's available.

It's June 15, and I'm trying to reduce the events of forty years into a twenty-five-minute talk for my daughter's memorial. It's difficult at best; with all the distractions, it's impossible. The young man seated in front of me is rapt, talking to a dark-haired woman in a pink sweater, smiling on his screen.

"Oh, darlin,' darlin,' I miss you so much. I wish you could be here with me."

I'm not sure whether despair or ecstasy will carry him away first.

The door opens and closes; more people come in. There are three people seated, waiting for a free computer. I'm doing my best to concentrate. I still see disapproving looks as I sit and try to collect my thoughts. I better do this with Yarra, where it's quiet, then come down here to type it up.

Arvind's Visit

I'd been invited for supper at the farm. Chiara stayed with Yarra at the hospital, and Chris was resting. Kris parks the car, walks back toward me. "Joanne, do you remember Arvind, the counselor Yarra and I went to see?

"I know him, Kris. I went with you once, remember? He helped you and Yarra so much."

Kris pauses and recalls, "I hadn't seen him for years. We drifted apart with the moves and all. Then one day last year, during the time when Yarra was getting colds and getting weak, he showed up at the farm. Arvind said to me, 'I drove out to tell you I would not be honoring Yarra if I did not ask you, when are you ready to let her go?'"

Kris and I share a silent moment. My heart wells up. I nod. "Another…" I choke. "Watchful, caring friend, Kris. So many."

Everything Connected

Melissa and nurse Carol, two precious friends of Yarra's, arrive as planned. Chiara and I immediately take advantage of their being with Yarra. We jump into Kris' car, and on his advice, drive off to the source of the Riwaka River. "It will do you good." Kris hands us a map. "It's hilly and curvy, but you're from Colorado. No problem."

First, we drive in silence, grateful for peaceful scenes: grassy hillsides, dark forests, and rivers. Then the road winds, curve after curve, uphill, 2,595 feet to the top of Takaka Hill. Also called Marble Mountain.

At the top, we park at a trailhead. The trail is lined with eight-to-twelve-foot-tall ferns and dark-trunked ponga trees on either side. Soon, I am reveling in greenery. The raised, stony track turns back on itself and drops us into a bush-cleared opening. A mat of layered, leafy sponge is a welcome treat underfoot. Before us, water sprays in white globules and liquid silver shards shoot in a wide sheath from a dark brown, fern-covered mountain wall. A thunderous blue-green cascade falls into a deep, clear pool and meanders off to become the Riwaka River. I stand with mouth open, breathing in the moist air, listening to the clinks, spits and rush of the waterfall. Kris is right; it does me good. I feel peaceful. I think of Yarra. She didn't get to experience this, so many lovely places out of her reach.

I tell Chiara, "When we came here, one of the first places Kris and Yarra took us to was a deep, clear, spring, New Zealand's largest, Pupu Springs. It was such a big deal to them. It looked like just a large green pond to me. Kris stood and stared out over the water for the longest time. Yarra couldn't stand in the heat, so she waited in the car. I didn't get it. I had a lot to learn."

Back in the car with Chiara, I read in the guidebook that Pupu Springs is only three miles from Takaka, right here where we are. Underground tunnels connect the Riwaka River at Takaka and Pupu Springs. I've come full circle.

We've been blessed by so many places of natural beauty—the beaches, ocean, waterfalls, caves, foliage, even The Brook in Nelson. How many times had we stood on the bridge just watching the movement of water over golden stones or listened to the trickling stream rushing downhill at the start of The Reserve, behind Kris and Yarra's house, or waited for the Morepork owl to hoot at night, as we fell asleep?

Water, greenery, and birds soothe our spirits. Like Kris and Yarra, we seek it. Is it because we more acutely need solace? Or are we reminded to seek it by now living in a culture where appreciating nature is a constant? That's what's kept us going, that and family. I wouldn't have made it without family.

Chiara and I drive home, tired but soothed by our outing. In the kitchen, we sort through the tea box. The doorbell rings in the hallway. Opening the door, I'm greeted by my friends Theresa and Karena with round-cheeked smiles.

I start to laugh, before I speak, and then I see in their soft eyes, *"It's almost over, dear friend."* My Guardian Angels have arrived.

"Come in, come in." I'm filled with joyful expectation.

Theresa holds out a bouquet of exquisitely arranged miniature buds encircled with lace, an appeal to the most hidden inner part of me. I sigh, press back tears. I want to protect the nosegay from the cold glare of the tall, ice-glazed windows. I reach out for the flowers, cup them in my hands.

Amid the rumpled piles of pillows and blankets on the couches, the stack of split logs, the empty black hole of the fireplace, the room lights up. I feel warmth.

Dear God, do we need light and warmth. Theresa opens her other hand where a red stone heart is nestled in her pink fingers. Theresa and Karena put their arms around me. My whole body softens, and tears flow. I cannot let go.

I introduce Chiara to these dear friends. Chiara offers to make tea. I'm grateful for her kindness. Then I think, "*How will she ever find all the bits and pieces for tea?"* Then I remember Chiara lived for a semester in England, and her hostess, Irene, brought her tea every morning. Chiara returns with a glass-lined, wicker tea tray and a smile.

We sit, talk with a soft, rapid patter and laughter and no attempts to assuage my sorrow, just love, understanding, camaraderie. In the presence of Chiara, Theresa, and Karena, I am surrounded by all the precious mothers in my life.

Come Be With Yarra

I awaken to the kitchen phone ringing over and over, from deep down in the back of the house. Becky doesn't pick up. *It's the hospital. I know.* Now, I'm really awake. I'd better get ready. Ready for this day. Behind the white lace curtains, dark rain slides down the windowpanes. Dark rain and white lace; that's the way this day will be, June 21, the Solstice. Yarra will know it in her bones. She often told me about delighting in going to Solstice celebrations with her friends. Yarra will leave today. This is the day she will leave her body.

No footsteps on the stairs. I'll get dressed for Mass. I slide to the edge of the bed, swing out my legs, and the cold hits me. I shudder and grab between the sheets for my underclothes, my New Zealand wool singlets and long underwear all warmed from my own body heat.

If this is my last day with Yarra, I want to wear something significant to her. Something that says *I love you, and, maybe, goodbye.* It's got to be her own artwork: the black tee shirt with the robust woman who looks like Yarra dancing with her hair streaming back and her arms flung out to the sides. It's stenciled in white with Yarra's bold slogan, "Create Your Passion." She'll see that. She'll know I'm acknowledging what she's been about all this time.

There's a knock on my door. Gosh, I didn't hear anyone come up the stairs. Maybe it's Becky, or Chris home early. I crack the door open. A woman stands, smiling. "Are you Joanne? I'm Dianne from the hospital. Chris wants you to come to be with Yarra now. I'll wait for you downstairs."

"Oh, thank you, Dianne. Wait in the living room in front of the fireplace where it's warmer. I'll be right down." I reach for my gloves and purse. *She's leaving...yes, be with Yarra while she leaves. That's why we came so we could be with her in her dying—today. I choke. I feel an old nurse response, "Just do it." It must be the cold. It tamps down my feelings.*

I hurry into the warm car. White puffs form in front of my mouth as I say, "I'm glad you could come for me, Dianne, thank you."

Dianne murmurs, "It's fine, no worries." We're silent and drive the familiar short drive to the hospital. We pass bicycling students in knit hats and mittens yelling to each other across the lanes. The exhaust from trucks and cars rises in a cloud as drivers stop at the red lights and peer out foggy windows.

We pass St. Peter Chanel Church, where the parishioners attending Mass will be praying for us. *God bless Yarra this day. God, help me to be steady, to be a strong mom. God help Chris and Kris. God bless all our children and those who will be praying for us today.*

Gravel crunches under my feet. My shoes clunk on the wooden porch. As I open the hospital door, a blanket of warmth hits me. No nurses about. An exotic bouquet of red-hot pokers and palm fronds brightens the dim entry. "New Cat" slinks toward the slightly ajar door to Yarra's room. He slips in and right back out as a nurse comes shooing him ahead of her. Now, the rose-colored doors are closed. I don't want to go in. My feet take me forward of their own accord. I want to wait for another day, but my hand reaches out, grasps and turns the cool metal handle, pushes the door inward.

The dawn dimness is softened by the salt lamps' salmon glow. I'm filled with gratitude; so many kindnesses. Chris sits beside the bed. He rises solemnly, leans over Yarra, and takes her hand. He shakes his head signaling me not to come in. "Yarra, Mom's here now, we'll be outside just a moment, then we'll be back in, OK?"

Yarra seems to be peacefully sleeping, her dark hair curls on the pillow framing her face. She is flushed. She did not respond to Chris' voice. We walk to the far corner of the corridor. He puts an arm around my shoulder, squeezes me, and whispers, "I think she's going. Since about 5:30 her breathing has been irregular and her pulse very rapid."

We glance at each other, see tears forming. We wrap our arms around each other's shoulders, lean together briefly…this is why we came.

Chris says, "I've called Kris. He's on his way. I don't think she will last much longer. I wanted you to be here." Chris looks at the wall clock. "I'll call the kids. They'll want to know, they'll want to pray."

I re-enter, sit in the morning dimness, bathed in the coral pool of light from the salt lamp. Joe's piano melody CD, a slow gentle tune, plays very softly. It is perfect as it keeps me company and provides shoring for all my thoughts.

The red scarf Chiara made is draped across Yarra's pillow. Her bed is a medley of colors and blankets. She looks fresh. The nurses must have just washed and changed her clothes and the bed.

Yarra opens her eyes. She watches me. I get out the red-lace skirt. "Good morning, Yarra. I'm putting your red-lace skirt on the bed. Here are your bears." I arrange the soft polar bear toys from John and Joe that support her arms and hands. I touch her hand. It's cool. I wonder if she can feel my fingers.

"I'm here, Yarra. I love you. Dad is here, too. Kris is on his way."

Yarra's eyes are steady, soft, still open, peaceful, so beautiful. Piano notes sound like small bells all around us. I see Joe's tall frame curved over the electronic piano, concentrating, his long fingers moving over the keys, loving his sister, his traveling buddy, friend.

"Do you hear Joe playing the song he wrote for you? Isn't it lovely? He's here with you. I'm going to put some lavender on your temples, Yarra. I know you love it…so soothing."

I take a drop of lavender oil on my finger and touch each temple. "You've done such a good job, Yarra. Your work is done, Sweetheart. You've done a long, difficult work…all done now, Honey."

Yarra closes her eyes. I fold her hand over "Little Bear."

Kris comes in, dressed in new, tan cords. He has prepared himself for this day and for Yarra. He has a new haircut and is clean-shaven, wearing the jade pendant Yarra gave him for their marriage gift. It hangs intentionally over a tan wool sweater from Chiara

Kris moves attentively to her bedside, as he has done so many times.

He strokes her forehead gently, bends to kiss her, gazes long into her face. He glances at me with a wan smile. Chris cracks open the door and signals with two fingers for us both to come out into the hallway. He tells Kris about her vital signs and that he thinks she will be going soon.

Kris says a friend of his has seen Yarra dancing around the "astral planes." Chris and I take that in. I envision Yarra dancing in the stars.

"Kris, I think any sign of Yarra dancing is welcome news, don't you?"

He nods.

Chris says, "I'll be back. I'm going to call the children."

Kris says, "I'll go to the kitchen for a cuppa. Rob is coming in soon with the coffin." He turns and walks down the hall.

I'm standing dumbfounded, hearing his parting words, "Rob is bringing the coffin."

Rob is bringing the coffin? Last time we talked, Kris said he and Yarra agreed on cremation. Don't tell me we are going to have a rehash session in these last moments. I watch his straight figure walking away, his arms hanging heavily, his steps, solid. Again I hear Leunig's words: "Let it go, let it out…let it all unravel. Set it free and it can be…a path on which to travel."

Please God, help us let her go.

I return to the room. The nurse manager, Jill, comes in. Her shining blue eyes look directly into mine. "How are you?" she asks, her voice full of concern.

"Full of gratitude," I breathe out.

"Crista will be in later," Jill says. "She asked to come in today." She looks gently at Yarra a few minutes and leaves. No need for physical caring now, just standing by to guide her passage.

Chris returns and goes to the bedside. He takes her hand. "Yarra, I've just talked to your brothers, Joe…Christian…and John…and to Ruby and Chiara. Chiara and Ruby are sending you an email. They all send you their love, and they are praying for you."

Yarra's eyes are partly open.

Kris pushes open the door. "Here's an email which just arrived from your sister." He holds out an eerily reproduced computer copy of Ruby's face. The white page is filled with grey and black halftones of Ruby's pale, pink skin. Her cheeks are white, her eyebrows black; her blue eyes are transformed into tones of misty grey, irises shiny, crackled onyx. Her blond hair, in white strands, wisps fairylike around her face. One white finger curls above grey lips, as if to send a kiss or say "hush." Ruby is the image of an angel bending in comfort, stunning to behold.

Yarra's eyes are partly open. "Yarra," I say softly, "Ruby sent you her photo on her new computer. Can you see this?"

Yarra's eyes pop open another quarter-inch. She's amazing. She's not going to miss anything. She stares at the photo intently and focuses her eyes. Yarra is seldom able to focus and stare. I think she has truly seen Ruby.

"She sends her love, Yarra, and Chiara, too."

It's eleven-thirty. I place my hands on Yarra's arm. Her flesh is getting cold higher up her arm. I slide my hand under the covers, her legs are blue, ice cold to mid-calf. I wonder, again, if she feels pain. She has medication and seems comfortable.

There's a tap on the door. Lawrence, a dear friend from Mosaic, peeks in, and comes in, bundled in layers. His bushy white beard hangs over his sweaters. He nods to Kris. He and Kris must have talked about his coming. He touches Yarra's arm and stands at her bedside a few minutes. He nods to Chris and me and goes quietly to a chair in the corner. He holds a music notebook on his lap. He begins to hum softly at first, then sings in his low bass voice the Latin words, "Bon homme es confidere en Domine" (A good man confides in God). It is a melodic, prayerful favorite of Mosaic choir, white-haired Lawrence's solo and his heart song. Peacefully, we join in singing and hum it through, over and over, soulfully.

Chapter 7—Yarra, Goodbye—June 21, 2007

So Many Goodbyes

The aroma of food cooking seeps under the door, reminding me I haven't had breakfast. I'm hungry. I glance at Kris, "Do you mind if I get some lunch?" He nods.

"I'll go to the staff dining room at the end of the hall."

A large metal tray of apple dumplings sits on the counter, thick crust wrapped around fresh New Zealand apples. "Oh, what a treat, and stuffed peppers." The cook looks into my eyes, smiles pleasantly. She knows what's going on with Yarra and her family today. She fixes me a fine plate of real mashed potatoes and a stuffed pepper.

"My favorite," I comment.

"Would you also like fresh string beans and carrots?" Her voice is so personal, friendly. I feel her words and service make up for compassionate phrases she would offer, if we were better acquainted.

Yesterday, three auxiliary staff personnel came separately and tapped on Yarra's door. They each said, "I asked permission to come in to say "goodbye" to Yarra before I go off for the weekend." They came in one at a time, smiling and at ease. Each walked to Yarra's bedside, each spoke a slightly different version of caring. "Yarra, I'm off for the weekend. I'm glad your mum and dad and sister are here. I'll see you next week, OK?"

Last evening, before nurse manager Jill went off duty, she told us, "I don't know how to explain it, that amazing daughter of yours… my cooks and cleaners…they each came to my office to tell me they receive something from going in Yarra's room. They asked for permission to say 'goodbye' to Yarra."

I am comforted. I say a prayer of thanks that we are blessed to have come to this compassionate facility. Bless the staff, all. Bless the administration. This is a healing place for all.

No one else is in the dining room. The nurses and aides are serving trays. I'm glad for a few minutes to meditate and collect myself. I have a few bites of food. Lawrence appears in the dining room doorway. His voice is urgent, "Joanne, I've just come from Yarra's room. Chris wants you to find Kris and come to the room now."

I push back my chair, fling open the veranda door, and scan the garden, then shuffle over the rough back yard. Kris finds solace in the bush, sheltered in the foliage. Not here. His van in the parking lot is empty. Inside the window of a patient's room I see Bernie, the music therapist, watching me hurry around in the yard. She would guess what's happening, I'm looking for someone. The sight of her interrupts my mission and reminds me: if Yarra is dying, I want to be with her. Kris could already be in the room.

I enter the side door and hurry up the hall to the rose-pink doors into the soft light. Yarra's been turned to face the door. Lawrence is gone. Kris is not here. The single piano notes from Joe's CD, "Song for Yarra," play softly. Chris stands at the head of the bed. He turns and comes to me at the door and murmurs, "She may have a few breaths…she breathed last just a minute ago. Maybe she is still here."

I move to her bedside. Yarra's fingers are curled under her chin. I reach my hand to cover hers. A long warm, perceptible exhalation washes over the back of my fingers, my forearm. Words spill from my lips, a heartfelt farewell. "Oh, thank you, Yarra, I love you. Goodbye, my dear. Goodbye. Go with God; Vaya con Dios, Yarra. I love you. I love you."

Internally, I begin to recite automatically, "Eternal rest grant unto her, oh God, and let perpetual light shine upon her." The Prayer for the Faithful Departed, memorized from Catechism as a child. "May her soul and the souls of the faithful departed rest in peace. Amen."

Silently, I call on my dear departed Mom and Dad, Alberta and Joe, my little sister Angela, Fr. Otto, all the grandparents. "Be there to receive her."

The door cracks open. Kris enters, looking calm. He comes to the bed, his eyes questioning. I wonder if he has spoken to Lawrence outside. Does he know?

Chris turns to Kris and says, "I think she may have just breathed her last."

He sinks into the chair where he has spent so many hours, days, weeks and months, watching with such tenderness her now peaceful, beautiful face.

We leave him to his goodbyes, each with a caress of our hands across his shoulders as we pass. "We'll be just outside if you want us," Chris murmurs.

In the hallway we turn to each other, wrap each other within our arms. We begin to tremble; a gasp, a sob, silent, spasmodic breaths of grief. No crying, no tears, just sighs and clinging to each other, and a soft sniffling of remorse and relief. *She's free. She's free at last.* We shake. We huddle side-by-side, holding each other's shoulders, gently swaying. There is not a sound in the corridor; not a person is in sight.

"Yarra's here, Chris, I feel her presence; she's leaving."

Chris places a hand around my waist, leads me to two plastic chairs against the wall. "Let's sit, Joanne." We intertwine our hands and arms and lean together.

Through the open door, we see Kris' broad shoulders curve toward Yarra, his face bent to her face, his hands holding hers. A glisten of light, high noon sun, catches the tears on his cheeks. A muted swath, through the sheer curtains, highlights his soft white locks bordered by her dark ringlets. Chiara's bright red swirl of beaded silk, her lovingly made gift to Yarra, Kris' tan Cargill jacket, the red-lace skirt…the well-worn toy polar bears from her brothers are resting on the bed sheets…John and Amy's yellow roses, a Vermeer painting of light, color, shadow and stillness.

We sit in the hall for timeless minutes. I'm peaceful…finished, grateful. Thank you, God. We walk to the far side of the bed.

Kris looks up, throws up his hands. Through a cascade of tears, his smile is glorious. "My…God," he pulses out in his deep, clear voice. "My…God…look…look…what…we've been able to do. Yarra made her peaceful passing," he chokes. His tear-rimmed blue eyes focus intently across the bed to where we stand. He spreads his open, encompassing hands, one to himself and Yarra, one towards us. "And we're all…still here…together."

I hear his strong, steady acclimation. It's true, Yarra died so peacefully, as she wished, as we intended, and we are here with her. No one else has entered the room. The nurses have left us alone with Yarra. I feel the spirits of all who have been with us on the journey swirling around.

Once Yarra said to me, "It's so amazing. I never thought that this life would be my life. I am so grateful. I can't believe this world. It's all so unbelievable."

Nurse Crista slowly opens the door, glances at each of us. She says softly, "You may stay. We're going to wait about an hour to prepare the body." My nurse's mind begins to peruse. *Why are we waiting? Because of body fluids settling? Privacy for Kris? Or some belief her spirit may be hovering? Then I hear the food carts rattling in the hall, and I think it's for practical reasons; staff is needed for feeding other patients. No matter….*

All these days of Yarra's dying, we have been treated with respect for our grieving, and gentleness for our privacy. No impersonal intrusiveness of bright lights, blaring TVs, noisy hallways, or mechanical adjustments of tubes and buzzing machines. No administrative requirements or unavailable nurses, which disconcerted us when we attended our relatives in the US hospitals.

We will have more time to sit with Yarra. I like that.

I say, "Crista, I want to help prepare the body." Until this time I hadn't committed myself, and Crista knew that. She looks at me directly and nods affirmatively. Chris says nothing.

Crista says, "You may go to the chart room if you want some privacy for phone calls."

"Oh, that's very helpful, Crista, we'll do that," says Chris.

Kris says, "Go ahead, make your calls. I'll stay here in the room with Yarra."

We phone Chiara. "We're here with Yarra, Chiara. Is this a good time to talk?

She cries, "Wait, wait, I'm at Ruby's softball game. I don't want her to see me cry. I'm going to go behind a truck."

"We're here with Yarra and Kris. She passed away peacefully just minutes ago."

Chiara's voice spills out, "I'm so glad Ruby and I came to New Zealand when she was little. I'm glad it's over. Just a minute, Mom, I need to get behind some bleachers where I can see Ruby, in case she goes to bat."

Her life goes on while we are reaching out from our private world of life ending. How difficult, trying to support her daughter and us and manage herself at a ballgame.

"Tell Ruby, Yarra saw her photo from the copier and computer. Ruby looked like an Angel. Yarra really opened her eyes wide and looked at it. It was a very special, last message she received from the family."

I envision Ruby in her gray softball uniform with the long-sleeved red tee and her hat pulled low over her eyes. Just as I saw teenaged Chiara and Yarra walking out of the house in their uniforms, so vibrant and energized.

As I lower the phone I hear Chiara's voice, "Mom, oh, Mom…"

"I'm still here, Chiara." I wait.

"Mom, it's the Solstice."

"I know Chiara, everyone here knows…Yarra picked her day to die."

When we reach Joe, he says, "I wish I was there. I'm sorry for… what the two of you are going through, but I'm also glad that you were there with her."

He pauses. "Yarra came to me in my sleep last night. I woke and wrote a new song for her. When I met my boss in the parking lot this morning, I told him not to be surprised if I was absent from work soon."

The Blessings of Anointing

Kris knocks on the chart room door, opens it a crack, and says, "Rob is here. He's come with the coffin," and leaves.

I'd seen the pine box at the yurt when I was there this week. Many people had painted their tributes on it. I thought it was symbolic, a good way for the farm kids to understand Yarra wasn't coming back. Why didn't I put my hand on it, too?

"What happened to the cremation plan? Did you hear of any changes?" I ask Chris. "Kris said he and Yarra agreed on cremation."

"No, he didn't say anything to me. He may just want to keep her beside him for a while."

Chris and I go to Yarra's room. Suddenly, Rob is in the room. His six-foot frame takes up space in the small room. Yet, his unassuming, gentle manner, his youthful good looks and soft voice bring assurance and calm. "I'm here to help carry the coffin in and out and up to the yurt."

I look at Kris in confusion. He says, "Yes, I know, Joanne, I just thought we'd bring her to the yurt for a few days."

I gulp. *A few days? Without embalming? Well, it's cold...I think of a line from the song "Poor Jud," in Oklahoma: "It's summer, and we're running out of ice."* Well, it's winter, and I've explained all I can or want to about the possibilities of decomposition. It's his decision now.

"I'll be outside, Kris," says Rob.

Crista comes in with washbasin, washcloths, and the three bottles of body oil Kris directed me to bring to her three weeks ago. She sets them purposefully on a stand near the bed. It's just as Kris said it would go.

Chris says softly, "I want to help."

Crista nods, "Chris, you stay over there with Joanne, OK? And Kris, you come on this side to help me turn Yarra."

She was so close to Yarra, how can she do this? She must be accustomed to her patients dying. She does this all the time, but she and Yarra were very close.

Crista looks at Yarra's body, looks across the room, her forehead furrowed. She comes to my side of the bed and then goes to the other, trying to organize. When she turns, I see her lips are trembling. This is too hard for her.

"Joanne, would you like to hold the basin while I wash Yarra's hair?" she asks.

I pick up the basin and go to the side of the bed. "Crista, we'll be all right here."

Yarra's hair, her "crowning beauty," has lost its luster and curls these past days, and I fear washing it will make it limp, but here we go. Crista lifts Yarra's head over the side of the bed, and I hold the basin while she shampoos and rinses her hair. Immediately the dark curls spring into place. It's looking beautiful again. I am glad to reach my fingers into her soft, wet hair, and form curls against her head. It feels good to be washing my daughter's hair.

Crista places Yarra's head on the bed, and she and Kris roll Yarra on her side to wash her back. I go back to Chris, and we hold Yarra while Crista presses a sanitary pad between her buttocks. I hope it will stay in place when her body is moved from the casket to the bed at the yurt. I don't say anything. Crista knows what she is doing.

It is then I notice Crista's hands trembling. Maybe her hesitancy is more than uncertainty about what to do next. According to the other nurses, "She was great with Yarra, best friends." I take a deep breath and begin to really help Crista; I stop observing and become a teammate. We are here to take care of Yarra.

Crista says, "We should get her nightie off and dress her before her limbs start to stiffen." Kris and Chris lift Yarra's torso. Crista and I inch off the red, flying angels nightie. We lay her down in the bed. The beauty of her body strikes me. Her olive-skinned body looks youthful.

My eyes are drawn to the deep rose-colored buttons on her small-cupped breasts, nipples I haven't seen in years. I feel my throat tighten. A young woman, she is still a young woman, not ravaged, as I expected. I imagine what it's like for Kris looking at his wife's body, nude and dead. I feel I am intruding even to think of it.

Crista says, "Let's scrub her armpits, Kris." She hands Kris a cloth with an indication that he should do the same on his side of her body. Crista sees his half-hearted attempts.

She raises her voice. "Kris, Yarra stinks quite a bit. She's been working hard. We don't need the yurt to smell of body odor."

Kris smiles and bunches the washcloth in the soap and gives her underarm another wash.

Crista grunts softly, under her breath, "We've had this conversation many times before."

Dr. Nicole, trim, with a short boy-haircut, comes in with her stethoscope in hand. She has come to verify the death. She nods her head in our direction, listens to Yarra's heart. Her eyes soften as she looks tenderly at Yarra, lifts her arm with her finger on the pulse. Looking at Yarra's pale body, she says as if quoting from a passage, "The loss of a child is the most difficult death."

Is that meant to comfort me? Many people have said that to me. I don't agree. I don't need her to tell me how I feel. Right now, I feel anger. I think she is trying hard, but I feel compelled to respond.

I hear my stilted reply. "At this moment, it is quite interactive, and that changes it a bit."

I wonder why I spoke. So silly. I laugh lightly, and that, too, puzzles me. I see Kris smile.

I'm glad Kris smiled, because I'm so surprised to hear myself. I sound rude and angry. You, doctor, can say your carefully chosen words, but I am her mother, and I can describe my own feelings. I am here doing the sacred work of washing and anointing her body. I don't need you to tell me how to feel. Why am I angry with her?

There you are, Joanne, right on target from Kubler Ross's stages of grief. Anger is one of the first. Am I'm using the doctor as a target? She's a stranger to me. Or is it leftover feelings that I had that she was too glib when she first met Yarra and "was willing to give the feeding tube six weeks"? It's been two and a half years, Joanne. Yarra and everyone here love Dr. Nicole. This must be about you, Joanne.

Dr. Nicole pockets her stethoscope and leaves.

Crista asks Kris to help hold Yarra on her side while Chris and I wash and anoint her back. We each wash a portion of her back and rinse it. Then, Crista opens the anointing oils and stirs them together. The heavy, lovely fragrances of frankincense, myrrh, almond, and orange fill the room. We dip our fingers in a small bowl and begin to stroke her soft skin. "*My child, my daughter, I'm so sorry to lose you.*"

The skin over her spinal knobs is intact. No bed sores, thanks to good nursing care, vigilance on the family's part, and the generosity of the New Zealand government for providing an oscillating bed since 2002. Crista and Kris are massaging her arms. Chris and I do her legs and feet. It feels so right, so holy, to be doing this anointing together, one last, loving, very personal act. We look at each other and pause silently.

There is one more task, to clothe Yarra. No mention of the red-lace skirt. It's to be the red velvet wedding dress from the celebration of their wedding party, which took place in the United States. She picked out the dress in Boulder.

Velvet has no elasticity. As the dress passes over her stiffening shoulders we hear a rip. No matter. We put on her deep green, black-and-red velvet jacket, which her dear college friend Anita gave her. We place Aunt Esther's turquoise necklace on her and draw Chiara's red scarf over her head.

"What about her feet?" Chris asks.

Immediately, Kris says, "No."

We look up, surprised.

He adds, "Nothing, no shoes, I want her feet bare." He pauses. "Free."

My throat clenches and tears form. *What love.*

Chris drops his head, puts his hand to his lips.

The Heavens Open

"There is just a handful of flowers left in the garden," Crista says. She approaches the bed, pauses to plan a design, then arranges her handful of blossoms. She places two pieces of fern up high on the corsage area of Yarra's dress and clusters two roses and a yellow aster on top. Some larger ferns she spreads across Yarra's skirt, and on these places more roses and lavender. Someone has made a little bouquet of rosebuds and lavender tied with a straw ribbon. Crista lifts and spreads Chiara's silk scarf across Yarra's right shoulder and places the bouquet on top.

Lastly, she replaces "Little Bear" under Yarra's hand. She has to have her bears. They went everywhere with her. Yarra's wedding ring glints on her little finger; Kris must have placed it there.

Crista looks appraisingly at her work and sees, as I do, that Yarra's jaw has fallen open, "I'll be right back," she says.

I believe her. I sit beside the bed to wait her return. If Crista had been my friend as a child, I would have nicknamed her Scout. She is competent and pleasant. One only has to look into her earnest blue eyes to feel compassion. Yarra must have been so comforted to have Crista around, as Chris and I have been today, confident that all will go well in her hands.

Crista is right back with a small red silk scarf in her hand. "We'll tie her chin up for a while, then later it will stay." I sit in a chair beside Crista to watch. Crista does her best, but Yarra's mouth falls open again. I stand.

Crista looks up, "Would you be willing to help me? We'll tie it real tight?" I remember my job, as a little girl, was to put my finger on the ribbon while mother made bows on presents. I hold the scarf while Crista makes a small bow, and it holds.

Yarra's eyelids have lifted a little. Crista says, "I could wipe them." She looks at me questioningly.

I say, "Do whatever you need to do."

Crista raises her arm to shield me from seeing what she is doing with the washcloth. I understand she is drying the sclera so it will adhere to the eyelids. Crista nods to Yarra and leaves. Oh, this must be so difficult for her.

In a few minutes, Yarra's eyes open again. I remember Nonna Angela telling stories about when she was a little girl in Italy, how the family members took turns sitting with the dead. They put coins on the dead person's eyes to hold them closed. I fish in my wallet for two New Zealand dollars. They are large as silver dollars and heavy. I place them gently on Yarra's eyelids.

Crista comes in, looks at Yarra and whispers, "So Spanish."

The doors open and Jill, carrying a handful of typed pages, comes in. Oh, probably release forms to sign since the body is going to a private party instead of a mortuary.

More nurses file into the room, and Chris follows them in. He's been on the phone with Joe and now gives me a "What's going on?" look. I shake my head and give my shoulders a slight shrug.

"Oh, did I tell you the nurses are going to carry out the casket?" Jill says. "How many other people will we need?"

Chris says, "Joanne and I will walk behind. We can't lift the weight, but there will be Kris and Rob, and perhaps Lawrence, that's three."

"We'll ask the auxiliary help if we need more," Jill says. "Now, we're going to practice a song so we can all walk out singing. You may join us if you like." She smiles at Chris and me and hands us song sheets. "Song sheets? "Walk out singing?" I'm overwhelmed.

Four graduate nurses gather around our daughter and begin to sing. "Dear friend, dear friend…." It's a lovely, simple melody we know. "Can we tell you how we feel? You have given us your riches…we love you so." It is a modified song we have sung in church. The nurses are not addressing their song to Jesus, they are singing their hearts out to "Dear friend…Can we tell you how we feel? You have given us your riches, we love you so." I am stunned. I look at Chris, his cheeks, like mine, are bathed in tears.

Rob enters the room with a wooden box, hand-built and gaily painted by friends, Yarra's coffin. Chris and I step out of the room.

The singing starts again. "Dear friend, dear friend...." the automatic doors swing open. Rob, Kris and the nurses shuffle out, straining under the weight of the casket.

Chris and I fall in line. Ahead of us lumber the nurses, one of each body type. There is model Carlyn, with her shoulder-length, white bob; petite Crista; sturdy Arleen; tall, slim Paula; and three from the other side whom I don't know. Each one hefting the weight, stretching or crunching their bodies to grip the handles on the sides, scuffling their feet, singing, singing.

My mind flies back to a hospital hallway in Pennsylvania. I wait outside my mother's room and another time my father's room, hoping to catch a nurse, in case one should momentarily step out of the computer-charting center, to ask them a question regarding my parent, or ask them to tend to them. The answer is the same, "The nurses are busy doing the charts; we'll send an aide."

Chris and I follow, weeping.

We process up the hall. All the rooms are empty, as the patients are in the dining room. *That's why we waited an hour to prepare the body. The nurses had all of this figured out. They had planned it all.*

We move haltingly across the wooden marae outside to a dark grey day, toward the open doors of the van. It came true. Yarra is being sung farewell like the Maori ancestors, as she is carried from the marae. A jumble of cocked arms lifts the casket up into the van. The bearers stand silent for a minute. Rob sways forward and slams the doors shut in a resounding clang.

We follow the van, bobbing and swaying on the straight, tarred road toward the hills. Black clouds billow and roil like several coal-fired engines spewing dense smoke. They rise heavily and churn into a water-laden, grey curtain, obliterating the hills and firmament, in heavy, deep tones. Rain pelts on the rooftop, flooding the windshield as wipers slosh water side-to-side. It's like peering through a kaleidoscope of translucent obsidian, smoke grey, jet black, and frosted glass. The van wobbles on ahead of us.

The rain lessens, and the screeching wipers grate on our ears. A narrow bolt of yellow light pierces the clouds in lightning intensity. Broad, parallel bands of sunlight curtain the menacing clouds. Two—not one—two, brilliant rainbows startle as they arch high across the sky. "Oh-look-look," we squeal in unison.

I hear Yarra's low dreamy voice on a crackly phone call from Peru: "Mom, they have the most beautiful double rainbows here... every time it rains. They call them "Arco Iris."

"Chris, do you remember? Yarra told us they always had double rainbows in Peru? Arco Iris, that's what she called them.... Here they are in the New Zealand sky, just a few minutes after...." I breathe in, look at Chris. He is gripping the wheel and staring at the sky, his mouth open, slowly shaking his head.

"I hope Kris saw them," he finally replies.

We drive along the Motueka River and descend along a flat valley covered with acres of kiwi bushes protected from birds by green netting. Rows of ten-foot-high, delicate hop vines twine up lath tepees. Red deer, fattened for butchering, placidly graze the fields, and sheep huddle under the weight of their sodden coats. Chris makes a sharp right turn up the hill under overhanging giant elm trees and up to Irma and Jan's acreage.

We brake to a halt as Kyle explodes off the porch. He runs ecstatically towards us, his long arms extended wide. "Joanne, Chris, did you see the double rainbows? We never see double rainbows. Twin rainbows for Yarra! Did you see them?" Kyle's face is glorious in joy and awe, a rainbow itself.

"Come, come to the yurt, Chris and Joanne, come to the yurt. Yarra's in there." Kyle, tall and straight, walks before us, leading the way.

Yarra's body is on a small bed, the remnant of garden flowers placed over her clothing, just as Crista prepared them. Flower vases flank the bed. The scarf and coins are gone. She looks so beautiful, with dark curls and eyebrows that accent her face. Her feet are bare; dainty blood red nails tip downward. There is no fire in the wood stove. It is cold.

The empty casket, conveniently beside the bed, serves as a seat for the silent, teary-eyed Kolff relatives. Hein and Johanna, Inez and Ralph, Lou and Chrissy, all bundled in coats and scarves. Kyle, Yiba, and Cella are quietly moving about the yurt. Kris looks tired and calm. Perhaps he is satisfied to have Yarra "home."

I am satisfied, too. Yarra is surrounded here by the people and things she loved. The well-traveled llama-wool serape she wore home from Peru hangs over the foot of her bed. She is dressed in her favorite clothing and jewelry; the "relics" are here.

Kris was right to follow his conviction. He would not "leave Yarra alone at the mortuary." This is so much better.

He moves toward me, looks with some amazement and says, "Can you believe it? She looks so beautiful…so beautiful?"

"Yes, Kris I see it, so beautiful, just as she is." I put a hand on his arm, squeeze my fingers lightly, feel the cold coarseness of his jacket. "You did good, Kris, all of it." I hear my words "all of it." He knows and I know how much, how very much that entails. Our eyes tear. "I hope you can get some rest before tomorrow morning at the mortuary. We'll go now, unless you need anything."

"Yes, OK; just remember to pick up the urn and the ashes for Sunday's celebration. The ashes will be in two boxes so you can take one home for your family."

"Yes, thank you, Kris. We'll do that." *Celebration? Ashes?* I sigh. "Speaking of boxes, we're emptying out Yarra's room tomorrow." Kris stiffens and nods.

Chris turns to Kris and says, emphasizing the words, "Kris, did you see the rainbows?"

Kris' eyes fill with tears. He presses his lips tight. Chris grabs his shoulders and gives him a long hug. "We'll be with you Saturday."

Chris and I leave the stillness of the yurt and walk over the wet grass to the car. It's cold, but everything feels fresh and clean. We hear footsteps. Kris is following us.

"Ah, Joanne, you…uh…might want to read something…Saturday…at the…mortuary…Saturday."

"*What's this? What's this I'm hearing?"*

"What are you talking about Kris? Is there going to be a service or something?"

He pauses and looks uncertain.

"Ah, I don't know. Some people are going to show up…the nurses…maybe you might want to read…a prayer or something."

I know he's trying to tell me something. He probably doesn't know any more than I do. I'm baffled. "At the mortuary…Saturday…there might be 'a service?'" I'm too tired to think about it.

"Yes, Kris, ah, I'll think, bring…something. *"Something?"* See you Saturday."

Empty

Yarra's room at the hospital is on my mind. I don't want to go there, but I know we must. "We need to clean out the room at the hospital," I say to Chris.

I notice I've said, "the room," not "Yarra's room." The room as neutral. Is this my brain's way of protecting me? "Your work is over, now, it's over." I'm surprised at my thoughts. I feel hard-hearted…empty.

The kiwi friends are taking care of the "Celebration of Life." Now we can just focus on finishing our tasks to close our stay here, go home to be with our children in the States and plan the memorial service there.

Walking into the room isn't difficult and sad, as I expected. The rose bouquet on the dresser from John and Amy is still fragrant. The curtains are wide open to the row of dense green hedges beyond the window. The three telephone poles Chris calls "crosses" stand tall against the blue sky. The bed is stripped and smells of disinfectant. Yarra isn't here anymore.

All sorts of paper cover every wall. Faded copies of photos from e-mails and the most recent copies of Yarra's paintings, posters. Handwritten and typed messages to Yarra are interspersed with fossicked seashells and twigs from beach and bush glued to paper or wood or strung together with ribbon. Once fresh and precious, they were mailed from someone who loved Yarra and to impart messages of cheer and encouragement. Today, powerless, they hang in limp disorder.

"Do we just get rid of these?" Chris said.

Without a thought, I say, "Here's a box, just drop them in here." *They served us well.* I'm surprised to hear myself concede they are remnants to be discarded…so unlike sentimental me. The friends will understand.

I glance at Chris as he folds the soft, worn shawls, ponchos and coverlets. They came from all over, and Yarra dragged them all over; from Colorado to a boxcar bedroom in Alaska, from a trailer in southern Georgia to a caravan under a Eucalyptus tree in Australia, onto a train across India, and stuffed in a crammed suitcase in Italy.

"Those fluffy ones are handmade from Chiara, Charlotte and cousin Phyllis. Put those in a separate box, the rest, we'll check with Kris."

On the wire screen close to the bed, her remaining jewelry is reduced to a few glass bead elastic bracelets that were easy to wear and bright enough for her to see. Kris gradually took home her good things; the necklaces she could no longer wear for their being too heavy, earrings which caused her ear lobes to bleed or were too uncomfortable pressing against her skin.

On the shelf of breakable treasures sit a swirly blue glass bottle sent by friends Irene and Betty Lou, from the Isle of Wight. Two American Indian pottery pieces, one a small black pot filled with cornmeal. In another small box are two entwined red clay rings, Yarra called them "two sisters' circles," made by another woman friend of Yarra and Chiara's.

How these fragile pieces survived three moves across the world, seven moves to residences in the US, Australia, and New Zealand, plus two nursing homes, I can't imagine. Spirit treasures, I wrap carefully and tuck into a box along with Stan Padilla's *Native American Chants and Prayers,* a book I kept in Yarra's room and often read to her. Writings for sharing sacred words in common. Maybe I will find something here for Sunday's celebration of Yarra's life.

I know where most of the clothing came from: hand-me-downs of friends, recycle shops and markets all over the US and New Zealand. Lace-edged camisoles from Ruth in Switzerland and sheer, colorful skirts from Colorado, India, and Australia.

Chris carries the boxes to the car. I walk to the nurse's station. I don't recognize the duty nurse. I say, "I'm Yarra's mom. We've emptied the room, thanks so much."

She comes forward, puts out her hand. "I'm sorry I haven't met you before. I'm Pauline." She folds both hands gently around my hand and holds it. "I'm sorry for Yarra's passing. It has been a pleasure to know your daughter. She taught me so much."

Tears well up in our eyes. "Thank you, Pauline, thank you. I know. Me, too. She taught me so much." I turn away quickly.

In the car, Chris asks, "What do you want to do? Wanna 'cuppa'?"

"No, I feel like a walk along the water. How about you?"

"That's good for me, too. Will we be warm enough?"

"We've got tons of scarves and hats. It's sunny. Let's see."

At the waterfront we park and step out into the sharp, fresh air. We wrap ourselves in layers of New Zealand woolens. We walk with our own thoughts, each in our individual rhythm. We have walked so many miles together that ours is a familiar and reassuring beat.

The immediate harsh crunch as our shoes grind seashells underfoot and the sting of cold across my face match my feelings. I place my feet deliberately. Why am I not wailing? I'm not debilitated, not broken in sorrow. Where are my tears? Is it the cold that condenses them? Holds me tight? Holds emotions and tears back?

After Yarra died, I sat with Yarra's body. Nurse Jill came in. She stood at Yarra's bedside, then asked me, "What are you feeling, Joanne?" I heard it as a clinical question. I searched my mind and body.

"Grateful. Grateful we were here with her."

That doesn't sound like a mother overcome with sorrow. Is it my nurse self that is holding me together? Am I going through the paces? Am I spent from losing her every day for fourteen years?

Chris' footsteps have stopped. Glittering light shatters my musing. A vermillion sun has transformed each wave into brilliant rosy-orange ribbons, which flicker across the blue-black water. Ahead of us, we've come to the turnaround place with the remnant spires of the abandoned merchant boat, silhouetted against a sunset sky.

"Are you cold?" Chris asks, looking down. "My feet are frozen."

"My toes are so stiff I can hardly feel them." We reach out and grab gloves in an awkward squeeze. We lean into each other and start walking back. I love this man with his gentle, wise ways, a treasure and a soul friend, a teammate and partner.

"Let's stop at Tally's to pick up some fresh snapper for supper; I don't feel like going out, do you?" he searches my face.

"No. Tally's is a good idea. We have baskets of veggies and feijoas in the kitchen. Thanks, Hon."

Back in our room at the B&B, I feel the intense cold gelling every bit of energy I have left in me. Chris and I flop on the bed, which faces a tall, dark armoire where our clothes are stashed. *We can leave! Our friends from Longmont, who are living here, have welcomed us in their warm, private apartment, anytime.*

"Chris! Firooze and Bernadette! Let's pack our suitcases, so we can go to their house right after whatever's happening tomorrow at the crematorium."

Chris is up and opening the wardrobe doors in a flash, tossing out our duffels. It's so easy. We're on a mission. I feel it. We don't even look at each other. We strip the hangers and stuff the suitcases. That's it, zip, zip. We're all done.

We plop down on the bed to stretch out for a few minutes, then go downstairs to the empty kitchen to prepare our supper. It feels good to be doing ordinary chores.

There's a loud knocking in the front hall, and Kris' voice calls out, "Chris, Joanne?"

Chris grabs a towel to wipe his hands. I turn to take the pan off the stove. Kris appears in the kitchen doorway, dwarfed in a heavy jacket, the collar pressed up, a scarf wound around his neck and wool hat all pulled down to his jaw. If it weren't for his voice, I wouldn't recognize him.

"Hi Kris." I give him a slow hug.

Chris walks to him and puts an arm around his shoulders. "Just in time, how about some snapper?"

I put the pan back on simmer and set another place at the table.

"Snapper would be good." He nods his head. "Yep, smells good." He scrapes out a chair and sits. We just look at each other for a few silent minutes.

Kris unwinds his woolen wrappings and drapes them on a chair back.

"Yeah, yeah, here we are." He sighs and looks across the table at us silently. He digs in his jacket pocket. " I was in town so I picked up the death certificates. You'll need one to get through the airport with the ashes." He pauses a moment, takes a deep breath. "Remember…when you stop at the morgue, uh…Sunday morning, there'll be two boxes of ashes—one box for me, yep, and one box for your family, for the plane." He pauses. "And the urn…for the celebration…Sunday. Pick up the urn for me, would you? We'll put them in front of the podium with some flowers." He sits down at the table.

This has been a long conversation for Kris.

He wants to get it done, or done right, off his mind. I don't know which, or all of them.

He looks away. "I'll keep the ashes for a while. Probably spread them at Kina Beach later."

We nod. "Will we owe them anything Sunday?"

"Let's wait and see. I think it will be covered."

We eat in silence, except for some murmurs of approval for the snapper.

Kris' knit hat has matted his curly hair into wayward spikes. He's oblivious. He looks like a different person now, with nothing to do next.

The clink of silverware accents our silence, calls me to attention. The heavy wool clothes, cold, sadness, the son-in-law coming back to visit the old parents after his wife, their daughter, dies. It feels like an Irish movie scene. I can't leave it there.

"We love you, Kris."

He raises his blue eyes and stares. Tears pool in his eyes. "Yeah, yeah, I love you…both of you. Here we are together again, huh?"

All Was Provided

On Saturday morning, we stop at the florist to buy an American Beauty rose.

The streets and sidewalks are dark with rain. My coat is stiff with cold in the few seconds of going from the porch to the car. *This cold will be good for something. It will hold us tight…just right… just right for tears and grieving.*

I carry my Ecuadoran bag for Yarra. In it, I bring the book of American Indian prayers and chants, Ella's black pot carefully wrapped, and the small packet of powdery fine cornmeal. I also have Fr. Patrick's stapled pages of Catholic prayers and a few poems written by the siblings, which I found in Yarra's loose papers.

Cars are pulling in to park on High Street. It's twenty minutes before nine, and people are gathering. Chris and I walk into the driveway leading around back to the crematorium. Oh, I hate that word. We see a flank of women, maybe a dozen or so, standing, looking towards us and waiting.

"There's Jill," Chris says. And we recognize some of the other nurses, bundled into various coats, scarves, hats and jackets, not as we usually see them, in white uniforms. Today, they are ordinary people who have come out on a blustery Saturday morning. Good. They'll know what to do.

We smile and say, "Good Morning." I lean in between Jill and Crista and whisper, "Do you know what to do here?"

Chris leans forward to hear their words, but they purse their lips, look at each other and shake their heads. "No, this is the first time we've ever been here," says Christa.

Chris gives a slight, Italian shoulder shrug and an over-turned hand, "What else is new?"

I look down the drive. "Here comes Erica and Irma with the kids, but where's Kyle?" Irma strides forward with blonde Yiba and Cella. Tousle-haired Yarren clings to Erika's hand and teenaged, sorrowful Shauna clutches her mother's elbow.

"Shauna's a young lady now," says Chris. "Looks like she's been crying.

"Yes, they were very close. Remember, she and Rene visited with Yarra every Friday. This must be hard for her,"

"Yes, they were her buddies until they moved up to Golden Bay."

A passel of men shuffle into the driveway, carrying the casket emblazoned in bright primary colors of handprints, flowers, mountains, suns, moons, and words. Kris, Rene, Jan, and Hans lead the way. At Jan's side, walks nine-year-old Kyle, his ever-investigating eyes flitting over the scene.

"Let's go in now." Chris places a hand on my elbow, nudging me forward. The crematorium is really a large, converted double garage. The walls are painted cream and the windows curtained in linen, with one whole side open and flanked by two garage doors propped wide. It's no kind of weather for standing in an open-sided garage with rain, wind and cold, but about thirty people have assembled. Chris and I walk through the crowd to where it's more protected. A grey metal structure covers most of the front wall.

Though they would never call themselves anything so formal as pallbearers, the men carrying the casket enter and set it on a raised wheeled cart. Erika steps forward and gently places a small bouquet on the casket, and a few others follow suit. The pine box, painted in unbridled splashes of gaudy designs, is an altar of color; unabashedly homemade, definitely, and uniquely Yarra; bright, front, and center.

Kris turns and looks toward the people assembled, nodding, acknowledging their presence. He wears his tan Carhartt jacket from the US and a hand-knit scarf from Chiara. He takes off his gloves and a wool hat and shoves them in his pocket. Curls fall about his face. His blue eyes glisten behind silver-rimmed glasses. I wish him well; this is an awesome task we are about to begin. He takes a breath and says in his clear, deep voice, "I thank you all for being here today for Yarra and me," he says, "and for Chris and Joanne."

Another pause, then he adds, "I think we'll just sing a few songs." His shoulders square, he plants his feet. His distinctive bass voice rings out, "Te..a..ro..ha…te whaka pono…." Immediately, the crowd picks up the tune. "…Te rangei ma ri e…ta tou, ta tou e." I understand the translation to be, "Love, faith, peace, all of us together." It's a Maori song so familiar it could be the New Zealand national lullaby. Everyone is singing in harmony and swaying to the Polynesian melody as little puffs of condensed moisture rise from their open mouths. Magic.

Kris looks our way, "Joanne and Chris, do you have something to read?" I'm vaguely surprised to be up so soon, but we were advised, and we may be the only presenters today. I am still holding the rose I brought to place on Yarra's casket. I step forward.

The melody and words of *The Rose* resonate in my mind and heart. That sentimental melody Yarra learned and loved during her high school year in Peru. I hear Yarra's phone call, "Oh mom, you have to hear this song. Every night, we sit on the bed waiting to digest our food.

"Carmella and the three girls and me listen to this guy, Julio Iglesias, sing it, and we cry and cry."

"What, Yarra? Why are you sitting in bed waiting to digest your food?" I'm more interested in that than a song.

"We're two miles high, Mom, and the heavy food we eat, there's not enough oxygen to digest it. We get a bellyache if we go to bed after supper. But, Mom, try to hear that song, 'The Rose,' OK?"

When I heard it, I fell in love with it, too. Ever since, it's a reminder to anyone in our family, whenever we hear it played—in a grocery store, on a radio station, a concert, we grab hands. Yarra's song…"love—it is a flower and you its only seed."

Yarra was the heart willing to take a chance, to learn to dance, unafraid of waking, of being taken, of dying, yes, yes, to all of that…. "When the night has been too lonely and the road has been too long…." oh yes, yes.

I peer into the deep lush redness of the American Beauty petals, which I hold in my hand. I step forward and place the rose on the casket. "This is for you, Yarra," I say softly. I swallow and hold back tears.

I look up to see Irma standing tall, Cella in her arms, with Kyle and Yiba standing between her and Jan. Erika and Rene shelter curly-haired Yarren, who presses himself against his mother's legs. These are Yarra's loved ones. They are her family here in New Zealand. Steady, practical, generous of spirit, and joyful, I breathe their strength in and begin.

"Yarra often said, 'If you live in enough places you could learn to love the whole world.' This morning, I believe that is true. When Yarra lived with her sister Chiara, in New Mexico, they became friends with Native American women who were artists. They enjoyed and absorbed their culture. Later, Yarra enjoyed hearing these Native American writings from Stan Padilla's book, *Chants and Prayers*, read to her. The first is a Navajo verse."

The mountains, I become a part of it.
The herbs, the fir tree, I become a part of it.
The morning mists, the clouds, the gathering waters,
I become a part of it.
The wilderness, the dewdrops, the pollen,
I become a part of it.

The crowd is attentive. "Now, an Osage/Cherokee verse." I pinch bits of finely ground cornmeal from the pot between my fingers and fling it to the compass points as I chant:

Look, I see the Sun…
He is my father
He is my beginning
Look, I see the Moon…
She is my Grandmother,
my guardian keeper
Look, I see the stars…
They are my friends,
my relatives.
Look, I see the universe…
I see myself.

I feel comforted, remembering the harmony I felt so many years ago as I watched my friend standing on her porch steps sprinkle cornmeal to the four directions. I rub the grains of fine, white, hand-ground cornmeal through my fingers and feel the silky curves of the little pot smoothed by hours of hand polishing.

With Yarra's every move, back and forth over oceans, it was packed into boxes of treasures, along with the finger-worn book of *Chants and Prayers*, which I bought for Yarra years ago. Much later in New Zealand, as I read it to her, the words provided a place in which she and I could share a mutual appreciation of the spirit world. How amazing it is to have them here today, the pot with the little bundle of cornmeal safely tucked inside and the book for her service.

I can see Yarra smiling and saying with a shrug, "See? The universe provided."

Chris takes a step forward, straightens two sheets of paper and looks at the crowd. They are quiet and still. These are people we know so little, and only know a portion of their support for Yarra, yet they are here for Yarra this morning, and for us. I feel a bond in their presence.

Chris says, "Over the years our children sent many offerings of their own writings and artwork to Yarra. Here is one of the poems."

Chris pauses, lifts his head, and recites:

"Transcendence"
Chiara Michelle Amoroso

Brushstrokes
Sing her Song
Her spirit soars,
As she paints colors,
On the canvas of life.

The end of the rainbow
Splashes down upon her paper
As she dreams,
And a thousand birds take flight.

She laughs
Shattered sunbeams and
Precious gemstones
Across the page.

Radiant and rare,
But none,
More precious
Than she.

Ocean waves
And sea sprays
Soothe her soul.

A million tiny feathers
And the prayers of little children
Whirl by.
Angels catch them
On their wings.

It is quiet; the rain has started up again. I step toward Chris and say, "We will finish with a reading from our Catholic heritage."

Loving and Merciful God,
We entrust our daughter, sister, wife, friend Yarra, to your mercy.
You have loved her greatly in this life.
Now that she is freed from all its cares,
Give her happiness and peace forever.
The old order has passed away.
Welcome her now into paradise
Where there will be no more sorrow,
No more weeping or pain, but only peace and joy.

I look to Chris. He nods his head, signaling "well done." The words, prayers, poems have melted over us.

The mortuary attendant, ruddy-cheeked, wearing a ubiquitous New Zealand Swan's Dry, a green plaid wool shirt, buttoned tight over his belly, crumpled work pants and heavy boots steps forward. He is ready to move on. He lifts his chin and asks, "Are we all right, then?"

No one answers. He says to the men in front. "If we are done here, would you carry the casket up to the door and push it inside?"

He turns the wheel lock handle and tugs open the heavy door. I feel I am watching a pageant in slow motion as Chris centers the casket in front of the door. The triangular form of men's shoulders as they lean and tilt the coffin into the cavernous opening evokes memories of other scenes. My imagination wanders. I see the united force of male shoulders in a rugby scrum; the image of the American soldiers leveraging their arms and legs to raise the flag at Iwo Jima; the obligation of male strength to duty.

Kris extends his arms to push the casket in, then further, following the attendant's instruction. *How can he do that?* The colors and the bouquets of flowers disappear into the narrow darkness. I feel fearful.

The attendant pushes the door slowly. A solid, irreversible "thunk" sends shivers up my spine.

Scanning the silent crowd, he raises his right hand over his shoulder and points to a doughnut-sized, shiny scarlet button, "Who will push the button?"

The words barely register…*Oh, no, who would choose to…?* In a flash, Kyle's slender frame shoots out from the wall of bystanders like an uncoiled spring. His long pale fingers reach up for the red button. Whack! He hits it hard. A collective gasp shatters the silence.

Kyle twirls. Smack! His red sneakers hit the cement floor, eyes bright, face alight with boyish accomplishment.

We hear a soft mechanical whoosh. I avert my eyes reflexively, and, over my shoulder, I see stunned, wide-eyed adults staring forward at an abrupt finality. Chris and I freeze, stunned by what has happened. We reach out to grasp hands.

Feet scuffle on the pavement. People peel away. Some are weeping, some slowly shaking their heads.

Chris puts a hand at my back, guiding me in the flow of people walking down the driveway and whispers, "Are you going to be all right, Joanne?"

I look up and see a group of smiling nurses waiting for us. *All right for you or not, take a breath, Joanne. These are Yarra's "friend" nurses, here on a Saturday morning.*

Jill says, "Joanne and Chris, we want to you to meet Grace. She was a special friend of Yarra's. She has been off for cancer therapy."

A smiling, round-cheeked, dark-haired woman comes forward. The gathered nurses move up to hear the conversation.

Grace says, "I loved to go into your daughter's room; she taught me so much. She looked so deeply into my eyes." Again, we hear the message relayed by many nurses, "she taught me so much."

Grace continues, "We had so many good times." She pauses, "The '*Walter*' book came from me."

I say, "Oh, Chris, remember when we first came to the room and saw that book on her bedside table?"

The nurses giggle.

I look at Grace. "We didn't know what this hospital would be like, we didn't know the nurses. We picked up that book and read the title, *Walter, the Farting Dog*, and said, 'Oh, they're onto her humor already.' So, it was you?"

The other nurses nudge her. “Tell them.”

They watch our faces as Grace says, “Oh, one of the nurses frequently has a little intestinal problem. One day, we called that nurse into the room to help us turn Yarra. She was busy and didn’t want to stay. She helped us, then left and tromped up the hall leaving little sounds behind with every step. I saw Yarra heard that, and Yarra saw my eyes and started laughing. Another day after we turned Yarra, one of the nurses hit the bed or something with her body and there was a sound; Yarra caught my eyes and laughed again.”

Chris reaches for my hand, gives me a squeeze, says, “Thank you, thank you for telling us that story, Grace. Wasn’t it wonderful when you could connect with Yarra? See her eyes sparkle, and you both could savor it?”

“Oh, yes it got to be quite the joke around here.” Grace chuckles. “Yarra was quite the celebrity for a while.” I see each nurse’s face is smiling, glowing as they look at us. Through Grace’s story they are saying, “This is how close we were with your daughter, shared with her, how we loved her.”

“Thank you, Grace. I’m glad you could be here today, glad to meet you, go well.”

Out in the car, we turn to each other. “Did we miss something in there?” I say.

“Joanne, I think it went very well.” Chris’ eyes show relief. “Kyle may have spared us a few pages of the last chapter.”

“Yes, maybe so.” *The pages where all the emotions I’m not feeling might have come tumbling out. Kyle may have saved us.*

“Tomorrow, we’re on to Yarra’s next request. Remember, ‘happy party, chocolates and B.B. King,’ and we’re not in charge.”

Back at the B&B, we find a folded note slipped under the door. It’s from Firooze and Bernadette. In a teacher’s firm script, we read, “We waited for you here today for an hour. We froze our asses off. The downstairs flat is ready for you. The stove is turned on. We will prepare your meal. We want you here. Firooze and Bernadette.”

We’re all packed and ready to go.

Pass Through

As we drive through Richmond, I see a dark, red-brick and white, wooden church, St. Paul's Catholic Church. It looks, to my American eye, more like a Protestant church, but there is a cross on top. I need Mass and communion tomorrow. I'll make it here.

Sunday morning, June 24, following Firooze's directions, I easily find the church and stop in the entry to get my bearings. The interior is dim, but intense morning sunlight gleams through red, gold and blue stained glass. I'm momentarily blinded. *Where do I want to sit?* I look away from the windows to the left. There in the back row, a curly, white-haired woman is cocking her hand towards me, patting the empty seat beside her.

Here is a New Zealand angel, if there ever was one. It's Theresa's dear, sprightly mom, flashing bright red lips in a welcoming smile. She mouths, "pass through," and I fully understand as she waves her cupped hand towards me. Warmth flows through me. I'm no longer "one of those people" if a pioneer like her welcomes me.

She pats the seat beside her, shifts over in her seat, moves her purse, and gives my hand a squeeze. She whispers, "I've been waiting for a friend, she's not come."

She grabs my arm and pats my hand like she's so pleased. She returns to her prayers.

The organ sends out its first soft chords. *Oh, come on, has this scene been scripted? It's "The Guided Tour" again...me a stranger in a strange town, at a strange church and a motherly, dear friend is waiting in the back pew. OK, OK. I get it. I'll take it. Thanks, God.*

Yarra's Life Celebration

Chris and I drive to Riverside community. I read Chiara's handwriting on the paper clutched in my hand. She has recorded Yarra's requests. My hands shake. *Take a big breath, belly breathe, compose yourself; this is for Yarra, Joanne, A Life Celebration, her last wishes.*

(62)

Yarra's Life Celebration
"A Happy Party" ✓
Red dress – any lovely one will do
Burgundy Velvet Skirt + Top
Daisies – white, purple
Chocolate cake

Songs – The Rose, On Eagle's Wings, + music by B.B. King ✓ – or whatever

Family and Friends to tell stories about moments with Yarra

Let balloons go (maybe with messages to Yarra)
Butterflies, if poss.
Rainbow colours piñata for kids – filled with chocolates

Would like to be cremated and family members each fling a few ashes to the heavens ✓ from Eagle's Head in Big Elk – or do with astos who

She does not wish to be kept alive if she can no longer participate in life – (see, hear, communicate, breathe, eat, etc)

program – ~~picture~~ drawing of dance spirit dance
black + white photo of Yarra

Readings for program and who to read them
maybe quote from diary – ask her or think of some for her

My stiff body lags behind as I come out of the car headfirst and groaning. The whole clear blue, sun-filled, sky opens overhead and my groan evolves into a gasp. An apparition rises above the hillside where the community center stands. The steeple and the white clapboard building sail forward like a cruise ship sailing over the sea. I shake my head. *Seeing things is not a good way to start the day, Joanne.*

I'm moving through molasses. I stomp my legs on the dry grass in the field where we are parked. Not quite done yet, one more day.

"Lots of cars parked here already," I murmur to Chris.

"I hear all Kris' relatives and in-laws will be here today, except his brother in Denmark, and all the farm friends, maybe Mosaic, too."

No one notices our arrival. There's a bustle about the place. People moving chairs clatter from the kitchen. Immediately inside the wide double doors, a few men manage a helium tank filling purple, white and yellow balloons. Yes, Yarra asked for "purple asters with yellow centers." Irma went looking. They're not available this time of year so she transferred the colors to balloons. Yarra would like it.

In the entry hall, colorful covered bowls of every size and pans of food are stacked on long tables. When the kitchen doors swing open, I see people with baskets and pots sliding between the doors, women chopping vegetables, stirring pots on the stove. The main hall is noisy with people dragging chairs into rows. *No soft organ music, no carpet under foot, no candles, and no hushed voices. Best to leave all your American and Catholic expectations of the word, "funeral" outside, Joanne. It's not a funeral. It's to be "A Happy Party," as Yarra requested.*

Kris' adult children, Bindia, tall and blond like her brother Mark, walk towards me, each carrying folding chairs. Tears stream down Bindia's face. She crinkles her brow when our eyes meet. I haven't seen her in ages. She nods, helpless to speak or greet me. I nod in return.

Johanna and Hein are working in front of portable school bulletin boards. They shuffle through packets of photos in their hands. Their cheeks are shining, wet. They are displaying portions of Kris and Yarra's life together. I see Yarra and Kris' faces, smiling over and over, from snatches of sun-filled, colored patches. All the Kolff family patiently, tearfully, attaching photos to bulletin boards, working side-by-side, quiet, pensive. I miss a step, falter. Chris grabs my elbow, steadies me. I look up. He looks as stunned as I feel.

"Thank you...so good of you." It's all we can say. All these people are openly grieving and working to prepare a farewell for my daughter. I shuffle toward the tall windows at the front of the meeting hall. It has been lined with folding chairs. Who did all this work? I can hardly breathe. Then I remember...this is where Kris' mother lived and worshiped. Her funeral was held in this very place, now it's Yarra's Celebration of Life. I feel weak. I head for chairs near a wooden podium. I feel I've been treading water too long. My head is above water, but my body is struggling to stay afloat. Chris holds me as I drop on a padded chair then sits beside me.

Sonia, a member of Mosaic, is waiting. She smiles, comes to show me a wreath of delicate greens and long thin ribbons. "It's my family's custom, Nordic, a 'Mitake.' I'd like to wear it to honor Yarra."

"It's lovely, Sonia, thank you. Will you introduce it to the audience?"

"Yes. I want to...I'll try." She walks away.

I take a deep breath, look up and out through the tall, clear glass windows. A haze of dust and particles of grass soften the light. There, that's real dust on the window. Just three days ago, Irma got permission to hold the service here next weekend. Only two days ago, she was told they had to move the program up to today. *And why are you thinking about dust on the windows? Distraction? Reality? It's all too quick, too final.* My eyes fall on the turquoise and purple urn...Yarra's ashes. Here beside me, next to a bright bouquet of long-stemmed flowers, *Yarra's ashes. It's your party, Hon.*

Rob strings electric wires across the floor and covers them with blue tape. He checks the sound system. I hear a few bars of B.B. King singing, "Come Rain or Come Shine."

Kris comes near, "How you doing?"

His eyes are tear-streaked and puffy. I glance at the urn. "Probably same as you are."

"Yes." He sighs and pauses. "Chris brought everything out from the mortuary, thank you. The urn looks good with the flowers, no?" He gives my shoulder a squeeze. "Lawrence gathered all the Mosaic people. They're going to sing."

I feel uplifted, just knowing our friends will be here singing. "Oh, wonderful."

"I'll be back." Kris adds as he walks away, "I'll see what I can do to help. Here's a copy of the program." I read Irma's handwriting:

Beautiful song by Mosaic choir
Welcome—Irma, How We Met
Chris—Talk of Yarra's Life, End-of-Life article, written for newspaper
Joanne—Talk of Yarra's life
Sonia—Presentation of wreath of "mitake"
Irma—Invitation to celebrate Yarra's life:
Candy-filled piñatas for children
A balloon release—chocolate for all
Followed by lunch and dancing to B.B. King
Music for Yarra "My Way" by Frank Sinatra

Wonderful! I'd given Yarra's requests for a "happy party" to Irma, and look what she and the friends have prepared. *It's your happy party, Yarra*. Good thing Irma took it on. No way we would have been able to pull this together.

I barely recognize the people as they enter, bundled in heavy winter clothing. As I glance over the crowd, among brightly colored casual jackets and sweaters, I note a row of dark, tailored coats. They are our neighbors from Brookland Terrace. Theresa and her mother are here, too. I feel a softness creep over my face and chest.

All goes as planned. Mosaic choir performs at its heartfelt best. I sigh with relief and gratitude. Irma sets a sprightly pace, a confident and pleasant telling of seeing Yarra in the market and saying, as many others have, "a woman in a purple wheelchair with long black hair and purple butterfly wings. I wanted her in my life." In the late nineties, she saw Yarra in Elko's and sat with her to share a coffee. It was an instant friendship, based on a conversation of riding horses. Irma began taking Yarra riding on therapy horses. She stayed by Yarra's side for all the rest of her life.

It's my turn to talk now. I look over the crowd. So many people have come today. A row of men in colorful wool shirts stand in the archway and one man in a long black coat. It's Fr. Patrick. He's spending his afternoon off to be here...so many good-hearted people and a real testimony to Yarra's many ribbons of connection. I want to tell all the stories. I tell many stories. *It's getting too long, Joanne. They came to honor Yarra and Kris, you and Chris. Be merciful, Joanne. But I don't want to stop. I want to keep talking about Yarra. I don't want it to end. Sonia, Joanne, Sonia is waiting.*

I motion Sonia to the podium. I return to my chair and sit down, feeling defeated.

Sonia makes the gentle presentation of a Nordic "mitake" wreath. She displays the delicate wreath and describes the custom. When I hear Sonia's presentation, I smile. Sonia, perhaps, does not know that, as descendants of Italians, we celebrate a similar custom on December 13th to honor St. Lucy. Chiara and Yarra, at least once, wore wreaths of candles in the morning to pass cinnamon buns to the family.

It is silent as Sonia walks back to her chair. A sudden loud clatter causes everyone to sit up and look around. It sounds like wooden boards being dropped on the bare floor, and indeed it is. Kyle pops up on wooden stilts.

"Oh, this is too much," I gasp. Kyle wears a tall, striped Dr. Seuss hat. He towers over the audience. He grins as he hands out Yarra's colorful, laminated, memorial flyers. I see glimpses of Yarra's photo and the color of her artwork. Irma's face is radiant.

No, Joanne, it's perfect. Yarra would love it. It's absolutely perfect.

As Yarra hoped, the New Zealand children, unfamiliar with the piñata custom, learned they have to swing the bat hard enough to break the gaily dancing "horsey on a rope." After many feeble bats, they understand the toy will have to be destroyed before the candies inside can come cascading down.

I join the crowd and release balloons into the sky, watching until mine becomes a pinpoint and disappears. *Yarra, my heart, this is for you.*

The crowd attacks bowls and platters of food, filling their plates with an enthusiasm and abandon that we have only seen in New Zealand. There is plenty for all. A swell of B.B. King's music fills the room. Diners jump up to clear the tables and the floor for dancing. Everyone, young and old, dances or strolls around to the beat.

Chris, who loves to dance, joins a few of Yarra's nurses, who twirl and fling their arms about in joyous abandon. It's a bewildering and amazing scene. Yarra's doctor/father and her nurses, who loved and cared for her, are dancing, crying, and smiling. Kris twirls by, eyes closed. *This is your happy party, Yarra. This is exactly what you wanted.*

People came to introduce themselves. Fellow students who met Yarra at The He-ART-ery, vendors from Nelson Saturday Market, clerks from the Dollar Store, people from the pool, the horse riding stable, nurses and caregivers—each has a special story to tell.

Arvind, Kris and Yarra's counselor, advisor, friend, comes when he sees I am alone having a cup of tea. "Joanne, it was a wonderful celebration. How do you feel?"

"You can imagine, I think, as you are also from another culture, it has been quite a day for me. Lots of letting go."

"Yes, and you've been at it a long time. You've been a wonderful mother."

His words stop me. He's not spoken so personally to me before. Arvind goes on, "I remember that day." I gaze into his deep eyes, see grey stubble on his chin.

"Yes, so do I. It was so intense." I see myself sitting motionless in his office as he, June and Kris tend Yarra. Today, he is personal. On "that day," he was a skilled professional, judicious and reserved. He leans forward and gives me a hug.

Yes, this is your party, Yarra. Well done.

My head is swirling. I'm watching my footing, feel confused. Chris is hugging Irma. She says, "You go now, everything will be taken care of."

Wonderful.

Kris appears from nowhere, leans towards me, wraps his strong arms around my shoulders. I grab the stair rail. I glance out at all the cars, still parked. Many friends who worked, prepared, came and are still working, still dancing. We slip away to the warm suite awaiting us at Firooze and Bernadette's.

"Chris, is it OK if we talk about what happens when we go home?"

"Yeah, I'm OK. What's on your mind?"

"We've been here in the daily presence of Yarra's imminent death for so long. We've talked, felt, and witnessed the feelings of grief for so long. The children have visited Yarra, they sense what we have been through, but mostly, they have been far away. I have such a strong feeling that it would be good to provide more than one day of being together for grieving. We can support each other. I doubt there'll be denial, but anger and depression, who knows? I know we can't control anything; I just want to provide an opportunity. I don't want them to go home after one day and grieve alone."

Chris listens, then says, "Good thinking, Joanne. What's your plan?"

"Let's talk with the kids; if they're OK with staying in the same place…probably, when we go back to Longmont, we'll plan the memorial service together. We can support each other. What do you think of setting up all Yarra's things—maybe ask for a room with a sitting room, at the hotel, and leave it open for them to come be there, look at her things, talk, whatever."

"You're right." Chris nods. "A safe place…for grieving."

Chris slows as he drives along the country road, "Yes, let's talk about it more when we get home and see what we can do."

This article was published in the local paper a few days after Yarra's death.

Farewell to Yarra/Angela
The Guardian, Motueka NZ newspaper, June 2007

Our daughter, Yarra Angela Amoroso, age 43, died peacefully, at the winter solstice in Motueka Community Hospital. Born in the United States, she lived in the Nelson area 9 years, the past 18 months in MCH.

When afflicted with Multiple Sclerosis, thirteen years ago, she responded with "I have M.S., it doesn't have me!" She lived life fully with openhearted, spirit-filled acceptance of Life's gifts, breathing them in and transforming them with her special passion for art as therapy, which she offered compassionately to help heal the suffering of others.

Seven and a half years ago, when her disease took away her ability to swallow, Yarra chose to accept artificial nourishment via a feeding tube. She did this to prolong her creative life, not to avoid death. Prior to losing her ability to communicate by speech, she established a Living Will with Advanced Directives and gave medical power of attorney to her husband to carry out her wishes. "I only desire life prolonging care, treatment, services and procedures, including artificial nourishment, if there is any reasonable hope of maintaining my quality of life, spiritually, mentally, emotionally and physically." At the time, she expressed those thoughts, for her quality of life to include, "seeing the sunsets, occasionally visiting a cafe, (being at that time, able only to observe and smell the food) meditating, looking out the window at the trees, being free of severe and constant pain and above all doing my art."

Yarra lost, one by one, each of these qualifiers, living zestfully, well beyond their parameters. The one exception was that, with one minimally functioning extremity, her right arm, she could, with assistance, continue to enjoy painting, until about 18 months ago. During the past four years, Yarra's method of communication has been through her art, her expressive eyes: blinking for "yes" and "no," and her earthy laughter.

In the past six months, she lost her ability to express herself through art, she suffered several minor medical problems, and two bouts of pneumonia. She indicated, through much conscientious communication, she no longer wished to be artificially nourished. In the fifteen days prior to her death, her advance directives were carried out via her medical power of attorney under the guidance of her physicians.

Two hundred thousand compassionately, respectfully observed breaths later, she expired for the last time. She voluntarily participated fully in her dying; she was aware, sometimes responsive, seemingly comfortable, pain free and peaceful. She was constantly receiving messages from visitors, loving friends and family from around the world via phone and emails and gifts of flowers and music. Her husband is Kris Kolff of Motueka. Her mother and father, siblings, friends and caregivers not only benefited from their association in her wonder-filled life, they were privileged to contribute to it, by comforting her in her transition from a disease-ridden body to a liberated spirit, eternally free.

We would lovingly and with deep gratitude like to thank the skilled and compassionate healing team of Motueka Community Hospital. I have been involved in the practice of medicine and consulting for half a century in numerous locations in the United States and Canada, my registered nurse wife, in the practice and teaching of nursing. Never have we witnessed any facility and staff that compares with the quality of skilled, dedicated, excellent care provided, compassionately and lovingly, by the healing team of Motueka Community Hospital staff and doctors. We, and her whole family, feel extraordinarily blessed to have had Yarra in their care for the last remarkable year of her life.

Chris Amoroso, MD

Epilogue

We return to Arizona. July 20, 2007 is stifling hot, even in early morning. I'm browsing the patio, hoping for a bird or a bloom to capture my thoughts. *Tomorrow, it will be a month since she died on the 21st. I want to do a Yarra thing...something she would do.* I go to my garage storage shelves, get out a sketch notebook, *I'll draw something New Zealand.* With colored pencils, in the cool garage, I try seashell. Not Ange's bright colors, but she loved any shells. And I have been thinking of her all the while. I don't want to forget her.

I show Chris my drawings, "Tomorrow's Ange's day. Let's do something she would do."

"Maybe Eskimo Pies?"

I laugh. "Yeah, she'd love that. She left us lots of options, don't you think?"

"How 'bout a 'Yarra' swim right now?"

One afternoon after Yarra's death, sunlight streams down through our Arizona skylight. It illuminates the painting on my wall. I notice one side of the heart, along the right lower edge, is darker than the rest of the painting. I peer into the dark shading, and letters, then words emerge: "Love Me Now."

Curious, I phone Kris in New Zealand. He tells me the significance of the painting. Yarra was devastated after an Jimmie Huega Adaptive Sports, Rock Climbing Class because, after repeated attempts, she was unable to climb over a large, reclining rock surface.

She came home shattered, was depressed for a time, then she picked up her chalk and with intense, colorful strokes created the vibrant heart and strengthened her own resilience. In a bold act of self-acceptance, she titled it "Love Me Now" and enabled herself to climb out of the experience of defeat.

Our family gathered in our hometown of Longmont, Colorado for a memorial service in August of 2007. Friends from our former church prepared the reception hall. Our children prepared the service. We shared chocolate and balloons.

Old friends, the children's school teachers, and community acquaintances arrived, embracing us and murmuring beautiful words of comfort about our daughter and our family.

"*Get thee to a nunnery*," Shakespeare's words kept repeating in my head during the previous weeks. After the memorial, as soon as the children were each on their way home, I said to Chris, "We need to find a convent, a retreat house or someplace quiet, just to breathe."

"I've been thinking about that, too," Chris says. What about a silent retreat for as long as we need, then we'll spend a few days reviewing our thoughts about what comes next? How about Camp St. Malo?"

"Great, see if they can take us."

"How long?"

"You decide, OK?"

Chris reserved nine days. Driving up Highway 36, our road to and from our cabin for years; the roadway abuts a red rock cliff on one side and overlooks a narrow river valley of orchards and ranches. How many times have we driven these traversing curves with crying babies, yappy kids, early morning rains and early evening snowstorms? The familiarity of the raw red cliffs is welcoming and settling.

Beyond Estes Park, Highway 7 curves to reveal a grey stone chapel, St. Malo on the Rock, with turrets and tall, narrow, stained-glass windows. Many times we've been here for Mass or conferences. We step inside for a few minutes' prayer. Beyond the chapel, the conference center and guest rooms beckon. We choose separate rooms in the same hall. We hardly speak as we unload the car and transfer our luggage; we are so willing to immerse ourselves in solitude, silence, meditation, prayer, nature, and reading. We are so ready to collapse on our beds.

I stretch myself out on the bed and cradle my head into the pillow. I immediately have a sensation I've never experienced before. I feel a current, like water or electricity, rushing full force, out of limbs, my trunk, my whole body. I lie very still for at least seven minutes. I feel tension drain away.

We pray and attend morning Mass. When we go for meals, we sit at the "silent table." No discussions, only a brief "feelings check-in" once a day. My mind is a white blank, and I aim to keep it that way for as long as possible. We have private space and our balconies face a forest of tall pines. At the edge of the sidewalk, a footpath leads into the woods.

Early in 2008, we are talking with Joe and his fiancé, Kelly, about wedding plans. They would like to schedule their wedding on the June 21st anniversary of Yarra's death. We are touched and welcome their suggestion. Before their festive beach wedding in Mexico, our family meets in a small state park. We eat chocolate and Mexican cookies while we sit under tropical foliage. We share remembrances of Yarra, which always include laughter. Thus, as the Solstice approaches every year, family emails pop up saying:

"Ruby is making chocolate chip cookies."

"I'm going for a horse ride."

"We're going camping."

"I'm doing a small painting."

We "keep" the Solstice for Yarra.

Sunday, July 5, 2009 an email from Kris arrives.

"Hi Chiara, and Joanne and Chris, just to let you know our midwinter gathering went well, enjoyed by all. I think. I was very moved by my daughter, Bindia's dance. 'This is for you, Kris.'

Bindia studied performance dance and created a dance enacted in a wheelchair, in honor of Yarra. I just wanted to see it again and again.

Carol, who lives down below here, played the harp and sang 'The Rose.' Bindia's David read some of his poems.

I told the story of Yarra's and my contract on the fourth of July 1997 at Estes Park: our declaration of independence from indecision—when we finally decided to come back to N.Z. after 12-18 months tossing up between NZ and Colorado. We wrote New Zealand on a helium balloon and sent it up and over the Rocky Mountains and far away!

Quite a few of us ended up sitting around the fire, eating Indian food from Motueka until 8pm. We gave everyone a chocolate wrapped in gold, from Yarra. Oh, and of course we played lots of my brother Hein's games. Chiara, it was another wonderful gathering of family and friends, once again brought together by Yarra."

Chocolate Kisses

Dear Yarra-
I still hang your art upon my wall,
so that when I have the need to listen,
to the still, small voice inside my head,
that says, "You can do this!"
I gaze upon your stumbling strokes,
the crazed colors, the falling composition,
all signed with a lipstick kiss,
and they remind me that
"Anything is possible."
If you try very hard
and keep pressing on
despite your disabilities,
and you smile wickedly,
while silently cursing your critics,
so that they mysteriously break out
in poorly matched clothes and silly hats,
and if you eat chocolate,
at the right time, at the wrong time,
or really, any time you can
and do up your hair just right, with flowers,
and put on your favorite maroon, crushed-velvet dress,
with a daring scarf, and a silver concho belt,
but most of all, you laugh,
inappropriately loudly, in a crowded room
so that everyone stops to look at you,
surprised, and they say, "Beautiful!"
and, funnily enough, by just saying it,
they will feel it, too.
Love,
Brother John
October 2017

In 2018, as I completed this book, once again, a message from Yarra appeared. Pondering the colorful heart painting hanging on our wall, I removed it and turned it over. There was a handwritten note, in Yarra's script. Bless Yarra for her last words

"Mom and Dad

This is a copy of a picture I did on a outward bound course—or inward bound! Then and since it has been a reminded to me to love my body now. Following this has been so rewarding! Learning how to listen, and try to respond! Thank you for sharing and all the help along the journey. Let us always be open to any healing by the way we live! XXOOLove You forever-Yarra

Angela Marie Amoroso Pisoni

Gratitudes

To Kris Kolf, all Kolff relatives, all Amorosos and friends in the United States, world wide, and countless New Zealanders, those known and unknown to us, who shared their caring visits, errands, phone calls, letters, casual chats, nail polishing, casseroles, untold numbers of favors, and cheered us and Yarra on our way.

To Vikki Lee, and the family of Jan and Irma Jager; Luka, Cella, and Yiba, John Arcus, Rob Leenheer, Melisso DeCino, Javan Stackley and Elija ; may all of you see yourselves as the generous, steadfast heroes and heroines you are.

To the members of Mosaic Choir, Nelson, New Zealand, and director Shannel Courtney, for shared hours of joy filled singing, and healing solace for Kris, Chris, me and the spirited performances, which Yarra could attend.

With unending gratitude to my husband, Chris, who constantly offered encouragement, thoughtful advice and organizational skills, which enabled me to complete the work of compiling my stories.

My heartfelt thanks to my daughter-in-law, Amy Amoroso, for her literary advice and for the system she devised which enabled me to proceed with transforming my memories of our experiences with our daughter, Yarra, into a book.

To my first reader, my daughter, Chiara Amoroso, who, cognizant of family events and times, astutely advised me. To Glenda Martin, book Woman publisher, editor, and discussion facilitator, who constantly encouraged me and heartened me with her responses. To friends Sharon Resigue and Sherry Blum who edited with thoughtful suggestions.

My heartfelt thanks to Meg Files, writing instructor at Pima College in 2011 and 2012, whose skillful teaching and wisdom-filled words encouraged my initial writing, and for her 2017 content editing and evaluation of the near-final edition.

With gratitude for the watchfulness and wisdom of my son Chris Amoroso, Jr., magazine publisher, for his role in guiding my book to completion and the help of his staff, Rosalie Hill Isom.

Thanks to my mother, Lucy Ambrosia Pisoni, who initiated my life-time hobby of reading and writing, and my teachers: Edith De Santis, Vaughn Marshall, Shirley Gaugher White, and Meg Files, who taught me that writing is much more than an assignment; it is a skill to be practiced, acquired, and cherished.

To my dear uncle, Fr. Otto Pisoni, who encouraged my reading and writing by gifting me with years of The Catholic Children's Book of a Month Club.

Books that were helpful to me

Women Living with Multiple Sclerosis by Judith Lynn Nichols, my first knowledge of MS.

Waist-High in the World, by Nancy Mairs, A Life Among the Nondisabled.

The Diving Bell and the Butterfly, Jon-Dominique Bauby. (His description of "Locked-in syndrome" provided me the awareness of Yarra's possible perceptions and feelings, and our varying understandings.)

Chants and Prayers, Stan Padilla.

On Death and Dying, Kubler-Ross.

Chris and Joanne Personal Lifetime Preparations

Cursillo Movement, 1965, Longmont, CO.

For Christian Family Movement, led by Fr. Francis Seriani, Aurora, Co. and Father Martin Arno, Longmont, CO. Weeklong summer program, 1976, with our children, at the University of Notre Dame, South Bend, IN.

Marriage Encounter, Aurora, Boulder and Longmont, CO, 1960-1985, Fr. Frances Bakewell.

Spiritual Eldering, taught by Rabbi Zalman Schachter-Shalomi, Naropa Institute, Boulder, CO.
The 12-Step Programs in the United States and New Zealand.
Non-violent Communication, Marshall B. Rosenberg, Albuquerque, NM, CO, AZ, NZ, 2000-2005.
Participants in National Race Walking competitions, 1970-2016.
Christian Amoroso, MD, internist, Pennsylvania School of Medicine.
Joanne T. Pisoni Amoroso RN, BA in Nursing, Certified English as a Second Language teacher; Elementary reading teacher; Amigos de las Americas, 1984, participant in eyeglass distribution, Guaranda, Province de Simon Bolivar, Ecuador.

Acknowledgement

Chris Amoroso, MD, husband, teacher, friend.
Kris Kolff, son-in-law, friend, teacher.
Mimi Farelly, art therapist.
Ethicist Monica Clark-Gill, Otago College, New Zealand.
Dr. Joseph Hassan.
Dr. Joseph Fennelly, and Lou Fennelly, RN, specialists in palliative care, dying and grief.

Personal Counselors and Friends

Dr. Margaret Sullivan, Dentist.
Dr. Edward Velayos, Rheumatologist, Physiatrist.
Dr. John Berson, Urologist.
Dr. Peter Holt, Internal Medicine.
Dr. Steven Nees, Hospice advisor.
Dr. Malcolm Clark, Neurologist, Nelson, NZ.
Arvind Pujji, Counselor.
Burke Hunter, Counselor.
National Multiple Sclerosis Society, Denver, CO.
Jimmie Heuga Center for Multiple Sclerosis, Avon, CO.
Betty Lou Zeller, RN.

Theresa O'Conner, RN.
Karena Shannon, Teacher/Speech Language Therapist.
Joan Van de Bos, RN.
Crista Strolly, RN.
Jill Dawson, RN.
Judy Totoro, RN.
Erika van Sint Annaland, Physical Therapist.
Fr. Jim Koenigsfeld, St. Columba's, Durango, CO.
Father Ed, St Mary's, Nelson, and Fr. Patrick Murphy, St. Peter Chanel, Motueka, NZ.
St Joseph's School, Nelson, NZ.
Staff of Desert House of Prayer, Tucson, AZ.
Mary Jaksch, Psychologist, Nelson, NZ.
Catherine Kelly, Psychologist.
Patricia York, Psychologist.
Shirley Gould, Psychologist.

Books We Shared with Yarra

(Most based on true stories of independent, strong-willed women.)

The Children of Babaka, Yarra Amoroso. A handmade storybook and line drawings, created from a New Guinea fable.

Tisha, Robert Specht. Based on true story of 19-year-old New England teacher, who goes to Alaska in 1927.

Mrs. Mike, Benedict and Nancy Freeman, 1947. True story of Katherine Marie Flannigan of Boston who goes to Alaska at 16 and marries a Royal Canadian Mounted Policeman.

Tracks, Robyn Davidson, pub. May 30, 1995. Young woman learns to train camels, makes solo trek across the Australian desert.

Follow the River, James Alexander Throm. Mary Ingles, 23, married and pregnant, living in a pioneer settlement in Virginia, is captured by Shawnee Indians and taken a thousand miles west. Unaided, she returns to her people.

Sacajawea, Ann Lee Waldo. Historical novel, Shoshone travel guide for Lewis and Clark.

Ada Black Jack, Jennifer Niven. True story of survival in the Arctic.

North Spirit, Paulette Jiles.

Love that Dog, Sharon Creech.

The Trumpet of the White Swan, EB White.

Two Old Women, Athabasca tribal tale.

NPR, "The Story Project, " a CD of three-minute, radio listener stories.

Books and Music Created for and about Yarra

DREAMS, Alice Austin, artist, book designer, and friend. Philadelphia, PA.

LIVING—The Inspirational Journey of Yarra Amoroso, by photojournalist and friend, Melissa A. DeCino, Longmont, CO.

"*A Song for You,*" Cheryl Homer and Cirrus Jaynes, Nelson musicians, neighbors, and friends.

Books by New Zealand Authors

From Lowlands to the Hills, by Tora Kolff, gift from Kris' mother, Tora; an accounting of the Kolff family's migration from Holland to Indonesia, their return to war-torn Holland, and finally settling in New Zealand.
Meg, by Maurice Gee, (Kris' first gift to Joanne).
An Angel at My Table, by Janet Frame.
Waiariki, by Patricia Grace.
The Bone People, by Keri Hume.
Believers of a Bright Coast, by Vincent O'Sullivan, (gift from Kris).

Books and discussions recommended and led by Glenda Martin and Molly Hoben, authors and publishers of BookWomen's Press, A Readers Community For Those Who Love Women's Words, which for nine years kept me whole and continues to do so.

About the Author

Joanne in Italy

Joanne Amoroso grew up as a small town girl in Brockway, PA. She lived the first fourteen years of her life with Italian-speaking grandparents in her home. Her playmates were the children and grandchildren of various European immigrants. In their homes, she learned to recognize, accept, appreciate, and eventually seek, culturally different friends and experiences in her life. During her childhood, her toddler sister, Angela, died after a prolonged, recurring pneumonia. Joanne believes all of these childhood experiences influenced her to become a registered nurse BA, and a certified Teacher of English as a Second Language.

Joanne and her husband, Chris, raised five enthusiastic children. She enjoys visiting with their families, reading, writing, travel and outdoor activities. Both Joanne and Chris participated in eyeglass distribution programs, Joanne, once, with Amigos de las Americas, in Guaranda, Ecuador and both in Khandbari, Nepal with Health Treks, a volunteer organization in Longmont, CO, of which they were founding members. She and Chris hiked the 486 miles of the Colorado Trail for their 60th birthdays.

Thus, when her daughter, Angela, a world-travelling artist, was diagnosed with Multiple Sclerosis, Joanne perceived the family would be entering into the cross-cultural world of illness, and that she and her physician husband, Chris, would be well prepared to accompany Angela and her husband, Kris, into that new world, as caregivers, in New Zealand. Joanne and Chris realize there are countless people who, generously or by default, live in that world of illness. To be present with Yarra on her journey became a gift. *Love Me Now* is Joanne's gift to her daughter's memory and to caregivers worldwide.

Yarra's Quotes

"Disabled! Who's disabled? I'm accepting what I have been given.

How are you doing with your life?

I hurt, and I love life.

The only answer is "Yes."

No matter what comes in my life, I'll deal with it. I may become clouded easily, but I can proceed in a healthy way, even in darkness.

The boredom is killing my Spirit. Please ask someone to take me outdoors each day.

I am a gypsy, Italian by blood, but let's not stop there…Colorado, Cusco, Peru, Alaska, Vermont, Australia, Papua New Guinea, Georgia, New Zealand…these are the places and the many cultures I have lived with. They helped make the "who" of who I am.

If you live in enough places, you can learn to love the whole world.

My learning to be more meditative with my inner search is making me honest with myself first, so I can love and be honest with others.

The daily choice is whether you want to live in heaven or hell now, not after death.

I'm in love with Life and the Mysteries it brings.

My Spirit is always there. If I see it, what am I supposed to do, throw it away? No, I just use it.

The one main thread through my travels is an immense love for life. Savoring every little bit of it, spitting out the bits which may have appeared bitter, always expressing myself through my art, in this life. I have a deep respect for life and trust that my art will always express those feelings. It is always mysteriously new and different. I've always found creativity in my own backyard.

It's been such a mysterious and incredible journey of letting go, accepting, and loving Life.

I can't believe I'm so in Love with Life…I AM. Yarra"

Only when you drink from the river of silence shall you indeed sing.
And when you have reached the mountain top, then you shall begin to climb.
And when the earth shall claim your limbs, then shall you truly dance.

– Kahlil Gibran

Made in the USA
Columbia, SC
07 May 2019